D1742413

The German Skills Machine

POLICIES AND INSTITUTIONS
Germany, Europe, and Transatlantic Relations

Published in Association with the American Institute for Contemporary German Studies (AICGS), Washington, D.C.
General Editor: **Carl Lankowski**, Research Director of the AICGS

THE GERMAN SKILLS MACHINE

Sustaining Comparative Advantage
in a Global Economy

Edited by

Pepper D. Culpepper and David Finegold

Berghahn Books
New York • Oxford

First published in 1999 by

Berghahn Books

© 1999 Pepper D. Culpepper and David Finegold

Library of Congress Cataloging-in-Publication Data

The German skills machine : sustaining comparative advantage in a
  global economy / edited by Pepper D. Culpepper and David
  Finegold.
     p.   cm.   (Policies and institutions : v. 3)
   Includes bibliographical references and index.
   ISBN 1-57181-144-3 (alk. paper)
   1. Occupational training—Germany.   2. Vocational education—
Germany.   I. Culpepper, Pepper D.   II. Finegold, David.
III.   Series
HD5715.5.G35G47   1999   99-23020
331.25'92'0943—dc21   CIP

British Library Cataloguing in Publication Data

A catalogue record for this book is available
from the British Library.

Printed in the United States on acid-free paper.

CONTENTS

LIST OF TABLES AND FIGURES

Tables

Figures

ACKNOWLEDGMENTS

This volume grew out of contributions to two conferences on the subject of the German training system that were sponsored by the American Institute for Contemporary German Studies (AICGS) in Washington, DC in 1997. The editors organized the second conference, which was designed exclusively with the purpose of ensuring the coherence of the volume as a whole. We would also like to acknowledge the efforts of Thomas Hinz and Kathleen Thelen, who organized the first conference, which was held in January, 1997. We thank the AICGS for financial support of both the authors during some of the time the book was being organized and redrafted, and in particular we want to express our gratitude to its director, Jackson Janes, and its research director, Carl Lankowski. We are also grateful to Susanne Dieper of the AICGS, who took care of the details of conference planning with aplomb. Mary Louise Dagenhart Culpepper exercised her considerable acumen with the English language to clarify the prose in several of the chapters. An anonymous reviewer from Berghahn Books made many suggestions that have helped us improve the volume. Finally, Michael Blackmore provided assistance with numerous editorial tasks in the book's closing stages, including the unification of the bibliography.

Contributors

Pepper D. Culpepper is Assistant Professor of Public Policy at the John F. Kennedy School of Government at Harvard University.

David Finegold is Assistant Research Professor at the Center for Effective Organizations at the Marshall School of Business at the University of Southern California.

Jutta Gatter is a Benefits Consultant at BASF in Germany.

Gary Herrigel is Associate Professor of Political Science at the University of Chicago.

Thomas Hinz is *wissenschaftlicher Assistent* at the Institute for Sociology at the Ludwig-Maxmilian-University, Munich.

Helga Krüger is Professor of Sociology at the Department of Vocational Education and Chair of the Research Program on "Status Passages and Risks in the Life Course" at the University of Bremen.

Eric Parker is a Research Fellow at the Project on Regional and Industrial Economics at Rutgers University and is a Research Affiliate of the Center on Wisconsin Strategy at the University of Wisconsin-Madison.

Joel Rogers is Professor of Law, Political Science, and Sociology at the University of Wisconsin-Madison, where he also directs the Center on Wisconsin Strategy.

Charles F. Sabel is Professor of Law and Social Science at Columbia Law School.

Karin Wagner is Professor of Business Administration at the Fachhochschule für Technik und Wirtschaft in Berlin.

Stewart Wood is Fellow and Tutor in Politics at Magdalen College at Oxford University and a Director of "Nexus," the UK-based policy and ideas network.

Introduction

STILL A MODEL FOR THE INDUSTRIALIZED COUNTRIES?

Pepper D. Culpepper

The German model of skill provision has been the darling of policy-makers across the capitalist democracies over the past two decades, and it is credited as being a significant contributor to the export success of German companies and to Germany's comparatively low youth unemployment. As the century draws to a close, though, the merits of this model, and even its viability in the face of technological and organizational change, are in doubt. This volume comes neither to praise nor to bury the model, but to unite contributions from across the social sciences that consider the relative advantages of institutions for skill provision that combine supervised in-firm training and theoretical instruction in out-of-firm centers. The German dual system of apprenticeship training is the exemplar of such a training regime, and our discussion and much of our evidence relates to the system as it functions in Germany today. But the ambition of the book is both general and comparative: what does this evidence allow us to say about the performance of German-style institutions for skill provision in advanced capitalist societies throughout the international economy? Is the German system of skill provision still a model for the industrialized countries?

The chapters in this book constitute a unique look at the effectiveness and distributive ramifications of the institutions of German skill provision as they functioned at home in the 1990s and as they served as a template for reform in other industrialized countries. The volume benefits from its reliance on multiple sources of data, including in-firm case studies, larger-scale surveys of companies, data on life course patterns, and historical and contemporary studies of the functioning of institutions in different settings, which themselves draw on interviews and secondary literature. The verification of empirical research always depends on the application of hypotheses to a variety of empirical cases and to different sorts of evidence, so the wealth of original research on which we base our findings allows us to speak with some authority about the contemporary functioning of institutions of skill provision in the industrialized countries. In particular, the reliance of several chapters on in-company research reflects the shared belief of the contributors in the methodological virtues of putting firms and their strategies at the center of political economic analysis (cf. Hall 1998b).

A Sketch of the Dual System

The theoretical interest of the German model of training grows out of an insight generated by the work of Gary Becker (1964): the market will in most circumstances under-provide the socially optimal combination of skills.[1] The theory runs that companies will be willing to pay only for those skills that are strictly firm-specific, i.e., much more useful for them than for other companies.

---

1. This discussion draws on Soskice (1994).

Individuals must bear the costs of providing themselves with general skills, those capacities that are transferable and of use to many companies. The best individuals, knowing they are the best, will pay to provide a greater proportion of their own training than will the less able, leaving the credit institutions that must finance this training with an adverse selection problem. If companies do pay to provide these general skills, they face the risk that other firms will poach their trained workers, paying them a higher wage based on the money they saved by not investing in the costs of training. Complicating matters further is the fact that, in the real world, it is often difficult to disentangle firm-specific skills from those with wider transferability (Finegold 1992).

The heralded achievement of the German model is that, despite these theoretical social dilemmas, companies nevertheless invest substantially and in large numbers in the costs of training apprentices, providing the majority of German youth with relevant, transferable skills. Yet the "dual system" – so-called because training takes place in both firms and public training schools – relies on the sharing of costs among companies, governments, and apprentices themselves. Companies provide the machinery, trainers, and low apprenticeship wages during the training period. The German federal states *(Länder)* pay for teachers and machinery at vocational schools *(Berufsschulen)*, which students attend one or two days per week (Münch 1991).[2] Apprentices invest in the development of their own skills in the form of their low wages. The system thus links this sharing of costs, of which firms nevertheless bear the greatest single proportion, with the future demand for skills by the economy, because companies are training according to their future skill needs.

Legally enshrined in the training law of 1969 but building on a much older craft training tradition, the dual system is reg-

---

2. Block release, in which students spend an equivalent proportion of their time at schools for several weeks at a time, is becoming increasingly popular in Germany; see Chapter 1 for a discussion.

ulated largely by institutions of private governance. The standard apprenticeship contract generally runs from three to three and a half years, depending on the particular specialty, and the content of occupational apprenticeship specialties is determined by negotiations between representatives of employers' associations and unions, with expertise also provided by the staff of the Federal Institute for Vocational Training (BiBB) (Streeck et al. 1987). Responsibility for supervising training in individual companies, approving those companies to train, and testing apprentices at the end of their training falls overwhelmingly to the chambers of industry and commerce or of trades, which are para-public bodies that all employers in a given industry must join (ibid; Münch 1991). Works councils have statutorily embedded rights of codetermination in questions of apprenticeship training at the firm level, although this supervisory power is de facto stronger as company size increases (Streeck et al. 1987). Thus, the dual system rests on a legal framework that guarantees that the social partners must negotiate all changes to occupational content and have the wherewithal to monitor the operation of training at the level of individual company. The state provides only this legal framework and a corps of experts through the BiBB.

The general interest of this particular institutional configuration results from four of its closely related characteristics: the aforementioned investment of companies in the costs of in-firm training; the market-conforming delivery of skills; the fact that those skills are defined by representatives of employers (who will use the skills) together with representatives of labor (who want to ensure that the skills are indeed general, not only firm-specific); and the fact that these same private actors are in control of monitoring the conduct of training. Companies are the best judges of what skills they will need in the future, so the first characteristic (that companies invest in skill provision) helps assure the second (that the provision of skill follows the needs of the market). Countries without a mechanism linking the skills offered through the educational system to those demanded on the labor market – the United States and France come immediately to mind – can only envy this trait of in-firm training.

However, the goal of firms is not to educate youth; the goal of firms is to make money. A system based purely on the demands of companies is therefore likely to result in the provision of only the skills immediately useful for companies, rather than a more broadly based vocational education. Unions have an interest in assuring that their constituents (and future members) receive skills that are broadly applicable, and they can assure that breadth if, as in Germany, their assent is necessary in order to change the content of training occupations. Finally, employers as a rule do not like opening themselves up to state intrusion (Finegold and Soskice 1988, Soskice 1994). Supervision by employers' representatives (the chambers), supplemented by the watchful eyes of labor representatives (works councils), offers a mechanism for monitoring that does not require the intervention of a state that may be both unwelcome and inefficient. These features have attracted the attention of policy-makers in different countries, who have tried (with mixed results) to adopt some of the elements of the German apprenticeship system. Their experiences constitute a rich empirical vein, which several of the contributors to this volume mine in order to draw conclusions about the necessary conditions for such a system to succeed.

Although the dual system is the linchpin of German skill provision, it is not the only element thereof. Higher education and company-level further training are also key components of German skill provision; indeed, one of the contentions made by chapters in this book (Chapter 6 by Jutta Gatter and the conclusion by David Finegold) is that these components are increasing in relative importance. Their articulation with the apprenticeship system, and the ability of their governance institutions to deliver the same performance as those upholding the dual system, are issues deserving much closer empirical analysis. However, these various features assume wider analytical interest only if a prior question has been answered: why is skill provision itself worthy of study? For if we could not demonstrate that skill provision was a central element in the functioning of advanced capitalist political economies, the audience of this book would not extend beyond specialists in vocational training and labor market policy. But, as the reader may have guessed, there are very good reasons to believe that the interest in the question of skill provision should in fact be much more widespread.

Skills in the Interdependent Global Economy

As barriers to trade and financial liberalization fall, the OECD countries are increasingly vulnerable to the effects of international competition. This economic openness has come at a time when the efficacy of Keynesian aggregate demand management appears to have faded away, leaving governments focused principally on maintaining price stability. This confluence of events means that the large states in the international system are casting around for effective ways to protect their citizens from the unpredictable shocks of the international economy and from the effects of the business cycle. For these large states, as has long been true for small states exposed to international trade (Katzenstein 1985), intervention on the supply side of the economy is one of the ways still available to governments to mediate the influence of exogenously induced economic change: both by enabling companies in the national economy to compete in international markets (as a result of providing them with collective goods like a skilled labor force), and to cushion the blow of economic change on those individuals it displaces, through active labor market policies (Garrett and Lange 1991, Garrett 1997).[3] Raising the skill level of the workforce is one strategy for

---

3. Torben Iversen (1997) has recently challenged the oft-cited causal link between trade openness and welfare state expansion, pointing instead to

productivity growth that appears to offer positive returns to both individuals and to the macro-economy (OECD 1994).

The focus of political economists on the possibilities for intervention in the area of skill provision has sharpened in tandem with economists' having reinvigorated the study of the role of knowledge more broadly, and of the role of in-firm training particularly. Proponents of endogenous growth theory in economics have shown that education and the knowledge base of a society are endogenous resources for innovation that may explain the persistent failure of per capita income in national economies to converge (cf. Romer 1986, 1994). More directly relevant to the problem of intermediate skills at the firm level is the work by Lisa Lynch on the returns of training to firms and to individuals (1994a and b). In the American firms studied in a comparative volume edited by Lynch, "informal training, or learning by doing, has relatively little impact on productivity growth in a firm … while more formal training increases productivity and a worker's ability to be innovative" (1994a: 18). For individuals, available cross-national evidence suggests that the pay of US workers does not benefit from informal on-the-job training received at a previous place of employment, while "company-based training and apprenticeships have higher returns than government-led or school-based training" (1994b: 85).[4]

---

the speed of de-industrialization as the real factor that drives welfare state expansion in the open economies. Whatever the real cause of perceived societal dislocations, however, strategies of supply-side intervention are an undeniably attractive way for governments to insulate their populations from these effects.

4. As a result of the cross-national study, Lynch makes three claims about changes to the system of vocational education that would increase the payoffs to training in the United States: "1. Greater employer participation in training to increase the probability that skills will be related to demand …. 2. Employee representation in determining the content of training, to ensure that the training includes more general skills as well as firm-specific skills. Absent such employee participation, training would be too narrow …. 3. Certification of skills through a nationally recog-

These data make clear that one road to productivity growth in the industrialized countries runs through improvements in the institutions for providing worker training.

Such findings confirm the general importance of skills for the political economy, for firms, and for individuals. Changes in the organization of production have reinforced further the centrality of skill in the advanced industrial economies. Piore and Sabel's (1984) landmark study of these changes demonstrated that the saturation of markets for standardized industrial goods and the rise of cheaper, mass-produced export goods in the newly industrializing countries has thrown the paradigm of mass production into turmoil in its heartland: the advanced capitalist democracies. To cope with the volatility of demand and the increasing taste for high-quality goods, Piore and Sabel argued that companies needed to build on the lessons of craft production to reintegrate conception with execution, reversing Taylor's dictum for scientific management. The practical concomitant of this strategy, which Piore and Sabel call flexible specialization, requires companies to make use of easily programmable machine tools for batch production, and to employ workers flexible enough to alter production techniques in response to rapid changes in demand. This work influenced (and was influenced by) the French regulation school and especially scholars of the "Third Italy," and similar themes have been developed notably in the work of Wolfgang Streeck on diversified quality production (DQP) in Germany (Sorge and Streeck 1988; Streeck 1991, 1992).[5] As Streeck has noted, the capacity for incremen-

---

nized process" (1994b: 90). As noted previously, these are exactly the features of the German dual system that make copying them an attractive prospect for other industrialized countries.

5. On *régulation* see Boyer and Mistral 1978 and Boyer 1986; on the Third Italy, see Brusco 1982 and the essays collected in Pyke et al. 1990. The difference between DQP and flexible specialization has more to do with the institutions supporting the system than the nature of production itself: flexible specialization takes its institutional cue from the communitarian

tal innovations in the production process in German companies depends on the existence of a skilled workforce trained in broad occupational specialties. The competitive advantage of the system, and of the export sector of the German economy that it supports, thus rests squarely on the skills of its workers.

Lean production moves away from some of the principles of flexible specialization and of DQP, placing more emphasis on the ability of workers to engage in productive teamwork than on the individual depth of each worker's skill. Womack et al.'s *The Machine that Changed the World* (1990) continues the emphasis on the capabilities of production workers, particularly in the area of quality control and feedback; but this capability comes into play in the context of team-based production. I return below to the potential problems this model of team-based production may pose for the German craft model, and Chapters 2 and 3 deal with this issue at length. The point of general interest as regards skill, however, is that the enormous amount of debate generated by lean production once again returns the analytical focus from the macro-economy to the company level. And at the company level, the growing involvement of production workers in the continual improvement in the work process puts worker capacities at the center of analysis. The nature of production has changed dramatically in the industrialized countries in recent years, and the stock of skills in the economy determines the alternative strategies that companies will be able to choose in this new environment.

As production has changed, so too has our understanding of the role of market and non-market coordination in the functioning of the political economy. Institutionalist analyses of political economy increasingly recognize that regimes of skill production constitute one of the core institutions that deter-

---

structures of the Italian industrial districts, DQP from the hard organizational structures regulating interaction between capital and labor in Germany; see Streeck 1991: 29-31 and Sabel 1994 on these differences.

mine the possible competitive strategies available to firms (Soskice 1990a, Hollingsworth and Boyer 1997, Hall and Soskice forthcoming, Kitschelt et al. 1998). This is an area of exciting ferment, yielding new insights about how economic outcomes are coordinated through a variety of market and non-market mechanisms. Skill provision is recognized in this work as a central institution of the political economy, and often as a prerequisite to moves to DQP or its variants: "flexible producers require a highly skilled work force operating with minimal supervision, general-purpose machinery, and intense coordination – even frequent collaboration with other producers" (Hollingsworth 1997: 272). One of the steps forward taken in our volume is to clarify, notably in the chapters in the third section of the book, the question of the chicken-and-the-egg with respect to a highly skilled workforce and a DQP regime: that is, which is the prerequisite of the other.

This question is part of another, larger one, which remains under-theorized in the work on varieties of capitalism: how do institutions change, and especially, how can governments or private actors encourage institutional change? Much of the work on non-market coordination uses equilibrium analysis, and its tendency has been to emphasize the self-reinforcing nature of existing institutional equilibria (e.g., Finegold and Soskice 1988, Soskice 1990a and 1990b). These self-stabilizing mechanisms have great explanatory power, which we recognize, but the contributions to the volume (especially those in Parts I and III) are often directly concerned with empirical instances of institutional change. And while this literature does a good job of predicting barriers to change, it is theoretically less well-equipped to explain the conditions under which change can occur. The contributions in Part I explore the responses of existing institutions in Germany to various shocks to the system, while those in Part III take up institutional experiments in which actors and governments attempt to change the behavior of companies in the area of training, trying to convince them to coordinate around a different equilibrium point. We do not put forward a comprehensive theory of institutional change, but our focus on attempts to change systems of skill provision highlights the variables that affect the probability for success of a reform: most importantly, the capacity of private sector associations (Culpepper, Parker and Rogers, Wood), but also the exit options available to companies (Culpepper), prevailing product market strategies (Culpepper, Wood), and institutional design (Wood, Parker and Rogers) have a systematic impact on the probability of success in a project of institutional change. These findings can inform modern discussions of market vs. non-market coordination and may serve as a corrective to the heavy emphasis on stability and path-dependence characteristic of recent institutionalist work in political science (Steinmo et al. 1992, Pierson 1997).

Problems in Germany:
Slow Growth, High Costs, and Institutional Rigidity

Systems of skill production are in the ascendant as variables for explaining patterns of economic adjustment. Yet Germany, the empirical referent of much of the work on the importance of skills systems, is currently stuck in a rut of persistently high unemployment and low growth that undermines confidence in the continued ability of the "high-wage, high-skill" German model to deliver widespread societal benefits. The chapters in the first section of this volume examine these contemporary problems of German skill provision in a comparative light, with particular regard to the ability of the system of skill provision to adjust to these challenges. For some liberal critics, the general rigidity of the German model constrains its growth and employment possibilities. Indeed, a recent report by the McKinsey Global Institute claims that German aggregate productivity is only so high because the low-wage service jobs that create employment in liberal market economies like the US are closed off in Germany by high minimum wages (1997: 2; cf. Scharpf 1997, Hall 1998a). Iversen and Wren (1998) draw similar conclusions about the Christian Democratic model, of which Germany is an exemplar, and its sacrifice of employment growth in the private sector services in the search for fiscal discipline and low earnings inequality.[6]

These structural problems were already emerging before German unification in 1990, which has only redoubled the pressure on the German system. Wolfgang Streeck has even asserted that, "while in normal circumstances the 'German model' may or may not have found a way out of its difficulties, unification may have so much exacerbated these as to make them insurmountable" (1997: 44). For the training system, rising costs and the strain of transferring the institutions of the dual system eastward have created serious problems; Karin Wagner's chapter opens Part I of this volume with a detailed analysis of these problems in the context of the generally increasing costs of the German apprenticeship system in the eastern and western states of Germany.[7] Wagner shows that the costs of apprenticeship to employers, which vary significantly with firm size (as large companies invest much more than small companies in training), were nevertheless counterbalanced through 1991 by the benefits derived by firms from apprenticeship. Since then, increases in the time spent by apprentices in training centers and the reduction in their time spent at productive work, along with increases in the wages of apprentices (exceeding the rate of increase of worker wages over the same time period), have

---

6. The data in Iversen and Wren (1998) do not take into account the exogenous fiscal shock of German unification, whose high costs caused German budget deficits to balloon in the 1990s.

7. A note on usage: throughout the volume, we use the terms East Germany and West Germany to designate, respectively, the German Democratic Republic and the Federal Republic of Germany before unification in 1990. We refer to these geographic areas as eastern and western Germany when discussing them in the context of the united Germany.

changed the cost-benefit analysis of many training firms. As a result, between 1990 and 1995 both the overall proportion of German firms that are training, and the proportion of apprentices trained by those firms that do train, have fallen. These pressures have been particularly acute in eastern Germany, where the feeble condition of the apprenticeship market has forced federal and state governments to intervene in order to soak up the excess number of would-be apprentices chasing too few apprenticeship places offered by companies. Although Wagner's conclusions are optimistic for the survival of the dual system, this optimism is conditional on the acceptance by the government and the social partners of the need to make the system more flexible and less costly for employers.

Her optimism is not shared by all observers of the German craft model of skill provision. In particular, Gary Herrigel and Charles Sabel argue in Chapter 2 that the craft identities intrinsic to the German system of occupational training create problems for companies trying to move toward new forms of production that depend on close shopfloor cooperation (cf. Herrigel 1996a, Sabel 1995). The emphasis in lean production on blending skill competencies in multi-functional teams asks a German mechanic not to rely on his technical virtuosity to engineer a solution to a given problem, but to collaborate with colleagues in different specialties to solve that problem. Herrigel and Sabel contend that workers embedded in a craft system like the German one, in which their very identities are tied up with their profession, will resist changes in the organization of production that sublimate the skill contribution of the individual in order to increase the efficiency of the team.

> Thus the acquisition of skills by way of apprenticeship typically depends on and reinforces the existence of a skill hierarchy. Once the pace of adjustment reaches the level where collaborative manufacturing makes economic sense, this division of labor plainly leads to paralyzing conflicts: the master technicians deprecate the

shop-floor solutions as technically inelegant, the shop-floor groups deplore the technical perfectionism of the higher-ups as an unaffordable luxury. (Sabel 1995: 23)

These jurisdictional conflicts thus increase the cost of production at the same time that they reduce its quality, which, Herrigel and Sabel argue, puts German manufacturing increasingly at risk if it does not reform itself.

They show both "maximalist" and "minimalist" strategies pursued in different German companies to overcome these problems. In the maximalist strategies, typified by the approach of carmaker BMW, companies ask employees (from managers to shopfloor workers) to abandon their occupational specializations in order to increase the efficiency of teams in production. These skill strategies are of a piece with supplier-assembler relations: companies abandon many functional divisions internally, as they reorganize on the basis of team-production, and they increase their collaboration with suppliers in order to ensure the closer integration of design and production. What separates the maximalist from the minimalist strategies is not so much the introduction of teams in certain areas of production – which many German companies have tried – but rather the extent of the transformation. Herrigel and Sabel note two sorts of minimalist strategies: one involves a few pockets of team production that become isolated within the overall organization of the firm, and the second conversely involves pockets of traditional craft production that refuse to bow to the widespread introduction of teams. In the first case, the isolated teams run up against obstacles in the extent of their authority and the failure of management to reorganize itself along similar lines; in the second case, islands of entrenched privilege fight the shift in production strategy, and the authors argue that the casualty of such a fight may well be the islands of tradition that refuse to go along with the changes.

Herrigel and Sabel see German companies and the German model as being capable of change; indeed, their examples of maximalist strategies demonstrate that change is possible, despite the inertia inherent in a system where occupational specialization is bound up with questions of individual identity. However, though they may be hopeful for Germany and the future of German production, they are not sanguine about the effects of the vocational training system. That system, they claim, is the one institution of the political economy that is inextricably wedded to the German craft system of production; if it is to enable German firms to reap the potential gains of lean production, the inflexible skill boundaries codified through the dual system must be loosened by decoupling skills from their strictly occupational definitions. The implication is that the skills system must transform itself so fundamentally that it is no longer recognizable as a craft model (Sabel 1995).

Chapter 3 tests this contention very concretely, confronting the hypotheses of Herrigel and Sabel with a rich set of data drawn from matched plant comparisons of 36 pump manufacturers in the United States and Germany. As Herrigel and Sabel's argument would predict, these data confirm that the German plants with the highest concentration of skilled workers have been the slowest to adopt multi-functional teams in the production process. While they relate this finding somewhat to the fact that the production of some companies is not well-suited to team-production, they also find that Herrigel and Sabel are right: German skilled workers do oppose the move to team-based production because of their desire to keep their technical skills at the forefront of the production process. Furthermore, among American pump manufacturers it is those companies with the highest proportion of skilled workers – skilled workers not burdened with the debilitating craft hierarchies that Herrigel and Sabel impute to Germany – which have moved the furthest towards team production.

A second finding of the chapter by Finegold and Wagner takes some of the sting out of the first: some German companies manufacturing for the more customized niches in the pump-making industry have been able to pioneer their own variant of lean organization without running into the dysfunctions created by the craft system. These companies have not moved aggressively to reduce the role of individual skill contributions through multi-functional teams, but they have instead flattened organizational hierarchies and devolved increased responsibility to individual workers in the context of group work. In this strategy, the high general skill level achieved through the German system of skill provision transforms itself from the obstacle of change to its midwife. The dual system and training for *Meisters* provide employees with the broad competencies necessary to take on a wider range of activities than previously. Moreover, in the German semi-skilled plants that have moved toward team-based production (thanks to the absence of skilled workers who would try to block this change), the moves toward lean organization have caused firms to increase their further training and/or to increase their intake of apprentices in the future. Moves to new forms of organization are not, then, precluded by the existing craft system of skill provision in Germany, even in its current rigid form. Indeed, once the work system has been transformed, the in-firm component of apprenticeships ensures that new trainees are prepared from the outset to work in teams. Those organizational diffusions, though, appear to depend for their success on being appropriated by actors in forms consistent with, rather than in fundamental tension with, the existing mode of skill provision (cf. Streeck 1996). Both systems of production and systems of skill provision need to adapt to survive, but there is no a priori reason to think that both cannot adapt while safeguarding their own institutional competitive advantage.

One other contemporary challenge to the dual system, which is not taken up directly by any of the chapters in this book, also merits mention: the ability of its institutional supports to withstand pressures for change brought on by European integration. Philippe Schmitter and Wolfgang Streeck argued in a 1991 article, in terms not specific to training institutions but appropriate to them, that the European principle of mutual recognition amounts to a de facto deregulation of social relations.[8] The argument runs that mutual recognition (based on the European Court ruling in *Cassis de Dijon*) has chipped away at nationally specific areas of private interest government, as less regulated national systems of intermediation crowd out those more tightly regulated systems. The specific training analogue of this move, against which Streeck warns, is the harmonization of skill profiles by the European Community (1997: 53). The more general argument of Streeck and Schmitter encompasses all heavily regulated and private interest-governed elements of the political economy, including the German dual system of apprenticeship.[9] There is no European authority that can reproduce the functions of the enabling national states that, in Germany and elsewhere, have provided the legal framework for associational governance to thrive (Streeck 1992). This institutional race to the bottom has been slow to materialize thus far, at least in the area of German skill provision. Yet the danger signaled by Schmitter and Streeck from the process of European integration is but a specific example of a more general question to which the chapters in Part III of the volume return:

8. The article originally appeared in *Politics and Society*, 19:2, 1991. A revised version was reprinted in Streeck (1992), and I refer to that version in the citations as Schmitter and Streeck (1992).

9. Schmitter reiterates this logic in a more recent article: "to the extent that the practice of integration remains confined to formal intergovernmental agreements … and to the extent that these agreements relies [sic] heavily on *mutual recognition* and *internal market competition* to resolve differences and govern exchanges between national economies, intermediate arrangements for sectoral coordination and governance would seem to have a dim future in Europe. They should be eliminated by market pressures or the formation of ever more extensive hierarchies among private firms. Only those countries that elected not to join the EC/EU could confidently expect to preserve their quaint practices of informal collusion, associational concertation, and private interest governance" (1997: 423-24; italics in original).

in an era of mobile capital and easily skirted national regulatory borders, what are the pre-conditions for national or regional institutions of private governance effectively to regulate systems of skill provision?

Distributive Outcomes and Institutional Choice

Like most debates about the structure of training systems, the previous discussion revolves largely around questions of efficiency: does the German training system continue to provide socially optimal outcomes and can it cope with changes in the organization of production? Yet institutions are not the product of social utility maximization; they are also "the by-product of substantive conflicts over the distributions inherent in social outcomes" (Knight 1992: 40). Systems of skill provision constitute bargained outcomes among different social actors, and once institutionalized, inertia enables these compromises to outlive the particular coalition of interest or governing ideas that first put them into place (cf. Goldstein and Keohane 1993: 20-21). Certainly with respect to research on the German training system, as in much of the work in contemporary institutionalist political economy, social scientists need to do a better job specifying what Peter Gourevitch (1996) calls the macro-politics of micro-reform. That is, what are the political processes by which national regulatory policies affect micro-economic forms of behavior, and which definitions of interest structure debates about institutional change?

In the previous section I have already alluded to the inability of Germany to create jobs in private-sector services (McKinsey 1997, Scharpf 1997, Iversen and Wren 1998). These recent findings confirm the long-standing stylized fact of the German model as one characterized by "insiders" and "outsiders" (Esping-Andersen 1996; cf. Blanchard and Summers 1986). The insiders are unionized German men who have received official skill certification through the dual system, for whom the high-wage, high-skill equilibrium is a happy reality. Outsiders are women, whom a variety of German social policies encourage to remain out of the labor force (Esping-Andersen 1990); foreign workers, who have historically provided a buffer for companies to lay off in lean times; and the unskilled and non-unionized workers, who have neither the labor market nor the political power to pull themselves into the virtuous circle of high skills and high wages. Training is but one of an interlocking network of German social institutions, so we must be cautious about isolating the effects of the training system on mobility and returns to skill investment over the lifecycle. Nevertheless, understanding the contemporary challenges facing systems of skill provision requires a better understanding of the distributive compromises on which they rest, their social effects, and the structural changes that destabilize these institutional products of past compromises.

Just as the economic conditions in which a model has been successful may change, forcing the model to adapt or perhaps just decreasing its ability to perform effectively, so do mutual understandings of what constitutes acceptable political consequences change over time, introducing political pressure on the system to change to accommodate newly powerful demands. The chapters in Part II do for the sociopolitical bases of German-style training what the chapters in Part I did for the economic viability of the system: they try to understand its consequences and to hint at the directions institutional change might take. In a debate often cast exclusively between proponents of convergence around institutional best practice versus the continued diversity of national institutional arrangements, focusing attention on these distributive aspects is an important acknowledgment that political economic institutions are not only the product of efficiency considerations, but also of political conflicts over the division of the economic pie.

The chapter by Thomas Hinz links the functioning of vocational training and of educational systems, and he argues that these two variables permit generalizable predictions about the likelihood for individual mobility between jobs and between classes in different societies. Standardized training systems like the German one function on the basis of occupational certification whose content is recognized by employers as being well-defined and largely invariant from one student to another. Stratification for Hinz refers to proportion of an age cohort that attends the maximal number of years in the general education system and the extent to which tracking dominates the system. Standardized training has the effect of limiting both occupational and class mobility: life course data indicate that average job tenure is longer in Germany than in Sweden and the US, and class mobility (downward *and* upward) is lower in Germany than elsewhere. Unstandardized vocational training systems exhibit greater mobility of both sorts, but Hinz argues that the stratification of the education system (in combination with the social policy regime) determines whether changes will be mostly upward (unstratified education) or downward (stratified education).

If these arguments are right, what are the implications for reform of the German training system? If reform were to go in the radical and unlikely direction of abandoning the occupational standardization of the dual system, as Herrigel and Sabel seem to advocate, then the social consequence would certainly be to introduce more individual risk into the system. Whether or not this risk contains within it as much possibility for upward as for downward mobility would therefore depend on whether there are simultaneous moves to "de-stratify" the highly tracked system of German general education. Hinz reminds us in Chapter 4 that the social effects of institutional engineering in one area of political economic regulation depend on changes in another; in social science-speak, the effect of educational and of vocational training systems must be assessed interactively. The open question, which Hinz himself raises, is to what extent these two variables in turn interact with (and thus depend for their outcomes on) the values taken by other institutional variables in the political economy.

Helga Krüger takes up in Chapter 5 the issue of how the institutions of training affect life courses, but in doing so she highlights a new institutional contributor to a well-known general feature of the German model: its gender bias. Male youths constitute two-thirds of those trained through the dual system and female youths only one-third. Where are the rest of the German young women? Krüger shows that many of them earn vocational qualifications through a school-based track, which she calls SVE, whose curricula are neither standardized nor negotiated among the social partners. The labor markets to which these certificates give access generally fail to provide the same rewards to individual investments in human capital as those of the dual system. Women predominate in this school-based track, although because it is not a standardized system, precise data about the exact numbers of participants in this system do not exist. But the news for gender equity is not all bad; the women certified through the dual system enjoy the benefits accruing to their male counterparts. Thus, the gender bias historically institutionalized by SVE is now somewhat de-coupled from gender, as one-third of the current dual system trainees are female.[10] However, the gender effect is still strong: firstly, the overwhelming number of those trained in SVE are women; and secondly, Krüger argues that school and employment agency counselors continue to push young women toward SVE if they are unable to get an apprenticeship in their first-choice occupation in the dual system. Although the dual system is not closed to women – especially its well-paying service professions like banking and insurance – the continued existence of SVE qualifications outside the highly regulated dual system allows its indirect effects on gender bias to persist.

10. In addition to its obvious gender effects, the existence of SVE highlights the existence of labor markets whose functioning provides *neither* women *nor* men the same return to individual investments in skill provision associated with other segments of the German labor market.

One corrective to the problems of SVE would be to inte-grate its occupations fully into the dual system, as has happened in a few, isolated occupations. Krüger suggests that the will to reform might in fact be weak in Germany, for reasons that are congruent with the "insider-outsider" stylized fact of German labor markets generally. The existence of a second-tier skill pro-vision system provides (yet another) buffer for companies to supplement the supply of skilled labor gained through the high-wage, high-skill system. Because SVE jobs do not typically lead to the sort of internal labor markets associated with apprentice-ships, they do not afford the statutorily and union-protected jobs of these internal labor markets. As Krüger notes, the sug-gestive data in her chapter will need to be confirmed by better hard numbers (and better public data collection) on the actual extent of the system; the findings of the chapter certainly indi-cate that more research on this issue is warranted.[11] If the SVE system does indeed still provide training to a significant propor-tion of women, then discussions of German skill provision will need to incorporate this little-known system into their consid-erations of reform.

In the final chapter of Part II, Jutta Gatter identifies a source of mounting pressure on the German skill provision system – the dramatic aging of the population – and she analyzes current weaknesses in the capacity of the further training system to respond to this change. As the population ages, working lives will need to be longer than today; Gatter argues that the rela-tively unregulated world of German further training has already taken on a greater role in the provision of skill, and it will con-tinue to do so in the future. Unlike the dual system, the German further training system is institutionally chaotic, described by

11. Krüger notes that the research institute tied to the federal employment agency (the IAB) has begun to track these data recently, as they recog-nize their lack of information in this area. A regional case study indicates that roughly half the female cohort of intermediate and foundational school-leavers pursues certification through SVE.

Gatter as a "jungle" of sectoral regulations that often lack clear mechanisms of implementation at the regional and firm levels. Two related problems bedevil the current market of further training measures in Germany: first, the quality of programs varies widely; and second, there is no standardized system for assessing these programs, in stark contrast to the situation in the strictly regulated apprenticeship market.

The rising importance of further training, combined with the lack of regulation of its supply, call into question the ability of the German skill provision system to constrain the growth of inequality. Gatter shows that company spending on further training varies dramatically across social groups. In general, the higher the initial education level of an individual, the more she is likely to participate in further training measures, such that further training spending exacerbates differences in human capital (and presumably in income) created by the system of initial training. But "she" is perhaps the wrong pronoun to use here, since women, who are disproportionately represented in the ranks of part-time workers, thereby suffer from the disproportionately low spending of companies on further training for part-time in comparison to full-time workers. In addition, older workers have been much less likely to participate in further training measures than have younger workers, which was partially a function of the growth in early retirement in Germany in the 1980s. Since the burden placed on the German pension system by this generous early retirement policy was heavy, the government has recently made early retirement conditional on the receipt of lower pension benefits. Thus, older workers face threats of declining relative income on two fronts: if they retire early, they will receive a reduced pension; if they stay in the workforce, and current investment trends continue, their human capital deficit relative to younger colleagues will increase. The differences between gender- and age-groups with respect to the time spent in further training measures are *lower* in the United States than in Germany, which is perhaps an ominous sign of the current trend of further training in Germany to increase inequality. Rather than minimizing inequality, lifelong learning and the growing importance of continuing vocational training may thus exacerbate further the existing insider-outsider character of the German labor market.

Institutional Experiments with In-Firm Training

While the German model of skill provision is under pressure at home, other industrialized countries have tried to import components of the model, particularly in the area of associationally governed apprenticeship training. The chapters in Part III critically examine these experiments, with an eye to answering two related questions: first, what are the social preconditions for a system of private interest-governed in-firm youth training to succeed in producing a supply of broadly skilled workers? The second question is the converse of the first: how plastic are these institutions, i.e., what sort of functions can be allowed to vary to suit local circumstances while maintaining the fundamental advantage of the German system? That advantage rests on the fact that a large number of employers have been convinced to invest substantially in the development of the transferable skills of their workers. The chapters in this section juxtapose cases of failure and success in order to draw reliable inferences about the conditions that increase the probability of achieving this objective.

My own chapter (7) opens Part III with a comparison of French and eastern German experiences in trying to import West German-style apprenticeship practices, classifying company training practices according to criteria derived from West German training patterns. To understand the factors that make firms more likely to gamble on high-skill training (given the risk that other companies will not also do so), the chapter uses information from 52 companies in the metal and electronics sectors to analyze the way these attempted changes of training regime look to individual firms. The framework conditions that turn out to be most important in influencing this choice are the modal organization of production and the availability of alternative options for recruiting skilled workers through the training system. The more the organization of production in an industry approximates the ideal of DQP, relying more on the broad skills of workers and less on price-slashing capability, the easier it will be to persuade individual companies to engage in high-skill training patterns.[12] The structure of the existing educational system also plays a decisive role, because it helps to determine if there are plausible alternative strategies to (exit options from) high-skill training. If firms have such exit options, then (other things being equal) they are more likely not to invest substantially in newly available training practices.

Yet other things are not always equal: these framework conditions are probabilistic, not deterministic. The capacities of regional and/or sectoral institutions of private governance affect the extent to which the training system responds to the evolving skill requirements of companies, and these institutions can serve as privileged conduits of information exchange between the private economy and the public authorities. In designing transitional aid to help ease the decision of companies to start down the high-skill path, this function of information circulation is the *sine qua non* of success. Moreover, institutions of private governance – preeminently, employers' associations – can create links among individual training companies that enable them to gain the fruits of cooperation (through high-skill training) while reinforcing their confidence that other firms, too, will begin to adopt favorable training practices in the new environment. The capacity of private interest governance thus mediates the influence of the framework conditions of the organization of produc-

---

12. Conversely, the closer the organization of production approximates to Fordism, the more difficult it is to convince companies to invest in high-level training.

tion and the structure of the training system. In convincing companies to invest in high-level training, private associations are the best placed to identify potentially cooperative firms and to mobilize them in support of the high-skill training effort. Thus, the process of training reform puts a premium on organizational capacity, and the capacity can be as important in determining success as are the "objective conditions" of the existing educational and productive systems.

If eastern Germany and France are challenging organizational environments for German-style training to take root, the American institutional ecosystem appears even more hostile. Lacking nationally strong organizations of employers or workers and devoid of a national certification system for training, American employers and governments have encountered serious obstacles in trying to establish high-level training among more than a few companies (cf. Lynch 1994b, Osterman 1994c, Bishop 1996, Cappelli et al. 1998). While some have pointed to the American network of community colleges as a resource upon which more firm-centered training could be constructed, such projects risk being captured by local employers such that the training provided ends up being only narrowly firm-specific. Chapter 8, by Eric Parker and Joel Rogers, explores these problems and analyzes how sectoral consortia, which organize multiple firms producing for related markets, have in some instances been able to overcome the inherently weak organizational fabric of the American political economy to put in place vibrant regional systems of skill provision. They identify three reasons why consortia are likely to succeed in getting firms to make high-skill investments: first, consortia are able to develop plans for many companies, which has the effect of making both the cost per plan low and the technical expertise of the consortia high; second, successful consortia are able to offer companies a range of services beyond those of youth training (such as further training or the building of supplier networks), which makes the consortia more valuable for the companies; and finally, the use of these training consortia links the companies more tightly to each other for the solving of wider problems, providing individual companies with an interlocutor for dealing with regional authorities, while also thereby giving firms a mechanism through which they can credibly commit to implicate themselves in projects of regional development.

This functional specification of these consortia, however, avoids the hardest question: how do such consortia get created in the first place, given the barriers that generally impede collective action among economic actors in the United States liberal market economy? The authors adduce various types of sectoral consortia that have begun functioning recently in the United States, usually building on the active involvement of both labor and business groups. In the case of perhaps the most successful consortia to emerge in the US, the Wisconsin Regional Training Partnership (WRTP), Parker and Rogers point to two conditions that seem to have allowed employers to agree to join their efforts in such a consortium: the fact that the targeted sectors were highly unionized by American standards, which provided employers with the advantage of a capable negotiating partner and the constraint of a strong opponent to low-skill strategies in companies; and the availability of technical expertise provided through the involvement of the Center on Wisconsin Strategy (COWS), which gave individual companies access to information about the potential costs and benefits of cooperation, information which is often lacking in the absence of employer organization. Wisconsin companies appear to have dodged the bullet of collective action because they were facing a game of coordination, in which the underlying conditions made cooperation an optimal strategy for individual companies, provided that other companies would also cooperate. In this game, COWS supplied and circulated information, letting companies know that the highest payoffs would accrue to cooperation. Recognizing that the weak organization of labor precludes this strategy from being mechanistically diffused to other regions of the United States, Parker and Rogers suggest that some combination of organizational reconfiguration of labor with public involvement may be the prerequisite for wider success. However, like the question of labor organization, some form of information diffusion to companies, as supplied by COWS for the WRTP, may well be necessary to convince many companies to invest in high-level training; and this function may also prove difficult to replicate in the organizationally weak American political economy.

Stewart Wood's chapter (9) deals with the failure of institutional innovation in another liberal market economy, that of Britain. At the end of the 1980s the Conservative government introduced Training and Enterprise Councils (TECs) as private governance structures whose principal task was to organize and provide training for regional firms. Loosely modeled on the German Chambers of Industry and Commerce, which regulate industrial training in the dual system, TECs are private-sector organizations tasked with linking public policy and the cooperation of private firms in training; Wood describes these organizational hybrids as "local-level deliverers of national public policy." Private though they may be, the TECs have failed to win the widespread confidence of either individual companies or of sectoral employer associations: the former see them as intrusive agents of the state, and the latter view them as organizational competitors. The TECs have thus alienated the constituency most crucial to their central mission (increasing skill provision by companies), even as the state has repeatedly deprived them of the financial and jurisdictional independence necessary to carry out that mission. Faced with the hostility of private enterprise to their training supervision, the TECs have retreated from their original goal of fostering training in the private sector, devoting their energies instead to the marginal function of connecting the public sector with existing government programs. Wood shows that some of the failures of the TECs stem from problems of internally inconsistent institutional design, but his chapter also recognizes a more fundamental problem for the

British government in its attempt to move away from the "low-skill equilibrium": as in France, the modal organization of production does not create a large demand for skilled workers by British employers. He notes that "weak demand for skills is certainly at the root of many of the problems faced by TECs in the local economy, and in many ways there is little that TECs, or tinkering with their institutional design, can do to overcome this problem."

Yet the news is not all bad for Britain and skill provision. The recent Modern Apprenticeship (MA) scheme has succeeded where past British policies have failed by linking substantial company investments in apprentices to the involvement of sectoral employers' associations in the development of standardized curricula, while also acknowledging a supervisory role for the TECs. There are not yet enough data to know if the success of the MA scheme is the result of a substitution effect, in which employers replace trainees they would have hired anyway with publicly aided apprenticeships, but Wood rightly points to the fact that the policy is promising because it relies on individual employer investment in standardized skills negotiated by employer representatives. The past failures of institutional design combined with the election of a new Labour government may prove salutary in leading TECs in the future to build stronger ties with local employers, employers' associations, and to local unions and education authorities. Without this proximity to private actors, the TECs will not succeed in helping Britain to supply the public good of a skilled workforce.

Taken together, the chapters in Part III yield clear predictions about the necessary conditions for institutions combining firm-specific and general training to succeed, predictions that correspond to some open questions in the political economy literature discussed earlier. First, in what seems like an obvious assertion, employers must demand broad skills for production. In other words, the causal chain in much of the current literature on non-market coordination has it backwards: a system for the provision of broad skills is not the precondition for DQP-style production; initial moves toward an organization of production based on incremental innovation and teamwork must already be under way in systems lacking these sorts of institutions of skill provision, such that employers will be willing to invest in institutions to create those skills. Attempts to implement such a reform based on a version of Say's Law, in which building the supply of a skilled workforce is supposed to stimulate the demand for those skills, are likely to fail. And just as employers must demand those skills, they must also have a dominant voice in the institutions that define skill requirements, in order to assure them that the skills certificates can evolve in line with changes in their demand for skill (thus confirming arguments in Finegold and Soskice 1988 and Soskice 1994). Building employer consortia that link employers to each other in the cooperative provision of training appears to be one of the most successful formulae for inducing employers to make an initial investment in skills and to build the confidence in the emerging system that is necessary in order for them to incorporate this type of skill provision as a permanent aspect of their human resource strategies.

Despite the centrality that all the authors attribute to employers in this process, the chapters in this section also demonstrate that institutions of skill provision controlled entirely by employers cannot assure that broad skills will be widely conferred along with firm-specific skills. Well-organized labor unions, as in the German case, provide the most obvious counter-balancing power to employers in such institutions (Streeck et al. 1987, Streeck 1992). In environments where labor unions have demonstrated some organizational capacity, but where they have historically been excluded from the skill formation process, our work suggests that their inclusion in the regulation of skill provision may provide the necessary countervailing power against employers. Yet in other political economies, the organizational resources or heritage of labor may make this strategy infeasible: the American South is one clear example. For such cases, our chapters do not provide answers, but they at least trace the contours of what an answer might look like. The chapters by Parker and Rogers and by Wood (8 and 9) suggest that one alternative mechanism for counter-balancing employer power is to involve community organizations generally, and especially public providers of technical education, in the process of curriculum definition and standardization. Providers of technical education can have both the necessary expertise and the credibility to defend the interest of broad educational objectives; they would be able to complement organizations of labor in the definition of skill certifications.

This point suggests another, on which most of our analyses converge: states cannot solve the problem of general and firm-relevant skill provision by throwing money at the problem. Wood's chapter is particularly eloquent on the way in which an overbearing state presence engenders the suspicion of companies. State aid is most likely to be effective in assuring the objective of broad skilling when it is harnessed to organizations of private governance, which have access to better information about the concerns of the private economy (cf. Culpepper forthcoming). Public authorities are unlikely to succeed in projects where they become the central instrument of implementation, rather than using their resources to enable private actors to negotiate the regulation of the system.

Our findings still leave room for considerable institutional variation, however. The chapters show that regions are often the locus for negotiated private governance that succeeds in providing a substantial group of broadly skilled workers; this finding challenges the conventional wisdom that systems of skill certification and standardization must be nationally uniform in order to allow for the provision of broad skills (cf. Lynch 1994b). While the national objective may be laudable, the best may be the enemy of the good when national skills certification faces many roadblocks before being introduced into a federal system like the United States. Our work shows that choosing the second-best option of regionally based certification does not necessarily entail a sacrifice of breadth of content. Moreover, Gatter's chapter reminds us that there are alternative mechanisms of skill provision that can compensate for weaknesses in the area of initial training. Political economies that have more highly developed systems of further training (like France) or of post-secondary education (like the United States) have the capacity to use their comparative institutional advantages to create functional equivalence with some of the institutions that in Germany help secure the provision of a broadly skilled workforce.

Some Unanswered Questions

Despite the extensive research represented in our work, this volume still leaves some questions unresolved. At the forefront of these questions is the ability of apprenticeship-style training to respond to the increasing growth of services in the economies of the advanced capitalist countries. The dual system has not produced the same profusion of occupational certificates for the service sector as it has in manufacturing. Yet these jobs now drive employment growth across the industrialized countries (Hall 1998a). Gatter's chapter includes evidence from service-sector companies on how they are using the current system of skill provision, but the ability of new certified occupations to keep up with new economic demands for skills is a large question mark hanging over the future of the dual system. The most likely path to reform will pass through a greater integration of the basic system of skill provision with the increasingly attractive (to young Germans) higher education track, an issue alluded to in several chapters and discussed at length in the conclusion. The answer to the question of services and German skill provision is still open, and the most that can be done is to signal it and to point to the area as one that demands more research in the future.

Even in manufacturing, the traditional area of strength of the German training system, disagreements remain about the ability of the system to adjust to new challenges. While the chapters by Wagner and by Finegold and Wagner give some grounds for optimism, they premise that optimism on the ability of the training system to reform itself. The chapter by Herrigel and Sabel provides evidence about the limits that the rigid German training system manifests in responding to rapidly changing firm demands for skills. With respect to the adaptability of the system, the issue here is really whether the dual system's glass is half-empty or half-full. Moreover, political change in Germany is slow, and thus the ability to push through reforms of the institutional underpinnings of the system cannot be assumed (cf. Katzenstein 1987).[13] Certainly, the commonly expressed need for reform does highlight a danger for the dual system, and we cannot yet know whether or not the system is flexible enough to respond to that need.

There is a larger question for students of political economy, to which this volume can only represent a partial answer: how much does functioning of the German model rest on the system of skill provision in its current form? The consensus of the current literature on non-market coordination in advanced capitalism seems to be, "very much" (cf. Hall and Soskice forthcoming, Hollingsworth and Boyer 1997, Streeck 1996); yet some broad processes of industrial transformation are essentially not decided by questions of skill provision. Systems of skill provision delimit the alternative strategies that firms can pursue, but

---

13. Pierson's (1994) study of welfare state retrenchment efforts in Britain and in the United States has demonstrated how policies create constituencies with an interest in their continuation, making the dynamics of establishment different from that of change. This finding in two liberal polities will hold only more strongly in the corporatist German policy-making system. However, the perception of crisis can indeed be a powerful stimulus to change, even in corporatist systems with welfare states analogous to the German one, as shown in Visser and Hemerijck's (1997) study of the Netherlands.

the most important causal variables in socioeconomic change will not always be skill-related. Moreover, the chapters in Part II of this volume reveal that some of the distributive trade-offs on which the system has rested in the past are increasingly untenable in the face of demographic change and of new understandings of equality. It is quite possible that changes to the model that attempt to reduce these distributive problems, as in the reforms to make the system work more flexibly, may generate unintended destabilizing consequences in other subsystems of the institutions of the German economy. We know that the political economy is complex, but our understanding of institutional interaction still falls short of the ability to know which elements of the German political economy are amenable to tinkering without fundamentally transforming the model itself.

This volume stands as a contribution both to ongoing debates in social science and to concrete problems of policy reform. Building on the convergence of findings about the increased importance of skill in the interdependent economy, we have tested a variety of hypotheses about how institutions of skill provision can provide the collective good of a broadly skilled workforce; the strength of our evidence has allowed us to correct some prevailing misunderstandings about the relationship of skill to systems of production; and the findings suggest further hypotheses for the next round of researchers to test. Yet we have also shown that these findings are not just of academic interest, but of relevance for the policy-makers in the industrialized countries that want to implement elements of in-firm training loosely modeled on the German system. Policy-makers can draw their own conclusions from the individual chapters, and David Finegold presents a synthesis of some of the policy-relevant findings from the individual chapters in the conclusion. It is our hope that this volume succeeds in straddling the worlds of social science and of policy reform by addressing with considerable methodological rigor questions that have important practical implications for the future of the advanced industrial economies.

Part I

THREATS TO THE GERMAN SYSTEM IN COMPARATIVE PERSPECTIVE

THE GERMAN APPRENTICESHIP
SYSTEM UNDER STRAIN

Karin Wagner

The Importance of the
Vocational Training System for the German Model

The German system has long combined a high level of competitiveness in world markets with a strong social cohesion
that fosters low levels of inequality in a high-wage economy.
This framework depends on a set of socioeconomic institutions
– including banks, employers' associations, and trade unions –
that support long-term commitments by labor and capital. One
important factor within this institutional framework is the vocational training system, which is seen by many authors to play a
key role in Germany's comparative advantage in the production
of high-quality, internationally competitive manufactured goods
through "diversified quality production" (DQP), which is based
on highly skilled craft workers and engineers (Sorge and Streeck
1988, Streeck 1997, Soskice 1997). Its high output of skilled
and well-educated employees is also seen to provide the basis for

Germany's export success and innovation (Carlin et al. 1996; Kern 1996; Wagner et al. 1997).

In the last few years, however, growing concern has been expressed about the viability of the German model. Globalization and the appearance of new forms of work organization are increasingly seen as a challenge (Streeck 1997). In the late 1980s new models of production were developed, and the training system began to be adapted (Kern and Schumann 1984). The new training structures have been updated and broadened so that the curricula contain improved technical content and require training in social competencies. Even with these changes, the German skill creation system in the 1990s has to adapt to new challenges, such as lean production, with its emphasis on team work, continuous improvement processes, flexible machine tools, close supplier relationships, and rapid innovation. Case studies show that the skills provided by the dual system along with the subsequent *Meister* training continue to be relevant in the new organizational context (see Chapter 3). However, the restructuring of the curricula has placed a greater burden on the shoulders of the employers by increasing their net training costs. A strong increase in the apprenticeship allowance at the beginning of the 1990s has further added to the cost of training. If employers investing in the vocational training system – as in other business processes – are to obtain an adequate return on their investment, then measures to reduce their net training costs are needed. The balance between the costs and benefits of training will be the first major point discussed in this chapter.

While the German training system might be coping with new forms of work organization, two further problems have affected the sustainability of the system: unification and a severe recession. The recession, which began in 1991, induced an unprecedented loss of jobs in manufacturing industry, and export performance has deteriorated sharply. Although the German economy is slowly recovering from the economic slump, many companies are still trimming their workforces and outsourcing more abroad, particularly in Eastern Europe. With the reduction in their overall employment, employers do not see a need for hiring new workers and thus refrain from offering apprenticeship places. This leads to a strong reduction in the supply of apprenticeship places, which is the backbone of the German training system. If supply does not cover the demand for training places, young people will not be trained, and the high skill strategy of the German system might fail. The balance between the supply and demand for training places will be the second major issue dealt with in this chapter.

The third topic is the transfer of the West German training system to eastern Germany.[1] At the time of unification, West Germany was one of the world's most successful high-wage economies (Streeck 1997). After unification almost all West German institutions – and with them the high-skill, high-wage model – were transferred to the former East Germany. Trade unions and employer associations agreed to raise eastern German wages to western German levels within five years to protect the existing high-skill, high-wage system of the west. Accordingly, wages soared in eastern Germany, while productivity lagged behind (Hitchens et al. 1993). The skills of eastern German workers were lower than those of western German workers, and technology was also in need of modernization. As a result, eastern Germany was not prepared to compete in high-quality markets demanding a highly skilled workforce (Wagner 1993, Wagner et al. 1995). Even with subsidies and training initiatives, the updating of skills and the efficient use of modern machinery will inevitably take a long time. In addition, the traditional market of the East German economy had been the Eastern bloc, which did not require and could not afford to pay higher prices for better products. Hence these markets broke

1. Eastern Germany here stands for the new federal states of the former German Democratic Republic (GDR) after unification in 1990; West Germany stands for the old federal states of the Federal Republic prior to unification.

away, and the eastern German manufacturers had to get into new markets which were already occupied by their western German counterparts or by other advanced producers. The consequence was a widespread collapse of eastern German manufacturing. Although each year more than 100 billion DM are transferred to subsidize the eastern German economy, a basis for self-sustaining growth has so far not been established (Carlin and Soskice 1997). The effects of the dismal economic situation on the supply of apprenticeships will be the third major topic of the chapter.

All these issues show the need for reform. Since the apprenticeship system is the major provider of vocational skills, the German model of high-quality production is highly dependent on it. It provides the comprehensive theoretical and practical training through the "dual system" for about 70 percent of German young people. Because of its central role, the growing debate – about whether the apprenticeship system is in need of reform – is quite controversial (Althoff 1994, Dybowski et al. 1994, Degen and Walden 1997). On the one hand, some fear that the demand for places will drop and criticize the fact that the dual system is not attractive enough for good school-leavers, losing too many of them to higher education. A large number of small companies (with up to 99 employees) are unable to fill their offered training places (Lenske 1997). On the other hand, it is argued (particularly in eastern Germany) that there is a surplus of would-be apprentices, and that the dual system will be decreasingly able to accommodate all applicants (Althoff 1994, Rüttgers 1996, Himmelreich 1996, Franz and Zimmermann 1996). Trade unions and the socialist party therefore demand that the system – which, to the present, has worked on the basis of completely voluntary participation by employers – should be financed through a levy scheme in the future. This proposal was put forward in the 1980s to accommodate the large increase in the number of young people seeking apprenticeship places, but has always been strongly opposed by employers, who claim that it will increase costs and lead to ineffective training. This chapter will seek to help to resolve the above controversial arguments, concluding with a set of measures to modernize the system.

Searching for the Break-Even Point in Apprenticeship Training

Gross Costs

Since Becker's seminal work on human capital (1964), the incentives for investing in firm-specific and general skills have acquired special interest. Employers in the dual system provide both types of skills and detailed surveys into the costs and benefits of the apprenticeship system have been conducted (Edding 1963, Noll et al. 1983, Falk 1982, von Bardeleben et al. 1991 and 1995). These studies show that German employers incur high gross training costs, which differ according to the size of firms, the type of apprenticeship, and the training year of the apprentice. The latest survey for 1991 found average yearly gross costs in the industry/trade occupations of 31,800 DM, and 24,900 DM in the craft sector; costs in the craft sector were thus on average about 20 percent lower than in the industry/ trade sector (von Bardeleben 1995). Gross costs are defined as personnel costs of the trainer while he or she teaches, wage costs of the trainee, and overhead costs. The study also shows that training costs of large firms, where the first two years of training are often conducted almost entirely in training workshops, are much higher, at 42,000 DM per apprentice. Small- and medium- sized enterprises, which do their training mainly on the shopfloor, report much lower gross costs. The difference in costs according to the size of companies is partly reflected in Table 1.1, as industry/trade companies are on average larger than craft companies.

Table 1.1   Gross training costs for different sectors and
training years in DM in 1991

	Industry and Trade			Craft sector		
	Total	Trainee wages as % of all costs	Costs for the trainer in %	Total	Trainee wages as % of all costs	Costs for the trainer in %
1st year	31,994	45.5	42.8	24,830	38.6	50.8
2nd year	33,102	49.3	38.2	26,254	45.9	46.3
3rd year	31,624	55.3	32.5	25,518	51.7	37.7
Average	31,824	50.0	37.7	24,889	45.4	43.7

Source: von Bardeleben et al. 1995.

Costs over the different training years do not vary greatly. While the wage costs for the apprentices increase over time and therefore make up a larger portion of total costs, the costs for trainers decrease at a similar level. The sum of wage costs for the apprentice and for the trainer account for almost 90 percent of the total costs of apprenticeship training in each of the three years.

Net Costs

Net costs are more difficult to assess, because the productive output of the apprentice is usually not systematically measured. In the above survey, net costs were calculated as gross costs minus the productive output of the trainee, which was equated to the wage costs for a skilled worker while he or she was producing the same output. These net costs were found to be about a third higher in large companies than in small ones. Net costs in the *Handwerk* sector, at 12,352 DM, are considerably lower than in the companies that belong to the chamber of industry and trade, at 20,509 DM, as shown in Table 1.2. Average yearly net training costs are 17,862 DM. These figures take into account a yearly output of 11,710 DM per apprentice (von Bardeleben et al. 1995). A comparison over the training period illustrates an increase in the productive output of apprentices as they advance from the first to the third training year, when the trainees are already quite skilled and spend a higher proportion of their time in real work settings. Accordingly, net costs decrease, while gross costs remain stable (see Table 1.2).

Table 1.2 Net costs of training in the industry/trade and craft sector according to training year in 1991

| | Industry and Trade | | | Craft sector | | |
	Gross costs	Productive output	Net costs	Gross costs	Productive output	Net costs
1st year	31,994	9,008	22,986	24,830	9,338	15,492
2nd year	33,102	11,036	22,066	26,254	12,020	14,234
3rd year	31,624	14,573	17,051	25,518	16,327	9,191
Average	31,824	11,315	20,509	24,889	12,536	12,352

Source: von Bardeleben et al. 1995.

Variable Net Costs

Another way to estimate the costs of training is to look only at the variable costs. This calculation differs from the full cost method in that fixed costs are not considered, but only the costs which are directly associated with the apprentice. The costs of trainer supervisors, who instruct apprentices as part of their wider job responsibilities, mainly at times when they are not busy with production themselves (in contrast to full-time trainers), and the costs of administration, which barely increase with the intake of an apprentice, are omitted.

Table 1.3 Variable net costs of training according to company employment size in 1991

Average	Up to 9	10-49	50-499	500+
6,339 DM	1,646 DM	3,609 DM	8,184 DM	17,886 DM

Source: von Bardeleben et al. 1995.

Using this method the average annual net costs to companies are reduced to just 6,339 DM per apprentice (see Table 1.3). A large variation, which depends very much on the organization of training in the firm, is again evident among companies of different sizes. Where training takes place predominantly on the job, as often happens in very small companies, variable net costs amount on average to just 1,646 DM. Companies with more than 500 employees – which frequently train in training workshops with full-time trainers (and full trainers' cost) – have more than ten times that net cost: 17,886 DM. With this method, which seems to match real costs more accurately, the variable net costs are negative for almost 20 percent of the trainees in the industry/trade sector and for 30 percent of trainees in the craft sector. It should be emphasized that (a) the training for some companies pays off immediately over the training period (without even considering further benefits) and (b) higher benefits than net costs are not restricted to the craft sector, as is often assumed. The overwhelming cost item are wages, which often account for about 80 percent of the total variable net costs. Consequently, the level of wages has a large impact on the level of training costs.

Further Training Benefits

ADDITIONAL FLEXIBILITY

In addition to the above estimated direct output of trainees, the benefits from employing an apprentice are often greatly underestimated. First, benefits are usually calculated only for those specific time periods during which apprentices are productive. Any corresponding slack times, such as waiting times that would occur if a skilled worker did the job, are not taken into account. Second, the added flexibility which an apprentice provides to the organization just by being available when a task comes up is often not considered. For example, she will answer the phone or take orders from customers at the time when they come in. For these tasks only her time spent taking the order is assessed as a benefit. However, if she were not there, another person would be needed to occupy the office full-time although this capacity would not be fully utilized. The same is true for occupations where some of the tasks can only be handled by two people.

SAVINGS IN RECRUITMENT COSTS

Companies that hire skilled workers from the market instead of training apprentices have to pay costs for advertisements, screening applications, doing interviews at different levels, and travel costs. These costs have been estimated by a large German company to reach 2,000 DM to 3,000 DM per hire (Cramer and Müller 1994). If the hired person fails to fit the job, then these costs will be incurred again in seeking a replacement worker. While there are also costs involved in recruiting apprentices, these are usually much lower as travel costs usually do not occur, there is no need for advertising since apprentices apply themselves or come from schools with close relations to a given company and it is less costly to test their skills since they will learn them on the job, and usually one person is sufficient to conduct the interviews.

NO ADAPTATION COSTS FOR NEWLY HIRED WORKERS

Newly hired people, even if they are skilled, need quite some time to acquire company-specific skills. Interviews in mechanical engineering firms have shown that newly hired people need between half a year and one year before they can work with full proficiency, depending on their qualifications, personalities, and their new jobs (Cramer and Müller 1994). If it is assumed that highly skilled people work during this time on average with half the productivity of a skilled worker fully adapted to the firm, the average loss in performance would be 27,000 DM, assuming average yearly wage costs of 54,000 DM in 1991. This loss is high if compared with the average net variable costs for apprentice training of 6,339 DM per year and it is still 1.5 times

the net variable costs of apprenticeship training in establishments with more than 500 employees. When a semi-skilled
person is hired to be trained for a skilled job, even higher costs
might be incurred, since training takes a much longer time and
the employer consequently loses a greater amount of output.
Companies that have tried to introduce a team organization
with a semi-skilled workforce have found that the higher
demands on the workforce require an enormous amount of new
training. To overcome these difficulties they have decided to
take on more apprentices in the future (Finegold and Wagner,
Chapter 3).

During their first two years, newly skilled workers are paid
the "young" skilled worker's wage. As about 50 percent of the
apprentices remain with their training company for at least two
years after the apprenticeship, companies gain additional benefits in comparison to hiring an experienced skilled worker (BMBW
1993). In larger companies the proportion of former apprentices
remaining in the company – and therefore the benefit – is even
greater. Many apprentices like to stay with their company for
one or two years after completion of their training, since training is not seen as being completed with the taking of examinations. After these years, the trainees as well as the employers
of smaller or medium-sized companies regard a change in firm
as an advantage for the technical and social development of
young people. This move is positive for the apprentices, as it
adds to their know-how about production processes, products,
and work organization, which differ greatly among establishments (Kloas 1988). It is also positive for the companies that
hire them, since they bring new ideas and methods into the
company and help to diffuse new working practices and technology. However, apprentices who leave their training company
directly after their exams are often regarded with distrust. The
potential new employer might suspect that the person was not
hired by the training company because of some negative aspects
in his/her apprenticeship.

AVOIDING THE COSTS OF POACHING WORKERS

Companies that poach skilled workers from other companies have to offer higher wages to entice workers to leave their current companies. If they have to pay 10 percent to 15 percent more than the average wage, it amounts to an additional 5,000 DM to 7,500 DM per year. Usually the higher pay for these newly hired people cannot be kept secret, and other employees will demand a comparable increase as well. Over time non-training companies will therefore face considerable additional wage costs (Soskice 1994).

HIRING PEOPLE WHO FIT

The risk of hiring a skilled person who does not fit the job, the team, or the company culture is much higher than hiring an apprentice who has been educated for over three years in the firm and whose personality and technical skills are well-known. Nearly three-quarters of the companies mentioned this consideration as an important advantage in training apprentices in the 1991 survey (von Bardeleben et al. 1995). With the increasing introduction of team work and closer cooperation, the personality factor will become even more critical. The pressure to hire the right person, and hence the benefits from the lengthy screening period apprenticeships provide, is particularly important in Germany, given the relatively high cost and difficulties of firing employees.

REPUTATION OF TRAINING COMPANIES

The willingness to train also affects the reputation of companies, both internally and externally. The large proportion of German employees who have gone through an apprenticeship know from their own experience how important training is for young people. For them it is hard to understand why their company should not give this opportunity to young school-leavers. In addition, employees are often looking for apprenticeships for their own children and expect that companies might offer training places to them. Large companies are well aware that offering apprenticeship places can improve their external reputation. Their annual reports almost always include long accounts of their training activities. They invest a lot in the quality of training so that their trainees score well on their exams. This can provide them with free advertising if their trainees are awarded a top mark by the chamber, which is reported in the newspapers and business magazines; many German readers associate well-trained people with high-quality goods. The correlation between training and reputation has recently been used in press releases of the ministry and of the chambers to increase the willingness of companies to train by publicly disclosing the names of those companies that do not train.

Conclusion for the Break-Even Point in 1991

According to the above cost calculations the German apprenticeship system has been very finely balanced; for many companies costs and benefits were nearly equal until 1991. Although costs vary according to sector, size of company, and occupation, many companies, especially smaller ones which do the bulk of training, might have come close to a break-even point, or even have achieved a net gain from training apprentices. For larger companies, variable net costs are much higher, but so too are the benefits after training. First of all, these companies have a choice among the better educated school-leavers, who prefer larger companies because of their better career prospects and greater fringe benefits. The larger firms apply more rigorous selection criteria in hiring school-leavers for apprenticeships. Thereby they ensure that they get very able apprentices who will fit the job, integrate well into the company, and who will not drop out of training. This helps insure that training costs are not wasted. Since the machinery in large manufacturers is usually more specialized, more delicate, and more expensive, a longer training period for newly hired skilled workers would be necessary; this makes it more worthwhile to train apprentices, who will then provide exactly those specific skills which are essential (Neubäumer 1993; BMBW1992; Schöngen and Westhoff 1992). This is supported by the higher retention rate of apprentices in large companies. In addition, training costs are tax deductible; with the higher tax rate of larger companies, the after-tax cost of training apprentices is further reduced.

Cost Increases in the 1990s

Weekly Working Time Reduction

For many years West Germany has had one of the lowest number of yearly working hours per worker of any industrialized country. In addition to about six weeks of annual vacation plus public holidays plus paid sick days, the average working hours per week are decreasing. This trend is well illustrated in the metal industry. At the beginning of 1980 the standard working time was 40 hours; a progressive decrease took place until a 35-hour week was agreed on in October 1995. While this decrease of 13 percent in working time affects workers and trainees in the same way, the time for productive work of the apprentice was squeezed. Given that the trainee needs instruction for the same amount of time as before – or even more because of more demanding training requirements (discussed below) – the reduced working time has led to a more than proportional cut in apprentices' productive work: fewer total hours, combined with the same time spent on theoretical training, leaves less time for work in production. A hypothetical example will clarify the impact of this change: given a decrease in working time from 38 to 35 hours per week, and assuming that theoretical instruction at school and work take up 18 hours, the decrease in time for an apprentice's productive contribution is 15 percent, falling from 20 to 17 hours.

Broader Training Requirements

The German apprenticeship system is subject to continuous modification. One distinct sign of change is the reduction in the number of occupations from 901 in 1950, to 606 in 1970, to 374 in 1995. The consolidation of older courses is even greater when we consider that new occupations have also been added over time. Since 1969 the skill requirements in all occupations have been modernized and intensified in scope and in depth. In 1995 the Federal Vocational Training Institute was working on updating 90 occupations (BMBW 1995). In the occupations of the metal and electrical industries, for example, not only an updating but a structural reform has taken place. Since the new standards were set in 1987, apprentices in all the metal occupations undertake a common course for the first one and a half years. Only then does a gradual specialization take place. In contrast to the past, companies must be equipped to train during these years not only for their own specialist occupation, but also in a much broader area. This leads to a reduction in productive time in two ways. First, the more general training takes longer and involves less hands-on production. Second, demands for deeper technical know-how have increased, which require more teaching time for new computer technologies, teamwork, communication competencies, and complex work processes. Continuing our example from the previous section, the requirement of only one more training hour reduces the time for productive contributions by a further 6 percent (i.e., bringing productive time down from 17 to 16 hours).

Increased Time for Vocational Schooling

These increased requirements consequently demand a better theoretical preparation and understanding, which leads to longer vocational schooling. Table 1.4 shows the sizeable decrease in the proportion of trainees in West Germany who attended fewer than eight lessons per week; the figure fell from 30 percent to 11 percent between 1980 to 1990, and it dropped a further five percent in 1994. The effects of this reduction are, first, that the increased time spent on theoretical training reduces the time available for practical work and therefore increases the net training costs to the company. Second, any schooling above eight hours per week generally requires that the trainee attend school for a second day. Since the schooling is occupation-specific and therefore often not available in smaller cities, many trainees have long travel times. The journey time back to the company on that day further reduces the hours devoted to productive work. A solution to this problem could be the more widespread use of block release,[2] which has in fact been increasing in recent years, or a different organization of the schooling time.

Table 1.4   Increase in weekly lessons at vocational schools in West Germany*

	1980	1990	1994
Less than 8 lessons	30.8	11.3	5.5
8 to 10	38.1	41.3	30.7
11 and more	14.3	29.8	31.4
Block release	17.6	17.6	20.9

*Missing percentages could not be placed in a category.
Source: Grund- und Strukturdaten 1995/96.

Higher Training Wages

While the above factors indirectly increase training cost by reducing the time available for productive output, the highest cost factor in the variable costs have historically been apprentice wages. The pay differs among occupations, training years, and regions. The highest wages are paid in the public service and in industry and trade: more than 1,140 DM/month on aver-

2. Block release denotes the system in which, rather than going to school one or two days per week, apprentices spend a period of one to several weeks in school, followed by a period of several weeks at the company.

age in 1996 in West Germany. At the low end are craft occupations – such as tailors, who received less than 340 DM per
month, and hairdressers , who got 680 DM per month (BMBW
1997). The average remuneration across all occupations was
1055 DM. For the first year the rate is about a third of a skilled
worker's wage, and then it increases by about 13-15 percent
each year on average.[3] This relatively low remuneration is seen
as representing an investment by the trainee in his or her career.

Between 1991 and 1995 the average wages for skilled employees increased by 16 percent in the industry and trade sector and
by 14 percent in the craft sector, while the corresponding increase
for apprentices was much higher at 20 percent and 31 percent
respectively (von Bardeleben et al. 1997). Explanations for this
increase may be found in (a) the general tendency to increase
the pay of low earning classes more than the higher ones, and (b)
the relatively high demand for apprentices between 1990 and
1992, when more than 100,000 apprenticeship places were
unfilled each year in West Germany (see below, Table 1.8). Since
wage costs account for 80 percent of the total net variable costs
of apprenticeship training, the increase in net costs is almost the
same as the increase in wages. The variable net costs increased in
the industry and trade sector by 20 percent between 1991 and
1995; however, in the craft sector they have gone up by 400 percent from the very low level of 1991 (von Bardeleben et al.
1997). The substantial increase in costs has had a significant,
detrimental impact on the willingness of companies to train.
Employers surveyed claim that a reduction or stagnation of
wages and a longer period of time spent in the company (e.g., 40-
hour week for apprentices, holidays according to legal minimum,
better organization of vocational schooling) will lead to an
increased provision of training places. They point to high training costs and short working times as the most important of ten
obstacles to increase training (BMBW 1997).

---

3. In East Germany the yearly increases are slightly higher (BMBW 1997).

In conclusion, we can see that until 1991 the variable net costs of apprenticeship training were relatively low for all types of companies. Since then, however, considerable cost increases have taken place. Germany experienced a short boom following unification while other countries like the US and UK were restructuring, but since 1992, Germany's economy has lagged far behind its key competitors. Most companies have undertaken serious restructuring efforts, using costs as a dominant variable in decision-making. Increasing training costs therefore has a detrimental effect on the willingness of companies to train. Although the training wages for apprentices are low in relation to German skilled workers' wages, the average wage per apprentice's productive working hour – if we assume 16 hours of productive working time per week and 69 hours per month – is 15.29 DM, which is higher than the wage of skilled workers in many of Germany's competitors. A weekly increase of just two hours in working time would reduce the hourly wage to 13.63 DM. This calculation reflects the sensitivity of training costs to wages.

The Problems of Unification and the Recession

Transfer of the Apprenticeship System to Eastern Germany

The transfer of the apprenticeship system to eastern Germany was in many ways easier than the transfer of other institutions, since a dual system of a certain type had existed in the GDR. In the GDR, about 65 percent of an age group – a slightly lower figure than in the Federal Republic – entered an apprenticeship after completing general schooling in the 1980s. In contrast to West Germany, the apprenticeships lasted only two instead of three to three and a half years. Apprenticeship was considered basic training, and so many former apprentices later took part in further education courses. As a result of the different industrial structure of the GDR, the proportion of trainees in different sectors was dissimilar between the two systems: 42 percent of apprentices were in industry and 12 percent were in agriculture in the GDR, versus 22 percent and 1 percent in West Germany. As the craft sector was relatively small, and private companies were limited in numbers, larger industrial firms were the principal providers of apprenticeship training. The opportunity to take the *Meister* examination played an important role in both systems. In 1989, 17,500 skilled workers passed this exam in the GDR and 55,500 in West Germany, which is roughly a similar proportion of the labor force.

Since unification, an immense further training effort has been undertaken to update the quality of vocational qualifications to the more modern technology of the Western world and to the more demanding aspects of work, e.g., to enable workers to accomplish a broad range of complex tasks without guidance and to retrain those who have lost their jobs in the restructuring process (Andresen 1992, Wagner 1993, Grünert and Lutz 1995). The institutions that support training in western Germany – such as the chambers, which supervise apprenticeship training (Franz and Soskice 1995, Soskice 1994, Streeck et al. 1987) – had to be built up in the new federal states. Trade unions and employer associations moved to eastern Germany, and experts from the western German chambers helped to set up the new system and trained the trainers. To compensate for existing deficits in the training facilities, external training centers were instituted in eastern Germany, at a cost of 450 million DM in 1991. Despite great efforts, the number of apprenticeship places was not sufficient, even in 1991, when the Treuhand kept many companies operating: 9,000 school-leavers had to be trained in external places that year. In 1992-93, the state provided 11 billion DM for retraining and further training. Large investments were made to bring vocational schools up-to-date.

With the transfer of institutions, adjustments to the West German working environment are taking place in the new federal states. Working time in eastern Germany was 40 hours per week in 1990, but it is moving relatively quickly to the western

German standard. In 1996 the 38-hour working week was introduced, while at the same time the vacation period increased from 20 to 30 days. The average wage level of a trainee, like the general wage level, lagged behind depending on the occupation. Apprentices' wages ranged from 39 percent to 75 percent of comparable wages in western Germany in 1991. The majority did not reach 65 percent of the western German level. Thus, the starting wage of a tailor was just 140 DM, of a banking clerk 500 DM, and of a metal worker 420 DM (BMBW 1992). Only two years later, in 1993, wages had reached 80 percent of the western wage level on average. As the western German wages grew strongly during this period the eastern German increase is even more dramatic.

Supply and Demand for Apprenticeship Places in Eastern and Western Germany

The supply of apprenticeship places has historically closely followed demand in recent history in West Germany. An enormous increase in the number of school-leavers at the beginning of the 1980s was absorbed by the dual system (Althoff 1994). Since then the number of school-leavers and apprentices has been declining (Table 1.5). Keeping this close relationship in mind, the fact that the supply of apprenticeships has been sharply decreasing over the last ten years is in itself no indication of a problem with the dual system. On the contrary, the elastic reaction of supply to demand is a very positive feature of the system. However, the relationship between unfilled demand and supply has changed dramatically since 1990. From 1990 to 1992, more than 110,000 training places could not be filled. At that time every school-leaver who had not found an apprenticeship place statistically had a choice among ten apprenticeship openings; in 1996 there were only 1.4 such openings left. Although this reflects a much more restricted choice, it is still higher than in 1975.

The Socialist Party (SPD) has proposed a levy system paid as a proportion of the wage costs to increase the number of apprenticeship openings. It would be implemented when, for each 100 persons looking for an apprenticeship, fewer than 112.5 openings were available, and if the average company training ratio (number of apprentices/number of employees) was less than 6 percent. The employers' associations argue that this would increase administrative costs and not necessarily lead to more apprenticeship places; as many employers might prefer to pay the levy (as has been the experience with the levy for handicapped employees). In addition, if public officials decide to expand the supply of apprenticeships in areas where there is no demand from employers, this will likely produce a labor market mismatch when apprentices complete their training and look for jobs. For example, in 1995 60 percent of the male apprentices wanted to train in just five occupations. The openings in these "dream" occupations, however, offered enough places for less than half of them. Sixty percent of the female apprentices also wanted to enter just five occupations; little more than half of them succeeded (BMBW 1997). Although not all apprentices can follow their wishes, the big advantage of a voluntary provision of apprenticeships by employers is that it closely follows the demand by the economy.

Table 1.6a shows the numerical development of apprenticeship places in different sectors in West Germany. The service sector exhibits steady growth, reflecting the increase in the services' share of the economy. The industry/trade and the craft sectors vary greatly, showing much flexibility in reaction to changing demand. Some authors have criticized the strong increase in craft apprenticeships from 1970 to 1980, when the school-leavers from the baby boom entered the labor market (Casey 1990, van Lieshout 1996). They argue that mainly the "cheaper" – i.e., the craft apprenticeships – were opened up, and that the industry/trade sector did not react. However, the interpretation depends very much on the base year that is chosen. If we consider the increase from 1975 to 1985, then the industry

Table 1.5 Supply and demand for new apprenticeships (in thousands)

	West Germany				East Germany			
Year	Supply of training places	Demand	Unfilled supply*	Unfilled demand*	Supply of training places	Demand	Unfilled supply	Unfilled demand
1975	480	486	18	24				
1980	695	667	45	17				
1990	659	559	114	14				
1992	623	512	123	12	99	96	3	1
1994	503	468	53	18	119	119	1	2
1996	483	473	34	25	126	139	1	13

*Unfilled supply: open apprenticeship places; Unfilled demand: school-leavers still looking for an apprenticeship place.

Source: Grund- und Strukturdaten 1996/97, BMBW 1997.

and trade sector exactly matches the 38 percent increase in the total number of apprentices, while the increase in the craft sector was slightly lower with 36 percent. Thus, the burden of the increase from 1975 to 1985 was almost equally split between these two sectors. A similar development can be seen in the decrease from 1985 to 1994, where both sectors took 33 percent fewer apprentices.

Table 1.6a Apprenticeships in different industry sectors and new contracts in West Germany since 1970 (in thousands)

Year	Total	Industry/ Trade	Craft	Liberal occ. *	New contracts
1970	1269	725	420	56	
1975	1329	634	505	103	462
1980	1716	787	702	114	650
1985	1831	875	688	131	697
1990	1477	756	487	130	546
1995	1250	561	470	143	450

*doctors, dentists, accountants, lawyers, etc.

Source: Grund- und Strukturdaten, various years.

In eastern Germany the supply of apprenticeship places has been increasing since 1991, but not as quickly as demand (Table 1.6b). Demand increased between 1992 and 1996 by 45 percent, but the supply of places increased by only a quarter. It has created a situation with a higher demand from young people for training than supply, a case which occurred in West Germany only in the middle of the 1970s (Table 1.5). This has led to the creation of considerable government programs offering apprenticeship places, which have not been taken into account in these figures. While at the beginning these programs were mainly undertaken in fictitious companies, in 1996 the majority of apprenticeships were done in close cooperation with real companies.

Table 1.6b   Apprenticeships in different industry sectors and new contracts in eastern Germany since 1991 (in thousands)

Year	Total	Industry/ Trade	Craft	Professional Services	New Contracts
1991	235	145	67	6	
1993	287	140	109	15	99
1995	329	142	146	17	123

Source: Grund- und Strukturdaten, 1996/97.

A comparison of the different sectors in eastern Germany shows that only in the industry/trade sector has a slight decrease in apprenticeships taken place. Unlike in western Germany, where the increase in different sectors over time has been stable, the underdevelopment of certain sectors of the economy in the GDR accounts for the over-proportional expansion in apprenticeship places in these sectors. The craft sector and the professional services have increased more than twofold, reflecting their increased business activities, but the growth in the demand for apprenticeship places was higher still. According to an employer survey, more training might be possible in the future: about 1500 eastern German companies that currently do not train could be mobilized to offer additional apprenticeships if they could get help to organize cooperative training and be supported by external training centers (BMBW 1996). Two-thirds of these places would be in the craft sector, 20 percent in services, 10 percent in the liberal professions, and only 2 percent in industry. In addition, companies that already train would do more if additional financial support were available and cooperative training partners could be found. To overcome these difficulties, the chambers have attempted to publicize cooperative training and funding opportunities.

The difficult situation in the apprenticeship system has also led to an increase in the drop-out rate. In 1995, 25 percent of the new contracts in western Germany and 21 percent in eastern Germany were dissolved, compared to just 16 percent in 1986 in West Germany. The more restricted choice of apprenticeship places might be one reason, as about 60 percent of the drop-outs occur in the first training year (mostly during or before the probation period). Half of these dropouts find a new training place. Another reason is the harsh economic climate – about 8 percent of trainees in western Germany and 27 percent in the eastern states had formally to enter a new contract because of a change in the ownership of their company (BMBW 1997).

Increase in Unemployment

After a strong boost to the West German economy from unification in 1990-91, recession hit Germany harder than in other industrialized countries. Employment in manufacturing declined by more than 10 percent between 1991 and 1994, whereas the total decrease in the previous decade had amounted to less than 3 percent. Total unemployment rose during this time from 7 percent to 9 percent. This figure would be even greater if many firms had not tried to hold on to their employees through the introduction of shorter hours, in the hope that the economy would pick up again after a short while. Table 1.7a shows this rapid increase in the number of short-term workers.

Table 1.7a Employment in western Germany according to sectors, unemployment rate, and short-term workers in mechanical engineering since 1991

Year	Manufacturing	Trade/ Transport*	Agriculture	Short-term workers	Unemployment %
1991	11,095,000	5,628,000	957,000	4,307	7.2
1992	10,897,000	5,713,000	909,000	5,593	6.3
1993	10,376,000	5,665,000	856,000	16,340	6.6
1994	9,969,000	5,587,000	815,000	180,232	8.2
1995					9.3

* and communication
** in mechanical engineering

Source: Statistisches Bundesamt 1996.

The contraction in eastern German manufacturing employment was far more extreme, declining by 25 percent in just three years. Short-term work was used extensively to maintain working places after unification but then decreased when it became clear that these places could not be kept (Table 1.7b). In consequence, products and production were restructured and hidden unemployment removed. As there was no demand for many products in the free market, and those firms with viable products were often very inefficient, the transition from a planned economy was difficult, and many companies went bankrupt. Eastern German firms lacked managerial and technical qualifications, sufficient equity capital, and the collateral necessary to secure bank loans (as the ownership of buildings and sites were not clear for a long time). The ensuing crisis would have been much more severe if managerial help and investments had not been transferred from western Germany (Wagner 1993, Hitchens et al. 1991).

The job losses in eastern Germany mainly affected workers in industry and agriculture, where employment has dropped by about two-thirds since 1989. It will be very difficult to turn this development around, since many companies are barely surviving, even with wages that remain substantially below those in

Table 1.7b   Employment in eastern Germany by sector, showing short-term workers and unemployment rate since 1991

Year	Manufacturing	Trade/ Transport*	Agriculture	Short-term workers	Unemployment %
1991	3,112,000	1,320,000	454,000	-	-
1992	2,450,000	1,244,000	282,000	165,648	12.2
1993	2,322,000	1,219,000	232,000	64,075	14.3
1994	2,342,000	1,213,000	226,000	31,294	13.7
1995					14.9

*   and communication
** in mechanical engineering

Source: Statistisches Jahrbuch 1996.

western Germany (Mallok 1996). The only increase in employment can be found in the so-called "liberal professions," many of which were almost nonexistent in the GDR. These include lawyers, tax advisors, and insurance agents. Even the trade, transport, and communications sectors have lost working places. Unemployment rose to almost 15 percent by 1996, which does not include the high number of people in early retirement, further training measures, and work creation programs *(Arbeitsbeschaffungsmassnahmen)*. If we add to the unemployed those in work programs or further education, along with those who are not registered as unemployed because they have become so discouraged that they are not seeking work, the figure reaches 28 percent. Adding those who commute to western Germany for jobs and who are currently in early retirement we can estimate that working places for about a third of the labor force are missing in eastern Germany. This does not even take into account those who went into early retirement before 1996 (Table 1.8).

Reduction in Training

The economic recession has had a big impact on the training system in both parts of Germany. First, the reduced employment

Table 1.8   Unemployment and people not in "regular" employment in 1996

Labor force	7,559,525	100.0%
Unemployed people	1,097,572	14.5%
People in work programs	287,316	3.8%
People in further education	490,583	6.5%
People not registered as unemployed*	265,000	3.5%
Sum		28.3%
Commuters from east to west	323,329	4.3%
Early retirement**	160,000	2.1%
Total		34.7%

*   *Stille Reserve;*
** at the beginning of 1993 almost 900,000 people went into early retirement.
Source: Bach et al. 1996.

means that fewer companies remain to offer apprenticeship places. Second, the continuing pressure to reduce the workforce makes it hard for the surviving companies to justify the intake of apprentices. Apprentices do productive work that the present workforce would like to keep for itself to secure its own employment, particularly if many of them have to accept reduced hours; and the trainees might not be retained after completion of their apprenticeships, and the related benefits for the firms could not then be included in the cost calculus. Third, at a time when firms are focusing on cost-cutting, the recent increases in training costs might lead companies to defer offering apprenticeship places. The impact might be particularly serious in the *Mittelstand* companies, which do no detailed cost/benefit calculations, but which are acutely sensitive to wage increases. Fourth, the large number of skilled people out of work reduces the hiring costs for already trained workers (see Culpepper, Chapter 7).

In eastern Germany the situation is more severe, and each of the above arguments has a correspondingly greater impact. In addition to the above-mentioned effects on training, the apprentices in eastern Germany are competing to a much larger extent with adults in further education programs, whose wages are largely paid by the government for their first period of employ-ment. Furthermore, not only is the relative supply of apprentice-ship places lower than in western Germany, but in contrast to the trend in western Germany, the demand for apprenticeship places from school-leavers is growing.

The adjustment of company training activities to the eco-nomic downturn differs by firm size and by industry. Overall, the apprenticeship training ratio in western Germany decreased from 7 percent in 1990 to 5.5 percent in 1995. Small plants have been and remain the most active in training, measured by training ratio (Table 1.9), since they can keep net variable training costs rela-tively low (as discussed above). Establishments with more than 500 employees have the lowest training ratio, as these companies have the highest training costs. A comparison of the proportion of companies in different size categories that are training suggests that large companies are very engaged in training. However, large companies are registered as training companies even if they just have one apprentice, so these data have to be considered together in combination with those on training ratios.

The effects of increased costs and the recession are also felt in the small companies, which have reduced their average train-ing ratio by more than 20 percent. Between 1994 and 1995 there was a slight increase in the number of training companies (Table 1.9), which is almost exclusively due to the small estab-lishments. For companies taking on an apprentice for the first time, there is a subsidy of 5,000 DM per apprentice. For smaller companies the subsidy may significantly offset net costs and allow them to break even.

Between 1990 and 1995 the proportion of enterprises provid-ing apprenticeships dropped from 28 percent to 24 percent (Table 1.10). Traditionally the metal-working, precision engineering, and leather, textile, and food industries have been most engaged in training. The strongest decline in percentage terms has taken place in the leather, textile, and food industries, where many plants have closed or transferred production to lower wage countries. As most large companies are engaged in some training (Table 1.9) the plants not doing any training are usually the smaller ones.

Table 1.9   Apprentice training ratio (apprentices to employees), number of training companies and proportion of companies training (by plant size) in western Germany in 1990 and 1995

No. of employees	Apprentice training ratio*		No of training companies		Percentage of companies training	
	1990	1995	1994	1995	1990	1995
1-9	10.9	8.0	217,055	220,354	21	17
10-49	8.3	6.6	119,883	120,621	52	47
50-499	5.9	4.5	42,779	42,658	74	68
500 +	5.2	4.3	4,304	4,241	94	94
Total	7.0	5.5	384,021	387,874	28	24

*   Number of apprentices as a proportion of all employees in a given size class. The ratio of apprentices to employees will be correspondingly higher in the companies that do actually train. Thus, these data suggest that in 1995, the mean apprentice ratio of training companies in the smallest size group – in which three-fourths of companies do not train any apprentices – is actually on the order of about 30 percent.

Source: BMBW (1997).

Table 1.10   Percentage of plants with apprentice training according to industry in western Germany

	Plants training as a proportion of all plants	
Industry	1990	1995
Metal-working	42.4	33.6
Precision engineering, optics, watches	39.0	34.7
Leather, textile, food	45.1	32.6
Trade	22.9	16.9
Transport, communication	11.6	10.3
Banks, insurance	22.2	18.8
Services	27.6	24.1
Total	28.3	23.7

Source: BMBW (1997) based on the employment statistics of the Bundesanstalt für Arbeit and calculations by the Bundesinstitut für Berufsbildung.

Measures to Ease the Strain on the Apprenticeship System

In the last few years, the pressures on the apprenticeship market have shifted from the demand-side (not enough young people seeking to fill apprentice openings between 1990 and 1992) to the supply-side (not enough apprenticeship places since 1993). In earlier years, concerns were raised that the apprenticeship system might not be attractive enough to entice a sufficient number of adequately qualified school-leavers in the future. With the rising costs of training and the recession, this situation has changed dramatically. The present high demand for apprenticeships by school-leavers indicates a greater need to think about measures to keep the apprenticeship system attractive to companies. Policy-makers must deal with the problems of both supply and demand.

Increasing Attractiveness of the Dual System to Companies

DESIGNING APPRENTICESHIP OCCUPATIONS FOR NEW MARKETS
AND UPDATING EXISTING QUALIFICATIONS

The globalization of markets, the restructuring of employment in manufacturing, and the increased importance of the service sector have had a variety of impacts on apprenticeship profiles. The introduction of new technologies and work organizations require integrated job structures for which job profiles have to be adjusted or almost completely changed. For example, in the metal-working industries the new requirements include, in addition to deeper technical know-how, the individual planning of work, interpersonal skills, diagnostic skills, and the correct response to problems and defects, planning of materials and tools, quality assurance, responsibility for delivery on time, and cost management (Geer and Hirschbrunn 1994). At the same time the restructuring across and within economic sectors leads to (a) a change in the demand for different occupations in each sector – the economic restructuring in eastern Germany shows this strongly – and (b) the need to develop apprenticeships in innovative business areas. While the restructuring among individual sectors is quantitatively managed by the increase and decrease in the supply of apprenticeships by the companies, the development of training profiles for new business segments has to be realized by the cooperation of the social partners together with the government. One such area is multimedia, where microelectronics have changed the industry and a considerable growth in employment is expected through at least the year 2010. This demand was recognized by the employer association and the trade union, and together with the Federal Institute of Vocational Training, five new apprenticeship occupations with integrated job profiles were created for the media market. In 1997, 5,000 apprentices have already registered in these new professions. Similar trends are observable in the fields of information technology, safety, leasing, environment, and fast food, where additional openings of apprenticeship places could be achieved once the job profiles are defined. Since the German system is based on cooperation and consent by employers, trade unions, and the government, the development of new job profiles can be slowed when the different interests cannot agree on a common set of skill requirements. The required consent also makes it difficult to update profiles quickly: for the metal occupations, this process took more than ten years. However, the pace of revision has recently quickened. In 1996, 26 new occupations were issued and 50 others modernized.

COOPERATION AMONG COMPANIES

Due to the increased breadth of training and the requirement for quality in updated apprenticeships, not all companies can fulfill modernized training requirements in the prescribed range. Therefore, cooperation among companies has developed to complement each other's capabilities. In some cases, larger companies with a wide range of activities and a modern training workshop offer training courses to other companies for which they pay a fee. The effect is twofold: the large company can increase the utilization of its training facilities and lower its unit costs, and at the same time the smaller companies can offer apprenticeship places despite their more limited range of work processes.

Another way of cooperating is when two companies that have differing operations split the training of a single apprentice. An apprentice spends a certain time at one company for one area of training and then continues at another company to learn a different skill set. A familiar example is the *Hotelfachmann* (skilled hotel clerk), who has to be trained in the kitchen/-restaurant as well as in the reception/rooms area at a hotel. Since many firms specialize in either restaurants or accommodation, they divide the labor of the training phases according to their specialties. In an effort to convince more companies to offer apprenticeship places, the government and the chambers have increased support for companies to find a training partner during the past few years.

TRAINING CENTERS

Cooperative training arrangements are not easy to set up, particularly for the large number of smaller companies, because the different elements of training requirements have to be met. Very often only a few elements are missing, making it more worthwhile to offer a few matching courses rather than to look for a company with which to enter a cooperative arrangement. To enable these companies to train, the state has supported the establishment of external training centers, where specific courses are offered to fill the gaps in a company's training capacity. The chambers, trade unions, and employers' associations manage most of these centers, supplying training modules that the companies cannot themselves provide. In 1991, 77,000 of these training places existed in western Germany. In eastern Germany they were built up quickly after unification to help stabilize the shaky training market: the number of eastern German apprentices in training centers increased from 25,000 to 32,000 between 1991 and 1994.

Attractiveness of Apprenticeship for School-leavers

THE APPRENTICESHIP EXAM – A MILESTONE FOR SEMI-SKILLED WORKERS

The apprenticeship examination is accepted as an important career step in Germany, and it carries with it a high reputation. Therefore it is important that persons who are disabled or disadvantaged, or who have failed to enter apprenticeship training directly after general school, have a chance to achieve this level. A number of measures exist to help disadvantaged individuals become qualified, such as a vocational preparation (or foundation) year to boost basic skills prior to entering an apprenticeship along with subsequent extra tutoring during the apprenticeship (see above). For those who have not previously entered apprenticeships, opportunities exist to take the examination at a later stage without attending vocational schooling. To qualify to sit the exam, semi-skilled workers must show evidence that they have experience for at least twice as long as the training period lasts in the corresponding apprenticeship training. The number of people taking advantage of this opportunity has been increasing over the last ten years: in the industry and trade occupations the number of people taking the exams externally increased from 19,000 in 1984 to 28,000 in 1994, which amounts to 8 percent of the exam participants (BMBW 1997). This increase reflects, on the one hand, the permeability of the system; on the other hand, the demand for this examination by outsiders shows its attractiveness as a milestone for lifelong learning activities, particularly for an aging labor force (see Gatter, Chapter 6).

FROM SKILLED WORKER TO MANAGER

The traditional career ladder for skilled craft workers is to take and pass a *Meister* or technician examination after at least two years of experience. The further training for *Meisters* is usually done in evening classes, while for technicians it is done in full-time courses (Prais and Wagner 1988). Most of the training comes at the expense of the participant, although in some cases subsidies and grants from the state are available (e.g., the *Meister-Bafög*). The number of occupations having the possibility of taking a *Meister* examination has grown; since the 1970s, when the *Meister* exams were only common in the craft area, *Meister* exams have been developed for different industrial areas. A wide variety of other further education examinations exist in other sectors (Keltner et al. 1996). This career ladder is an important incentive for better-qualified young people to enter the dual system, as they can move into supervisory or middle-management positions without the need to complete the demanding top educational track and without studying at university. In 1993 45,000 skilled workers passed the *Meister* exams in the craft sector, 15,000 in the manufacturing sector, and another 45,000 corresponding levels in the clerical area. These 105,000 further training certifications can be compared to the 530,000 apprenticeship exams passed in the same year, which suggests that about 20 percent of apprentices take this career step. As is the case for the apprenticeship examinations, the need for modernization of the further education profiles has become clear. Recently, negotiations to give the chambers more flexibility in the creation of new or the modernization of existing further training regulations were completed successfully (CEDEFOP 1997).

Drexel (1995) has expressed skepticism as to whether the *Meister* position will still be viable after the introduction of modern work processes, in which front-line workers take over many of the traditional responsibilities of the *Meister*. However, research based on in-firm studies has shown that an increasing demand exists for more highly skilled individuals to perform a variety of tasks, from quality control to group facilitator, for which people with *Meister* qualifications are sought (Finegold and Wagner, Chapter 3; Mason 1997). The curriculum for the

Meister examination is adapted to new requirements so that the progression route remains open and even more attractive.

It should be noted that passing the *Meister* exam is not identical with having a *Meister* (supervisor) position. Despite the high number of *Meister* exams passed, only about one-third of the industrial *Meister* positions are occupied by a person with a *Meister* examination. Although a pass in a *Meister* exam does not automatically qualify someone for promotion to a *Meister* position, only one in seven of those who pass has a position below his/her qualification (Steedman et al. 1991). *Meisters* might have moved to a technical position of comparable status to manager or opened their own business, which is encouraged by German law – it allows only people with a *Meister* certificate to manage a craft business. A survey of newly qualified technicians and *Meisters* conducted by the Federal Institute of Vocational Training has shown that skilled workers take *Meister* or technician training courses in order to achieve a higher or better position, to differentiate themselves from other skilled workers, and to reduce the possibility of being laid off. Only a few *Meisters* expect that persons coming from the higher education route, such as graduate engineers, would be competitors for their positions.

EQUIVALENCE OF GENERAL AND VOCATIONAL TRAINING

Anxiety has been expressed that the most able school-leavers increasingly go to university and that not enough people with a good school qualification remain in the dual system. Although a career structure exists for apprentices to the *Meister* and the technician exams, there is no direct formal path of career advancement beyond this point. Entering university currently requires individuals to pass courses in general education, but a new law is now being implemented to allow for more flexibility between general and vocational schooling. In the future, people with the *Meister* or technician certificates may enter university without any additional testing. This change will potentially attract those school-leavers who are undecided about their occupational choice and who choose the Gymnasium track just to keep open the possibility of a university education. With the new regulations, they might enter an apprenticeship to learn the practical aspects of an occupation first, and if they do well, they can continue at an institute of higher education. Given a continuous increase in the qualification level of apprentices over the long-term (with 15 percent of the apprentices now already having passed the university entrance exam), the concerns about the declining popularity of apprenticeship might be overly alarmist. Moreover, statistical analysis shows that the vast majority of the changes in demand for apprenticeships observed between 1980 and 1996 were due to demographic changes, reduced supply of apprenticeships, and structural changes in the economy; these variables explain 97 percent of the variation, leaving only 3 percent unexplained (Behringer and Ulrich 1997).

However, in comparative terms the German system still lacks flexibility between work and education for the adult workforce. In the US, for example, it is quite common that people leave work and to go back to college, full or part time, which is still rare in Germany. Given the growth in knowledge work, which requires lifelong learning on and off the job, a greater flexibility of the schooling, university, and dual system is a precondition for remaining competitive in a changing world.

Creating More Training Places

Shortly after unification the German government promised that each school-leaver in eastern Germany would get an apprenticeship. To fulfill this promise, a program was begun that gave small enterprises 5,000 DM for each additional apprentice they hired. Companies that took trainees laid off by bankrupt companies received a larger sum, 8,000 DM for each apprentice. However, the decreasing employment in eastern Germany made it difficult to meet the increased demand for apprenticeship places with even these generous subsidies. Although by 1994 15,000 eastern German apprentices were trained in western German companies, the number of training places was still not equal to the demand for apprenticeships. In 1994, 35,000 apprentices were full-time trained in training centers financed by the government, of which 14,000 were new places to accommodate every school-leaver from that year who had not found a place in a firm. Similar numbers were taken in 1995 and 1996. To maintain a strong incentive for school-leavers to search for in-company training places, the wages in external training places – which are funded under §40c *Arbeitsförderungsgesetz* (Work Promotion Act) – were restricted to 460 DM in the first, 483 DM in the second, and 507 DM in the third training year in 1996 (BMBW 1997).

To motivate more companies to offer training places, more than 9,000 career advisers from the labor offices and the chambers have been sent to companies to campaign for new apprenticeship places and training cooperation. They visited more than 110,000 companies throughout Germany and were able to persuade firms to create 27,000 new training places. A fund of 54 million DM was established to support this kind of activity and to finance up to 150 training place "developers" for the period between 1995 and 1998.

Reducing Costs

As discussed previously, the costs of training and the reduced hours of apprentices at their companies have been pointed to by employers as major obstacles to increasing the supply of apprenticeships. The greater time spent in the classroom limits the apprentices from doing productive work, and hence is a major driver in the increase in the net training costs of employers, to which several policy responses have been developed. First, the federal ministry has proposed increasing the working time of apprentices at companies by reducing schooling to only one day in the second and third years of apprenticeship, hoping thereby to increase the willingness of companies to take on apprentices. Two states – because the authority in educational matters lies with the states (Länder) in Germany – have taken this proposition on board, and have increased the number of school lessons per day from eight to nine. This restructuring of schooling leads to an increase in the presence of apprentices at the company by 20-30 working days per year, which is quite large if it is seen in relation to the productive time of the trainees (iwd 1997).

A second response to the problem of high costs has been a wage increase of only 1.8 percent in 1996. While this is a first step, any further increases in apprentice wages must be watched carefully. For many companies, wages are the most obvious and usually the largest cost item. A decrease in the remuneration of apprentices in relation to skilled workers might increase the willingness of companies to offer more training places. The social partners should therefore try to keep the rises in wages for apprentices lower than the rises for the skilled workers. Third, the chambers have also contributed to a decrease in training costs by waiving or reducing their collection of examination fees for additional training places (BMBW 1997). For the other training places, the chambers have agreed not to raise the fees for the next few years, although the fees cover just 50 percent of the costs incurred by the chambers. Fourth, the training in large companies could be more work-oriented; apprentices prefer to do "real" work instead of producing training pieces which are then thrown away. The earlier involvement of apprentices in production has decreased the gross training costs by 10-15 percent at companies like Volkswagen. They could also be involved in developing solutions for particular problems on the shopfloor, using team approaches. Companies that have tried this technique cited as examples the improvement of the lighting on the shopfloor or designing and producing new logo signs. The benefits from these 'exercises' more than match the training costs.

Conclusions

In the last few years the pressures on the German apprenticeship system have grown. Because of the high interdependence of social and economic factors it is difficult to identify a single cause. From the above analysis we have seen that, until 1991, the costs of training were finely balanced with the benefits accruing to the training firm during or shortly after apprenticeship. Up to that point, the supply of apprenticeship places consistently exceeded the number of school-leavers seeking apprenticeships. Since 1990, however, the wages of apprentices have risen more rapidly than those of skilled workers. Simultaneously, higher training requirements and shorter working times have reduced the time apprentices devote to productive work. In response to the increases in cost, the supply of apprenticeship places decreased much more quickly than the demand for places.

Some small steps have already been undertaken to remedy the high costs of training. If continued, these changes might bring the system slowly back into equilibrium. For a faster adjustment more rigorous measures would have to be adopted. Splitting one wage between two apprentices has been suggested as a proposal to reduce costs and to entice more employers to offer apprenticeships. This suggestion – which implies halving the wage of apprentices – is probably too radical to be politically palatable. However, a reduction of fringe benefits to the legal minimum and a reorganization of schooling to become more effective might decrease net costs considerably. If this balance cannot be achieved, the poaching problem, which is familiar from the Anglo-Saxon context, might come up in Germany as well, hindering early investments in human capital.

In eastern Germany the economic situation is much more severe: the loss in working places there has been more drastic, the real unemployment rate is extremely high, and the threat of future unemployment increases is very real, as productivity is still very low and wage increases continue to outstrip productivity gains. Therefore it will be even more important to keep the wages of apprentices relatively low so that companies can break even on training and thus remain motivated to offer apprenticeship places. Even then, a long period of dynamic and persistent growth will be required before the eastern German economy is healthy enough to offer a sufficient number of training places; a continuing need for state support can be expected in order to place all apprentices over the next few years. In western Germany, an upswing of the economy and a reduction in the costs of training by various methods might result in a situation like that at the beginning of the 1990s, characterized by a high supply of apprenticeship places and a low demand because of the depressed western German birth rates. In this situation an internal migration of eastern German school-leavers to enter western German apprenticeships should be encouraged.

To ensure sufficient demand for apprenticeship places in the future, it is important that the training system remains attractive to school-leavers. It has to provide up-to-date skills that will lead to good jobs with a promising career. The modernization of apprenticeships should closely follow leading technologies and the development of new industries. The contact between schools and companies should also be improved to facilitate an efficient training program. The equalization of general and vocational training certificates will widen career choices and attract more able school-leavers. Additionally, it will improve the flexibility of the educational system and remove a disadvantage in further education of the German system, which otherwise would hinder the lifelong learning requirements of an aging workforce.

The restructuring of German companies in response to globalization – a process sped up by the recession – has forced them to become leaner in their work organization, with fewer hierarchical levels but with higher demands on technical and communications skills placed on each employee along with the ability to do team work. The consequently higher complexity of work will lead to a demand for better skilled personnel. Broadly based apprenticeships seem to be capable of providing this functional flexibility and are a good basis for lifelong learning and relearning, such that the dual system remains an important asset for the German economy. The biggest danger to the sustainability of apprenticeship, however, may lie in current and future company investment strategies, with many companies concentrating future growth in production facilities outside of Germany because of concerns about cost competitiveness. Therefore, employment growth in new markets has to be promoted, for which new occupation profiles have to be created rapidly.

Considering all these factors the German dual system is not in crisis, but it must react flexibly to changing market conditions. Over the past decades the system has proven that it is able to adapt. However, the strong recession in western Germany combined with the collapse of the eastern German industrial working places put a higher level of strain on the apprenticeship system than it has experienced previously. The favorable economic situation at the beginning of the 1990s and the scarcity of demand for apprenticeship places have also led to cost increases that the system cannot bear, and which need to be reduced quickly. All social partners have to strengthen their efforts to overcome these difficulties and to adjust the system. Most of the problems have been acknowledged by the government in accepting the report on "the reform project for vocational training – for more flexible structures and modern occupations" in April 1997 (Schmidt 1997). However, these insights have to be converted into actions.

Chapter 2

CRAFT PRODUCTION IN CRISIS

Industrial Restructuring in Germany during the 1990s[*]

Gary Herrigel and Charles F. Sabel

During the 1980s, the system of organization in which German (then West German) manufacturers were embedded and through which they competed on world markets was touted in popular and scholarly literatures as an important potential alternative to the "Fordist" forms of organization that then existed in the United States and other older, advanced industrial countries. Whereas the old "Fordist" system was rigid, slow to innovate, and focused on the mass production of standardized goods, German firms, the argument ran, were more flexible, focused on quality products, and capable of jumping from market

* An earlier version of this chapter appeared in LeeJay Cho and Yoon Hyung Kim, eds., 1997, *Hedging Bets on Growth in a Globalizing Industrial Order: Lessons for Asian NIEs*, Seoul, South Korea: KDI Press. This updated version is reprinted here with permission. The chapter is based upon a month's worth of interviews conducted in southwestern Germany.

niche to market niche. Nearly every dimension of the German political economy was praised (though rarely by the same authors at the same time): large German firms, with their intricate forms of internal decentralization, complex systems of code-termination and reliance on highly skilled and flexible workers in production looked to some as if they could provide an alternative, more social democratic, model for the corporation (Streeck 1991). Small German firms, equally reliant on skilled workers, embedded in dense networks of sub-contracting relations and sustained by a broad array of supporting public and private institutions, were held by others to be examples of an even more radical possible future in which decentralization, cooperation, and trust would triumph over corporate hierarchy (e.g., and mea culpa, Herrigel 1989, 1993a).

The German dual system that supplied the well-trained workforce for these large and small firms was seen by many countries to offer the best possible solution to the public-goods problem of creating a large base of intermediate skills (e.g., Soskice 1991, Streeck 1991). Still others presented the German system of industrial relations, with its strong yet cooperative unions, to international labor audiences, hungry for such evidence, as a way to imagine a place for trade unions in the future within internationally competitive capitalist economies (Turner 1991, Thelen 1992). The list of imitable German practices can easily be extended: from the chambers of commerce that governed the dual system to the decentralized, indirect incentives in Federal technology policy, all kinds of observers with all kinds of interests found something to admire in the German political economy (e.g., Streeck 1992, Katzenstein 1989, Ziegler 1990).

There may be some who continue to hold up these German institutions as a model for others today. But very few of those who do can possibly have been to Germany recently. Times have truly changed, and by all indications, German producers, large and small, as well as the many institutions that support them, have had a great deal of difficulty changing with them.

All of the pearls of German industry registered deep losses in profits and sales throughout the beginning of the 1990s and have only managed a moderate recovery, despite an upturn in the European business cycle. Huge cuts in employment rocked all of the major sectors. Even more disconcerting, the districts of thickly networked small and medium-sized producers, in Baden-Württemberg, the Bergisches Land, and elsewhere, also suffered: flagship industries such as machine tools have fallen into crisis, and unemployment rose in regions that used to be considered immune to such things. Trade unions have not exactly stood by idly as the crisis has unfolded, but they have not been able to do anything to arrest its onset: indeed, in many cases they have been able to do little more than protect their own by making sure that layoffs strike the most vulnerable elements of the workforce first (such as foreigners and women). So detached, in fact, have German trade unions become from the adjustment dynamics in factories today that, in many cases, even workers themselves are beginning to view the unions as part of the problem rather than part of the solution.

What happened to the German industrial system? Were the optimistic accounts in the 1980s completely off the mark or did something drastically change in the 1990s? The argument of this chapter will be that the arguments of the 1980s were not so much off the mark as they were one-sided. The changes that began in the early 1990s and that have continued to plague economic actors and institutions throughout the decade brought other, more problematic, dimensions of the German system to light that were not especially apparent a decade ago.

In a nutshell, the German system constituted a specific kind of craft production-based alternative to the rigid, hierarchical Fordism that collapsed in the first great postwar crisis. The key to the German advantage over the old system was its ability to gain flexibility in production by reuniting conception and execution at various levels: above all in the person of the skilled worker in batch production process and in close, cooperative subcontracting relations. Large-scale American Fordism had grown rigid by radically separating conception from execution within the hierarchical corporation and the mass-production process. In a global competitive environment that demanded flexibility, the Germans had an advantage. The playing out of this advantage during the 1980s is what generated all of the attention.

Changes in the international competitive environment, however, particularly the entry of Japanese, American, and other producers deploying variants of an alternative, more open, and lower cost kind of flexible system unearthed rigidities in the German system that were not apparent in competition with the old Fordist producers. Two factors in particular were most important: first, the continued practical and cultural salience of skill distinctions within German workplaces imposed limits on the speed with which German firms could introduce new products and technologies and change the organization of production. Competitors abroad who have been unencumbered by such fixed identities in the workplace have achieved a more profound reunification of conception and execution throughout the entire production process, making it possible for them to make products that are more elegant in design and less costly than their German counterparts. Second, this basic problem of fixed, clearly bounded skill identities was exacerbated by a host of bureaucratic elements within the German production system that separated production from development and design labs as well as different parts of production from one another. These structures developed and/or were imposed during the long period in the mid-twentieth century when the main competitors of the Germans were large-scale, highly Taylorized, mass producers.[1]

1. In other words, in comparison to a mass production system in crisis, what stood out about the Germans were the elements within their workplace arrangements that differed from that system. Now, however, when the alternative is a more open system, the striking aspects of the German system are the characteristics it adopted from and shared with the historically older system of rigid, hierarchical production.

This has been a serious problem for the Germans, for it has not been immediately apparent how existing German practices and institutions could adapt to meet the stringent organizational, logistical, and human-resource conditions that production along more open, leaner, and lower cost lines requires. The German skill-based or "craft" industrial system,[2] in both its large firm and small firm variants, contains not only a wealth of previously hidden rigidities, but a broad array of institutionally entrenched actors who stand to lose a great deal in any move away from the old system. The process of adjustment during the 1990s has consequently involved greater micro-level social conflict and social transformation than has occurred in Germany for quite some time.

Though we believe these problems are great, we in no way intend to suggest that they constitute an absolute bar to successful adjustment in Germany. For one thing, some of the Germans' most intense competitors, most notably the Japanese, are experiencing severe adjustment difficulties of their own in trying to overcome rigidities and implement more open and flexible production arrangements. This both provides some space in competitive markets for change and underscores the openness of the current international moment of experimentation: there is an international race to construct the most open and flexible production arrangements possible. All of the competitors bring to the contest a host of cultural and institu-

---

2. In using the word "craft," one has to be careful not to confuse the German system it is intended to denote with the British and American understanding of craft and a craft system, which connotes a more specific reference to the control of labor markets within and between firms by coherent craft organizations. In the German case, the organizations in the labor market along skill lines are absent. For this reason, it might have been reasonable to refer to the German system as the "Skill" or "Beruf" system, but we rejected that idea because it emphasizes skill too narrowly and loses the other dimensions of the German system, such as specialization, small batches, and small firm or producing unit cooperation, that we intend the general term "craft" to convey.

tional advantages and disadvantages. A second reason for optimism in the German case is that there are already clear examples within Germany of extremely successful producers who have taken radical steps to move beyond the traditional German craft system. Though these cases are at the moment isolated ones and to a certain extent the product of unique conditions that cannot be generalized to other German producers, they do point to the possibility of a very interesting new German production system that combines some of the strengths of the old German system with the flexibility and low cost of the new open one.

This chapter will elaborate the above argument in the following way: the first section will outline what Fordism was in ideal typical form and then contrast both the German and alternative open, flexible systems to it – the latter being primarily illustrated with Japanese examples. The second section will then examine how the German system has come up short against the alternative. The third section will then look at current efforts at adjustment within Germany: it contrasts successful and unsuccessful cases of adjustment, and suggests how the former may be leading to a system that also overcomes some of the limits of the Japanese version of the alternative system.

Fordism and Its Alternatives

By Fordism, we mean an historically specific orientation toward production that emerged first and diffused most broadly in the United States, but which also had an important time in the sun in Europe during the early and mid-twentieth century. Fordism, as an ideal type, involved the mass production of standardized goods, strictly Taylorist organization of work in production (i.e., highly specialized tasks), and heavy reliance on unskilled and semi-skilled workers. All of these features of direct production were governed by a segmented set of hierarchies for production, development, finance, marketing, etc. The logic of Fordism involved two fundamental principles: control over market and technology and the rigid separation of conception from execution in all aspects of production and its governance.[3]

Control over markets, in the form of oligopoly or monopoly, and over technology, through long product cycles, were defining features of Fordism. It was only through the exercise of such control that the relatively rigid and large scale investments involved in mass production could be justified. Competition and innovation undermined pre-microelectronic automation mass production because production was so rigid it was always vulnerable to competitors who could offer a slightly more expensive custom product that provided precisely those things that the standard mass produced wares could not. Innovation that replaced existing products had a similarly undermining effect.

The second principle, the separation of conception from execution in product development, production, and work, was both a cause and a consequence of this kind of control. Product development and production planning were hidden away from outside suppliers and production management and workers in bureaucratic departments, for example, so that neither of those groups could run off with trade secrets and turn themselves into competitors of the organization. At the same time, the stability that market control afforded meant that the division of labor could be extended to achieve economies of scale in production, tasks requiring skill and manual expertise could be transferred to machines and the production process could be peopled by unskilled and semi-skilled workers who knew little of the larger process of which their jobs were a part. Such extreme fragmentation of knowledge and action was itself a way for top manage-

---

3. This is a relatively narrow definition of Fordism that focuses primarily on the organization of industrial production. We want to distance ourselves from the more inclusive definitions current in the neo-Marxist Fordism debate. On that, see Jessop (1991).

ment – the only part of the corporation with an overview of the entire production and development process – to exercise control and direction over the process.

In its time, this system was enormously productive: it contributed to the tremendous growth of the middle class in advanced industrial countries during the twentieth century and it was arguably responsible for winning at least one of the two world wars. By now, however, it is clear that for all the things Fordism was, one thing it clearly was not was invincible. Indeed, Fordism's hegemony within the industries of advanced industrial countries began to wane in the 1970s and fell into bona fide crisis in the 1980s.

The key vulnerability in the system revolved around principle one above: the capacity to achieve and maintain the kind of control necessary for stable Fordist growth depended upon either the existence of a clear hierarchy of technological sophistication and industrial development in the world economy, or the existence of relatively sovereign national (or supra-national-regional) markets in which competition from foreign producers was a minimal threat. By the 1970s, it was clear that the formerly war-ravaged economies of Europe and Japan had assimilated the technological advances that had been pioneered earlier in the century in the United States, effectively eliminating any previously existing developmental hierarchy among the most advanced industrial economies. At the same time, each of those countries (or groups of countries) had grown to a point where they could no longer grow on the basis of their internal markets alone. They thus aggressively invaded the formerly sovereign market domains of the others, but especially that of the United States. Suddenly it was no longer possible to maintain control of markets or technology anywhere in the advanced west: competition that gave rise to ever more rapid product and technological innovation became the rule. In such an environment, the rigid, hierarchical principles of Fordist organization began to come under extreme stress.

Germany and Japan

In turbulent, constantly changing market and technological environments, flexibility is an asset. During the 1980s, countless case studies showed over and over again that those organizational forms – in firms, regions, and countries – that had a modicum of flexibility in production performed better than those that did not (Pyke and Sengenberger 1991; Dore 1986; Piore and Sabel 1984, Streeck 1991). This is the context in which the German and Japanese systems of production became so interesting to outsiders. Producers in each of these economies demonstrated a degree of flexibility in production that was dramatic in comparison to the ossifying and rigid structures of decaying Fordism and moreover, they were very successful in international markets.

The key to the success of both systems lay in their ability – in different ways – to reintegrate conception and execution in the development and manufacture of products. In both systems this reintegration occurred within firms and between firms.

The German System of Decentralized Craft Production

The successful components of the German industrial system during the 1980s revolved around the principles of craft-based manufacturing and cooperative subcontracting among specialized producers. The essence of craft manufacture as a general type of production is the deployment of general-purpose machinery tended by broadly skilled workers. In a craft production process different groups of skilled workers in different segments of the production process receive from management general instructions for how and what to produce. They must then rely on their skill and experience to devise a way to make the part – or in finding that it cannot be made in its given form, go back to management and participate in its redesign.

In most industrialized countries, the coming of mass production undermined the craft organization of production. But in

Germany, the craft idea became more deeply embedded in the society during the twentieth century through its association with the concept of *Beruf,* the notion that all forms of industrial production contain naturally within them broad distinctions that require different and distinctive skills. This concept became a constitutive feature of the way in which workers organized their career paths and the way that managers conceived of the situation in production. A dense network of institutions for vocational training, workplace codetermination, and collective bargaining monitored and reproduced the system, providing apprentices with intensive training and the holders of skill with the imprimatur of official recognition. This kind of public distinction accorded to holders of those who succeeded in achieving a distinctive skill *(Beruf)* created a set of public norms that made trust in the workplace possible: managers could delegate decisions to skilled workers because they could be confident that the institutional system that provided the worker with his or her skills had done its job.

Even though there is considerable trust and cooperation within German craft production, there is also hierarchy and fragmentation: skilled workers do not design what they produce, all do not have the same amount of experience, and the production process is divided among different kinds of skills (e.g., tool maker, mechanic, electrician, etc.). Identities within the production process, because they are so embedded in a system of institutional certificates and processes, are relatively fixed. Nevertheless, and this is crucial for understanding the flexibility of the German system over the more rigid Fordist one, the contribution that each group of skilled workers and managers makes to a final product is not fixed: indeed, it is continuously renegotiated in the heat of production. New orders and new products require new shopfloor arrangements: workers are given considerable autonomy and discretion on the shopfloor to respond to the new situation, and there is a high degree of cooperation between labor and management in the firm concerning the reorganization of the production process. During the nineteenth century, this kind of labor-management cooperation within the craft system occurred in a direct, face-to-face manner between shopfloor workers and managers. By the end of the twentieth century, however, after many German firms had themselves moved into mass production, this labor-management cooperation was removed from the immediate shopfloor into the institutions of workplace codetermination; but it was still very remarkable and extensive cooperation, which accorded German producers an enviable flexibility advantage over more rigid mass producers with more adversarial and contentious shopfloor environments in which workers were more narrowly trained.

Relations between German firms (or individual workshops within larger companies) and their subcontractors (internal or external) involved a similar balance between the autonomy and discretion of specialists and cooperation among them. Typically, subcontractors (workshops) were approached with a general set of specifications (sometimes nothing more than a vague array of needs) and were expected to apply their expertise to the resolution of the problem. As with the skilled workers, conception is reintegrated with execution not only in the invention of the specific details for producing the part or subassembly, but because the process of devising a solution frequently involved close cooperation with the designers in the contracting firm.

Relations between subcontractors and their clients were not quite as embedded in a system of training and monitoring as were individual workers acquiring a *Beruf*, but there was significant institutionalization nonetheless. All producers in Germany are required to register with the Chamber of Industry and Commerce and provide that body with basic information about the firm's activities. Frequently, subcontractors and clients belonged to the same trade association and met with one another in standards bodies in which negotiation took place about the quality and identity of products, production techniques, etc. Such institutional affiliations provided a

weaker imprimatur than the *Beruf* system of vocational training. But membership and participation in such organizations
provided not only publicity for the firm, but also, crucially, sig-
nified its membership among the community of respectable
producers. In this weaker sense, norms of trust were also institutionalized in this system.

Producing in this way is very flexible. Since there are few
specific work rules within the skill specialties, workers and managers can relatively cheaply and rapidly turn from the production of one thing to another, within a given set of parameters.
German producers were widely known to be expert customizers,
easily able to build into their products a broad array of special
customer requests, including the construction of unique products. The process also contributed to high-quality manufacturing, because the participation of producers in both the conception
and execution of products had the beneficent side effect of
engendering learning among all the participating parties about
what was right and what was wrong about the part being produced and the process producing it. Improvements in the production process could be implemented continuously.

This craft system always made it possible for the Germans to
become the world's most successful manufacturing exporters,
through their dominance of low-volume and/or premium niches
in world markets, even during the heyday of Fordism. The flexible craft production process was very good at producing premium high-quality goods that reflected sophisticated customer
desires – sometimes precisely. The strategy was more expensive,
however. German production costs and products were always
higher than producers in other countries in similar industries.
But as long as there was a gap between standardized and very
high-volume mass markets and lower volume, higher-quality
specialized markets, the Germans were able to flourish. During
the turbulent 1980s, when commodity product markets began
to fragment and customer desires became more particular and
demanding, it appeared that the special characteristics of the

German system were ideally suited for the new environment. The new terms of competition were related in many ways to those that had guided production in Germany throughout much of the industrialization process.

Open and Flexible Production: The Example of the Japanese

The German craft-based system was not the only system to flourish during the 1980s. Another one was the Japanese system, which deployed forms of organization in production that diverged quite significantly, both from Fordism and from the skill-fractured system of the Germans. The system of production in Japanese manufacturing is also extremely flexible and, like the Germans, this flexibility is achieved through the reintegration of conception and execution both in development and in production. Unlike the German system, however, which retains considerable hierarchy and fragmentation within its organizations, the principles underlying the Japanese system aim for a more thoroughgoing integration of conception and execution.

Rather than relying on groups of differently skilled workers with general knowledge of their specialty to solve problems that arise in production, the Japanese attempt to respond to problems that arise in production by creating groups appropriate to the task. There are no fixed vocational identities in the Japanese production process. Unlike German workers, who come into the production process only after a long apprenticeship within a particular *Beruf,* Japanese workers enter the factory with relatively little knowledge of specific kinds of work. They enter groups within the factory that are actively engaged in collectively solving problems that they encounter in fulfilling orders in production. Apprenticeship is replaced by participation in collective problem solving on the shopfloor. Identities at work associated with craft skill are replaced by identities at work associated with the capacity to contribute to the competitiveness of the company.

In this system, conception and execution are blended together in much the same way that they were in the German system: production workers receive general instructions for which they then have to devise a concrete solution. The crucial difference is that in the Japanese workplace, there are no jurisdictions that predetermine the specialties of interlocutors as there are in the German system. The Japanese get a tremendous amount of extra flexibility from this: they can virtually redefine the production process and reallocate roles within it with each new set of instructions or product change. Moreover, learning is built into the system, not only in the sense that newcomers are trained collectively by the group, but also in the sense that this contin-uous self-redefinition on the part of production workers causes them to monitor their activities in a way that allows them to engage in continuous improvement and innovation.

Relations between workshops within Japanese firms and between firms and their subcontractors involve a similar kind of reintegration of conception and execution. Here the key is the *Kanban*, or no inventory production system, which, because it eliminates all production buffers, places all workshops and col-laborating firms under collective pressure to find solutions for their production problems; a problem in one area of production becomes apparent immediately throughout the whole produc-tion chain. This not only constrains work groups to come up with effective solutions to their particular production problem; it provides an incentive for horizontal cooperation as well. Everyone benefits from a smoother production flow.

The interesting feature of this horizontal cooperation is that it is structurally induced. It does not depend for its operation on the existence of trust, in the sense of shared membership in and public recognition by a community as in Germany. Coopera-tion, though it is important in both systems, actually differs very substantially between them. The Japanese system differs from the German in that the systematic pursuit of low inventories forces more systematic collaboration about the entire production process among all the participating groups. Thus where the German system induces learning through collaboration in dyadic relations within pieces of the production process, the imposed interconnectedness of low inventories induces collaborators to learn by monitoring the flow of the entire production process (Sabel 1993).

German vs. Japanese Flexible Organization

Both of these alternative flexible systems flourished during the 1980s, while economies and corporations that had been committed to the old hierarchical Fordist system floundered and struggled with adjustment. At the time, much was made about the counterintuitive character of both systems. The flexible systems seemed to be redefining the very character of efficiency: instead of looking to lower costs through ever greater specialization in the organization of production coupled with standardization and economies of scale, the Germans and especially the Japanese seemed to be showing that an emphasis on local autonomy and generality in production, coupled with greater integration between the development and production of goods, was actually a more efficient way to produce (regardless of scale). Specialization in the division of labor was expensive because it involved the construction of rules and elaborate hierarchical organizations filled with people either following rules or making sure that the rules were followed. The general and more locally autonomous, cooperative systems had fewer rules and thus fewer levels of middle level rule enforcers. Less hierarchy and more autonomy turned out to be cheaper (Aoki 1988, Piore and Sabel 1984).

This principle, as it happens, also holds true among the flexible producers. That is, the system with the least formal hierarchy, specialized identities, and fragmentation in the production process, and fewest fixed rules dictating particular kinds and preventing other kinds of behavior among members of productive organizations is the most flexible and lowest-cost approach to manufacturing. The giant losses that German producers, large and small, incurred during the first half of the 1990s suggest that they came up on the short end of the stick in this contest. German companies, despite some signs of improvement at the end of the decade, have been unable to keep up with the torrid pace of new product introduction and technological innovation that the Japanese – and now especially their many "lean" American imitators – have been setting, and the many improvements in the organization of production have still not been able to bring German costs down to the competitive levels of American producers.[4] German products in a range of manufacturing sectors – machinery, electrical equipment, automobiles, optical equipment – are still unattractively expensive and, notoriously, "over-engineered." Japanese and American producers are now able to produce with the same kind of quality in the same kind of high-value-added markets that used to be the sovereign province of German producers, and the newcomers are proving to be better in quality and less costly producers than the veterans.[5]

If the claim is that hierarchy, excessive fragmentation in production, and rigid rules are the problem, where are these characteristics located in the German system? As we saw above, the

4. See the very frustrated and pessimistic summary article by Michael Schumann and Horst Kern, summarizing advances in German production organization, especially in automobiles, during the 1990s, and the continued difficulties German producers have meeting international benchmarks for lowest cost and best practice: "Kontinunität oder Pfadwechsel? Das deutsche Produktionsmodell am Scheideweg," *SOFI Mitteilungen*, Number 26, 1997, which will appear in Cattero (forthcoming).

5. The remarkable thing about this claim is that it holds true of Japanese producers in branches such as automobiles despite the tremendous problems that have beset their financial and political systems. But American producers have been pressing European producers with their low-cost structures and alternative forms of organization not only through competition in export markets, but also through direct investment strategies in Europe and especially eastern Europe. See Schumann and Kern (1997).

craft system itself involves hierarchy and fragmentation: divisions between separate *Berufe* are considered to be virtually natural divisions within the production process and in the system of social differentiation in society. Masters, moreover, are the superiors of apprentices and of newer and younger skilled workers within their *Beruf*. This generic fragmentation and hierarchy, we saw, was then further exacerbated by the evolution of the German industrial economy during the long mid-twentieth-century flirtation with Fordism: the institutionalization of the vocational training system reinforced the hierarchical relations between masters and apprentices and among older and younger skilled workers while at the same time reproducing clear social distinctions among workers in different *Berufe*. Similarly, the formal institutionalization of workplace codetermination structures imposed a formal hierarchical apparatus within plants that involved significant bureaucratic mediation between management and individual workshops and *Berufe*. Masters, foremen, shop stewards and works councilors, and their counterparts or superiors in the formal structures of plant management, had significant governing authority in production.

The disadvantage of *Beruf*-based hierarchy and fragmentation in the German system comes to light under conditions of extremely rapid product and technological change. Each time a new product or a new technology is introduced – as opposed to an old one that is customized for a customer – the various roles that each of the categories of skill will play in the manufacture and development of the new product must be bargained out. Each will want to participate; each will have its own ideas and solutions; each will defend its turf against encroachments from the others. Electrical masters and technicians will fight with mechanical ones both on the shopfloor and in the design studios.

If the new product involves the increasing interpenetration of formerly distinct areas of technology and expertise – such as microelectronics and mechanical engineering – it will take some time to iron out all of the potential areas of conflict. If the market is stable for the product and does not change very rapidly, it might be possible to wait until all of these conflicts have been resolved before deciding upon the final design of the product. But if the market is turbulent and unstable and the lifespan of the current technology is clearly going to be limited, firms are forced to bring their products on to the market while the internal conflicts are still being worked out. More often than not, impatient and nervous senior managers under time pressure but with no greater knowledge of the technology or the market than the contending specialists, will be forced to broker a compromise between the players in a way that allows the solutions of each – to the extent that they are not contradictory – to be built in to the product. It should not be surprising that such products will appear to the customer as inelegant, overpriced and over-engineered – they are.

This is what is going on in German factories today. Jurisdictional disputes driven by the need to accelerate new product introduction at a moment when the boundaries between traditional *Berufe* are being technologically eroded is driving up the cost and driving down the quality of products. Such jurisdictional conflicts do not exist in the Japanese or most advanced American systems because there are no fixed jurisdictions or occupational identities. The Japanese can combine the work of development departments and production (simultaneous engineering) and they can continually redesign their production processes to accommodate new products by utilizing U-shaped lines and group work organization.

This is extremely difficult to do in the German system as it is constituted today: to implement more boundary-blending forms of cooperation in development and production, the traditional structure of the craft system has to be deconstructed and its elements recomposed in a new more flexible (not to say Japanese) way.[6] Given the centrality of craft as a form of social

6. One has to be careful here. We call the alternative system "Japanese" because it is the most familiar example in international discussions of flexible alternatives to the craft system. Nevertheless, two things must be

organization in German industry, as well as in the institutional environment that surrounds, supports, and governs that form of social organization, the current adjustment period has been one of extremely dramatic and pervasive social transformation.

German Adjustment

German industrial producers have been well aware of the competitive problem that they face. Most have been deeply involved in attempting to amend their internal structures of organizations in ways that, to a greater or lesser degree, depart from the craft system and implement more open and flexible arrangements within the organization of management and production. Indeed, at the moment it is possible to say that the debate in Germany is not about whether or not the old *Beruf*-based system and its supporting institutions need to be amended and made more flexible. Instead the debate is about how much needs to be changed.[7]

In this sense it is possible to distinguish between minimalist and maximalist strategies. In the former case, producers attempt to reform the old system only slightly, by cutting costs, reducing overheads and implementing some of the most basic

---

noted: first, the Japanese system is itself not bereft of hierarchy and fragmentation, which cause rigidities in the current environment, nor is it proving easy within that system to move away from such rigidities. Second, German producers themselves tend to have in mind an even more radically open system of flexible production in their own discussion of reform. They recognize the limits of the Japanese case and are not interested in reproducing its limits in their own systems. Interestingly, many of our interlocutors felt that their most advanced, lowest cost, and flexible competitors were now in the United States.

7. This is not to say that there are not niches where the kinds of competitive pressures being discussed in the text do not (yet) apply; the case of pumps discussed by Finegold and Wagner in Chapter 3 strikes us as one such exceptional niche example.

elements of the alternative "Japanese" system. This is a top-down strategy, often initiated under financial duress and under the instigating and watchful eye of the firm's bankers. Typically the aim is to improve the bottom line by "getting costs under control." In the latter, maximalist case, producers have radically departed from the traditional structures of management and work organization and have implemented their own versions of open and flexible production organization throughout most areas of the firm. The reasons for this larger step vary considerably: in some cases, a crisis occurred very early at the firm and at a point in the business cycle when the rest of the economy was flourishing, and management implemented the radical changes in a piecemeal manner – not even realizing themselves what they were doing until the process was very far along. In other cases, reform is more radical because crisis at the firm resulted in a change of management and the newer reform managers came from places where they had had bad experiences with the minimalist reform strategy.

In the current, very unstable, environment, we find it impossible to declare any of the cases we have observed to be a trend: the minimalist strategies could evolve into maximalist ones, and the maximalist ones that we have observed may not work. That said, we think that the conceptual fermentation and experimentation that exists today, and the striking departure from past practice that we observed in some of the maximalist plants, has the potential to transform the old German craft system and produce a version of the new that could be more open and flexible than the traditional Japanese system.

We begin this section with a discussion of some of the maximalist plants and then turn to the minimalist cases and the troubles they encounter. The final section will consider possible trajectories away from the minimalist strategy and how the openness the Germans seem to be striving for in production combines the strengths of both the old and new.

Maximalist Strategies

Perhaps the most impressive and advanced example of restructuring along more open and flexible lines within the entire German economy is the BMW Corporation. This company saw in the beginning of the 1980s that its luxury automobile market niche was going to be vulnerable to new competition from mass producers seeking to move up market in quality. It was also clear to the company that addressing such new competition would be complicated by the proliferation of a host of new technologies, such as microelectronics and new kinds of plastics. The company needed to lower its manufacturing costs, improve product-cycle turnover and innovation while maintaining or improving its manufacturing quality (Sabel et al. 1991, Herrigel 1996b).

BMW's response was to attack internal hierarchy and over-specialization within its organization (in all areas of management and production) while at the same time attempting to lower its level of vertical integration and decentralize production. Old functional departments within the company were recomposed and integrated with one another so that they could both scan and identify new technologies and potential suppliers at the same time that the new ideas were being modified to accommodate market tastes and adapted for production. For example, at the end of the 1980s, a new committee, known as the *Bezugsartenkreis*, was formed, which brought representatives of engineering, purchasing, and controlling (finance/accounting) departments together to facilitate systematic discussion of issues concerning product development and the location of production inside or outside the firm. In the early 1990s, production was added to this group of interlocutors and the committee was transformed into an integrated department in its own right, under the direct supervision of the top managing board. By incorporating production into discussions of product development and location, the company was seeking to reintegrate conception and execution within its organization and hoped to ensure that the development and production of new cars would occur simultaneously (*Manager Magazine* 1993).[8]

Part and parcel of this restructuring has been the redefinition of managerial careers and expectations.[9] BMW wants to avoid the "Chimney Effect" of managers envisioning their career paths in functionally specialized terms – e.g., by making a career in marketing, development, or in purchasing. Instead, managers are increasingly expected to move horizontally through the organization, gathering experience at a variety of posts in a variety of locations. The more varied their experience, the greater is their flexibility and their capacity to collaborate with others both within BMW and with its subcontractors. Commitment to the goals of the organization, rather than to those of a narrow functional specialty within it, is the goal that BMW is trying to achieve.

The reorganization, simplification, and decentralization of the management structure to facilitate boundary-crossing exchange and cooperation has its analog in the decentralization of production away from the firm and the reorganization of the

8. "Codewort Pretoria," 60-71.
9. The following paragraphs draw on interviews conducted by the authors at BMW in Munich and Regensburg in the winter and spring of 1989, as well as published sources in the press as indicated. It is interesting to note, as a reviewer of this chapter pointed out to us, that training for the managerial occupation, *Industriekaufmann*, now has been redefined to incorporate many of the multi-functional qualities of the system described in the text at BMW. Apprenticeship training for people who go into marketing, purchasing, and other specialties is identical, including rotation among these different departments in large firms. What is not clear is how this corresponds to changes in practice in the firms. The reviewer seemed to think that there was a difference between those who entered the firm as apprentices and those who entered as managers, suggesting that residual rigidity of the sort we describe is still very much alive in German firms. We are happy to acknowledge the *Industriekaufmann* example, however, because our argument is not that the German system can't change; it is about the character of conflicts and obstacles that are arising in the way of redefining the system.

production that remains within the firm into U-shaped lines manned by work teams. Over the course of the 1980s, the company increasingly redefined the automobile as a system of subsystems (modules) and its role as the manufacturer as one of "Systems Integrator."

Figures on vertical integration vary considerably, even when the same measure appears to be used. But by the beginning of the 1990s, it was clear that somewhere between 55 and 75 percent of the total production costs at BMW came from outsourced parts. People in purchasing at that time claimed that over 80 percent of the parts purchased involved important collaborative work with a specialist subcontractor which supplies BMW with know-how and design. Moreover, the firm was insisting that its suppliers deliver their modules on a just-in-time basis with exacting quality and cost targets. No single part or module of their automobile was considered to be, in principle, inappropriate for outsourcing. Workshops in BMW's plants were made increasingly autonomous and obligated to prove their production efficiency according to market standards: i.e., also on a low-cost, no-inventory, high-quality basis.

The effects of this new more porous and collaborative system on the performance and organizational identity of BMW have been remarkable. Output of automobiles increased between 1984 to 1992 from approximately 350,000 cars to nearly 600,000, while sales increased during the same time period from slightly more than DM9 Billion to DM31.2 billion – all with steadily increasing profitability (*Manager Magazine* 1993: 68, Bluethmann 1992). Above all, the new structure made possible radical reductions in development time. The first indication that the reforms were bearing fruit came with the introduction of the Z1 sports car in the late 1980s. Construction of this car was an experimental effort to shorten the eight-year model-development cycle that the company carried throughout the 1980s. The new engineering subsidiary, ZT Technik GmbH, did the engineering for the new car and BMW subcontracted out mod-

ules worldwide to firms that did the final design and development of the automobile. Within two years, the company was
producing a limited edition of the car at the rate of roughly sev-
enteen units per day. The company required another two years
before the car could be produced in series. On the whole, the
project did much to demonstrate that with the new system
BMW could potentially reduce development times to the range
– 43 months – previously attained exclusively by world-leading
Japanese producers. As the decade has progressed, moreover,
BMW refined the system even more: the company introduced
the third completely redesigned iteration of the Z1, the Z3, at
the end of the decade. The rapid launch of this new car was
among the most successful in BMW's history.

Predictably, many of the best additional examples of successful movement away from the traditional craft system in Germany are BMW suppliers, like the medium-sized family firm,
Getrag, located in northern Württemberg. This manufacturer of
high-performance gear units for standard-shift automobiles
began to initiate major changes in its organization in 1987 in
order to meet the stringent cost and quality terms of a new contract from BMW. According to a spokesman for the company,
the reorganization was guided by the idea that the new organization would be defined more by a process of change, than by a
specific organizational structure. The company literally and
somewhat naively set out to constitute trusting relations among
all actors within the firm, regardless of role or position in the
organization of the firm, which were informed by mutual respect.
It discouraged thinking in terms of hierarchy and status and
made all information about the company (its finances, its products, its suppliers, its customers) available to everyone within it.

To realize this vision, product teams were created that combined the previously separate departments of development,
planning, purchasing and production. The many levels of management hierarchy in the old system between top management
and shop floor were reduced to three. Relations with Getrag

suppliers were also reformed so that their parts and materials would be delivered according to the stringent cost and quality standards of the *Kanban* system.

It is in the production process, however, where the departure from the old craft system can be seen most clearly. In the restructuring, the production process was broken down and completely reorganized. All line and workshop organization was eliminated and production and assembly islands, governed by autonomous work teams, were introduced. Members of the teams allocate work amongst themselves and take responsibility for most aspects of their quality control and maintenance. Island teams possess a small budget to help them perform these tasks. Teams also have the option of turning to different suppliers – inevitably also outsiders – to ensure that their quality responsibilities are met. Workers in the teams are multi-skilled and are not constrained by old craft categories: their responsibility is to keep the island performing at exacting cost and quality standards in the best way that they can.

Clearly, one of the central ways that they do this is to interact with the other work teams and with suppliers so that the entire production flow can be continually optimized and improved. In an effort to encourage this kind of cross boundary communication both within and across teams, even the old apprenticeship system is being broken down: rather than training workers in specific trades away from the production process under the stewardship of masters, the firm attempts to integrate the apprentices into the teams from the start. Rather than learning a specific craft skill, newer apprentices are trained in the much more demanding trade of general problem-solving and cooperation.

The new system, which the firm has been introducing piecemeal over the last decade, has been tremendously successful. The firm has rates of machine utilization above 80 percent in the teams, while serviceability rates on the same production machinery (time not spent in repair) are over 90 percent. More-

over, over the course of the last seven years, the firm has introduced three new generations of its product.

A third example of successful adjustment is the small
machinery firm Mettler Toledo, a maker of electronic scales and
weighing devices on the Schwäbische Alb in southern Württemberg. This firm has nothing to do with BMW or the automobile industry. Rather, reorganization at Mettler Toledo was
brought on by a financial crisis associated with an unsuccessful
shift to new microelectronic variants of their product during
the mid 1980s. The crisis brought in new management with a
mandate to radically restructure the company. Management
made two major moves: first, all production was shifted onto
area suppliers so that the company could focus its energies fully
on product development, product assembly, and sales. Relations
with suppliers, which were already very close and cooperative
before the reorganization, were intensified so that important
providers were drawn directly into the development process.

Second, all remaining activities within the firm were reorganized into teams: no functional divisions or departments
survived the reorganization and all levels of formal middle management associated with those areas were dissolved. The company was reorganized around products and processes. Teams
were fully responsible for the development and production of
new products and dealt with the continuing needs of existing
customers. The emphasis was on total process optimization and
improvement. Teams maintained intimate and open contact
with the assembly workers about individual orders. Assemblers
worked as individuals and had responsibility for the complete
assembly of a product. They could call on team members for
advice and service at any time. As at Getrag, this reorganization
at Mettler Toledo led the firm to attempt to get away from the
old craft system of apprenticeship. By circumventing the archaic
specialized roles of the dual system, the firm found it could integrate apprentices right from the beginning into production and
team work.

None of these successes was achieved painlessly. Virtually all of the above cases of restructuring were initiated in periods of financial and market crisis for the firms. The elimination of hierarchy involved the dislocation of many unnecessary jobs in middle management. The introduction of teams made it possible for fewer workers to perform more operations, thus making many others redundant, although generally this was accomplished through early retirements and attrition rather than mass layoffs. Still, hundreds of workers and managers lost their jobs at Getrag and Mettler Toledo, as did thousands at BMW over the course of the long transition to the new system. Though their situation was unique in that they began the shift away from the old craft system in the mid-1980s because of the early onset of crisis, the dislocation and job losses they experienced when moving in the new direction have subsequently become commonplace across German industry. In any case, these are important examples to note because their early and ultimately quite successful movement toward the new system makes it difficult to claim that the Germans cannot change and that they must live or die by the craft system.

Minimalist Strategies

That said, the obstacles to change have been extremely great in the 1990s and the situation facing firms just beginning the restructuring is much graver than it was for the three firms noted above. Those firms got to restructure themselves in a reasonably healthy economy surrounded by producers in the late 1980s who were thriving. Now, after a decade of deep recession and permanent restructuring pressures that have continued despite a moderate upswing in the business cycle, those once happy producers have all been forced to deal with the kind of financial and market crises that the above producers experienced much earlier. And with far greater intensity. The open and flexible "Japanese" system has diffused and been adopted and adapted by producers in a broad array of countries – notably in the United States – often in ways that make the system more flexible and efficient than it is even in Japan. All of these developments make the level of competition and the rapidity of technological and product change in nearly all market segments unimaginably intense. Thousands of the finest industrial producers in Germany have all been struggling throughout the decade to make themselves cheaper, higher quality, and more flexible producers, or be competed into oblivion by those who can.[10]

The earlier argument and the three examples just given, however, suggest that achieving the kind of transformation in the organization of production necessary to remain competitive in the current environment must involve far more than laying people off or shifting production outside of Germany to lower the wage bill. In many ways a whole way of life needs to be changed. The deconstruction of craft jurisdictions involves the elimination of traditional ways of envisioning one's career and narrating one's vocational life to oneself – and to one's peers, employer, and even employees. Very important forms of social status and understandings of achievement (the élan of the accomplished skilled craftsman, the prestige of the master, the accomplishment of the technician and applied engineer) will be threatened with devaluation by efforts to break down hierarchy and construct an environment of polymorphous collaboration in which those forms of achievement make no useful contribution to competitive success.

10. For fine examples of the struggles, successes, and continuing frustrations despite significant alterations of the German system we have been describing, see Schumann and Kern (1997). One is tempted to characterize the problems that the Germans face – and these are elaborated in the minimalist cases discussed in the text, as well as in the reflections put forth by Kern and Schumann – that they have been capable of altering the degree of hierarchy and fixity of role positions within the production process very dramatically over the course of the 1990s. The problem is that they are competing with producers who have developed a form of organization that differs not in degree, but in kind, from the German system.

Similarly in the ranks of middle management, expertise at ensuring that rules and guidelines are followed by those to whom they apply loses its value when rules are permanently provisional and constructed by the very people who then follow them. What is true of the middle management is also true of the German works councils, who by law are charged with participating in the construction of rules and in practice oversee the overseers: what is a works councilor to do when production is divided into self-governing and self-redefining groups that interact independently and systematically with different levels of the firm?

This kind of social and institutional destabilization is by no means confined within the boundaries of firms. Relations between subcontracting workshops and firms are also affected as are relations between firms and supporting institutions. Among firms and sub-contractors, for example, the shared understandings of career and the shared experiences of education and training that helped make it possible to maintain the kind of trusting collaboration across parts of the production chain are undermined by the introduction of boundary-blurring production organization. Where in the old craft system, engineers and technicians with similar degrees (even from the same school) facilitated the collaboration of two craft producers, in the new system work groups deal with work groups in a manner that they collectively establish. Bonds of trust that stood on the firm ground of shared jurisdiction have to be reforged in an environment that continuously redefines the roles of the collaborators.

Between producers and supporting institutions restructuring creates a disjunction between the services offered and the kinds of problems that consumers of such services confront. State agencies (such as the Steinbeis Foundation in Baden-Württemberg), trade associations, and technical universities, for example, were quite expert at facilitating technology transfer to healthy craft producers: they knew the structure of firms and industries, frequently had stable ties to particular departments within firms and, in the case of trade associations and technical universities, often developed departmental structures, career paths and curricula of their own that mimicked craft jurisdictions and functional divisions within firms. The current situation contradicts the old one at every level: firms are in crisis, not healthy, and their problems are organizational, not technological. Moreover, neither the firms nor the industries are sure of what their structures are likely to become, yet most are convinced of the need to attack existing craft and functional divisions and foster cross-departmental integration.

In this context, there is a great danger of the supporting institutions becoming either irrelevant to the needs of the emerging new system or obstacles to the emergence of the new system. For example, trade associations, driven by their own internal bureaucratic jurisdictional inertia, can offer services along no longer existing functional lines. Or, worse, they could sanction firms by withholding resources or cooperation when producers seeking to redefine their own boundaries participate in collaborative projects organized by producers and an association from a traditionally separate industrial sector. Likewise, professors and departments in technical universities can sponsor research projects and dissertations on topics that follow the outdated disciplinary agendas of university departments and professional associations, rather than the incipient discipline crossing needs of industry. Those professors pursuing interdisciplinary agendas can be ignored on the job market or released and denied tenure in a difficult financial climate.

Given the extent to which efforts to move away from the craft system are likely to destabilize social, institutional and professional relations throughout the German political economy, it is no surprise that we found that firms are reluctant to throw the old system out *in toto* and replace it with something new. Instead, what one finds is that producers are taking piecemeal steps away from the old system: boundaries are being tested and conflicts with entrenched interests entered into on only a number of fronts. In most cases, reformers themselves do not have a precise idea of how far they need to go and how much needs to be changed – they only know that lower costs and greater openness and flexibility in production and management are urgently needed. Few are either interested in or capable of defending the old system from criticism however, and nearly all firms and institutions are at least talking about moving toward more open, team-based organizational forms. Yet it is equally true that few within those organizations are able to resist calling for the deconstruction and destabilization of somebody else's department or of finding an extremely compelling technical ground for the continued existence of their own traditional privileges and duties. Adjustment is proceeding along this slow path of vision, experimentation, prudence and desperation.

Within this context, two characteristic bottlenecks have emerged among the many German firms that have recently initiated minimalist or piecemeal efforts to break from the craft system and implement more "Japanese"-like arrangements. The first is that the new forms of organization become isolated within the firm, making it difficult for the new forms of organization to work in ways that will maintain the commitment of those involved in them. The second is that the new forms of organization succeed in colonizing all elements of a firm, except for a few islands of tradition. In the first case, the viability of the entire firm hangs in the balance, in the second case the long-term attractiveness of the island of tradition to the rest of the firm does.

A good example of the first problem developed at a large machine-tool company in Baden-Württemberg that manufactures large-scale stamping machines for the automobile industry. This company has made tremendous strides toward completely revamping its production process through the introduction of integrated product islands and group work. The traditional workshop system has been modified so that machines are now grouped around the production of particular groups of products rather than around parts for all products. All set-up, production planning, and delivery scheduling tasks, which formerly were performed by the masters and foremen of the individual machine shops, or by a level of middle management located directly above the floor of the plant, have been integrated into the new product islands. Members of product development teams, moreover, now continually move between activity in the production teams and the relocated engineering rooms on the shopfloor. Technicians, programmers, engineers and skilled machine operators now work side-by-side in close cooperation and to some extent interchangeably within the teams. Groups within the islands have begun electing their own representatives to facilitate the coordination of their own internal duties and to maintain contact with the operations of the other groups and other product islands.

There are two factors within the firm, however, which significantly disturb the operation of these islands and constrain their ability to produce significant gains in efficiency and cost reduction. First, the changes in production have only been introduced in the areas of direct mechanical production; areas of work preparation, such as tool-making, as well as materials purchasing have neither been organized into teams nor adapted to the needs of teams. As a result, teams have only limited control over their overhead costs. Since the idea of the introduction of teams is to devolve responsibility for holding down costs to the teams themselves, lack of control over overheads engenders frustration on the shopfloor – and skepticism regarding the effectiveness of the new system. Changing this arrangement, however, involves attacking the privileges of some of the most highly skilled workers in the plant (toolmakers) – something the management of the firm, at least until now, has been unwilling to do.

Second, changes in production have not been accompanied by corresponding efforts to deconstruct the hierarchical relations between top management departments and the newly emergent product team structure. Management has retained the right to veto group decisions that it believes will not result in the cost savings it desires. It has also retained control over the budgets of the product islands: company management, not the teams, make team investment decisions and ultimately evaluate the performance of the teams. A spokesman for one of the product islands as well as the head of all manufacturing at the firm claimed that this limitation on local autonomy and the continued existence of hierarchy threatened to undermine the effectiveness of the product islands and teams. When members of the group believe that their success or failure is the direct result of their collective efforts, all have an incentive to make continuous improvements. Without local autonomy, however, such incentives do not exist and the commitment of team members to the success of the team is undermined.

Both examples show that the partial movement away from the principles of craft organization risks making the new organizational principles appear to be a charade. Making a full commitment, however, means taking privilege and authority away from those with little desire to give them up. Clearly there is no equilibrium with the current arrangement: doing nothing will lead to the gradual erosion of morale and enthusiasm within the new product islands, returning to the old craft system will price the firm out of the market, and moving forward will involve the spilling of blood. Someone is going to lose this battle, and the stakes in the world market at the moment are such that it may be the firm itself.

The second characteristic obstacle to restructuring along more open and flexible lines reverses the forces of the previous example: rather than boundary-blending and cooperative organization being isolated in production, production is isolated within the firm as the last bastion of traditional organization. Unlike the previous case, this situation redounds to the disadvantage not of the entire firm, but to the island of tradition.

A good example of this occurred at the electric turbine subsidiary of a large European multinational in Mannheim in the north of Baden-Württemberg. The parent company was well known as a very progressive company, at the forefront of globalization as well as of the decentralization of management structure and control. Subsidiaries throughout the entire global concern have been given tremendous operating autonomy, encouraged constantly to bring out new products and utilize collaborative relations with sub-contractors as well as encouraging other subsidiaries to do so.

Like BMW, the company has tried to cultivate a new kind of management career in which individual managers move throughout the organization, cross functionally, accumulating knowledge of the company, its products, its suppliers and its customers. Promotion within this company has increasingly become contingent upon having successfully participated in cooperative product development teams that involve members of different departments as well as key suppliers. To encourage this, the Mother company introduced what it calls a Customer Focus Program (CFP) in all of its subsidiaries. This program brought managers together across subsidiaries as well as across functional departments on a regular basis to foster dialogue on the improvement of company products and the development of new technologies. This is not simply a discussion group, however; CFP also, because it has constituted itself regularly, acts as a kind of monitoring forum for projects and subsidiaries throughout the organization. In many subsidiaries, this collaborative, team, and product-oriented organizational practice has been taken right down to the shopfloor in the form of group work and product oriented, low inventory production.

Not so in the Mannheim Turbine works. Hierarchy flattening occurred within the departmental structures above the shopfloor, where a number of CFP groups were created. But the production process itself remains dominated by the old workshop-based craft system and the old craft hierarchies. The plants in Mannheim continued to be organized around specialized machine and/or part production. Typically, any given work station operated with an inventory of up to five days. Operators working on particular machines dedicated to the production of a specific range of parts had little idea where their work object fit into the larger product the plant was constructing – one machinist had no idea where the parts he was making were going to go next in the line of production. Masters and foremen set up machines.

Why this continued existence of the old craft system beneath an increasingly open, flexible management structure? In part the answer stems from the strategy that the local firm pursued after the Mannheim plant was merged with the larger European mother company in 1988. Prior to the merger, the Mannheim plant was capable of making complete electrical turbine generators. After the merger, the plant was broken up and parts of the production process were shifted to parent company facilities in other locations; Mannheim was specialized in large part production. Thousands of layoffs resulted from these changes. Perhaps understandably, given the massive job losses, the works council and trade unions were reluctant to engage in additional restructuring within the production lines that remain for fear of additional layoffs. The local labor representation was persuaded that additional losses would redound to its disadvantage and therefore defended its traditional jurisdiction over how jobs were defined. As labor resisted the new structures, management, which is committed to the European parent company, not Mannheim, became increasingly frustrated and focused on finding other more profitable locations for production.

A final example shows how restructuring can go in a more robust direction. A producer of automobile gaskets outside of Stuttgart profited from its relationships with local automobile producers for many years. But complacency and poor management, coupled with changing fortunes among German auto producers in general, gave rise to a deep and wrenching crisis at the firm. Indeed, so bad was the crisis, that the old management was removed and replaced with managers with broad restructuring experiences in their past. The new managers explicitly set out to restructure production and management organization in a way that avoided the pitfalls of piecemeal reform and minimalist cost-cutting, because they had been frustrated by the mixed results this kind of adjustment had yielded in their previous employers. As a result, from the very beginning they made it clear to the workforce and to the works-council that dramatic departures from the craft system would be implemented: U-shaped lines were to be laid out throughout the plant, group work was to become the norm, and development and production would increasingly occur simultaneously.

This kind of clarity on the part of management encouraged early acceptance and involvement on the part of works councils in the internal restructuring of the workplace. Works councilors, skilled workers, and plant managers all worked together to set up the new arrangements: many made a number of trips to the United States to observe the more open and low cost production arrangements of the firm's major competitors. Given this kind of cooperation in radical change, restructuring has proceeded very far at the firm – though progress has still been piecemeal. There are still islands within the firm that produce in the old manner, but the climate, even among those who work in the old-style arrangements, is that these arrangements will not last long. Indeed, so advanced is the new system in the firm that the works council, which has traditionally been strongly identified with the IG Metall metal-workers union, has devoted itself to winning team members over to the union. Its biggest challenge is to get the elected speakers of groups to become shop stewards-or vice versa. So far, the results are mixed.

Conclusion

The above minimalist strategies show how difficult and treacherous the current restructuring process is in Germany today.

Efforts to implement new structures in specific areas of the firm and not others run the risk of being undermined by the resistance to change elsewhere in the firm. Attachment to old jurisdictional ideas of functional right, entitlement, and authority are frequently the primary obstacles to change. Even in those cases, however, where actors with central roles within the traditional system are intimately involved in the restructuring process, such as the works council in the third example above, it is not at all certain that the new structure that it has helped to create will have a place for it. The stakes in this process of adjustment are high indeed: if the restructuring does not succeed, it could mean the very survival of the firm. If it does succeed, it is not at all guaranteed that there will even be a place in the new system for those who play a central role in bringing it into being.

The particular kinds of conflicts outlined above are unique to the German system. Problems and conflicts around the deconstruction of hierarchy and the smoothing over of fragmentation are not at all unique to Germany. The Japanese are finding that their own system of flexible production has internal problems that inhibit producers' ability to keep pace with the intensity of technological and product change in today's extremely demanding international markets. In particular, an over-identification in the Japanese system with the community of the firm has placed a limit on the capacity of larger producers to recombine production and take advantage of the specialties and flexible practices of its own suppliers – much less many of its competitors. There is little institutional infrastructure beyond the boundaries of the firm, as there is in the German system of Chambers of Industry and Commerce, trade associations, and state monitored vocational training, that can help structure the recombination of workers, producers, and assets that the desire for greater flexibility seems to make necessary.

Indeed, when seen in this context, the German situation, as uncertain and wrenching as it is, can actually be understood to contain a ray of hope. The more decentralized, extra-firm, and public character of many dimensions of the German craft system provides producers with the raw material for the construction of an even more radically open system than the Japanese. With the exception of the vocational training system, most of the institutions that facilitated cooperation among independent producers in the old German craft system were not themselves implicated in the direct reproduction of the craft system in production itself: instead, they facilitated communication about the quality of production or the capacity of a specific producer to perform up to a particular standard. The more that internal restructuring within firms and among firms emphasizes local autonomy, responsibility for costs and continuous improvement, the less significant the boundaries of a given firm will become to the newly created pieces. And, correspondingly, the more significant will the social and economic realm between producers become for the regulation and governance of production. Even if many of the current institutions that occupy this space are themselves committed to the old craft system, the fact that the space itself is a very familiar one to the Germans could turn out to be an advantage in the long run. Time will tell.

Chapter 3

THE GERMAN SKILL-CREATION SYSTEM AND TEAM-BASED PRODUCTION

Competitive Asset or Liability?[*]

David Finegold and Karin Wagner

Introduction

The German manufacturing sector is at a critical juncture. The sharp drop in output and employment during the last recession precipitated talk of a crisis in the metalworking industry. While the economy has recovered somewhat from the depths of the recession, the high current levels of unemployment and decisions by leading German corporations (e.g., Mercedes, BMW, Siemens) to concentrate investment in new

* We would like to thank the German Marshall Fund of the United States and the US Department of Labor, which provided the funding for this research, and the many pump companies that gave us time and access to data. We would also like to thank Pepper Culpepper, Arndt Sorge, David Soskice, and Jay Tate for comments that helped improve the chapter.

plants outside Germany are signs that the crisis may be structural, rather than cyclical.

Experts on the German system have argued that the source of the problem lies in major changes in the basis of competitive advantage in the world economy. Germany's traditional success in capital goods manufacturing was built on a system of "diversified quality production" (DQP), where highly skilled craft workers and engineers were able to design and build technically superior machines that could command a price premium in global markets (Streeck 1989). The success of the DQP strategy, however, now appears to be threatened by the emergence of a new paradigm – lean production (Womack et al. 1990). First perfected by the Japanese and then emulated by leading American companies, lean production enables manufacturers to turn out goods of comparable quality to German products far more quickly and less expensively. It does this by combining the benefits of flexible machine tools, close partnerships with suppliers who deliver on a just-in-time basis, and a system of continuous improvement built into a team-based production process (Best 1990; Levine 1995). Herrigel (1996a; Herrigel and Sabel, Chapter 2) contends that not only is lean production proving superior to DQP in increasing segments of manufacturing industry, but also that the very sets of institutions, skills, and organizational culture that made DQP thrive in Germany may undermine the capacity of German firms to adapt to the new lean-production paradigm.

This chapter focuses on whether the German skill-creation system remains a competitive strength that can help German firms adapt to the challenges of the new competitive climate or a liability that is hindering manufacturers from undertaking necessary restructuring. We explore this issue through a comparative analysis of how German and US manufacturers are reforming their work processes, concentrating in particular on that aspect of lean production – the use of multi-functional work teams – that has been cited as most problematic in the

German context (Herrigel and Sabel, Chapter 2; Kuhlmann and Schumann 1997; Streeck 1996). Among the key questions which the chapter addresses are:

- What changes in market conditions have compelled firms to restructure?
- How did the skill base of German and US manufacturers compare prior to this restructuring effort?
- How has the adoption of multi-functional teams differed across countries and different product markets and are these teams appropriate in all contexts?
- What impact have the US and German skills-creation systems had on the use of work teams?

Our answers to these questions are based on data gathered from nationally representative samples of carefully matched pump plants in the US and Germany. Pump manufacturers were chosen because on key dimensions they are broadly representative of the industrial machinery sector in the two countries. Industrial machinery is perhaps the archetype for the DQP model on which German export success has been built. The pump industry features a wide spectrum of different product types; indeed, the differences among products are so great that the pump sector is better conceived as a collection of different market segments, each with its own producers and a relatively small number of users, rather than a unified industry. The products range from highly specialized, engineered pumps or pumping systems produced to precise customer requirements to standardized products for the consumer or small commercial market. This distinguishes it from automobile assembly plants, where much of the recent research on workplace reform has been conducted (e.g., Shimokawa et al. 1997). The pump industry in both countries is dominated by small and medium-sized companies. Despite their relatively small size, most pump companies need to be active in the global marketplace to serve their specialized customer niches on a worldwide basis; a few firms also have global production capabilities.

To preview our main conclusions, we find that both product market segment and national institutions have an important impact on skill levels. Prior to restructuring, German and US pumpmakers in the same product markets had a remarkably similar skills mix, although the skills were produced in very different ways. After the advent of lean production and other changes in the competitive climate, however, we see that national institutions have a powerful influence on how plants respond: in Germany, plants with a higher percentage of skilled workers are less likely to adopt multi-functional work teams, while just the opposite pattern exists in the US, with American plants more likely overall to adopt lean production practices. Several of the more skilled German manufacturers, however, were adopting alternative restructuring strategies better suited to their existing skill base and customized production requirements.

Understanding the Pattern of Workplace Restructuring: Two Types of Lean Organization

There is a large and growing literature in political economy and management on how new production strategies, such as lean production, evolve and diffuse across countries (e.g., Piore and Sabel 1984; Kogut 1991). Typically one company or a small set of firms develops a new organization of production that represents a significant competitive advantage over its rivals. As this firm gains market share, other organizations and researchers will seek to study the organization and understand the factors underlying its success. The attempts at emulation of these new organizational concepts are likely to occur first in those companies most closely connected to innovating firms: direct competitors in the home country, foreign competitors, and suppliers or customers. As the new ideas gain wider currency, then firms in other industries with similar production requirements are likely to experiment with them. In the process of diffusion, however, the original concept will be modified to fit the particular context of each adopter (Tenkasi and Mohrman 1994).

As a consequence of the different levels of variation, the production regimes described in the literature – whether lean production, flexible specialization, or DQP – were never accurate representations of the majority of firms in a country. Rather, they are best seen as ideal types of organization based on the experience of some leading companies that can serve as models for other firms to adapt to their own circumstances. The value of such models is that they can illustrate how a complex configuration of mutually reinforcing factors – e.g., management strategy, organizational design, work processes, uses of technology, skill levels, reward structures and the external institutional context – can come together to form a new organizational logic (e.g., Lawler 1996; Meyer et al. 1993).

In the case of lean production, if the automobile is *The Machine that Changed the World,* then lean production, as described in the MIT-led study that coined the term, may be described as "The Idea that Changed the World," at least the world of metal manufacturing. Lean production has had such a major impact on the metalworking sector because it appears to offer a means to satisfy two seemingly irreconcilable manufacturing objectives, combining the economies of scale of mass production and customization to individual client needs typically associated with craft of diversified quality production (DQP). In the process of *mass customization* it is possible to generate dramatic performance improvements in cycle times, productivity and quality, and to reduce inventories. Lean production achieves these objectives through a fundamental redesign of the production process.

Many of the individual concepts contained within lean production are not new; what is new is how Toyota gradually combined earlier production innovations from the US (such as scientific management and total quality management) with its own insights to create a distinctive production system (Fujimoto 1994). Given its evolutionary nature, some of the recent attention focused on the lean production "revolution" has struck German managers as odd. Major elements of the lean production model have always been part of the typical German approach to production or were contained in the *new production concepts* (Kern and Schumann 1984) introduced in the mid-1980s: e.g., high levels of training for the workforce, direct worker control over quality, cellular manufacturing, and increased sharing of information on performance, the production process, and the wider business. Other parts of the lean production paradigm, such as the *kanban* or demand-pull system for driving production based on customer orders and partnering with suppliers to enable the high-quality, frequent deliveries needed for just-in-time production, are innovations that seem easily reconciled with the DQP approach. What is potentially more problematic in the German context, is the shift under lean production in the basic organizational unit for performing work from the individual to the multi-functional team. The team is responsible for all of the tasks needed to produce the component and to satisfy the needs of its internal or external customer. Individual team members are cross-trained, often through job rotation, to perform all of the work within the cell.

Alongside lean production, an alternative vision of a team-based, lean organization has evolved, where "lean" entails flattening the organization by removing layers of management and pushing authority and information down to frontline workers.[1]

---

1. There are two distinct strands to the literature on organizational flattening. The first, sociotechnical strand focuses heavily on employee satisfaction and quality of work life, with removal of managerial layers seen as a way to increase empowerment and only secondarily, corporate performance, while the other, led by management consultants, focuses on *re-engineering* business processes to cut out waste, with the normal consequence of downsizing the organization.

This version of the "lean" organization emerges from the long history of work on employee involvement (EI) (e.g., Passmore 1988; Lawler et al. 1989) and its most recent manifestation, the "high-performance workplace" (HPW) (Osterman 1994b; Applebaum and Batt 1994; Lawler et al. 1995). The EI/HPW model places far more emphasis on the human, rather than the technical, side of the work process.

The crucial distinction between the two models lies in the nature of organizational change and the power given to teams (Lawler 1994). Lean production, as practiced in Japan, relies on a top-down model of change, with teams reporting to a multi-tiered bureaucracy. Adler and Borys (1996) argue that managers in this bureaucracy perform the vital functions of developing and refining standards and sharing information across teams, essential elements in the continuous improvement process. In contrast, the EI/HPW model of change is bottom up, centered on self-managed teams whose members assume the traditional responsibilities of managers (e.g., production scheduling) and staff (some maintenance and human resource functions) along with a wider array of technical tasks. Lawler (1994) illustrates this distinction by contrasting the relatively limited work tasks and span of control of teams in Toyota and other Japanese carmakers with those in Volvo's Kalmar plant, where a self-managed team assembled an entire car. The EI/HPW model also places a greater emphasis than lean production on the use of reward practices, such as pay for skill and team performance, that can motivate employees to maximize their discretionary effort to improve company performance, a piece of the organizational strategy that large Japanese corporations may have found unnecessary historically because of their lifetime employment model.

This study is an attempt to explain variations in the use and types of teams in Germany and the US and how these are affected by the existing skill mix. Where variations in work organization are apparent, we attempt to analyze more systematically what factors account for different approaches to restructuring. The study focuses on the relative importance and inter-action between two main potential sources of variation – national institutions and products' technical requirements pre-dicted by theories of comparative political economy (e.g., Hall 1986; Broedner 1990; Streeck 1996) and technological change (Gerwin 1987). A third important level of variation in restruc-turing arises among individual firms in the same country and product segment; this is in effect the residual in our analysis, since we do not have systematic data to analyze these sources of intranational variation.

National Institutions

Each country and the regions within it have different institu-tional structures and cultural values, creating a set of capabili-ties and constraints that affect a company's choice of production organization. Some elements of the institutional environment that will shape how managers adapt their current practices in response to lean production are the structure of capital markets, the strength of the local supplier base, the power of employer associations and/or unions, labor market regulations, and the quality and quantity of the outputs from the education and training system (Finegold and Soskice 1988; Sorge 1990b). As noted, we are particularly interested in testing how the last of these factors – differences in the US and German skill-creation systems and the existing supply of skilled workers – has affected the adoption of multi-functional work teams in the two country samples. Specifically, we want to test Herrigel and Sabel's con-tention that the high degree of specialization among skilled workers and the narrow functional orientation of German man-agers from different disciplines – e.g., manufacturing engi-neering, product engineering, marketing, purchasing – make it difficult to establish the multi-functional teams on the shopfloor and integrated product teams or concurrent engineering in the product development process. The obstacles, he argues, are not only structural, part of the organization of the firm and VET system, but are also part of individual identities, as skilled workers and managers have come to define themselves based on their relatively narrow functional capabilities.

Product Market/Technical Requirements

Lean production was developed for high-volume manufacture of a relatively standardized product. As the success of Toyota's Lexus line has demonstrated at the expense of Mercedes and BMW, however, it is also possible to apply these same techniques to the production of luxury automobiles which were previously thought to be the sole purview of DQP. The relevance of the lean-production approach to pump manufacturers is still likely to depend on which type of product market segment they serve. It has traditionally been possible to distinguish three main product segments within the pump industry: standardized goods that are typically built to forecast, assemble-to-order pumps that are produced based on a set of product features and specifications that a customer has chosen from a catalog, and customized or engineered pumps or systems which are designed to meet a particular customer need.[2] As noted, lean production may be beginning to blur the distinction among these categories, enabling standardized producers to assemble to order with large savings in inventory and minimal loss of efficiency,

---

2. It is important not to equate standardized goods with lower quality production. Pumpmakers in all segments are required to make products that are very reliable and durable; the difference between segments relates to product size, production volumes, and the extent of customization required. We operationalized the distinction among product types by grouping plants in the two countries based on the number of pumps produced annually per production worker: custom (3-50), assemble-to-order (51-400) and standardized (401-5,000). This categorization based on batch size corresponds closely to a division of plants based on the percentage of production that contained new engineering content, but provides greater distinction between standardized and assemble-to-order plants.

while customized producers may be able to reduce lead times and production costs through greater use of product modules. Nevertheless, there are large differences in production volumes and technical requirements of products across the three segments, which prior research suggests should have an important impact on work organization (Gerwin 1987). Specifically, those plants specializing in very large, custom pumps produced in batches of one or two are likely to find multi-functional work teams less applicable than those that manufacture large runs of standardized pumps for the commercial marketplace.

Individual Firm Capabilities

A more idiosyncratic level of variation is likely to occur based on the particular circumstances of individual companies or plants, e.g., the strength of their existing managerial and worker capabilities. Within any random sample of plants of this type, there will inevitably be some managers who are more open to new concepts and more successful at implementing radical change. In addition, comparisons of closely matched firms in the same country (e.g., Federal Express and UPS or McKinsey and Boston Consulting Group) have shown that there is more than one path to success in a given business segment, with direct competitors pursuing very different organizational and human-resource strategies (Cappelli and Crocker-Hefter 1996). The nature of the ownership structure – e.g., is a company privately held, part of a larger conglomerate, or independent and publicly traded? Is it foreign or domestically controlled? – is also likely to have an impact on how much pressure a plant feels to undertake major restructuring and whether it has the resources needed to implement such changes.

In summary, given the differing technical requirements between the pump and automobile industries, some features of lean production, such as the division of production jobs into a narrow range of tasks, would neither be feasible nor desirable for many pumpmakers. Rather, we would expect to observe a distinctive organizational response in each national setting and product market segment given the capacities and constraints facing pump companies. In the case of German firms, managers' decisions are likely to be shaped both by the existing capabilities of apprentices and *Meisters* and the constraints imposed by the high labor costs and restricted work hours in the German institutional environment.

Research Methodology and Sample

This study employed a matched-plant method that has been used successfully to compare a variety of other sectors across countries (e.g., Daly, Hitchens, and Wagner 1985; Mason and Finegold 1997). We focused on identifying the different responses to team-based organization in nationally representative samples of German and US pumpmakers. Pump manufacturers were chosen, as noted, to provide a representative picture of the changes taking place in the wider metalworking sector, as the sector features plants with a wide array of product markets and skill demands. Relative to the automotive sector, pumpmakers' variety of product types and typically small and medium-sized plants differentiate them from car assembly plants, but they have much in common with the second- and third-tier auto suppliers. The pump industry (liquid and vacuum pumps and compressors) is also important in its own right. It represents approximately 25 percent of total employment (46,500 workers in 1995) and output in the German general industrial equipment industry, a vital contributor to German exports and a slightly smaller proportion of US general industrial machinery (VDMA 1996, United Nations 1995).

In order to understand the extent and pace of workplace restructuring in each plant and the main sources of variation in work-restructuring strategies, we gathered data on a set of key elements of lean production: new relationships with suppliers, workplace redesign (cellular manufacturing, multi-functional work and product-development teams, frontline-worker responsibility for quality, uses of new flexible machine tool technology) and human resource factors (skills/training, reward systems, information sharing) that could affect the adoption of lean techniques. To assess the success of these restructuring initiatives, we identified a number of dimensions along which lean production has been said to improve performance: reduction in new product development time, lower inventories, improvements in on-time deliveries and quality levels and enhanced productivity.

The primary means of gathering data were half-day visits to matched pairs of German and US plants by the research team from the US and Germany. The visits consisted of interviews with the general manager, and in many cases other members of the senior management team (e.g., manufacturing manager, human resource manager) and observation of the shopfloor to get further details on the production process, machinery layout and utilization. The detailed interview protocol was developed based on the researchers' previous studies in metalworking and then refined through pilot visits in each country. We then sent a short survey to all participating firms to gather additional data and document changes over the period from 1993 to 1996 on the extent of adoption of different elements of the new production organization. Follow-up phone calls were used to obtain any missing information.

Because of our particular interest in the relationship between skill levels and changes in the workplace, we also distributed a two-page individual questionnaire to a random sample of machine operators, setters and supervisors in a sub-sample of US plants to obtain information on their career histories, qualifications and how they had acquired the skills needed for their current job. We received 220 valid, completed surveys from eight plants. In addition, we conducted a set of interviews with education and training providers and standard-setting bodies in the US and Germany. The purpose of these visits was to gather information on the comparability of qualifications across countries at both skilled worker and technician/supervisor levels. We compared the curriculum, forms of provision, and the standards expected of students (through comparison of examination questions) as well as the educational background and post-course career paths of trainees.

The sample of firms was identified through trade directories, including manufacturers producing a wide array of different size and types of pumps (e.g., centrifugal, rotary, vacuum). The visits were made in two rounds in 1995 and early 1996. The first set of visits were to plants concentrated in Berlin and Southern Germany. These plants were asked to identify direct competitors or the most comparable producers of their pumps in the US. We then attempted to visit these matched plants in the US along with other US pumpmakers in close geographic proximity, requesting that they in turn identify comparable firms in Germany. This led to a second round of visits in both countries. The German establishments were scattered across Western Germany, while US visits were concentrated in four regions: California, the Pacific Northwest, the Midwest, and mid-Atlantic. We limited the sample to western Germany because the eastern German mechanical engineering sector is still in a transition process to a market economy (Hitchens, Wagner and Birnie 1993). In all, the sample included eighteen German and eighteen US pump manufacturers that appear to be broadly representative of the industry as a whole. This sample included eight companies that operated production facilities in both the US and Germany (see Table 3.1).[3]

3. In several cases, the production capability was relatively limited outside of the home country, with some machining and a focus on assembly. In many cases, the plants in the two countries were producing sufficiently different types of pumps that they did not produce a good match, so we sought other competitors. Three of our matched pairs came from within the same organization; in general, the foreign owned plants in Germany appeared more advanced in their restructuring efforts.

Table 3.1   Distribution of shopfloor employment in the sample by type of production

	Number of companies		Proportion of employment	
	US	Germany	US	Germany
Standardized	6	6	54	51
Assemble-to-order	6	6	19	28
Customized	6	6	27	21
Total	18	18	100	100

Note: Standardized pump plants produce 401-5,000 pumps annually per worker, assemble to order = 51-400/worker, and custom = 3-50/worker.

Industry Overview and Dynamics

The pump industry has undergone substantial restructuring in the last decade. US pumpmakers were hit hard in the recession of 1991-92, with employment dropping by nine percent in a two year period (see Table 3.2). Since 1993 there has been a substantial growth in productivity as output has recovered, while total employment has continued to fall. The sharp drop in indirect workers has been partly offset by a rise in production workers.

Table 3.2   Trends in the US pump industry (SIC 3561, 3594) (Base Year = 1987)

Year	Employees	Output	Output per employee	Production workers	Non-production workers
1987	100.0	100.0	100.0	100.0	100.0
1989	105.4	106.6	101.1	104.5	106.6
1991	104.4	106.3	101.8	102.8	106.6
1993	95.4	101.1	106.0	97.6	92.5
1995	94.2	107.0	113.6	101.7	84.0

Source: Bureau of Labor Statistics web page, 1997.

After the initial boost that came with German reunification, the German pump industry has suffered an even more significant decline than its US counterpart. In the three years from 1990 to 1993 employment in the West German pump industry dropped by 11 percent, reflecting the general recession that had gripped West German manufacturing (see Table 3.3). By the end of 1994, total employment in the eastern and western German pump sector stood at 49,500, ten percent below the West German level of four years before, reflecting both the effects of the recession in Germany and the strong decline in eastern German engineering industry (Carlin and Soskice 1997). Real output fell even more sharply, declining by 20 percent for West German pump manufacturers between 1990 and 1993, with a corresponding decline in productivity and capacity utilization. At the same time, the ratio of imports to exports grew considerably, reflecting a decline in competitiveness, although German exports (at 3.4 billion DM) were still more than double imports (1.6 billion DM) in 1995 (VDMA 1996).

Table 3.3   Output and performance of the German pump industry

	Nominal output per employee in DM	Real output per employee in DM	Capacity utilization %	Export orders as % of all orders
1990	164.000	164.000	91	41
1993	172.000	149.000	78	40
1994*	188.000	165.000	79	46**

*   united Germany;
**   an increase of about 3 percentage points has been added by the eastern German manufacturers.

Source: VDMA 1996, Statistisches Handbuch für den Maschinenbau, liquid pumps.

Despite the retrenchment in both countries, the US and Germany continue to be the world's top two pump producers (see Table 3.4). Germany retained its position as the world's leading exporter of pumps, with 21 percent of the world market for liquid pumps in 1994, ahead of the US (16 percent) and

Japan (15 percent), Germany, however, saw a significant decline in its share of world markets between 1989 and 1994, while the US maintained its market position and Japan and some smaller nations expanded production.

Table 3.4   Shares of world pump trade

	Liquid pumps		Vacuum pumps and compressors	
	1989	1994	1989	1994
Germany	24.7	21.4	25.1	19.0
US	15.9	16.3	20.4	17.9
Japan	12.6	15.1	11.3	11.2

Source: VDMA 1996.

Pressures for Restructuring

To remain competitive in the global marketplace, US and German pump manufacturers have been compelled to undertake major restructuring. Like many segments of capital goods production, pump-makers have traditionally prospered by targeting market segments where buyers were willing to pay a price premium in return for high-quality, very reliable, customized products. In the 1990s, the increasing intensity of global competition and the pressure on their customers to cut costs have substantially eroded this price premium. High product quality continues to be particularly important in Germany, where it was cited by 39 percent of all German managers we interviewed (compared to 29 percent of US managers) as their primary source of competitive advantage, more than twice the percentage they cited for any other competitive factor (e.g., price, delivery time). Customers, however, now increasingly assume quality as a minimum criteria for firms to be considered for an order and focus competition on price. "Where in the past we could expect to win an order if we cost 20 percent more than our competitors because of our reputation for quality, now we are lucky if we can get a 3-5 percent price premium," said one general manager. The growing influence of large engineering contractors, key customers for many pump companies, has contributed to this price pressure; in the past, German manufacturers could justify a higher initial price based on an engineering advantage – e.g., a pump with greater energy efficiency or reduced maintenance requirements – that produces lower lifecycle costs. It is now more difficult to obtain this price premium because it would cut into the already thin margins of their customer, who is often not the ultimate end user of the product, and hence cares more about cost than performance or reliability.

The emergence of new, lower-cost competitors has further intensified pressure to reduce costs if firms are to maintain any profit margin. In some standardized market segments, low-cost producers in Asia and, more recently, eastern Europe, are manufacturing complete pumps that compete directly with US and German products so that German manufacturers were forced to move to a higher segment even in the standardized product group. However, for the majority of pumpmakers which are in more specialized markets, the impetus for change is focused on rethinking the production organization or increasing the sourcing of labor-intensive components.

One pressure for restructuring that was much more strongly evident in German pump manufacturing has been the significant increase in total labor costs. German manufacturers have been accustomed to operating with shorter working hours and higher labor costs than their rivals in the US, Asia and southern Europe. With the reduction in the length of the work week to 35 hours in 1995, however, German firms suffered a significant further reduction in competitiveness that has forced managers to rethink their use of labor and future investment strategies.

Several factors, however, have shielded the pump industry from the full effects of the crisis felt in some other segments of metal manufacturing. Differences in technical standards – the German DIN standard is dominant in Europe while the US API standards are common in North America and Asia – have placed some limitation on direct competition between US and European pumpmakers; this difference in standards is reinforced as a barrier-to-entry by the accompanying test requirements, with large pumpmakers obliged to have costly test equipment on site to certify that each pump meets the required standard. In addition, pumps – like razor blades – are a form of annuity business, with manufacturers often selling the initial product at or below cost in order to get the lucrative business in spare parts over the life of the good. Thus, firms with a large installed base have a steady revenue stream even when current orders decline, although competition in the spares market is also increasing.

The Supply of Skills Prior to Restructuring

National differences in skills

The German vocational training system provides a high supply of skilled workers, which stems from the well-known dual system and has often been cited as a model for the reforms of US school-to-work programs (e.g., Hamilton 1990; OTA 1990). The German dual system ensures not only a high quantity of skilled labor (roughly two-thirds of school-leavers complete an apprenticeship), but also a high and relatively uniform quality of skills; to obtain a nationally recognized metal-working qualification, young people must complete a 3.5 year course and a set of rigorous final exams that demonstrates their mastery of all the main areas of metal cutting and forming, including material on CNC programming and pneumatics/hydraulics that were introduced with the broadening of the metalworking qualification in the late 1980s. In addition to these occupational skills, the general content of German apprenticeships has been expanded to include knowledge of the whole enterprise, communication skills, and problem-solving and basic math skills; these revisions to the content of qualifications support the new approach to quality, production scheduling, machine maintenance, planning, controlling and assessing work, and personal responsibility (Geer and Hirschbrunn 1994). With the new apprenticeship curricula, young people are spending proportionately more time studying a broad set of core subjects together and less time on a narrow functional specialty. The change in requirements has mitigated the rigidity of the identities within the production process that Herrigel and Sabel (Chapter 2) cite as being rather fixed. The broadening of training requirements, with the institution of a common curriculum for the first year in all mechanical apprenticeships – electrical occupations have also adopted a common core – has improved individual mobility and postponed occupational choices, enabling all young people to get an overview of the entire production process. For toolmakers and mechanics, the common, initial foundation of the course has been extended to cover the first year and a half of the apprenticeship period.

Our interviews with training providers in the US and in Germany and detailed comparison of curriculum and examinations revealed that the US adult apprenticeship system offers a similar amount of both on and off-the-job training and breadth of practical subjects as the German dual system. We also found at least five major differences between the systems. The most obvious difference between apprenticeships in the two countries is the scale of the systems, with Germany's dual system training roughly ten times as many skilled workers relative to all production workers as the US (Broadberry and Wagner 1996). Second, the US does not include the same focus on generic skills, with individuals spending most of their classroom training learning about the different occupational areas along with technical math and blueprint reading. Third, the US does not have any mechanisms for overseeing the quality of the supervision that individuals are receiving during the bulk of the time they spend in on-the-job training, as occurs through the German *Meisters* and trade unions. Fourth, while US apprentices generally follow a common curriculum set by the Department of

Labor and/or their state apprenticeship office, there is no mechanism yet in place to insure comparability in the testing of the skills they acquire,[4] as occurs in Germany; indeed, some of the "apprenticeship" programs we observed were customized training packages designed by a community college to meet the needs of a particular firm, while providing its employees with a qualification. And finally, US apprentices are, on average, roughly ten years older than their German counterparts, typically undertaking the apprenticeship after they have already been working for several years in the metal-working industry. None of our US sample plants had any youth apprentices (e.g., individuals under 21 who were still classified as full-time students at a school or local college). Our interviews with the designers of these pilot programs in several states indicate that youth apprenticeships are not geared to provide the same amount of occupational training as in Germany, but rather to provide young people with some exposure to the workplace and a broader educational foundation onto which they may later build more occupationally specific skills.[5]

In the German sample plants a much higher percentage of the production workforce had craft or higher level vocational qualifications than in US establishments (see Table 3.5). For the sample as a whole, more than 70 percent of production workers and supervisors in Germany had completed an apprenticeship compared to roughly 11 percent in the US. Likewise, 15 of the 18 German plants were training apprentices at the time of our visits, accounting for 6.3 percent of all production workers, while apprentices accounted for under one percent of the production workforce in the US.

4. The US has established a National Skills Standards Board that is charged with putting in place a system of voluntary, national skill standards which would cover the metalworking occupations.
5. In some cases, it is still unclear whether youth apprentices would receive any credit (e.g., permission to skip some courses) for their studies if they later undertook an adult apprenticeship.

Table 3.5   Percentage of apprentices in relation to shopfloor workers

Product Type	US 1993	US 1996	Germany 1993	Germany 1996
Standardized	0.6%	0.9%	3.0%	4.0%
Assemble to order	0%	0%	6.0%	5.0%
Custom	2.4%	0%	14.0%	10.0%
Total	0.7%	0.7%	7.71%	6.3%

The difference in the number of workers with apprenticeship qualifications, however, greatly overstates the actual skill differences we found between Germany and the US. Approximately half of all US production workers appeared to be functioning at a skilled level even if they did not possess a formal craft qualification – e.g., they were capable of operating a variety of different machines, editing programs using a CNC control, checking for quality using SPC and performing basic maintenance tasks. Several factors explain the unexpectedly high levels of shopfloor skills found in US plants. The US has a much wider array of education and training routes open to individuals than in Germany. Close to half (47 percent) of all the operators, setters and supervisors we surveyed in the US had a relevant vocational qualification, and another 11 percent (predominantly supervisors) had a four-year college degree (see Table 3.6).[6] Some of these qualifications, like vocational certificates from public or private colleges, may indicate a much narrower set of skills than that provided by apprenticeships; others, such as military skill certificates and associate degrees, generally signify a level of training more comparable to the German apprenticeship. Furthermore, over a third of the individuals surveyed had at least two or more different vocational qualifications.

6. We asked that employers distribute the short, written skill survey to all or a random sample of individuals in these occupations. Eight US plants distributed the survey and 220 individuals responded. The individuals responding may have been biased toward the more highly qualified.

Table 3.6 Highest qualifications of US shopfloor employees (percent)

Qualification	High School	Post-secondary vocational training	University	other
%	34	49	11	6

Comparing the skill requirements of frontline workers in the pump industry with other occupations in US manufacturing indicates that they are far more skilled than the average machine operator or assembler, and very similar to other skilled craftsmen or precision production workers. For the US as a whole, 62 percent of individuals engaged in precision production, craft, or repair jobs reported that they needed some formal training to qualify for their jobs in 1991, while only 38 percent of machine operators and assemblers required some form of qualification (US Bureau of Labor Statistics 1992).

The US also had a significantly higher percentage of two- and four-year college graduates working directly in production or in key supervisory or cell leader positions than was found in Germany. In many cases these graduates had received employer support to obtain their qualifications through tuition reimbursement schemes that pay the course costs for individuals studying in their own time. These programs were operating in virtually all of our US sample plants, and approximately five percent of the workforce was enrolled in a course that the company was paying for at the time of the survey in 1996. In contrast, German skilled workers wanting to obtain the *Meister* qualification typically had to finance the course themselves (Prais and Wagner 1988).

One element contributing to the high levels of skills in the US pump industry was the surprisingly low level of employee turnover. The average tenure of production workers in our sample was thirteen years, and no plants – even those operating in very tight local labor markets – reported serious problems retaining skilled workers, although several managers indicated difficulty locating new recruits with suitable metalworking skills when they had a vacancy. These pump plants were often the largest metalworking employer in a local area, and they typically offered wages, benefits, and employment security that were equal or better than those available at the job shops competing for skilled labor. In addition, wages were often informally tied to seniority through the annual performance review process, thus creating an additional incentive for individuals to remain with their employer. The high degree of employment stability meant that many workers had accumulated skills through informal on-the-job training and gradual movement through different jobs in the plant, with 86 percent of workers surveyed indicating that their current employer was the main source of the skills they used on the job.

The Relationship between Product Strategies and Skills

The differences in plants' traditional production strategies – customized, assemble-to-order, or standardized – were strongly related to plant-level differences in the existing skill mix and levels in both country samples. Prior to the recent restructuring initiatives, producers of standardized pumps in both countries employed a largely semi-skilled workforce performing a relatively narrow range of tasks, with degreed engineers and supervisors taking responsibility for control of production and any process improvements. This type of production system is commonly found in the US (see Mason and Finegold 1997), but is not frequently associated with German metalworking firms (e.g., Streeck 1989). Of the six standardized pump producers in the German sample, two outsourced most of their machining (one to a subsidiary in eastern Germany); in three of the other four plants, an average of 25 percent of the workforce was skilled. This was a much higher percentage of craft-trained workers than we found in comparable US plants, but a dramatic difference from the norm associated with the German system of DQP.[7] These standardized plants also illustrated the strong gender divisions in the workplace – women were strongly represented in the more routine, semi-skilled jobs in Germany but were largely absent from the skilled positions in both countries.

At the other end of the skill spectrum, the high degree of product variation and more limited automation in plants building pumps to fit particular customer needs required a highly skilled, more flexible workforce in both the US and Germany. In German assemble-to-order and custom plants over 80 percent of production workers were skilled on average.[8] Since US producers could not readily hire from a pool of apprenticeship-trained workers, they used a variety of mechanisms, including hiring those with other relevant qualifications or experience, formal and informal on-the-job training, and outside courses, to create the necessary skill base; one custom manufacturer estimated that 80 percent of its machine setter/operators were performing at a skilled-level equivalent to a journeyman machinist, and most US plants in this product segment had at least half of their workforce operating at the equivalent of a skilled worker level.

Workplace Restructuring

Adoption of Multi-functional Work Teams

For most US and German pump manufacturers the use of teams on the shopfloor is a relatively recent innovation; the majority

---

7. This figure may understate the supply of general skills in Germany, insofar as some of the production workers in semi-skilled positions in the standardized plants had completed apprenticeships in occupations unrelated to metalworking (e.g., baking, clerical) and were counted as semi- or unskilled.

8. The other German pumpmaker we have classified as standardized, based on relatively large production volumes, produced a more sophisticated, costly pump and had a skill structure more closely resembling the assemble-to-order and custom producers.

of the production workforce in both countries is still not organized in teams. German plants were the first to introduce teams,
beginning in 1982. Most of the early experiments with teams
were conducted by assemble-to-order plants between 1985 and
1990 and were confined to a small part of the production
process. These experiments occurred well before lean production concepts had been popularized in Germany. The adoption
of teams was part of an earlier restructuring movement – the
plant in plant principle – that focused on reducing throughput
time and improving quality by simplifying the plant layout and
giving workers more responsibility for meeting customer needs
(Wildemann 1987, 1989; Kern and Schumann 1984). By 1993
when lean production concepts were beginning to gain widespread attention, 22 percent of German shopfloor workers were
in teams, with standardized manufacturers now leading the way.
In the US, by contrast, only a few plants had introduced teams
by 1993, covering just 11 percent of the workforce on average
(see Tables 3.7 and 3.8).

Table 3.7 Penetration of work teams (percentage of
shopfloor employees covered)

	US		WG	
Product type	1993	1996	1993	1996
Standardized	9	31	28	41
Assemble to order	12	36	23	29
Custom	15	55	18	19
Total	11	37	22	27

In the ensuing three years, however, US plants in all three
product segments undertook aggressive restructuring of the
shopfloor, increasing the percentage of the production workforce in teams by more than 200 percent. During this same
period, most German pumpmakers made very little further
progress in implementing teams, with an average growth of 23
percent in the use of teams across all three segments. As a result,

by 1996 37 percent of US shopfloor employees were working in teams compared to 27 percent in Germany; approximately equal number of plants in the two countries had introduced some work teams by 1996, but the American establishments had generally progressed further with diffusing teams across production and assembly. Only one plant – a German standardized manufacturer – had fully integrated a set of teams across the entire operation (e.g., closely linking production teams with integrated product teams and order processing groups for particular lines of pumps), with a few others in each country moving in the direction of a team-based organization.

Table 3.8   Inception and incidence of teams

Product type	Average year introduced		Percentage of plants with some teams in			
	US	WG	US		WG	
			1993	1996	1993	1996
Standardized	1994	1991	20	83	75	100
Assemble to order	1993	1988	20	66	50	66
Custom	1993	1991	50	80	20	50

In Germany, the lower the percentage of skilled workers, the more likely the organization was to adopt a team-based structure. The inverse correlation between the percentage of skilled production workers and the percentage of shopfloor employees in teams was .46 (P value = .07), a relationship normally considered significant for a small sample size such as ours (N=16 excluding the two plants that outsourced most production). This was true both comparing across and within plants: plants that produced for more standardized markets (and thus, as noted above, with a smaller supply of skilled workers) were more complete adopters of multi-functional work teams. Likewise, within individual German plants, we found that those parts of the production process where skilled workers were most concentrated were slower to diffuse multi-functional teams. It was not, as noted above, that these assemble-to-order and custom producers did not attempt teams, but rather that their early experiments with teams had not been extended across the shopfloor. In perhaps the most notable example, one German assemble-to-order pump-maker had successfully introduced a work team in the receiving and shipping department, the lowest skilled part of the plant. The team was able to boost productivity by 30 percent. The next year when management attempted to replicate this success in the machine shop, however, they encountered unexpected obstacles. The plan was to move from the traditional plant lay-out, where machines were grouped by type of function (e.g., turning, grinding, cutting, etc.) to create component cells. Two years later these cells were still not operating as planned. The main stumbling block has been resistance from the plant's skilled machinists. The technical director explained the source of their opposition as rooted in the way individuals define "skills":

> They view it as a reduction in skill because they focus solely on the technical skills and not the other responsibilities that would come with the move toward cellular production. For them it means producing one range of parts on a few, CNC machines, where in the past they could produce any part on any machine in the plant. What they fail to take into account is the other skills that the team requires – production scheduling, ordering, manag-ing supplier relations, programming and the communication required to make a team work effectively across several shifts. This is the change in mindset we're trying to bring about.

We must be cautious in generalizing too much from these exam-ples, however, since there is still a high degree of variation across plants in the extent of work redesign: more than two-thirds of the companies in the sample had introduced some team work and/or cellular production, but only 6 of the plants had a substantial por-tion (i.e., more than 30 percent) of shopfloor workers in teams.

There appear to be two main explanations for this relation-ship between skills and teams in Germany. First, teams are not appropriate in all contexts. Where task interdependency is low and the specialized competencies required for performing tasks are high, then it may not make sense to invest the time and effort required to establish and run a multi-functional team (Mohrman and Mohrman 1997). This appeared to be the case for many German custom pump manufacturers. In these cases, a strong identity with a certain *Beruf* may help, rather than hinder, the effectiveness individual workers within the production process, as skilled workers have the depth of technical expertise required for complex tasks, while also having sufficient general skills necessary to assume additional duties like quality control or dealing with suppliers. Several of these plants had redesigned the shopfloor into mini business units, giving workers greater responsibility for meeting quality, cost and schedule targets, and where physically possible had created large cells to improve the flow of components. But the specialized expertise required for complex sets of production operations differed substantially between individual orders and often required many years of on-the-job learning even for already skilled workers, and thus was not economical to share among workers in a cross-functional team. Second, as Herrigel and Sabel argue in Chapter 2, German skilled workers were more likely to resist the moves toward cellular manufacturing and multi-functional teams that they viewed as threatening to the specialized set of skills that were an essential part of their identity and their authority within the production environment.

The resistance to Japanese style-work teams has also been apparent in the German auto industry, where skilled workers failed to recognize the new responsibilities associated with teams as a significant enrichment of their job (Jürgens 1997) and opposed efforts to standardize or simplify their technical tasks (Springer 1997). Kuhlmann and Schumann (1997), however, draw a distinction between the teams associated with lean production in Japan and the US, and the debate over group work (*Gruppenarbeit*) in Germany, which began with the sociotechnical movement in the 1970s (Kern and Schumann 1984). In contrast with the US, German workers did not see teams as necessary to enhance employee participation, which had long been statutorily guaranteed through the works council (Hofstede 1980). Instead, the focus was placed on group work, which closely resembles the restructuring that took place in custom pump plants, preserving the autonomy and technical competencies of the frontline workers in a reform that could command the support of both labor and management in the German auto industry.

Just the opposite pattern was apparent in the US with the more highly skilled plants making the most significant moves toward team-based organizations.[9] The more highly skilled workers in most US assemble-to-order and custom plants did not pose the same obstacle to teams as German skilled workers, because of the nature of their skills and the way in which they acquired them; as noted above, most of these US workers did not come through an apprenticeship program, with the craft identity it instills, but had instead completed school or college vocational programs followed by ongoing on-the-job training.[10] They were thus far more likely to value the additional responsibilities that came with team structures and the opportunity to advance into management that the new cell leader positions sometimes offered. In contrast, it was the relative lack of skills or the need for them in some US plants that appeared to be the primary deterrent to the implementation of teams. Some of the most standardized US plants had sufficiently large batch sizes to continue to maintain assembly line production, and hence the

---

9. We are not able to test for this statistically since we do not have sufficiently detailed data on the skill mix of all US plants.

10. In contrast with Japan, where job rotation in lean plants is carefully planned and systematically provided to all shopfloor workers, ojt in the US is far more informal and individually driven, with those workers who showed initiative acquiring the skills gradually by working in different parts of the plant.

worker tasks remained narrow and the opportunities for coop-eration in teams were limited.

Given the recent move toward teams in most pump plants, it is a sign of the relatively high skill level within the pump indus-try that these teams were often given major responsibilities, much greater for example than the skills of teams in automobile assembly plants (MacDuffie and Krafcik 1995). In the US pump sample, almost all plants that had introduced teams put them in charge of their own quality control and cross training team members (see Table 3.9). In addition, 75 percent of US plants with teams had given at least some of these groups responsibility for their own scheduling, maintenance and relations with sup-pliers, while over half had some teams also assuming responsibil-ity for preparing capital budget requests and their own hiring. In Germany, when teams were set up they were given somewhat more authority than their US counterparts, with all plants giving their teams responsibility for quality control and scheduling, and a higher percentage giving teams responsibility for maintenance (88 percent) and proposals for new machinery purchases (70 percent); it was less common, however, for German teams to work with suppliers (40 percent) than their US counterparts. Where German teams were introduced with an already high per-centage of skilled workers, there was less need for and time devoted to cross-training existing employees and rotating them through different production tasks than in the US.

Table 3.9   Responsibilities of teams (percentage of plants with some teams reporting)

Team responsibilities	US	Germany
Scheduling	75	100
Hiring	55	N/A
Quality control	100	100
Supplier relations	75	40
Maintenance	75	88
Proposals for new machinery	55	70

We also observed a significant increase in the responsibilities given to teams across plants as they became more established. The percentage of US teams responsible for their own production scheduling increased sixfold from 1993 to 1996 (7 percent to 43 percent). Similar trends were observable in hiring (12 percent to 37 percent) and relationships with their suppliers (3 percent to 34 percent). The growth in the number of teams that had responsibility for their own maintenance (3 percent to 23 percent) or preparing proposals for new capital equipment (6 percent to 19 percent) was somewhat lower, but still significant.[11]

Only a couple of plants in each country plants had experimented with self-managed work teams, where the traditional supervisor position was removed and the team members either appointed their own leader to assume these responsibilities or shared the roles among themselves. Interestingly, although the German plants on average had fewer teams in 1996, the two most advanced examples of team-based organizations were found in German manufacturers of standardized pumps.[12] Both plants had come under severe pressure to move toward leaner, more team-based organizations and to introduce slightly more complex products because of direct foreign competition in this price-sensitive segment of the pump market. In one, the self-managed work teams consisted of 8-15 workers across three shifts assigned to the same component cell. The teams performed all of the tasks described above, including a continuous improvement process that entailed analyzing the main sources of defects and working closely with suppliers to increase the consistency of materials they were receiving. The teams also prepared proposals for the purchase of new capital equipment,

---

11. We do not have similar figures for Germany.
12. As noted, several of the other German standardized plants responded to these same competitive pressures by outsourcing a high percentage of their production.

which entailed calculations of payback rates and strategic justification based on careful tracking of quality problems or production bottlenecks caused by existing machinery. Although
the plant was only halfway toward the full introduction of a cellular production system, the restructuring had already produced
dramatic results. On-time deliveries improved from 82 to 98
percent, inventory fell by 25 percent, with the main reduction
coming in finished goods and work-in process, and the cost of
quality was halved.

In the other highly innovative German standardized plant,
teams were more like mini-business units in which approximately twenty individuals, including sales, procurement and
engineering experts, were given complete responsibility for a
product line or key component, from the processing of a new
order to delivery of the end product. The focus of the new organization was on providing better service to the customer, either
internal or external, and teams were empowered to go outside
the organization if their internal suppliers were not responsive.
The restructuring resulted in a 300 percent increase in productivity compared to six years earlier.

Increase in Skill Requirements with Restructuring

Plants that were shifting toward a team-based structure generated a clear increase in skill demands and hence a need for further training if the teams were to succeed. In the US, where
further training has always been more important for skill development than in Germany, workplace restructuring led to a major
increase in training in all product segments (see Table 3.10). On
average US production workers received 3.2 days of training
per year in 1996, up from 1.8 days three years earlier, while
training for managers and professionals increased from 2.3 to
4.3 days per year during this time period. And nearly two-thirds
of US shopfloor employees reported receiving some formal
training in the 12 months prior to our visit.

Table 3.10   Annual days of further work-based training (per worker)

Product Type	US		Germany	
	1993	1996	1993	1996
Standardized	2.7	3.2	1.4	1.7
Assemble to order	0.6	3.3	3.4	1.6
Custom	2.8	3.0	2.1	0.5
Average	1.8	3.2	2.3	1.5

Those US plants that had progressed furthest with the adoption of teams had significantly increased their levels of skill investment, in many cases making training a requirement for the entire production workforce, not just a select group of machine setters and tool-makers as in the past. The training effort was often substantial, including both on- and off-the-job training and typically featuring a broadening of technical skills and an emphasis on interpersonal skills needed to make groups function effectively. In addition to other responsibilities, team members were typically required to perform all of the different machine operations in the cell. The team itself often took responsibility for multi-skilling its members through ojt and planned rotations. If a team-based organization is to succeed, according to one US manager, "Four years of training are needed to implement fully teamwork." Typically, however, the company training did not lead to certified skills and thereby helped employers to safeguard their investment in often transferable skills by keeping the capabilities of their workers less transparent to other firms.

Similar training needs were clearly recognized in the German standardized pumpmakers that had shifted from semi-skilled, narrow jobs toward multi-functional work teams. Indeed, a key reason that the employees in these plants were more supportive of the adoption of lean production practices is that it led to a clear increase in the skill requirements of their jobs, and consequently the wages they could earn. One plant that was in the process of introducing a team-based structure had accompanied the change with the introduction of a customized "mini-apprenticeship" including a total of three months of further education spread over a year for the shopfloor workers, most of whom had not been skilled prior to the restructuring. Much of this training took place in the workers' own time (and hence, like US tuition reimbursement programs, is not counted in the figures in Table 3.10 on work-based training). In another plant, there was also a large increase in internal training for the introduction of team work but their skills were still deemed to be insufficient; the workers were very receptive to the changes, but did not have the foundation skills needed to bring about continuous improvement or succeed in a team environment (see Hartmann et al. 1994 for similar findings in the garment industry). As a consequence this plant, like other German standardized producers that were attempting to restructure the work process, not only increased further education but in addition expanded their apprentice intake to build the desired skill base.

Both US and German managers also recognized that it was vital to increase the training for cell leaders if teams were to succeed, often training the prospective team leaders in advance of the work restructuring. The new position of cell leader typically requires a new set of skills, shifting from traditional supervision and control to greater emphasis on coaching and facilitation (Mason 1997). In Germany, supervisors were already well equipped to play this role, having taken courses on pedagogy as part of their *Meister* qualification and had experience in coaching apprentices. In the US, the shift in roles has often been accompanied by a move toward recruitment of two- or four-year college graduates for team-leader positions, rather than the past practice of promoting the best skilled workers into supervisory roles, since the former were thought to possess the necessary leadership/people skills.

The impact of introducing work teams on skill requirements in German plants that already had a higher percentage of skilled workers was more ambiguous. As in semi-skilled plants, the introduction of teams, particularly if self-managed, required that workers master some new competencies: e.g., production scheduling, and in some cases, capital budgeting and supplier relations. In these more custom-oriented plants, the workers were already multi-skilled and had basic communication skills, so that they could take over widened responsibilities regarding quality, delivery times and the philosophy of the 'internal customer' without much further training. At the same time, however, a move toward product or component teams typically reduced the variety and complexity of the traditional machining tasks, hence prompting the resistance from German skilled workers referred to above. With the high existing skill base and lack of change in the work process in German assemble-to-order and custom plants, there was little need for training. Both managers and workers received an average of just over one day per year of formal further training in 1996 and had experienced a real decline in the amount of training on offer in the last three years. Indeed, the majority of German plants offered no regular further training to production workers. Typically, further training was only seen to be required when new machinery was purchased, when the vendor would be expected to train a small group of *Meisters* and skilled workers.

The lower and declining levels of further training in the higher end German plants appeared to be related to three factors. First, many of the technical and interpersonal competencies required for teams are already included in the training that apprentices and *Meisters* receive; second, the downsizing of the workforce was associated with a general cutback in investments in worker skills; and third, the earlier timing of some of the major moves to team-based organization meant that much of the training had already been completed. As seen in Table 3.7, there was virtually no change in the work organization between 1993 and 1996 in the customized plants, and hence little need for further training the already skilled workforce. A couple of plants had undertaken large restructuring efforts prior to this period. One plant in particular had negotiated a systematic further training program with the union as part of an agreement to temporarily raise work hours from 35 to 40 hours/week; 1.5 of these extra hours were set aside for further training, meaning an additional 60-80 hours of training per worker each year. When this restructuring was completed, the extra hours agreement ended along with the investment in further training.

Conclusions

Well before the phrase "lean production" was coined, German manufacturers, including some pumpmakers, were experimenting with many of the "new production concepts" now associated with the Toyota production system (Kern and Schumann 1984, Wildemann 1987). Despite the early German lead, American plants, on average, had made significantly greater progress than their German counterparts in the adoption of lean practices by 1996. This included both greater reorganization of the work process into cells and work teams and more investment in further training needed to make the new organization work.

These broad findings, however, mask a striking range of diversity in the extent of work reorganization across plants, which lends some support to Herrigel and Sabel's thesis, but which also reveals that extensive changes are underway. At the time of our visits in 1995-96, the majority of plants in both of our country samples were still in a state of major organizational change; over half of the plants had implemented some form of multi-functional work teams. Two German standardized producers had responded to severe competitive pressures by going further than any plants in our sample toward implementation of fully team-based organizations. At the same time, several plants in each country sample had attempted little or no redesign of the work process. The typical plant fell somewhere in between.

It had begun restructuring 3-5 years ago and thus far had reorganized some of the machine tools into cells for certain key components and had some of the workforce in teams, but was still trying to convert the rest of the production process. The highly uneven diffusion of lean production practices that was apparent in the auto industry both in Japan and worldwide (MacDuffie and Pils 1996) has if anything been magnified in the pump industry, which is divided into dozens of highly specialized market niches, each with only a few main competitors.

In seeking to explain the source of this variation, it is clear that the technical requirements of production interact with the differences in national institutions to shape pumpmakers' strategies and skill levels. Prior to restructuring, the work organization and skill profile of German standardized pump manufacturers resembled that of US standardized pumpmakers far more than it resembled that of German assemble-to-order or customized pump manufacturers. These low-end German manufacturers typically had a relatively low skilled, often predominantly female workforce that mostly had not been through metalworking apprenticeships and performed relatively narrow repetitive tasks. And the adoption of a more team-based production system by standardized manufacturers was associated in both countries with substantial increases in skill demands and more firm-based training. In the customized end of the pump industry, US plants have had to create a highly skilled workforce functionally equivalent to the German apprentices so that they are capable of dealing with the high level of variability and technical proficiency required in the work process.

Differences in product markets have also had a clear impact on the pressure for restructuring. Producers of standardized pumps were subject to the most challenge from lower cost foreign competitors, and hence felt the greatest need to restructure; in Germany, standardized producers either outsourced an increasing percentage of production or had undertaken radical redesign of the work process to become more cost competitive.

At the other end of the product spectrum, customized producers faced relatively few new challengers in either country. Perhaps the pumpmakers under greatest threat in the immediate future are the traditional assemble-to-order manufacturers, which have the most to gain potentially from lean production, but thus far have been relatively slow to restructure.

National institutional differences have led to some significant differences in the organizational and human resource strategies of German and US pumpmakers and their use and types of teams. The dual system provided German plants with a substantial advantage over their US counterparts in obtaining new skills through the supply of production workers with intermediate (craft and technical skill) qualifications. This gap, however, was much smaller than indicated by national-level comparisons of skill levels. While skill development in Germany continues to be heavily concentrated on initial training for young people, US manufacturers rely on a more diverse array of sources to obtain already skilled workers (e.g., community/technical colleges, the military, other employers) and invest more heavily in the ongoing development of their workforce.

The importance of national institutions for explaining workplace restructuring was highlighted by the comparison of moves toward team-based organizations in the US and Germany. In the US, having a more highly skilled workforce facilitated the adoption of multi-functional work teams, by ensuring that the capabilities existed on the shopfloor to make a team-based organization effective. Since only a small percentage of the US functionally skilled workers had come through craft apprenticeships, the reorganization of the work process into teams appeared to be received by most workers as a chance for broader responsibility and greater autonomy. In contrast, confirming the thesis of Herrigel and Sabel, most German assemble-to-order and customized plants had made relatively little use of multi-functional teams, at least in part because the personal identity of German skilled workers appeared to conflict with the blurring of individual roles and narrowing of some technical skill requirements that can accompany the move toward a team-based organization.

While some aspects of Germany's training system may impede the use of Japanese-style multi-functional teams, our study revealed a few examples of highly innovative German firms that could potentially serve as the forerunners for the development of a new, distinctive German form of lean organization. These plants have adopted an alternative plant-within-a-plant concept that achieves many of the advantages of lean production, along with the additional benefit of a much flatter hierarchy, while preserving individual worker skills and autonomy. In creating these new organizations, German firms have built on some of the strengths of the existing skill system. The reformed, modern metalworking apprenticeship provides individuals with strong theoretical and applied training that is highly valuable when a broader set of work tasks and traditional supervisory responsibilities are shared among members of self-managing teams. To obtain the full benefits from these skilled workers, however, managers need to stress the broadened responsibilities that individuals are being given and create reward systems that value these new, non-technical skills.

Likewise, while the adoption of flatter hierarchies reduces the need for traditional supervisors, the existence of a large supply of individuals with the *Meister* qualification in Germany can help firms' restructuring efforts. During the transition to a more team-based structure, *Meisters* have been trained in the right set of skills – both pedagogical and technical – needed to coach frontline workers to become effective team leaders. And as this transition continues, they are assuming new responsibilities in flatter organizations, such as fostering continuous improvement, overseeing process standards and production planning, and contributing to new product development.

If German companies are to complete the process of adopting new production concepts to their own organizational context – and most of our sample was still in the early phases of this transition – then a number of issues regarding the skill system will need to be resolved. One issue that the German dual system faces is the relatively slow pace of change in the formal skill standards and accompanying curriculum for apprenticeship. The large firm-based training component is able to adapt flexibly to the new needs of the work environment, but this can create a growing gap between the workplace and what individuals are learning in their days at school. The school-based education – both the formal curriculum and the way it is delivered – will have to be adapted to the technological and organizational requirements of lean enterprises. This could entail standards that include a greater focus on areas that are already part of the curriculum (e.g., continuous improvement techniques, broader business understanding), somewhat reduced time devoted to hands-on technical areas that are becoming less important with the spread of CNC, and a shift from lectures to more group instruction and action-learning that would help reinforce the skills needed to operate in a learning organization. Efforts have been underway since the mid-1990s to update the curriculum more quickly, and the process for changing courses is itself being streamlined to facilitate more frequent updates in the future (Schmidt 1996).

While the above changes represent relatively marginal improvements on the existing system, a potentially greater threat is whether the employers will continue to supply the places required to sustain the system. The upgrading and broadening of the apprenticeship program has made it more expensive and difficult for small firms to participate in the system, leading some small and medium-sized employers to form partnerships to share the costs and different expertise required to deliver apprenticeships. Greater attention will need to be paid to controlling the costs of apprenticeships, in particular trainees' allowances, to maintain the incentive for firms to participate (see Wagner, Chapter 1). The biggest danger to the sustainability of apprenticeship, however, may lie in current and future company investment strategies; with low employee turnover and many companies concentrating future growth in production facilities outside Germany because of concerns about cost competitiveness, there was limited demand for new skilled workers and hence less incentive for them to continue to train apprentices.

To retain its strong manufacturing base, and the apprenticeship system that supports it, Germany needs to develop its own set of production concepts that builds on the country's existing strengths. This entails creating an organizational and reward structure that enables firms to fully utilize the potential of their highly skilled workers and newly-deployed *Meisters* by pushing greater responsibility to teams of frontline workers and aggressively restructuring the rest of the enterprise to match the functional flexibility on the shopfloor (Womack and Jones 1996).

Part II

DISTRIBUTIVE OUTCOMES
OF THE
GERMAN TRAINING SYSTEM

Chapter 4

VOCATIONAL TRAINING AND JOB MOBILITY IN COMPARATIVE PERSPECTIVE*

Thomas Hinz

Introduction

An oft-neglected aspect of the German vocational training system is its close linkage to the system of general schooling: the combination of stratified general schooling and standardized vocational training fits within German labor market structures and the broader institutional context, e.g., social policy and law. The main thesis of this chapter is that general education and

* I would like to thank David Finegold, Pepper Culpepper, Jutta Gatter, Kathleen Thelen, and Jim Witte for their valuable comments on a previous version. Additional thanks to Jutta Allmendinger – her conceptual work is a central element in this research. Important ideas are based on our cooperation (Allmendinger and Hinz 1997). Nathan Lillie helped me to gather statistical material and was a helpful informal discussant. Jeremiah Riemer and Mary Louise Culpepper supported a thorough editing.

vocational training, and their institutional environments, create job mobility patterns that can be identified by analyzing the stratification of the educational system and the standardization of the system of certification for vocational training. The starting point of the argument is the proposition that general education and vocational training determine how jobs and individuals are matched at the time of labor market entry. Additionally, education and training have a long-term impact on individual careers. General education and job training structure life courses by preselecting young men and women for different paths of job mobility (for a review, see Kerckhoff 1995).

What does it mean to speak of stratification and standardization? In Germany, schooling is standardized: the structures, institutions, curricula, and leaving certificates are roughly comparable in all the states *(Länder)*. More importantly for occupational careers, German general education is highly stratified: the great majority of German pupils attend schools in a tracked system. Pupils are selected at about age ten for either four, six, or nine years of additional schooling. This decision is seldom subject to review, and later transfers to higher levels are difficult to effect. The stratified general educational system in Germany (where in 1995, only about one in four students in any given birth cohort attained the highest school credentials) is matched by the "dual system" – that is, a standardized vocational training system. Within this system, there are well-defined occupations with curricula that structure training partly in the workplace and partly in school. Although the firms that train have some freedom in organizing the work-based part of the training program, all the apprentices in each occupation have to pass the same final examination. Certificates of further occupational qualification *(Meister)* can only be achieved if one has already successfully completed an apprenticeship.

Looking at other countries, one can find sharp contrasts to the German arrangement of stratified schooling and standardized vocational training. In the US, for example, general education is unstratified, in that about 85 percent of a cohort receives a high school diploma. However, it is often necessary to meet additional selection criteria if one wants to attend the more prestigious institutions of higher education. For selection processes at colleges and labor market entry, it also matters that the US system of schooling is unstandardized. The variation of high school funding and quality is extremely broad – from a very high standard of education in some public and private high schools to a low level in some badly equipped public schools. Vocational training is also unstandardized; there are thousands of local programs of vocational training, mostly within the high schools or in community colleges, and the vocational high school tracks often work more as a negative selection of students than as a real training experience. Although some states have tried to establish vocational routes which involve the participation of employers, these programs still have an experimental character (see Parker and Rogers, Chapter 8): they are under permanent evaluation and revision and are far from being institutionalized.

This brief comparison of general education and vocational training has implications for several labor market outcomes. The system of general schooling and vocational training can be classified along the axes of *stratification* and *standardization*, and this typology has meaning for two aspects of job mobility: the stability of occupational careers and the "boundedness" of class positions (Allmendinger 1989b, Allmendinger and Hinz 1997).[1] A further important issue in understanding career patterns is how stratification and standardization of schooling and vocational training are related to a broader institutional context. The structure of general education and vocational training depends on processes of institutionalization with deep

---

1. "Boundedness" refers throughout this chapter to the extent to which individuals move from one class to another. High boundedness implies low mobility between classes, and low boundedness implies high interclass mobility.

historical roots: institutions are built over time by corporate actors like unions, employers' associations, and governments. The German training system is characterized by a high degree of coordination and consensus; its labor market structures and the coordination of economic processes are parts of a complex interrelated institutional system which has been characterized as an "occupational labor market" (Marsden 1990) and a "flexibly coordinated economy" (Soskice 1990a). The German dual system contributes to this occupational labor market (compared to an internal labor market) by enabling career mobility based on occupation, rather than just through a given firm's hierarchy. The deep institutional embeddedness of vocational training may restrict a successful implementation of the German system in other countries, even if there is a high level of public support for transplanting aspects of the German vocational training system.

This chapter is divided into four parts: first I discuss the analytic dimensions of stratification and standardization with respect to important training issues. Vocational training is a process of investment in human capital, so I try to understand how the investment decision is shaped by levels of stratification and standardization. Both dimensions also influence the school-to-work transition. The central aim of the chapter is to look at mobility outcomes of the German schooling and training system in a comparative perspective, so in the second section I therefore present empirical life course data from Germany, Britain and Sweden, focusing on two measures of career mobility: job shifts and class shifts. These measures are indicators of the stability and boundedness of occupational careers. The third section discusses shortcomings of the empirical analysis and connects education and vocational training to other institutions of the economy. The final section briefly discusses pressures on the German system, and whether or not the characteristics of a standardized and stratified education and training system may change as a result of these pressures.

Stratification of General Education
and Standardization of Vocational Training

Looking at standardization and stratification gives us an instrument to analyze the broad empirical variation among schooling and training systems. One can find different degrees of selectivity in general education, and one can distinguish school-based, work-based, and hybrid forms of vocational training. Based on the research of Allmendinger (1989b), I will use the axes of standardization and stratification and relate them to theoretical issues of vocational training (see also Allmendinger and Hinz 1997).

Standardization is defined as the degree to which the qualities of education and training meet the same standards nationwide. The standardization of general education means that schooling does not differ within one country: curricula are well-defined and exams are the same for all students, and passing a standardized exam automatically provides access to further education. The standardization of vocational training refers to the expectations of employers and trainees, who can rely on the information given to them by (standardized) certificates. *Stratification* is expressed by the proportion of an age cohort that attains the maximum number of school years provided by the educational system and by the degree of differentiation within given educational levels (i.e., tracking). Stratification affects the match between education and social structure. In stratified educational systems, the educational system is tightly coupled with a differentiated occupational structure, in which access to certain jobs depends on the attainment of a given degree; in unstratified systems, the coupling between the educational system and the occupational structure is loose.

The dimensions of standardization and stratification raise two theoretical issues for vocational training: first, how is the individual decision to invest in his or her human capital development influenced by the different extent of standardization and stratification? This is a very important question in light of strategic problems generated by the transferability of general human capital. Second, how is the transition out of education and into the labor market shaped by the structure of the educational and vocational training system?

Problem of Investment

Human capital theory defines skills as individual assets. A person's productivity depends on the amount of training and the degree of its specificity. According to the theory, there are two forms of human capital: general human capital is a matter of schooling, and specific human capital is accrued through on-the-job training. Individuals make their investment decisions according to a rational calculation, in which costs, opportunity costs, expected returns, and different talents are crucial factors. Regarding general education, investment decisions are generally made by parents, not by children themselves. The more parents have to invest directly in the education of their children, the more likely it is that the educational system will reproduce a social structure that distributes resources according to the inequality characterizing the parents' generation. A comparison of different schooling systems has shown that intergenerational inequality in educational degrees is present even in a formally unstratified educational environment such as in the US (Shavit and Blossfeld 1993). "Unstratified" therefore does not mean "equal."

In vocational training the transferability of skills creates problems of strategic behavior. A trainee acquires skills that can be used by different employers, while a single employer pays all the costs of training. Transferability of skills is generally high in a standardized training system.[2] There are two ways to handle the problem of transferability: first, training in transferable skills

---

2. An unstandardized vocational training system would avoid this sort of strategic situation.

can be organized in (publicly financed) schools or colleges, thus removing it from the work place. In this case employers (and others) pay for vocational training by taxes. Second, employers who train in transferable skills can be compensated by paying their trainees wages below their marginal utility. Trainees pay for a share of the training costs by accepting a lower wage. It is important to note that a close linkage of vocational training to general education could make decision processes easier. Stratified general education helps to select applicants for training slots by school grades. Those who apply for apprenticeships are sorted between the ages of ten and fifteen and have certain expectations of their future careers. For them, access to higher education is more or less blocked and their best choice is to pursue transferable vocational training.

A problem of opportunism exists if one looks at the employers' side. Why should an employer provide transferable training if he or she can profit from the investments other employers make? This strategic situation is referred to as poaching. In the case of the German vocational training system, standardized apprenticeships usually take two to three and a half years, much longer than is usual for initial on-the-job training in the US. During these years, both employers and trainees invest considerable time and money in training the apprentice in specific occupational areas. Evidence shows that about 80 percent of German firms with more than 500 employees offer training for apprentices and pay average net costs of about $10,500 per year.[3] How can the process of investment in transferable skills be stabilized? How does cooperative action emerge between employers and employees, as well as among the employers themselves? An answer motivated by analyses of trust relations would argue that institutions have to reinforce long-term perspectives. In the employer-employee relationship, a clear and mutually understood career system in the internal labor market together with the transfer-

---

3. For calculation see Harhoff and Kane (1996).

ability of skills gives rise to a long-term perspective. It is important that former apprentices have the chance to enter the internal labor market for skilled workers with prospects of further upward mobility. As long as employers offer such long-term career paths within the firms, apprentices have incentives to stay.

The transferability of skills functions as an assurance against low internal career prospects. As Fukuyama (1996) remarks, such a design works only with a high degree of consensus between management and workers and, in turn, enhances labor management relations even more, leading to a high degree of reciprocity and generalized trust. In standardized systems of apprenticeship, considerable autonomy and responsibility are given to trainees and future workers, who share a high degree of pride in their work and a sense of professionalism and identification with their social class, management, and industry. The employers use the apprenticeship system as a thorough screening system for long-term employment relations, obtaining a variety of other benefits from participating in apprenticeships that offset training costs (see Wagner, Chapter 1). The young men and women who have completed an apprenticeship do not have to pay high search costs since they know enough about their current employers to decide whether or not the job is attractive. Finally, standardization of vocational training gives employees an option to change employers, while firms can rely on (nationally recognizable) certified skills when hiring graduates of the "dual system."

Comparing the US and Germany, one has to note that the institutional environments dealing with the problem of investment differ in terms of their time-related character. The German system has a deeper commitment to a long-term relationship; it is more "trust"-based. Institutions built to reduce the strategic problems of transferability and poaching are interdependent to a high degree. Hence, a rather costly standardized vocational training system has an important side-effect: it goes hand-in-hand with a longer time horizon.

Problem of Transition

A problem closely related to the time structure of educational institutions is the transition of young people from education into employment. The educational system structures this first step into the labor market. A work-based vocational training system facilitates a transition into a job for several reasons: (1) contacts with employers function as network resources; (2) work-based training creates more realistic expectations about the workplace and reduces the probability of a mismatch; (3) in a pedagogical sense, work-based training gives young people a sense of the general virtues (e.g., discipline) that help in finding employment. The US discussion about reforms of the youth training system concentrates on these aspects of the school-to-work transition.

The degree of standardization of the system clearly influences this transition, since employers will hire applicants with adequate occupational training. From the employee's view, beginning an apprenticeship means a stronger pre-selection for potential jobs. As argued above, the search costs when the apprenticeship is completed are lower, and employers have lower screening costs as well (see Wagner, Chapter 1). Comparing the US and Germany, Büchtemann et al. (1994) demonstrate that the transitional unemployment of young people who are entering the labor market is considerably shorter in Germany than in the US. One year after leaving school the unemployment rate for young people in the US is about 10 percent, while it is only 4 percent in Germany. By its in-firm nature, the German vocational training system creates labor market access for apprentices. As expected, about 80 percent of those who have completed an apprenticeship find a job in the occupational field in which they were trained shortly after completion of their initial training. Twelve years after leaving school, about 60 percent of the apprentices work in the same occupational field; the recognition of the qualification in the external labor market is shown by the fact that two-thirds of those with completed apprenticeships change their employer within eight years after initially entering the labor market (Büchtemann et al. 1994).

Evidently, these data fit the "occupational labor market" model. In the US, by contrast, 70 percent of a school-leaving cohort work at jobs without formal skill requirements five years after they have left school. Empirical studies of school-based vocational training show that the risk of youth unemployment also decreases when young women and men take part in vocational courses at high schools (Arum and Shavit 1995). However, most vocational training is done on the job and often in a very short training period. At the beginning of their careers, young employees in the US frequently change jobs. Employers' searches for employees rely on different kinds of information in the two countries: in Germany, certificates serve as credentials, while in the US, employers have far less standardized information, relying instead on job histories and the ability to screen new hires before offering them full-time positions. From the view of employees, work-based vocational training creates better network resources before entering the labor market. In sum, the German vocational training works as a better "integrator" into the labor market. The firm-based system of Germany has a higher "social" value because apprentices learn general and practical skills in real work settings, which is to say, they get "socialized" to the workplace (Witte and Kalleberg 1995: 312). This advantage of the German system only covers more established occupational fields. The more market based system of the US, however, fosters integration into "new" (high-tech) jobs (see Finegold's conclusion in this volume).

The Stability and Boundedness of Occupational Careers

The previous section showed that the manner and quality of labor market entry are influenced by educational qualifications.

Sociological theory often refers to education as a "sorting machine," one that is a key factor in explaining social stratification. A stratified general education system is generally coupled with hierarchical points of labor market entry, such that formal education becomes a prerequisite for entering certain career paths; this is true across economic sectors within a country with stratified schooling. In Germany, for example, careers in the public and in the private sector depend on the level of general education. Unstratified educational systems lead to a higher degree of societal "openness": selection for different school tracks does not take place as early as in more stratified systems, and the only negative differentiation occurs in dropping out. The American combination of an unstratified and unstandardized educational system reflects the history of the US, where parents and local communities have greater influence on the schools.

In an "occupational labor market," employees are bound to their occupations: standardization channels mobility. The German system of standardized vocational training creates strong incentives for employees to remain within occupations, since changing tracks means that acquired skills, which are transferable within an occupational field, are lost. Büchtemann et al. (1994) report a difference in patterns of relative earnings in Germany and the US over a twelve-year period after leaving school. The relative difference in earnings between groups of employees with different general human capital remains stable in Germany, while in the US, there is a reduction in the relative distance between groups in the first twelve years after leaving school. In other words, how individuals perform in school appears to have a more lasting effect on labor market outcomes in Germany than the US. However, further analysis shows that a perfect fit of skill requirements and learned skills does not seem a relevant factor in explaining differences in earnings (Witte and Kalleberg 1995). The difference in job tenure is significant, as German employees stay with a single employer longer than US employees (Harhoff and Kane 1996). At the age of twenty-five, about one-quarter of Germans with apprenticeship certificates have a job tenure lower than three years. In the US this proportion is significantly higher (about 55 percent).[4] The difference in job tenure remains over the life time. Higher job stability in Germany, which is additionally influenced by other institutional factors – i.e., laws which increase the costs for dismissals and make hiring more expensive, as well as a smaller difference in wages between and within industries – is an indicator of "job security" (Abraham and Houseman 1992). Recent studies confirm the picture of stable careers for Germany in the late 1980s, while stressing the lower variance in earnings compared to the US (DiPrete and McManus 1996). Standardized vocational training could be described as one important individual port of entry to a system of "job security" which seems to be far removed from a "risk society" (Beck 1986) in a comparative perspective. Admittedly, this is true only for the insiders of the German system, as it excludes a (slightly growing) group of outsiders who did not receive school-finishing certificates or did not complete vocational training. For these young women and men "job security" is a fiction.

The next section will analyze whether the stratification/ standardization schema is confirmed by empirical data. As argued above, a nation's educational environment is defined by its educational and vocational training systems. Career mobility is conventionally indexed by the number of jobs held over the life course and the extent of movement within and between hierarchical levels. Due to the limited availability of life course data, the following empirical analysis has an illustrative character only and will be restricted to a comparison of three nations: Britain, Germany, and Sweden.[5] As we will see, the three countries con-

---

4. For calculation see Harhoff and Kane (1996).
5. Because of sparse comparable data on occupational careers, country selection was severely restricted. Even more consequentially, internationally comparative data on occupational trajectories of women were not available. The data considered in this article are part of the "Euro-

stitute a practical range for studying the interplay between general education and vocational training.

The dimensions of stratification and standardization should be applied separately to education and vocational training. Comparing their relative importance for intra-generational mobility outcomes shows that stratification is primarily relevant for general education, while standardization is more relevant for vocational training (as depicted in Figure 4.1 below). In stratified educational systems, people exit with school-leaving certificates that differ according to the time spent in general education and how well they have performed on different final examinations. Each level of general education is then matched by specific types of vocational training. People with high educational certificates may enter vocational training that is "lower status," but people in the lower ranks of general education can rarely enter high-status vocational tracks without taking a detour back to general schooling to get the "right" certificate, a path that is long and burdensome. Hence the stratification of general education preserves class lines and makes upward class mobility over the life course unlikely.[6]

---

careers" project, directed by Karl Ulrich Mayer. Together with Jutta All-mendinger, who was the co-author of a previous article (Allmendinger and Hinz 1997), I was able to use mobility tables from the following data sets: the German Life Course Study (observation period: 1981-83; cohorts born 1929-31, 1939-41, and 1949-51) of Karl Ulrich Mayer; ESRC SCELI (1986; cohorts born 1926-34, 1935-44, 1945-54, and 1955-61) of Colin Mills; and the Swedish Level of Living Survey (1991, cohorts born 1925-34, 1935-44, 1945-54, and 1955-65) of Michael Tahlin. Available data lead to restrictions of the direct comparability among the data sets, due to the different times of observation and the different age groups. Moreover, the distinction between voluntary and involuntary job shifts is impossible to glean from the data.

6. This chapter focuses on intra-generational mobility in terms of job and class shifts. I do not analyze the role of general education reproducing intergenerational inequality. Recent studies show that almost all the systems of general education pertain to intergenerational inequality (see the volume by Shavit and Blossfeld 1993).

Figure 4.1 Stratification and standardization of educational and vocational training

Educational training ("Boundedness")	Vocational training ("Stability")	
	Standardized *- stable -*	**Unstandardized** *- unstable -*
Stratified *- bounded -*	Germany	Britain
Unstratified *- not bounded -*		Sweden

Source: Allmendinger and Hinz (1997).

The transition from school to work is sequenced and "orderly": the educational system and the labor market have complementary hierarchical structures, and standardized vocational training does not confine workers to a single employer. There are also limitations known from research on occupational labor markets: in the long run, trainees are bound to one occupational field and have restricted access to further training at advanced levels. The stratified educational system requires that higher education – needed for eligibility for higher vocational training – usually can be acquired only by passing through advanced levels of general education. Although stratified general education in itself would allow for downward class mobility, combining it with standardized training – which shields against downward mobility – leads us to expect stability over the work life, with hardly any changes in class positions or occupations.

This combination of standardization and stratification characterizes the German system. Standardized vocational training should lead to a smooth transition between the educational and occupational sectors, as well as to "orderly" occupational trajectories with few occupational changes.[7] Within given occupa-

---

7. It has often been claimed that standardized, occupation-specific training considerably restricts workers' flexibility to change occupations. At the

tional areas, however, broad and marketable skills facilitate job changes. These job changes may involve moderate upward (but usually not downward) mobility, mostly linked to seniority.

The system of general education in Britain hardly differs from the German one. It is stratified and, in 1995, only every fifth student of a given age cohort attained the highest school credentials. Vocational training, however, differs sharply between the two countries: in Britain, vocational training, outside of the much smaller apprenticeship system (see Chapter 9) is of relatively short duration and is primarily in the hands of companies (Soskice 1990a, 1994; Hutton 1995). It thus qualifies as relatively unstandardized. Once acquired, vocational training serves for a single job but not for a lifetime; the time horizon is shorter. New employers are likely to ask for more and different training, again offered within the (new) firm. In the British case, we would expect many job changes (because of the unstandardized training system), little upward class mobility (due to the stratified school system), and considerable downward class mobility (again, resulting from unstandardized training). In sum, the British system suggests unstable and upwardly bounded occupational life courses.

In Sweden, the situation is different again. More than two-thirds of each birth cohort attain the highest educational level, meaning that general education is relatively unstratified. Vocational training is unstandardized, leading to unbounded and unstable career trajectories. Because Swedish vocational training does not involve a "dual system," as in Germany, the dominance of the occupational labor market model is less pronounced, and frequent job changes are to be expected. In addition, because of the unstratified school system, class position should be less fixed.

---

same time, such training increases the flexibility of the ways in which workers operate on the shop-floor. The former is seen as a severe disadvantage, the latter as a distinct advantage vis-à-vis global competition, because it enhances group work and creative group innovations (Fukuyama 1996).

Figure 4.1 displays these expectations graphically. Note that in Figures 4.1, 4.2a, and 4.2b, one cell is empty: there is no state with an unstratified educational system and standardized vocational training, for reasons having to do with cost. If a state invests in broad and extended educational systems, fiscal limitations are likely to deter it from providing a lengthy phase of publicly sponsored (standardized) vocational training.[8]

For empirical analysis I will focus on two different indicators: the average yearly rate of job shifts[9] and the average yearly rate of changes in class positions.[10] The rate of job changes stands for "stability;" the rate of class changes serves as a measure for the "boundedness" of work trajectories. Do nations differ according to the rate of job changes and changes in class positions? Figures 4.2a and 4.2b, using the same format as Figure 4.1, provide some preliminary answers: Figure 4.2a presents the data for all cohorts covered by the three national studies, while Figure 4.2b pertains only to 50-year-old men.[11] In both cases, I report the rate of job changes followed by the rate of class shifts.

8. Current discussions on reforms of education and training ironically concentrate on this empty cell. An optimal educational and training system should provide broad basic skills and a solid – not too specialized – vocational training. The question how to organize (and to finance) this best solution is still unsolved.

9. I report the rate of job and class changes because absolute numbers are misleading as a result of international differences in the time of labor market participation (as discussed above).

10. A job episode is defined as an employment spell without a change in occupation, occupational level, and employer. Class positions were classified on the scheme developed by Erikson and Goldthorpe and available only in a very condensed form: I+II: higher and lower divisions of the service class; III: low service class; IVab: self-employed outside agriculture; IVc: self-employed in agriculture; V+VI: skilled workers; VII+IVd: unskilled workers. Because of its very low absolute numbers, class IVc was not considered in the analyses.

11. The decision to report numbers based on all cohorts was necessitated by the fact that the Swedish researchers did not provide the rate of class changes by cohort. This problem becomes even more evident in Table 4.1.

Figures 4.2a and **4.2b**   Rate of job changes and changes in class position

Figure 4.2a   All cohorts

Rate of class changes ("Boundedness")	Rate of Job Changes ("Stability")	
	Low	High
Low	Germany (. 13/. 07)	Britain (. 25/. 11)
High		Sweden (. 23/14)

Figure 4.2b   50-year-old men

Rate of class changes ("Boundedness")	Rate of Job Changes ("Stability")	
	Low	High
Low	Germany (. 09/. 04)	Britain (. 17/. 07)
High		Sweden (. 16/not provided)

Note: Numbers indicate, respectively, the average number of job changes or class changes that an individual experiences per year. Thus, the numbers for Germany in Figure 4.2a mean that on average an individual male with an employment duration of 10 years has 1.3 job shifts and has 0.7 class shifts.

Source: Allmendinger and Hinz (1997).

Data: Eurocareers, Mayer.

When we look at all cohorts, the rate of job changes over the life course conforms to our expectations of the labor market consequences of unstandardized (Britain, Sweden) and standardized (Germany) vocational training systems. Britain (a rate of .25) and Sweden (.23) do not differ much, but the rate of job shifts is considerably lower in Germany (.13). Although markedly lower than the rate of job shifts, the rate of change in class positions over the life course also varies internationally:

Sweden has the highest (.14) and Germany the lowest (.07) rate of class changes, and in Britain we find a rate of .11. Again, results fit the expectations based on consequences of unstratified (Sweden) and stratified (Germany, Britain) general education. Differences between Germany and Britain are explained by British unstandardized vocational training, which does not protect against downward class shifts. Results for the cohort of 50-year-old men are similar: in comparison with Germany (.09), the rate of job shifts is higher in Britain (.17) and Sweden (.16). Because of missing data on Sweden, the findings pertaining to changes in class positions are limited. The British-German comparison shows marked differences, with British men having a rate of .07 class shifts over the occupational life course while German men have a rate of .04. Again, this result is explained by differential rates of downward mobility.

These findings can be supplemented by an analysis of mobility tables, which depict the proportion of men remaining in their initial class position over the life course; again, Table 4.1a pertains to all cohorts, and Table 4.1b only to the cohort of 50-year-old men. We limit our analysis to three class positions: the higher service class, skilled workers, and unskilled workers.[12] When we look at data pertaining to all cohorts, Germany consistently has the highest proportion of immobile workers – 92 percent of those starting in the higher service class also end in this class position. The figures pertaining to Britain (82 percent immobile) again can be attributed to a higher downward mobility in this country: close to six percent of those initially employed in classes I and II (higher service classes) move to the position of unskilled workers. In Germany and Sweden, we find less than one percent downward moves.[13] The ranking of immobile

12. In all three countries, most men are working in these three class positions; for more details see Allmendinger and Hinz (1997).
13. In addition, in Britain skilled workers suffer the highest risk of moving to the position of unskilled workers (22 percent), while this percentage amounts to 10 percent in Germany and 15 percent in Sweden.

unskilled workers also stays well within our predictions: it is considerably higher in Germany (48 percent immobile) and Britain (43 percent immobile) than in Sweden (28 percent immobile). More than in any other class, the long-term effects of stratified general education, in which additional general education is a prerequisite for getting access to higher levels of vocational training, become visible. Results pertaining to the cohort of 50-year-old men are limited to Germany and Britain and basically support the conclusions given above.

Tables 4.1a and 4.1b   Men remaining in the initial class position (by occupational class)

Table 4.1a   All cohorts

Class position	Britain	Germany	Sweden
Higher service class	82%	92%	84%
Skilled workers	40%	59%	46%
Unskilled workers	43%	48%	28%

Table 4.1b   50-year-old men

Class position	Britain	Germany
Higher service class	74%	90%
Skilled workers	32%	56%
Unskilled workers	51%	46%

Note: Data for Sweden were not provided by cohorts.

Source: Allmendinger and Hinz (1997).

Data: Eurocareers, Mayer.

The mobility patterns analyzed so far have been derived from an abstract model of stratification and standardization of education and training. To get a more complete picture of the marked differences in job and class mobility, it is useful to place these findings in the context of the wage differentials that separate different groups in a society. We now ask, regardless of the opportunity structure, what does the incentive structure look like? How much doe job and class mobility pay? To give an idea of an answer, I will briefly describe the wage level of skilled workers and the wage compression between different groups of workers in the three countries analyzed in this chapter. Firstly, it is important to get an impression of differences in absolute wages. With official statistical data (Statistisches Bundesamt 1996) we can compare wage levels for workers in manufacturing. Calculations are based on gross wages for the year 1992 and take into account differences in purchasing power. The average hourly wage for a skilled worker in manufacturing is highest in Germany (DM 22.87). In Sweden, a worker in manufacturing gets DM 20.83, while the wage level in Britain is significantly lower (DM 16.39). The pattern of stable careers in Germany is accompanied by a high absolute wage level for (mostly) skilled workers. As previously mentioned, the range of wages in Germany is restricted, as a result of labor market institutions (DiPrete and McManus 1996).

Next, we will look at relative wages for three class positions: higher service class workers, skilled workers, and unskilled workers, in order to see how job mobility pays in relative terms. There is one important restriction for the following comparison which is done with the ISSP 1992 data set (International Social Survey Program, see Table 4.2). Unfortunately, different categories of earnings were represented: in Germany, we have data on net income (after taxes and social insurance), but for Sweden and Britain only gross earnings were reported (before taxes). Wage positions were calculated only for males (not older than 60 years).[14]

The wage differential between skilled workers and higher service class workers is similar in all three countries; the relative wage position of higher service class workers is about 60 percent percent higher than in the class of skilled workers. Note that in

14.   One may compare relative differences only *within* the three countries.

Table 4.2   Relative income chances and class positions

Class position	Britain	Germany	Sweden
Higher service class	165	151	160
Skilled workers	100	100	100
Unskilled workers	89	72	98

Note: The income of skilled workers (full time) is taken as a baseline for each country. For example, a member of the higher service class receives on average 165 percent of the mean income of skilled workers in Britain. Income serves as a proxy for wages. Note that one may only compare figures *within* countries. For international differences please refer to the data reported in the text. Raw differences between different categories of workers are not a reliable indicator of overall inequality, because these data ignore the magnitude of the spread between groups of wage earners, and because they ignore the relative frequency of different sorts of workers. On the first point, note that income inequality is higher in UK than in Germany if one compares ratios between the top and bottom deciles of the net income distribution. In the UK, those in the highest decile have incomes about 3.8 higher than those of people in the lowest decile; in Germany, this factor is 3.0, and in Sweden it is 2.7 (OECD 1995). On the second point, there is a higher proportion of unskilled workers in the UK than in Germany, a difference whose magnitude varies by cohort. In the cohort of 30-year old men, in the UK about 30 percent of the male sample are unskilled workers, whereas in Germany, the proportion is only about 10 percent (Allmendinger and Hinz 1997).

Source: Own calculations, males only (not older than 60 years).

Data: ISSP 1992 Social Inequality.

Sweden, progressive tax rules diminish this differential between classes, and these data do not include these redistributive effects; likewise, in Germany, the differential for gross income (before tax) would be higher than that reported in Table 4.2. The intranational differences of income positions between classes are more distinct if one compares the relative wages of unskilled workers in the three countries. In Sweden, there is hardly any difference between the average wage of a skilled and an unskilled worker; the wage differential in Britain is more pronounced (an unskilled worker in Britain gets 89 percent of a skilled worker's wage). Yet in Germany, an unskilled worker earns only about 70 percent of the average wage of a skilled worker. Note again that we only have data for net incomes in

Germany and the differential in gross (before tax) wages should even be more glaring.

These data provide some context for understanding the implications of job and class mobility in different countries. Job stability in Germany has marked negative implications for the lowest classes; unskilled workers receive significantly lower wages than do skilled workers. Obviously, those who did not complete vocational training or cannot make use of it are relatively worse off (compared to other skill groups) in Germany than in Britain and Sweden. Obtaining skills pays under German labor market conditions: the wage differential between skilled and unskilled workers and the high absolute wage level for skilled workers create incentives to invest in vocational training, even if chances for upward mobility are low.

Let us now summarize the work trajectories in comparative perspective. In Britain, with its stratified educational and unstandardized vocational training system, we find – as expected – unstable work trajectories with many job and relatively few class changes, but with a relatively high level of downward mobility. In Germany, with a stratified educational and a standardized vocational system, stable and bounded occupational careers dominate, with few job changes and little crossing of class boundaries. Sweden, with an unstratified educational system and unstandardized vocational training, has occupational careers that are relatively unbounded by class. This structure results from an unstratified educational system and a higher level of redistribution within society.

Although lacking data for a systematic comparison of Germany and the US, we should try to determine where the US is located in this typology. The US has an unstratified system of general education and unstandardized vocational training. According to the typology the US is in the same box as Sweden. Do occupational careers have similar patterns in the US and Sweden? Müller et al. (1996) demonstrate in their recent comparative study of thirteen countries that Sweden and the US indeed have some similarities regarding occupational place-ment. Vocational training qualifications in both countries do not increase chances of entering the labor force in skilled jobs compared with chances of starting a career in an unskilled job. In addition, probabilities of entering the higher service classes are very similar across the two countries. In Sweden and the US, a vocational training degree does not matter in this respect. In Germany, completion of vocational training raises individual chances of entering the labor market in higher service classes (versus the probability of entering the labor force in unskilled positions). Other findings indicate that US society seems more "open" when one considers career mobility. Kappelhoff and Teckenberg (1987) report dramatic differences for "long-distance" mobility (e.g., changes from the class position of unskilled workers to higher service class) between the US and Germany. They emphasize that chances for both upward-mobility and for downward mobility are higher in the US.

One significant difference between Swedish and US general education is the degree of standardization. The Swedish educational system is highly standardized, in line with a policy of strong central government. The lack of standardization in US education promotes social differences among regions, individual schools, and social classes. Broad variation in the formally unstratified system of general education brings educational inequality back into the picture. Parents seek to pass on the legacy of their social advantages via school choice. The importance of standardization for schooling is reflected in the recent discussion about establishing national standards in the US (Ravitch 1995). Greater standardization is mostly intended to enhance the national skill level, but it also plays an important role creating equal educational opportunities (cf. Krüger, Chapter 5). Moreover, large differences in inequality in the two societies result from the fact that Sweden represents a different welfare regime, as we know from the comparative analysis of welfare states (Esping-Andersen 1990).

Institutional Context

What are the shortcomings of the empirical evidence presented here? I have used aggregate data to identify national types of "stability" and "boundedness." The results indicate that national differences do indeed correspond to the proposed typology, but it would be desirable in future research to study individual movements between jobs and occupational classes in detail in order to confirm the underlying propositions about different national types suggested by this aggregate analysis. In addition, differences in overall job and class mobility reflect other national particularities besides education and vocational training – like the variation in the size of different economic sectors, the size of the public sector, the strength of internal labor markets, etc. And of course, mobility patterns are highly dependent on broader institutional contexts of labor market and social policy, and these factors need to be approached in a more integrated fashion.

There are plausible arguments that the links among the educational system, the labor market, and social policy are interdependent and cumulative in their effects. This interdependence would cause a structural inertia of institutional settings and impede the transfer of some elements from one institutional environment into another. The German vocational training system and its job placement function, for example, are linked with strong labor unions and the traditional corporatist involvement of employers and unions in skill formation policy (Thelen and Kume 1997), which limits the poaching of skilled workers by employers. Industrial relations create a more rigid wage structure, which is responsible for a lower rate of return on job-seeking efforts. Laws make dismissals more expensive than in other nations. Finally, there are considerations of prestige that motivate businesses to participate in the "dual system," at least in regional labor markets (Harhoff and Kane 1996).

Moreover, the institutions of social policy have their own time-related characteristics. In Germany, social policy programs can be described as continuous – in contrast to situational wel-fare programs in the US or in Britain (Allmendinger 1994). Ger-man social policy aims to secure a given position in an occupational hierarchy in times of unemployment or old age. Educational and vocational policies "match": both stress conti-nuity, security, predictability, and trust. Members of the society tend to share a clear sense of what they may expect and where they stand in the occupational hierarchy, given their educational credentials. People can trust such systems. The institutionally ingrained belief in continuity is structured by more factors than just education and social policy: labor unions, trade associations, and other "communal organizations" (Fukuyama 1996) also play a part in this process. The same fit between social policy pro-grams and educational system can be found in nations that mostly employ situational policy programs: in the US, training is mostly given on-the-job, with a limited time horizon and limited security, and assuming instability and occupational change.

Social policy also regulates labor force participation rates. Examining the different participation patterns in Germany and the US can enhance the analysis of occupational opportunities and incentives: labor force participation rates are indicators of the transition between education, the labor market, and retire-ment. An early entry increases the duration of labor force par-ticipation and increases the opportunities for mobility; likewise, if labor force participation ends early, the "duration of risk time" for job and class movements is shortened. Figures 4.3 and 4.4 show labor force participation rates (1975 and 1995) for Ger-many and the US.

For the age group between 25 and 54 years of age, there are only small differences between Germany and the US for both points of measurement. The participation rate of men is slightly higher in Germany than in the US, whereas the participation rate of women is higher in the US. Looking at the age group of those 16-24 years-old, however, we find significant differences between the two countries. In 1995, both for men and women,

Figure 4.3 Labor force participation, 1975

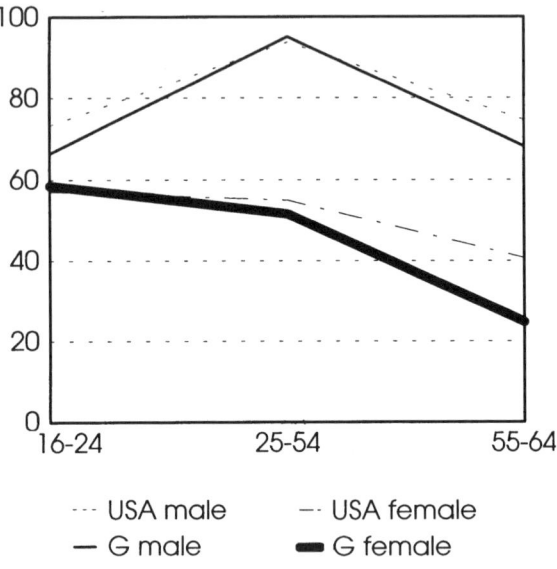

Source: OECD Labor Force Statistics.

participation rates are lower in Germany. If we look at age groups over 55, the German activity rates, both in 1975 and 1995, decline significantly. Among the 55-64 year-old men, the labor force participation was only 68 percent in 1975 and 55 percent in 1995 – this is 7 percentage points below the US rate in 1975 and fully 11 percentage points below the US rate in 1995 (see Gatter, Chapter 6).

The differences in activity rates by age and gender are closely related to the types of educational and vocational training systems, and to the character of the welfare state. The US liberal market model (Esping-Andersen 1990) is empirically identified: activity rates of both the very young and the very old

Figure 4.4 Labor force participation, 1995

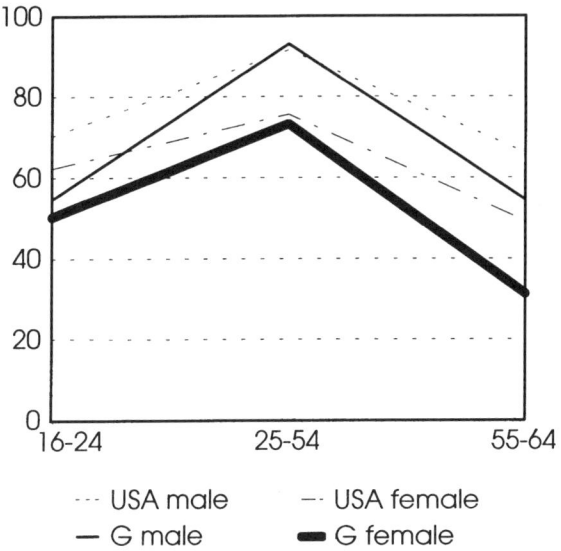

Source: OECD Labor Force Statistics.

are higher than in Germany. This is true for both sexes and an expression of "commodification" in which the life course is more centered on labor force participation: early entry matches late exit. There is a longer "risk time" for upward and downward mobility. The high activity rate of young men and women is connected with on-the-job training; the high labor force partic-ipation of older people reflects a lower level of social security in the US welfare system. Germany represents the opposite with regard to age- and gender-specific activity rates: late entry matches early exit, and women still have a relatively low partic-ipation rate. Education and vocational training systems result in late entry into the labor force. Especially for the unemployed, pension entitlements that can be claimed early lead to a shortening of the activity phase at the other end of the lifecycle. The structure of the German welfare state thus favors the "male bread-winner model."

In addition to the institutional context, we should take labor market dynamics into account. The changing economic situation as well as social trends – i.e., the increasing labor force participation of women (see Figures 4.3 and 4.4) – influence the relative importance of education and vocational training. Sectoral changes are probably the most obvious indicators of a dynamic environment for occupational careers. The number of jobs in the industrial sector is shrinking, while the service sector is expanding. Skills gathered in a diminishing industry are obviously devalued. Studies of dynamics and their impact on job mobility need to include more detailed information about the "social units" (firms and organizations) that determine career paths: they grow and shrink, new businesses are started, and others are shut down. Davis et al. (1996) report high rates of job turnover in the US resulting from economic dynamics. High job mobility is increased by the dynamics of the economy (for international comparisons see Schettkat 1996).

In conclusion, further research on career mobility should consider the following aspects:

- Institutional setting: we should analyze how different institutions within one country interact with respect to the stability and boundedness of careers.
- Organizational change: careers are embedded in organizations (Carroll et al. 1990). We should try to incorporate the idea of organizational development into analyses of mobility. Often, organizational changes might be the most important factor in determining mobility chances. Empirical studies could profit from a multi-level approach integrating the organizational environment into the analysis of mobility.

Pressures on German Vocational Training

The German vocational training system is currently under pressure, as evidenced by a reduction of applicants for apprenticeships and a reduction of firms offering apprenticeship slots (Mayer 1996; Wagner, Chapter 1). These trends partly reflect economic and demographic changes. More importantly, the German system worked well in the past because it depended on a pre-selection by the stratified school system and a closed labor market segment for skilled workers *(Facharbeiter)*. As long as these conditions continue to exist, the system performs the matching function. New hiring procedures and new skill requirements have opened up the closed market segment. Highly skilled "outsiders" – i.e., those with a university degree – have a chance to enter internal labor markets, and thus they block traditional promotion paths of skilled workers. As a consequence of these developments combined with organizational restructuring, employees with an apprenticeship have lower chances of upward mobility than in the past. Additionally, dismissed workers with outdated qualifications are at risk of swelling the ranks of the long-term unemployed. This is the dark side of the job stability system: if one loses a job in an occupational labor market, it is more difficult to find a new one just by changing occupations.

One change already underway within the German stratified system of education is the increasing proportion of students who receive the *Abitur* and enter higher education. This change clearly illustrates the decline of career chances for apprentices. Moreover, the lowest level of school completion (*Hauptschule*, nine years) has lost its traditional character as the regular degree qualifying for an apprenticeship. In the larger cities the *Hauptschule* has become a school for children from a disadvantaged social background, the children of ethnic minorities, and for children of refugees who might leave the country again before they have finished school. Employers who seek apprentices often require a better school degree. The relative rates of return for higher grades might decrease, despite the fact that these higher grades have now become a necessary precondition for many careers.

Another currently discussed problem of vocational training is its gender-bias (see Krüger, Chapter 5). Apprenticeships and occupational skills are highly gender-segregated; women suffer disadvantages on the labor market since a higher proportion of them are trained for occupations with low chances for upward mobility and a higher risk of mismatch with labor demand.

How can German institutional actors react to the changing labor market? There are discussions about changing the specific fit between stratified education and standardized vocational training. One possibility for the dual system to regain attractiveness would be to increase its permeability (Hamilton and Hurrelmann 1993). The completion of an apprenticeship should be an alternative way to gain access to higher education. The paths that already exist, which are really more like detours, could become a more regular track to universities. Moreover, vocational training itself is under revision. One possible reform could aim at changing the depth of standardization. The vast variety of occupations could be rearranged into occupational fields containing groups of occupations with similar training programs. This could increase individual's flexibility in reaction to labor markets trends. German occupational careers will likely be more "open" and less "stable" in the future.

Chapter 5

GENDER AND SKILLS
Distributive Ramifications of the
German Skill System

Helga Krüger

Defining the Issue

Internal criticism of the German training system, which is primarily directed at the formalized linkages between training and developments in the labor market, is as old as the system itself. Furthermore, the number of proponents and detractors of the dual system falls and rises in line with economic upturns and downturns: they do not constitute a unified camp, and they are in no way equally distributed across all sectors. Whereas the electronics and chemical industries have tried to undermine the dual apprenticeship system from its inception, considering it inadequate for their labor force management needs, the engineering industry, the trades and crafts sector, and the civil service have always favored the system, emphasizing its importance for skill formation and for organized vocational socialization. The latter sectors appreciate its effects on competence and the internalization of quality standards visible in the execution of daily tasks (Enquête-Kommission des Deutschen Bundestages 1990).

Evaluations of the training system differ, depending on the weight given to its various social, political, or economic functions in general, or on the particular interests of businesses, which are subject to different pressures for innovation and follow different modernization strategies, different forms of cost management, and different strategies for developing customer loyalty. Fully independent of these considerations, but also as old as the training system itself, is the criticism from the woman's perspective, which reveals a gender bias in both the skill provision system and the debates concerning it. These critics point out that it was and still is solely oriented around male youths' benefits, whereas some central questions of vocational education for female youths remain neglected. They start from the well-proven fact that while the educational grades of young women have surpassed those of young men, two-thirds of the female labor force are situated in the bottom third of the labor market. Some claim that this discrepancy results not only from continuing sexual discrimination in the labor market, but also from gender bias within the youth training system itself (Sattel 1989).

Indeed, introducing gender into a consideration of the German vocational training system reveals some important blind spots in the current discussion of skill provision. The debate has concentrated on just one of two co-existing, but completely different types of vocational training route in Germany: the well-known vocational and educational dual system (VED), in which male youths predominate, and the school-based vocational educational system (hereafter SVE), in which female youths predominate. Both systems consist of an average of three years of vocational learning, and both qualify individuals for the same level of position within the strongly hierarchical German labor market. The systems are also clearly gendered.

The usually neglected, gendered segmentation of the German occupational and employment system ties into the different formal integrational linkages between the educational system and the labor market. In consequence, the comparison of two types of organization for occupational training in one country highlights the issue of standardizing transitions from school to work. Analyzing these two systems provides evidence of the extent to which tracking systems matter for life chances, and this analysis uncovers the largely forgotten structural content of the two systems in shaping gendered life-course patterns.

Since with respect to educational and labor market linkages, SVE-tracking resembles that provided by technical colleges in Anglo-American countries, but contrasts to VED, the feminist perspective is of general, not just particular, interest (i.e., not only for researchers in gender studies). It provides an opportunity for those not familiar with the German training system to start to understand the German "obsession" for standardized regulatory systems. It focuses attention on the power of institutions over personal behavior and the fact that institutions often structure a society without the conscious awareness of individuals operating within them. The question here is, then, in what manner and to what extent do they define behavior? Therefore, in the following I shall not discuss female discrimination by looking at distributive outcomes, but rather I shall take these outcomes as a starting point and an indicator of the institutional ramifications of the system itself. These ramifications include the sustainability of return to prior investments in human capital, and, for the labor market, the development of horizontal and vertical segmentation and the very different policies for labor force adjustment to firms' demands.

This chapter begins by describing how occupational skill provision is part of an intricate educational system that incorporates cultural, economic, and social policy, and which led historically to the formation of a double structure of occupational training in Germany, in the form of VED and SVE. Thereafter, it considers the effects of this double structure on (a) the shaping of the life courses of women and (b) the function of the gendered structuring of tracking for the employment system. Finally, it turns to the different strategies employed by companies to adapt their labor force to the changing demands of the job and question why women (still) play along.

Standardization, Linkages, and Their Historically Frozen Institutionalization

Although social action is often seen as a matter of individual choice and accomplishment, social institutions such as the educational system, the family, the labor market, and the social security system structure the life course by standardizing individual labor market entries, positions, career paths, and long-term perspectives to a high degree. It was Marcuse (1964) who first defined history as a frozen framework of action when referring to the importance of institutionalized molds (institutions and their internal pathways and external networks) for change as well as the reproduction of a given society. Indeed, in order to understand the central principles of the German training system, it is necessary first to locate it within the ensemble of educational ramifications – and to think in terms of state regulations, which may be hard to imagine from an American perspective. Nevertheless, the inevitability will be clarified when we, in a second step, go back to the historically rooted differentiation of VED and SVE.

The German Education and Training System and Gender-Specific Distributions: An Overview

The data on the distribution of men and women in the German system of skill provision usually refer only to parts of it. But, in order to decipher the data adequately, it is important to differentiate between phases, stratification, and linkages between them and to the labor market.

PHASES

In Germany, education consists of two differently, but nonetheless highly structured sequences. The first phase of general education is immediately followed by a second phase of occupationally specific learning. A minority of youths will attain their labor market qualifications via the university track, while about two-thirds of German youths participate in occupational learning. This majority would, in the US, consist of "The Forgotten Half" (the title of the Final Report on Youth and America's Future in 1988), who finish high school without entering university.[1] In contrast to the United States, occupational training and education schemes of the VED and SVE types train for the major group of work positions, i.e., for nearly 498 officially recognized different occupations. In 1996, 370 of these belonged to VED (Alex and Stooß 1996) and 128 to SVE (Stooß 1997). The overall distribution of gender in both training systems is shown in Figure 5.1.

Although SVE trains for fewer than one-third of all occupations, the high number of VED occupations is deceptive. As the most recent data show, some 100 VED regulated occupations have fewer than ten apprentices nationwide, and a further 60 have fewer than twenty (Alex and Stooß 1996: 16). In contrast, similarly low numbers in SVE lead to the immediate closure of a program. The ranking of numbers in typical female occupations reveals that the most frequent SVE occupation is in the third position, behind two female-dominated qualifications from VED (Bürofach-, Bürohilfskräfte; Warenkaufleute; nichtärztliche Gesundheitsberufe (Alex and Stooß 1996: 41)). Therefore, within

---

1. In decade since the publication of this report, the "Forgotten Half" has dropped to 40 percent, as an increasing percentage of American young people attends some form of higher education.

Figure 5.1 Dual (VED) and school-based (SVE) vocational education systems compared

VED (370 occupations)		SVE (128 occupations)
two-thirds male youths circa 70% concentrated in 18 occupations, e.g.:	one-third female youths 70% concentrated in 15 occupations, e.g.:	female youths dominate in all occupations, e.g.:
- electrician	- sales personnel	- child minder
- car mechanic	- middle level office worker	- laboratory assistant
- fitter	- hairdresser	- nurse
- toolmaker	- medical/dental	- interpreter
- brick layer	practitioners' assistant	

Source: Heinz et al. 1985; BMBW 1994; Alex and Stooß 1996; Stooß 1997.

the second phase of education, SVE is clearly feminized and not an insignificant part of the German system of skill provision.

STRATIFICATION

Both phases within the German education system exhibit institutionally structured stratification. The first phase stratifies through three levels of diplomas: only 35 percent of youths finish *Gymnasium* (13 years; equal proportions of both sexes); 34 percent finish *Mittelschule* (ten years; intermediate level; two-thirds are female); 25 percent finish *Hauptschule* (nine years; foundational level; two-thirds are male); and 6 percent drop out (again, more male than female) (BMBW 1994). While the last two levels both provide access only to the vocational training track, the highest level gives direct access to university and also access to the vocational training system. Twice as many female as male school-leavers with the highest level diploma complete occupational training in VED *before* entering university in order to better their chances in the labor market afterwards (HIS 1991).

The second phase tracks into five labor-market entrance levels: university graduates (research, top managers, lawyers, teachers, top civil servants, etc.); polytechnic graduates (upper-middle management, upper middle civil servants, etc.); further training graduates (master craftsmen; top secretaries, etc.); VED and SVE graduates (skilled workers, nurses, carpenters, hairdressers, etc.); 3-6 percent leave without any certificates (unskilled and those trained on-the-job without an occupational title).

The tracking selections in the first phase of education occur very early (when pupils have not even reached their teens) on the basis of their apparent ability and orientations. But the large proportion who enter the vocational training track may have a second chance to attain university access certificates via the "second *Bildungsweg*," a system of vocationally based upgrading via special learning opportunities, which can even give one the qualification required to study at a university. This very complex system provides Germany with an effective instrument for tracking, orienting and motivating youths to undergo long periods of different types of learning; for dealing with different abilities and late developers; and for smoothing out youth labor market transitions in times of unemployment risk by integrating them via phased education, which is linked to the promise of improving labor market chances. And again: more girls than boys try to better their chances by means of attaining higher levels of education.

STANDARDIZATION

Phases, stratification, and allocation in the labor market produce an intricate system for distributing chances and opportunities in which every part is highly standardized. In the US, the existence of a decentralized and unstandardized education and training system leads to large regional variations (with respect to the organization of schools, their curricula, and their teachers' qualifications), as a result of which certain segments of the population are disadvantaged because the quality of local components of the educational system vary (Hinz, Chapter 4; All-mendinger 1989a). By way of contrast, the German educational system is based on universal, binding, standardized curricula, and at all levels a highly qualified teaching staff is employed that has to complete an academic course of study in their sub-jects (which lasts four years) and two years of probationary on-the-job training. The standards for the training of teachers and the school curricula for phase I are laid down by the KMK-Rah-menverordnungen (a standing committee of the educational ministers of all the federal states). Therefore, the stratified Ger-man system assumes that pupils' performances vary in spite of equal teaching conditions, and that these differences should match position and status in the labor market.

Whereas the stratification in the first phase of education is important for the tracking in the pathways of the second phase, this second phase is in turn important for tracking in the labor market. Although women surpass men in the entrance levels for occupational training, women end up in lower labor market posi-tions than men. Part of the reason lies in the area of formative labor market entrance qualifications.

Within the frequently discussed VED, the internal and external stabilization of the system relies on a shared responsibility for the quality of apprenticeship, which is absent in the SVE sys-tem, although at first glance this is not apparent. Both systems combine learning at school and the workplace; the common variant of block-release rather than day-release in SVE can also be found in industrial VEDs, as opposed to those in force in the trades and crafts. What makes all the difference is the lack of the state's and employers' shared responsibility for training and its internal and external standardization. Skills and curricula for each of the occupations in VED are strictly defined on a supra-company level, and each occupational title corresponds to a prescribed specification of skills *(Berufsbild)* that is fixed by the Federal Institute for Vocational Training *(Bundesinstitut für Berufsbildung)*. Yet the curricula in SVE are not standardized: they change from state to state, sometimes from one school provider to the next, as a great number of SVE places are offered by private organizations. While the occupational descriptions in VED are the result of negotiation processes between the educational administration, the employers associations and chambers of commerce, crafts and industry representatives, and the trade unions, in SVE the schools for training often belong to the employer's enterprise (as is the case in all health-care occupations, including nursing). The certificates in VED entitle the holder to fixed entry wages when entering the corresponding occupation, which is to say that they imbue the certificate with a specific labor market value (Giddens 1984), are publicly supervised, and establish a standardized labor market below the labor market for university graduates. In contrast, the occupational titles in SVE do not codify the skills required, nor, in some cases, the length of school-based vocational education.[2] Teachers have often not undergone university training corresponding to the occupational field taught and pupils are paid much less or even nothing at all by the employer during the training (Meifort and Becker 1995; Krüger 1991). Consequently, SVE exhibits much looser linkages to labor market positions.

Krahn (1991), who is very familiar with the German scene, stresses the sharp differences between the North American market-based system – which he calls a "non-system" with reference to Hamilton and Hurrelmann (1994: 329) – and the highly institutionalized German system of vocational training. When he writes that the German system "produces a highly-skilled workforce, ensures standardized qualifications, and reduces much of the uncertainty of school-work transitions for youth" (1996: 45),

2. The content of the SVE certificates is defined by the Ministry of Education of each federal state, or, in the case of nursing, by a special federal law for health occupations.

we can agree, because both VED and SVE train for and track to specific occupations in the labor market. We also accept that he has grasped the important point when he states that the system is based on a "shared commitment to training goals by the state, educators, and employers," and that these actors "define it as their long-term interests to pay for the training of youth, unlike the North American situation where it has been assumed that training is primarily the responsibility of schools." But we also have to underline that this last statement does not capture the entire truth: SVE, which is female dominated, steps out of line – a specific skill-providing segment, tracking to specific occupations and to a specific segment in the labor market.

Even official statistics on education in Germany do not adequately measure the relative proportion of youth trained in SVE- and in VED-occupations. The official reports on vocational training include the proportion of female youths in VED, which fluctuated between 35 and 38 percent in the 1980s, in line with the overall demand for apprentices (Born 1989); this figure reached a peak of 42 percent immediately after unification in 1990. But these data do not quantify the numbers of male youths in SVE; moreover, we lack reliable figures related to SVE, because large parts of this subsystem function outside the statutory framework of the educational system and are not documented. An earlier regional study of the distribution of cohorts of female school graduates with foundational and intermediate level school-leaving certificates showed that only about 32 percent of the cohort entered VED, while about 55 percent went into SVE (Heinz et al 1985).[3] Case studies confirm that the allocation of training certifications to either SVE or VED is not a function of the quantitative importance of the occupational track: the transfer of just one SVE qualification – the dentist's assistant *(Zahnarzthelferin)* – into VED in 1956 (which also

---

3. A further 10 percent had different types of upgrading offers; the remainder of the cohort was not findable.

means adding it to the official statistics), moved the certification immediately into the top ten certifications among females in VED, a position which it has maintained ever since (Born 1989). Studies of specific occupational statistics prove that other certifications that remain in SVE cannot be of negligible size: the number of childcare-workers (*Erzieherin*, SVE) equals the numbers of primary school teachers (University-degree) (Rauschenbach 1986); the number of persons in SVE health care occupations surpasses by a factor of six that of physicians (Statistisches Bundesamt 1994: 72);[4] and given the extremely short average stay in nursing (three to five years; cf. Prognos AG and Dornier GmbH 1989), the raw number of nurses recruited must be very high.

Due to the wide range of different occupations, official statistics offer only aggregate figures, without reference to the type of training per occupation. The cases mentioned above refer to only a few of the 128 SVE-linked occupations. They give some indication of the importance of SVE-linked occupations but unfortunately do not offer comparisons to VED-linked occupations. Only recently have researchers from the Federal Institute of Research on Labor Force and Occupational Development (IAB) begun to be concerned about this blind spot in occupational training research and documentation, and they have consequently started to register at least the number of different training schemes in SVE (Stooß 1997). With regard to pupil participation in VED, the overview of Alex and Stooß (which is the first of its type) adjusted the range of the 370 VED training

4. These include the following health care professions: *Krankenschwestern/ -pfleger, Krankenpflegehelfer/-innen, Kinderkrankenschwestern/-pfleger, Medizinisch-technische Radiologie-Assisten/innen, Medizinisch-technische Laboratoriums-Assistent/-innen, Krankengymnastinnen,* and *Funktionsschwestern/ -pfleger im Operationsdienst,* as well as ambulance and anesthetic technicians (Statistisches Bundesamt Bonn 1997: 190, with reference to Bundesärzte-kammer 1994). In 1995, there was one doctor for every 266 inhabitants of Germany (Statistisches Bundesamt 1997: 187).

offers to only the 210 relevant ones, i.e., with more than 50 pupils nationwide, while the 128 registered SVE-offers all cover more than this (1996: 16). That adjustment transforms the ratio of SVE- to VED-linked occupations to 1:2. This overview of the official statistics and the mainstream literature on the German vocational education system, and its perception abroad, sustain the feminist reproach: the lack of data demonstrates that Germany does not care about its SVE system, or more exactly, that some insiders are only now discovering this system anew.

The neglect of SVE makes it worthwhile to explore its historical roots, an exploration which supports the thesis that in Germany training policy forms an important part of general social policy.

Vocational Training Ramifications and Their History

It was at the beginning of this century, a time of high unemployment in Germany and insecurity for the state as a result of large numbers of people turning to communism, that the proponents of VED achieved their first success in extending the medieval system of training into the trades and crafts and transforming it into a state-based institutionalized system. Their interests coincided with the political goal of the government to fill the time between finishing foundational level schooling (which around 70 percent of pupils did) and military service in a manner that would prepare young men for both their long-term commitment to a working life and the duties of citizenship (Kerschensteiner 1901).[5] Since this time, the German system of skill provision has had a number of interrelated mandates including creating knowledge, distributing knowledge (and, therefore,

5. Bismarck repeatedly underlined that nothing would reconcile the workers better with the state, and thus lower the risk of a proletarian revolution, than the perspective of a stable life course with a public guarantee of material security (Ritter 1983).

life-course chances), and enriching skills with "civilizing" attitudes to occupational attainment and the sociopolitical demands of democracy.

This was also the time of heated debates about the male and female "nature-bounded" character and the consolidation of the family as the basis for economic development (Hausen 1978). The state and business were united in the view that along with the needs of producing not only a qualified and loyal, but also a healthy and stable workforce, the family must be stabilized. Furthermore, the trade unions also saw the benefits of negotiating wages appropriate for a family breadwinner with responsibility for maintaining a wife and children.

The historic act was the "discovery" of occupational training as a pivot for gendered life course differences. Its effects in "*producing gender*," in the structural sense of the cultural noun of "*doing gender*" (West and Zimmerman 1987),[6] lay in the division of youth groups into two types of occupational transition pathways to adulthood, one leading to "existence-securing" positions and the other to "natural vocations" – to use the nomenclature of that time (Mayer 1992). To prevent reliance solely upon socialization processes in their occupational choices, which are clearly in the foreground of today's research about women's distribution in the labor market, the distinction between "existence-securing" and "natural" occupations was cemented into the internal structure of vocational and educational training itself. For female youths, school-based vocational education (SVE) was designed to develop skills for caring, nursing, dressmaking and repairing, and, at best, assisting in male-dominated territories, but without consideration of the market need for supporting themselves; for male youths, the dual system, with its contractually guaranteed skill protection and remuneration, was

6. West and Zimmermann use the term to describe the gendering effects of every interaction that cannot be done without attributing and deciphering behavior in accordance to the sexes of the actors and consequently stabilizing gendered frames of action.

based on the structural ties to the corresponding existence-securing career, as described above. In consequence, the market value of SVE qualifications was not fixed in collective agreements nor were the occupational specializations recognized in standardized wage rates; they were set apart from the building-blocks for an occupational career (Kleinau and Mayer 1996). The teaching offers lacked clear occupational boundaries, but corresponded to the broad areas of social support associated with family life and, in case the search for a partner was unsuccessful, should prepare the young woman for assistance, auxiliary services, and commitment compatible with public social engagement.

Historical research shows that the first German women's movement protested against this two-track system, but in vain (Nave-Herz 1997; Kleinau and Mayer 1996; Brinker-Gabler 1979): women's participation in the labor market was at best conceptualized as a pre-familial intermediary stage, with the politically motivated and thus consciously intended consequence of keeping women out of the contractually-secured educational and career system, which simultaneously was established for the male part of society (Lüsebrink 1993; Schlüter 1987; Bednarz-Braun 1983; Nienhaus 1982). The second phase of education fixed individuals for their prescribed roles in family life: for women in their role as home-makers, and for men as breadwinners. The lack of state interest in female occupational qualifications resulted in the rise of private providers of vocational education which charged tuition fees, and in the establishment of "on-the-job" training offers (without any pay for the trainee). And even the state's offers of school-based vocational training defined it as primarily a cultural task that should concentrate on femininity and family orientations (Kleinau and Mayer 1996). The consequences were a lower social status in the labor force, a lack of career structures, and the low market value even for further education (Teubner 1989).

Nowadays, women are found in both systems: in times of labor shortage, a small number of female occupations have over time been transferred to the VED system: e.g., the approximately fifteen female dominated positions in the dual system today, such as "*kaufmännische Berufe*" (mid-level office workers, which were originally designed for men), sales personnel, hairdressers, and dentist's assistants. Others still remain in SVE, which in the meantime also have expanded in line with the growing personal-service sector, such as the numerous, increasing nursing and "caring" occupations, catering to pre-school children, hospital patients, the elderly, the handicapped, the long-term and chronically ill and also to certain auxiliary services such as physiotherapy, and massage (Krüger 1991). Even the classical women's SVE assistant qualifications (such as chemical or electronics assistants, introduced at the beginning of the century and promoted by the firms in these industries) had expanded by 1986 to include 28 different assistant types, all of which lead to dead-ends in the labor market, because firms' internal training schemes favor people who have come through VED (Frackmann and Schild 1988). Still other qualifications have remained subject to immediate consumer interests and largely stayed in the hands of private training schools (for example, beauticians, photographers, gymnastic teachers, speech or physical therapists), and they continue to demand high tuition fees. In addition, as an entrance qualification, most of them require at least an intermediate level school diploma (*Mittelschule*, which demands, in addition to achievement, one more year of learning at school in phase I) or a two-year preliminary vocational school training with upgrading by means of the "second *Bildungsweg*."

In Germany, when a person acquires a job corresponding to her/his occupational certificate, wages are usually a function of the individual's initial investments in education. But the ramifications of history are still felt today. In spite of the higher preliminary educational qualifications required for most of the SVE occupations, which in phase I demand an extra year of learning compared to those required for VED, and in spite of the existence of tuition fees for a number of SVE offers – once again, in contrast with VED, which is not only tuition-free, but which also provides wage supports to apprentices – the certificate's corresponding market positions and pay hardly surpass those linked to VED (Krüger 1991; 1998). In other words, women's higher investment of time and money in initial education and training and their higher levels of attainment in general education are eaten away by the time they enter the labor market.

History reveals to what extent gendered notions about family duties mattered at the time the two types of vocational education and training systems were established. But not every female-stereotyped occupation remained in SVE, and not every woman will enter the SVE track. Although men in SVE are estimated to be largely underrepresented, women today are found in *both* VED *and* SVE. The different structures of training, once established, have lost their obvious link to a person's sex. This fact provides the chance to differentiate between gendered structures (SVE vs. VED) and actual gender (male vs. female) in order to estimate the different outcomes of both systems as such, e.g., the effects of their originally gender-related different market values. With reference to Giddens (1984) these might be defined as: a higher versus a less stable definition of occupational skills boundaries; a higher versus a lower regulation of workforce recruitment; a higher versus a lower rigidity of linkages between educational investment/attainment and career perspectives. The question would then be whether VED benefits women in contrast to the respective disadvantages of women trained in SVE, and the outcomes will give some general empirical hints as to the importance of the type of skill provision with respect to occupational rewards.[7] By comparing the effects of both training systems on

7. These questions cannot be answered through overall comparison of male and female income rates. The incorporation of gender into two skill providing structures with different linkages to income and internal career patterns also transforms the question of obvious pay inequality (which is blocked by law) into a structural one: educational investments and

female employment patterns throughout their careers we can show the extent to which the system acts as such even in female (i.e., family-interrupted) labor market participation patterns.

Effects of Both Types of Vocational Training on Female Life-Course Trajectories

In our research on female life-course sequences between family and employment we included women from VED and SVE. Since this project aimed to filter out family influences, we focused a second study on the trajectories of these women's husbands.[8] The design followed a stepped theoretical sampling in order to select the variables in question and to allow for a combination of quantitative and qualitative research methods. In the following, the data set will not be used as evidence of the (well-known) differences between male and female life course patterns, but since we can fully control for the intervening effects of their family situation, the data provided us with the opportunity to fully filter out VED and SVE influences on these women's life courses. The sample consisted of:

1. Women who were in their sixties and had completed their vocational training in 1948/49. They belong to the

---

incomes differ between SVE and VED, as well as the corresponding continuity- and career patterns, but are linked to the type of skill provision and the respective occupation, not to the sexes of their students/the workplace holder. In order to prove sex discrimination in income we would need investment and income statistics per VED- and SVE- linked occupations and proportions of gender per occupational group, which do not yet exist.

8. Both projects formed part of the Special Research Center Program, "Status Passages and Risks in the Life Course," at the University of Bremen; the first was conducted from 1988 to 1991, together with C. Born and M. Scholz. The second was conducted from 1991 to 1993, together with C. Born, H. Stenger (part time), G. Braemer (part time), and C. Erzberger.

first living generation that could refer to a whole and
non-war-troubled adult lifespan.

2. We selected equal numbers of women who, in 1948/49,
had completed vocational training in one of the top five
occupations within the range of female-dominated
ones, including one in VED (middle level office worker)
and one in SVE (child-minder).[9]

3. We included only married women with children, and in
order to control for family orientations we selected
equal numbers from two culturally contrasting regions
in West Germany, an urban Protestant and a rural
Catholic one.

Out of the data on 220 women – who completed the postal
questionnaire on further qualifications, date of marriage and
birth of children, grandparenthood, retirement, and the beginning and end of employment phases[10] – we selected 53 of them

9. It may be astonishing for American readers, but in Germany both jobs
require three years of learning and training, e.g., a child minder's education includes knowledge about the psychology of early childhood, about
possible disabilities, diseases, child development training, etc. Both educational schemes figure among the 498 occupations for which training is
offered in the second phase of education. Both still remain within the
ranks of vocational training schemes of today. The respondents'
addresses came from the chambers of industry and commerce and of
crafts, where the names and addresses of candidates who sat final examinations for the different occupations in VED are stored, and from
schools for the SVE-based training scheme.

10. To uncover possible bias in our sample (which with 220 cases was rather
small), we compared their life-course data with those from larger data-
bases (official statistics and other large-scale data collections) by means of
reliability testing (Prein et al. 1993); this testing showed that our data did
not contain any bias, either with respect to the average distribution of
familial events according to the age of women in this cohort (marriage,
birth of children), with respect to the number of children and the divorce
rate, or with respect to the rate of participation in the labor market
according to age and family composition (Born et al. 1996). In the second

for in-depth interviews on their vocational choices and on turning points in their lives, again proportionally distributed according to region and occupation. In addition to some surprising outcomes of combining quantitative and qualitative data (all these women were convinced that their lives were shaped by their husband's family life needs), the findings of particular relevance to the subject of this chapter are the following:

1. The comparison of their "decision making" about what type of vocational training to enter showed no evidence of differences between the occupational groups, nor between the two regions. All had actively sought and experienced great difficulties in securing an apprenticeship, and they widely described their interest in avoiding remaining unqualified. Child-minders did not connect their vocational training with their (presumable) devotion to their own children but (no differently than the other interviewees) showed an equal desire for securing a living on their own (for more details on the qualitative interviews see Born et al. 1996). All these women developed career perspectives and all characterized their entry into a specific occupational training scheme as the result of "mere chance" (having heard about an open training position from their advisers, neighbors, newspapers, etc.). But the result of the accidental training allocations showed strong effects on their whole adult life, as documented in the following.

2. The women were compared on the basis of duration of employment in the occupation trained for, in jobs other than the trained-for occupation, and in jobs which are outside the statutory social insurance scheme.[11] When contrasting women

---

project the husbands' employment trajectories also proved to be non-biased within the range of the parameters of this cohort (educational levels, employment rates, upward mobility, income; cf. Erzberger 1993).

11. Duration of employment was taken as the sum of all periods in the respective type of employment, expressed as a percentage of the total

with training for middle level office work (VED) and those with child-care training (SVE) we discovered the following:

Mid-level office workers form the occupational group with the most frequent interruptions,[12] but they nevertheless accumulated an average of twenty-seven years of employment in the field of their initial training, distributed differently over their life spans. In contrast, women who trained as child-minders only accumulated an average of five years of employment in that occupation, and these years occurred before their first interruption. When returning to the labor market their qualifications lost their value. Ten years after the end of their training, none of the child-minders was employed in the occupation for which they had initially been trained, but 76 percent of the office workers were. Even twenty years later still 54 percent of mid-level office workers were working in the sector, while 83 percent of the child-minders were in jobs outside the statutory social insurance scheme.

3. The factor that best accounted for distributive patterns of types of employment (and associated with remarkable differences in women's incomes) crystallized as the type of first occupation trained for. The qualitative interviews showed that all the women (*including* the child-minders) acquired a high level of identification with their occupations during their vocational training and subsequent employment. The two groups did not

---

duration of employment overall. In view of the high number of interruptions, we decided to stick to descriptive methods of analysis. The preparation of the data in the form of a cluster analysis served to test, with the help of analysis of variance and contingency table models, the visible influence of all types of primary occupation on the female life course, and showed a significant correlation between occupational group and cluster membership (significant beyond the 95 percent confidence level). Instead of referring to all groups I will concentrate on the comparison of just the *two* of interest here (for more details, see Born et al. 1996).

12. Nearly half of the women displayed between three and twelve changes between paid employment and staying at home.

differ in the average number of children, nor did the employment patterns follow regional contours, nor were the significantly different life-course patterns explained by family lifecycles. Interruptions and returns differed within each trained group, but overall they did not correspond to family phases of child-rearing and caring. And despite the fact that interruptions put at risk every woman's continuity patterns in their acquired occupation in the labor market, the comparison showed that women from SVE are much more disadvantaged than women from VED.[13]

4. The employment patterns of the women during their life course clearly depend on whether or not they were certified through the VED or SVE training systems.

This finding is puzzling even for current attainment theories in Germany, according to which the level of training is assumed, for men as well women, to be the variable that structures the employment trajectory (Blossfeld 1987). Such an interpretation holds true for their husbands' employment patterns (Erzberger 1993), but it cannot explain the typical differences between occupations in the manner and level of paid employment in the life course of the spouses, because the *qualification levels* of the population investigated are equal. Another widely propagated variant, with respect to different basic resources for structural effects, refers to the external opportunity structure, i.e., the expansion of the female labor market (Blossfeld and Mayer 1988). But in our case, both the trained middle level office work-

13. In the intensive qualitative interviews we checked all individual preferences related to decision-making relative to initial vocational training and compared them in order to reveal cultural differences (urban Protestant and rural Catholic), as well as between people with different occupational titles. The results showed no differences in orientation. With respect to the qualified office workers and child minders, this finding again underlines that both did not so much choose, but rather they took what they could get without foreseeing the effect of these choices on their lives.

ers and the trained child-minders faced a labor market that was expanding in line with the general increase in prosperity and in the change of norms about exclusively family-centered child caring, but most members of the latter group still did not return to their labor market sector.

The third commonly used variable for structural explanations – that the low income of the husband that drives women back into demanding positions in the labor market – would mean in our case that child-minders were significantly more successful at landing themselves rich husbands, while the others failed to find a good match. But analysis of the husbands' life-course data excludes this explanation (Erzberger 1993). The coupling of the standardized life course data and qualitative interviews from both projects makes clear that whether and to what extent women stayed in or returned to the labor market did *not* depend on the husband's income, but instead on the different labor market values of VED or SVE.[14]

These values are based on the relationship between a looser or stronger standardization of vocational training and the associated recruitment practices within the corresponding labor-market segment: because of expansion in the sector and the scarcity of labor for commercial work, employers tried hard to bring qualified office workers back into the labor force and provide job-related internal further training, whereas child-minders' qualifications were quickly dismissed, even by those who provided the SVE, as nothing more than "every woman's natural qualification" (Notz 1989). Employers conflate, to a high degree, traditional female occupations in the personal services sector with the *personal* features of women. Very soon, the child-min-

14. That women's labor market participation can be proved to be almost independent of their husbands' career patterns (Born 1993) differs from Anglo-American findings (Davies et al. 1992; Marx-Ferree 1991; Yeandle 1984; 1991; Mason 1987; Bird and West 1987; Oppenheimer 1974), but also to what was previously thought by German researchers (cf. Lauterbach 1994).

ders in our sample had to compete with every woman who was just *willing* to do childcare. As the qualitative interviews showed, they denied having undergone any training when trying to re-enter the labor force in order *at least* to get positions outside of the statutory social-insurance scheme. In the case of child-minders, it is the internalized reference to social commitment that historically was not reconciled with collectively bargained qualificational and payment standards (Möller 1987). Thus, the comparison shows to what extent the internal and external stabilization of vocational training matters for life chances. And it underlines that gender-sensitive research into opportunities does not merely imply being sensitive to income differences between men and women, but also being sensitive to institutions, i.e., sensitive to the "stickiness" of historically developed organizational differences in the education and career system.

A lot of research has been done into the effects on stratification of the German education and training system over the life course (Mayer 1990; Müller et al. 1983). During economic downswings, the dependence of young people seeking training places on the supply of apprenticeship places can lead to lifelong disadvantages in the labor market career of an entire cohort (Blossfeld 1987, 1989). In accordance with mainstream life-course researchers, Blossfeld did not differentiate according to gender, nor between VED and SVE, but attributed his findings directly to a low supply of apprenticeships. He neglected the fact that in times of recession the state's policy is to smooth down the negative effects on youth by offering more SVE places. The flexible instrument of SVE allows for an increase in the number of classes, and in those times, the number of male youths in it will grow. But its function as a buffer of business cycles does not change its institutionalized nature – and Blossfeld is right without knowing about these mechanisms, because male youths in SVE will share its disadvantages with the female youths in it. Mainstream research also remains blind to the fact that the number of disadvantaged youth fluctuates, but not the underlying structuration principle. During economic recessions even the most highly qualified young women – who at other times can compete successfully for places in the VED system – will have worse chances than their male counterparts in finding a VED place (as discussed more fully below). Thus, although the number of women in SVE will also fluctuate, women will always take up the majority of the offers in this system.

Vocational Training Differences and Labor Force Advantages

The growing service sector, while female-stereotyped, opens up new chances for women. And indeed their employment rate is growing while that of men declines (Häussermann and Siebel 1995). The variety of life-course patterns within our research's sample of women occurs despite the fact that their occupations all belong to this labor-market segment. The extremely different results raise the need for a more careful debate about the internal structure of the service sector and the role of SVE and VED within it.

Both training systems define labor market positions. Comparing the vocational education and training systems in Germany, Austria, Switzerland, Canada, and the US, Heinz (1996) discusses the different structuration principles of the labor markets in these countries and concludes that VED (the only system that he took into account) corresponds to an *occupational* labor market with vertical and horizontal boundaries between the occupations, and occupation-specific career paths within the firms' internal organizational structures (cf. also Drexel 1993). He argues (1996: 5) that

> The examples of Canada and the USA demonstrate that where internal markets *dominate*, preparation for work occurs at school

and by on-the-job training. Occupational markets operate on more formalized procedures of skill training that are more or less independent from any particular employer's needs; where occupational markets are important, there is a specific institutional network of organized vocational socialization. Internal labor markets, in contrast, rely on more informal training which is required to serve specific job assignments. Occupational markets permit workers' mobility between companies because they recognize certified vocational skill profiles.

The identification of an occupational labor market in Germany, which includes recruitment, placement and company-internal career organization, detracts attention from the co-existing SVE that also trains for specific occupations, but nevertheless largely exhibits the internal market characteristics described above. Heinz refers to different recruitment practices from VED in which the certified skill's definition by occupational title permits workers' mobility between companies. This does not diminish the fact that, once entered, the initial skill's definition is linked to the firm's occupationally defined internal career structure, which will reduce personal mobility. The immobility of workers can contradict the employer's innovational needs. But here is where the chances for recruitment via SVE, and not via VED, come into play.

If we look at different within-firm segments *in the productive sector,* we must consider that in addition to the company-internal career paths, they also operate on short-term positioning. Namely the chemical and electronics industries, as discussed earlier, alternatively profit from both systems of recruitment: they recruit their laboratory assistants (SVE, mostly female) for dead-end positions *("Stabs-Positionen"),* and the other work force for long term positions *("Linien-Positionen")* from the dual system (VED). While the assistants' employment duration, despite the high entrance qualifications from the first phase (usually higher level *(Gymnasium),* but at least intermediate level *(Mittelschule),* is on average only 5-7 years, in general they are replaced with fresh SVE graduates after the first interruption, and they are excluded from internal programs for further training and qualifications (Bednarz-Braun 1983). These opportunities for career development are officially reserved for the VED graduates and therefore formally exclude SVE graduates. The combination of access pathways allows a calculated flexible personnel policy. According to the company's new requirements, the relations between the two training systems for recruitment are starting to change. With the introduction of ever more SVE assistant training programs (primarily in information science), more employers across sectors are making this shift (Enquête-Kommission des Deutschen Bundestages 1990).

The boundaries for this practice depend on firms' chances to escape the denomination of positions as defined and standardized by VED. Employers' interest in, as well as the number of, VED positions may be shrinking (Häussermann and Siebel 1995). Corresponding to the rapid obsolescence of knowledge due to the innovation rate in production, a furtive undermining of VED via recruiting from SVE is taking place, a fact as yet hardly discussed. The official debate still considers only VED, which diverts attention away from this development.

And indeed in VED itself some change is becoming obvious: companies are seeking to reduce the training costs associated with VED and the resulting fixed minimum wages as well. Some are not offering apprenticeship positions at all: during the actual recession, less than one in four German firms trains in the hope of recruiting sufficient qualified labor from neighboring training firms (poaching). Others compare their firms internal costs to the benefits VED offers of a tight coupling between schooling and labor market (see Wagner, Chapter 1),[15] and stick

---

15. On the lower extra costs of German firms in comparison with Anglo-American ones, including the costs of controlling work quality, cf. Häussermann and Siebel 1995; Esping-Andersen 1990; Allmendinger 1989.

to VED, but try to raise entrance-level qualifications for it from the first phase of education.[16]

Apart from these strategies in the occupationally-structured productive labor market segment, the greatest dilemma of the SVE occupations will be in employment in the private-public mix of welfare, which is managed directly by the state, and where positions below the academic level are entirely SVE dominated. Large parts of this sector correspond to Heinz's classification (1996: 5) of "the casual labor market where skill requirements are low and job security is minimal," which he, along with Ashton (1993) and Marsden and Ryan (1991), argues is widespread in the US. People qualified through SVE in the welfare sector encounter a situation in Germany that is less regulated by vocational training structures, but still by the normative assumptions about women's "vocations" that dominated when SVE was established (GEW 1988; Rabe-Kleberg 1993).

It is this segment that is expanding most rapidly in the German employment system. Experience from the US and other countries suggests that, with an increase in the number of jobs in the personal-service sector, workers are protected less than ever from poverty. German data also show that, apart from the more slowly increasing number of qualified jobs in its civil-service sector (cf. below), the numbers of officially registered unskilled or on-the-job trained workers with bad pay and low job security in the personal service sector is growing disproportionately; in 1991 for example, 64 percent of the whole service

16. Indeed, in balancing supply and demand, firms are free in selecting among those seeking apprenticeships, and in times of good supply, particularly medium and large enterprises and public employers are successful in bettering the quality of their prospective recruits by restricting access to their VEDs to only the best qualified school-leavers from Realschule (ten years) or Gymnasium (thirteen years). In these times, less well-qualified young people from Hauptschule (nine years) are referred to small crafts and service firms which tend to use their apprentices as a source of cheap labor and usually cannot offer job security and promotion prospects; or they are referred to SVE.

sector workforce was classified as unskilled, significantly higher than the 30 percent proportion of the same type of labor in the classical production sector (Cornelsen 1993).

The relationship between qualified positions and precarious jobs is increasingly shifting (Manske 1995), but unfortunately there are no studies about this shift in the quality of jobs in relation to the distribution of SVE and VED across the service-sector segments. However, it is known that the proportion of SVE-qualified women in the personal-service sector is particularly high (Fricke and Schuchardt 1987). They predominate in the nursing and caring occupations, for which research evidence demonstrates that the striking and rapid solution is to cope with the high quantitative demand by means of downgrading the tasks and changing them into badly paid jobs (Landenberger and Kuhlmey 1993; Rauschenbach 1986; Stooß 1986; Prognos AG 1980). The linkage of women with SVE (including the assumption that they do not need "existence-securing" employment) and, conversely, the linkage of women to care provision as a (practically) natural vocation have thus been maintained since the start of the SVE system, despite the significant changes in family structure and labor market requirements that have occurred in the last few decades (Rabe-Kleberg et al. 1991).

The advantage for the welfare state, as the major employer in this sector, lies in the maintenance of a double marshalling yard with cost-reducing effects that allow it to cling to SVE. On the one hand, according to the size of its coffers, the state can shunt an entire range of tasks onto women who will remain at home, due to the low utility of their vocational training. On the other hand, these women can be shunted back into employment in auxiliary services in public-welfare institutions in order to compensate cost-effectively for personnel shortages when the economy is booming (cf. Heintze et al. 1997; Braun and Jung 1997; Pfau-Effinger 1990; Prognos AG 1989; Offe 1984).

The mixture of training and gender-specific philosophies in this sector has negative consequences not only for the employees, but also for their patients/clients and, not least, for the structural development of the sector itself: the openness of quality definition according to area of tasks can become a significant risk for the quality of the work itself.[17] Furthermore, for the skill-providing programs in SVE, the transfer between scientific developments and daily practice by means of university-trained teaching staff, which is guaranteed for all VED occupations by the laws governing training, is blocked. But the disassociation of daily practice from more general, systematic knowledge in nursing is becoming increasingly problematic.[18] Consequently the current debate about VED or SVE in this sector of personal services is starting to shift into the direction opposite to the one in the productive sector: pressure from women's and consumers' pressure is directed to transforming SVE into VED in order to guarantee the quality of the services as well as equal chances for long-term perspectives of the work force, who have acquired appropriate qualification (Görres et al. 1996).

VED comprises mainly men, but also women in the civil-service sector and mid-level office work (including high-paying sectors like banking and insurance). Here indeed, the enormous expansion of positions has bettered the chances for qualified women to a remarkable extent (Esping-Andersen 1990). As reflected in our data on the employment patterns of the female mid-level office workers over their life courses, women could profit remarkably from this change in the occupational structure, and it is interesting to link this development to the training system: qualified office occupations are the only ones where predominantly female work is fully integrated into VED. The

17. Becker and Meifort (1994: 18) speak of "dangerous care," referring by this term to a general debate on "careless care," due to time-stress and a lack of knowledge about competency-preserving and -restructuring techniques in care-giving activities.

18. It is only in the 1990s that, in reaction to public pressure and international standards, German universities have witnessed the rise of nursing science and connected teachers' training (Robert-Bosch 1992; 1996).

historical inheritance here was that women should be prohib-
ited from these careers by forcing them to undergo a one to two
years special school-based training (Handelsschule), while men
got offers in VED immediately after having finished phase I. But
these "extra-offers," which still exist today and are frequently
used by women before they seek a corresponding apprenticeship, also provided women with better competitive chances and
very quickly they caught up with and overtook their male competitors, up to the point where the traditional male occupational title ("Kauf*mann*") has been changed into a female one
("Kauf*frau*") in everyday language. Only the high positions for
top secretaries remained school-based (and require the highest
level qualification from phase I).

With reference to the developments in this sector, again, we
must reiterate the structural importance of the vocational training system, which Beck and Brater (1977: 32) declared to be the
"bones of the life-course corset" *(Korsettstangen des Lebenslaufs)*,
and which once established are not easily broken. In the case of
mid-level office work and the civil service, with its high rate of
further training and its requirements for reliability, nobody
wants to do this. But due to the openness of quality standards
that operate in the personal-service sector and its historically
inherited SVE system, there is little political interest in relieving
these services of their hybrid status between female responsibil-
ity/all-round competence and qualified activities. The benefits
to employers of a cheap and flexible labor are obvious, although
this system cannot guarantee minimum quality standards nor
prevent participants, right from the start of their practitioner's
phase, from being deployed as required. And in this case, the
weak market position of the consumers, to require quality and
define occupational competencies (as in VED) has not prompted
the state to implement and standardize skills and the internal
occupational needs.

Nevertheless, all three sectors under scrutiny showed the
structural importance of the training system for labor-force and

labor-quality development. The macrosociological view on women's life-courses reveals that women's employment trajectories are shaped independently of their husbands', but not at all independently of the type of their initial vocational training, and that the variety in female life-course patterns corresponds to a high degree with whether or not classical female occupations were integrated into the VED or left in SVE.

But if the effects of educational attainment on occupational rewards are mediated by the education and training system (for an international comparison cf. Allmendinger 1989a), why do women not assume male standards of costs and benefits? Why do women make bad choices? We have to face the question: why do they not escape SVE?

Tracking and Counseling

As suggested by Figure 5.1, the distribution of youths in training schemes and in occupations in Germany varies in line with gender. But research concentrates widely on female choices in order to explain to what extent their labor-market disadvantages can be reduced to personal preferences and consequently to self-disadvantaging behavior.[19] The corresponding literature turns on contradictory arguments: on the one hand feminist researchers stick to the thesis that the disadvantages women face are

19. The well-known campaign of the beginning of the 1980s about bringing girls into male-stereotyped occupations ("Mädchen in Männerberufe") had no equivalent about bringing boys into female-stereotyped ones, although the concentration of boys in male-stereotyped occupations mirrors the figures for their female counterparts (Alex and Stooß 1996). As male-stereotyped occupations all profit from VED, boys have nothing to be worried about in their career "choices." In contrast to the government's expectations, the results of evaluation studies on girl's behavior raised severe suspicions about the term "choices" itself, at least in the case of *girl's* allocation processes (Lemmermöhle-Thüsing 1992) (cf. discussion below).

due to their choosing *"female fitting"* occupations (Flaake and King 1992; Ostner 1989) and that Germans should re-evaluate what women do. Others point to their family orientation, which may lead women to discount the long-term consequences of occupational choices (Geissler and Oechsle 1996). Both are difficult to reconcile with results of research that show that the primary worry of female youths is finding a good apprenticeship (Seidenspinner and Burger 1982; Heinz et al. 1985; Lemmermöhle-Thüsing 1992), that more women than men invest extra years in their education in order to compete with at least intermediate level diplomas on the apprenticeship market (Heinz et al. 1985), that they accept losing money instead of earning it when entering SVE (Krüger 1992), and that they undergo more (state-provided) further training than men (Axhausen 1992).

In order to understand these contradictions we have to take into account that, due to the institutionalized pathways from school to work in Germany and the US, even "tracking" and "counseling" are only similar on superficial inspection. Here again, the underlying structure matters much more for individual behavior than personal preferences; that is, individual choices are heavily constrained by the stepped decision-making in Germany's entire educational system with its division in phases, as well as in its internal stratification, and the variability in the supply of SVE places that serve as a buffer for VED. Careful longitudinal studies on transitions from school to work prove the cooling-off effects of personal choices by a system that matches options and realities at different turning points: (a) after four years in the first phase of education in regard to the choice of more theoretical or more practical orientations; (b) in the second phase of vocational education, the choice of what occupation to pursue, and (c) during the short period of seeking an appropriate training position, in balancing precise options and offered apprenticeship places (Heinz et al. 1985). These studies clearly indicate an enormous difference between girls' personal options at the beginning of these trajectories and their training positioning at the end of it. As Goldmann and Müller (1985) outline, only a quarter of all women in vocational training for sales personnel indicated this occupation as their personal preference when leaving school at phase one. Three-quarters had tried in vain to enter other, more prestigious apprenticeships. The most recent longitudinal study on "selection processes in the German vocational training system" (1988 to the present) shows that the 184 girls surveyed in the first phase of education wished to enter fifty-nine different occupations, of which only twenty were female-stereotyped. Their distribution in VED, two years later, showed 60 percent were training in four female-stereotyped occupations. The largest number were concentrated in sales personnel, which only 6 percent had originally wished to enter (Dietz et al. 1997).

It is also true that male youth are not predominantly placed in the training scheme of their first choice (Heinz et al. 1985; Dietz et al. 1997), but they then enter another training scheme in VED (and will at least profit from its structure), while female youth who have tried in vain to enter VED, then enter SVE as "better than nothing," i.e., better than remaining unqualified (Heinz et al. 1985; Born et al. 1996). Even if, during an evaluation of their labor market chances, their preferred strategy was to better their options by attaining higher certificates in the first phase of education (one reason why they may do better at school than their male peers), at the end of a long series of failed attempts in the apprenticeship labor market many of them end up with an offer in SVE – and will join the small group of pupils with preliminary options for it (also in the case of nurses, as shown in Piechotta forthcoming). Standardized cross-sectional studies, which concentrate only on the outcomes of this career search process, and not on the process of "choosing," can thus yield misleading interpretations: due to the fact that vocational choice is largely defined culturally as personal management, girls entering SVE transfer their existing opportunities to their own preferences, and they show satisfaction with any training program whatsoever, if questioned *after having entered* it (Heinz 1995; Lemmermöhle-Thüsing 1992).

Consequently the gate-keeper's role in the gendered distribution of apprenticeships remains partly hidden; but it should not be underestimated. In periods of scarce apprenticeship offers, employment counselors try to convince girls to make a better choice when entering SVE in order to preserve the VED benefits for male insiders by reducing the number of female competitors. They assume it is easier to turn females' mind to the (female-stereotyped) SVE than males, which is accepted by the trade unions and hence they only mildly protest against this practice (Drechsel et al. 1988). And research on distributions of gender and qualification levels shows that as well as insisting on high entrance-level qualifications, the recruitment personnel of firms in Germany have a surprisingly tenacious preference for male youths in classically male-stereotyped VEDs, even if female youths can compete on the basis of higher entrance levels from the first phase of education (Heinz et al. 1985).

It is not by chance that female youths dominate in female-stereotyped occupational certifications in VED and in every occupational category in SVE, even though they tried to better their chances for preferred occupations again in the second phase of education by participating much more frequently than their male peers in the special programs of the "second *Bildungsweg*" (though mostly with disappointing results).[20] Structurally fixed career patterns, incorporated into the organizational patterns of the corresponding firms and service sectors, will do the rest; this shows the power of tracking via two institutionalized alternatives and gendered perceptions of work.

In Germany it seems to be extremely hard to break the gendered structure of recruitment, and achievement helps only in those fields that are not male-stereotyped *and* that are integrated

---

20. Schober and Chaberny (1983: 17) conclude: "It is better to be male with foundational level qualifications than female with intermediate level qualifications."

in VED: banking, insurance, administration in firms, the civil service sector (Dorn and Rozema 1992). With the rise of these segments the size of the qualified female labor force increases, but it does not break the rules of gendering in the welfare state's practice, which is reinforced, last but not least, because in male-stereotyped segments the increasing opportunities for assistant qualifications via SVE offer firms the double recruitment strategy described above.

Conclusions

In a discussion of the sustainability of the German system of skill provision in international comparison, the question of gender is particularly relevant in order (a) to show the extent to which educational institutions matter for both the life course and in determining the boundaries in the occupational structure of the labor market; and (b) to destroy the myth about the presumed uniformity of the German system of skill provision. It is remarkable that the full-time schooling system – with quite high educational standards and clear occupational skill provision, but with low qualificational boundaries for corresponding occupational positions and with short-term career prospects – produces a type of transition into the labor market similar to that found in graduates from Anglo-American technical schools. In Germany as well it mainly tracks into a labor market segment that is much more regulated by "free market forces" than male-dominated labor-market segments that are linked to VED. And whereas the Anglo-American technical school system proves to be the most occupationally guided one in these countries, in Germany, SVE shows in comparison to VED to what extent even this type of transition wastes private and social investments in training.

But whereas in the Anglo-American countries, the general deficit of institutionalized pathways from school to work puts at risk the employment fate of both sexes, in Germany, gender and occupational structure produce overlapping effects. Here, we have to differentiate between gendered occupations and gendered fixations of the pathways. In doing so we are able to discern clearly the pathways' effects. Where SVE, which was historically linked to female occupations, has been changed into VED, the female-stereotyping of the occupation did not completely disappear, but it does not eat away the positive effects of the VED pathway type. In cases of addition of both structures, the negative effects for personal job security are cumulative. In countries where the training system has not become a sociopolitical shaping force for the life courses of either men or women, the boundaries for stereotyping and allocation of activities according to gender are much weaker (Fels 1989) and we will find a more equal distribution of the disadvantages of market dependence of competencies. Correspondingly, in Germany it is much less a question of "equal pay for equal work," but much more the debate of "equal" institutional regulations of work and skills between gendered labor market positions that would diminish sex discrimination. And indeed, the careful analysis and comparison of the employment trajectories of women with a qualification that was moved into the VED system with women possessing a qualification that remained within the SVE system also shows that the cultural historical gendering has become "structure," i.e., that it today operates according to a gendered logic, but indifferently to the actual sex of their participants. Women who escape SVE benefit from the VED advantages, and men who enter SVE will have to fight its disadvantages. And again: it is not the fact that apprenticeships combine learning at school and within the firm that makes the difference, since this is also the case in SVE, but the lack in SVE of formal integrational standards and linkages to career patterns that puts personal investments in training at risk of later being useless.

The analysis above has concentrated on structural outcomes of both training systems and has shown the surprisingly great labor force advantages of VED over SVE. The question whether SVE training schemes *could* be transformed into VED within the German system can easily be answered with "yes," as earlier transformations have shown. Yet if we question the *chance* to transform all of them, i.e. to give up SVE as a whole, things become more complicated. Due to the concentration of debate on VED both within and outside Germany, up to now too little research has been done on the impact of SVE on VED; and we might speculate about whether SVE effects – intended in historical times but from the equal opportunities standpoint unsupportable today – have become necessary for the sustainability of the VED system over time. This draws attention to the interdependence of the two systems for the German social model of labor-force management – is VED's success also dependent on the existence of SVE? A definitive answer to this question will require much more additional work. Undoubtedly, VED works successfully in favor of a lifelong career within the occupation for which a person has trained, and it tries to meet long-term basic qualifications for general economic development. But historically coupled with a gender gap in relation to securing an existence by employment, the German model also hinges upon the incorporation of its virtual and norm-based perception of family policy. SVE's adaptability for relieving the strain from the apprenticeship market, its low qualificational standardizations for corresponding occupational positions in the personal service sector, and its short-term career prospects in the productive sector transformed SVE into a three-fold buffer: (a) of educational policy; (b) of welfare policy; and (c) of qualification management within firms.

New barriers against SVE's transformation into VED may result from the multiple functions fulfilled by its co-existence with VED: the historical analysis of the educational sector showed SVE's buffer effects for VED in times of low supply of apprenticeships, but also its persistence during economic booms; this fact corresponds to and also uncovers a great deal of the spe-

cific characteristics of German welfare state policy and its structural alliance with the employers, unions, and the church with
respect to family policy as well as to the organization of the
personal service sector (Pfau-Effinger 1997; Esping-Andersen
1990). And it goes a long way towards explaining the relatively
low rate of participation of women in the German labor market
in comparison to other industrialized countries (Esping-Andersen 1990; Hinz, Chapter 4). But the linkage of SVE with one
particular political regime, such as the Christian Democrats,
proves erroneous; under Social Democratic governments only
the ideological part of women's exclusion from the career systems
shrank, not its SVE-linked structural background.

Compared with the relatively low inter-firm mobility of the
VED trained workforce, the mobility rate of the SVE trained
workforce is much higher, but is never analyzed outside of sectoral frames (Häussermann and Siebel 1995). History reveals
again that companies long ago discovered women as a flexible
source of labor with good qualifications from SVE, and the co-
existence of both systems opens up different strategies for
employers to deal with innovational needs: in the case of VED
recruitment, by firm-internal further training; in the case of
SVE recruitment policies, by labor-force replacement.

I have sought to focus attention on SVE because it is usually overlooked in international comparisons. When examined
within its multi-dimensional cultural, social, economic and biographical effects, the persistence of the two types of training,
and SVE's resistance to social change is not astonishing, despite
the demand of German women for the transfer of all feminine
occupational training to VED since the beginning of this century. One system supports the other, and only during the expan-
sionary phase of the labor market in the 1950s did the readiness
to transfer the standardization effects of VED for further female-
stereotyped occupations grow. This indicates again to what
extent the solidarity between companies' and the state's interests in integrating youth into society by means of establishing a

standardized sequence of general education, skill acquisition, and occupationally linked prospects in the labor market benefits the current system of regulation, and why this solidarity tends to exclude women when the unemployment figures imply that remaining in the family is more functional for the state, at least in the short term. Companies see no reason to change their dual strategy (Negt 1997), as long as it allows them to differentiate between flexible and fresh-from-school marginal employees, and long-term core employees who form the candidates for the companies' internal training programs, as discussed above.

Whether meeting technological challenges really is hindered by the formalized standardizations of VED, and whether it is not much more a question of the qualifications of company-internal management, may remain open. But the question cannot be avoided as to why, since the beginning of the system, the ever-recurring opposition to VED has never led to the insight that one possible solution to the much-decried inertia of modernization in Germany could also be the transfer of all VED training schemes into SVE, i.e., the part of occupational training that was developed for women. That the SVE alternative never did enter the arguments of proponents and detractors of the VED debate may indicate that the status quo is deplored as the best alternative, and that in view of its societally stabilizing effects nobody wants to swap the benefits of a strongly regulated VED for a weakly regulated SVE – which again reinforces the assumption that the official complaints are only of strategic, not fundamentally transformative, significance.

Chapter 6

CONTINUING OCCUPATIONAL TRAINING IN AN AGING GERMAN ECONOMY*

Jutta Gatter

Introduction

Industrial economies are currently under siege on several fronts. The main challenges faced by business and government are external: rising competition within an increasingly global economy, the collapse of the former communist states, an overall internationalization through enhanced tradability of goods and services, and the spread of new production concepts. Another longer-term problem for the sustainability of welfare states is the graying of their populations and the concomitant aging of the workforce. In Germany the pace and volume

*   An earlier draft of this chapter was presented at the AICGS, Washington D.C. in June, 1997. I would like to thank Michael Breuer, David Finegold, Joel Rogers, Ulrike Schneider, and Martin Seeleib-Kaiser for their very helpful comments.

of this change is expected to exceed the graying of most other advanced industrialized nations.

The state has already begun to deal with demographic issues through pension reform and the introduction of a long-term care insurance. However, at the firm level, only the short-term problems have been recognized thus far. These have significantly contributed to the debate about the *"Standort Deutschland"* (German competitiveness). The discussion has largely focused on reducing labor costs (including social security contributions) and the need for continuing training of workers to sustain or even regain international competitiveness. It is highly unlikely that Germany, an oft-cited example of a "high-skill equilibrium," will initiate successful wage competition with low wage countries. Thus, the competitiveness of industries and single companies will increasingly depend on the ability of workers to innovate: human capital will become the key factor for competitiveness (Reich 1991, Thurow 1996, Buttler and Tessaring 1993). It seems that broad knowledge and communication skills – so-called key qualifications that represent general rather than firm-specific human capital – will be crucial in the future. Only these unspecified, "redundant" capabilities can be put to many different, previously unknown uses, enabling companies to respond quickly to unpredictable new demands without a loss of quality (Streeck 1992).

Structural change can be carried out either through internal or external flexibility. Whereas internal adjustment comprises retraining and further training for people already in the workforce, external flexibility means exchanging older workers for younger ones. In times of high unemployment, the latter seems to be a rational and politically attractive solution. Thus, a rising percentage of older workers in Germany retires early, avoiding sometimes necessary, yet socially unacceptable layoffs, while offering opportunities for younger people to enter the (internal) labor market. However, with a decreasing number of young people leaving the educational system, structural change must be increasingly accomplished with middle-aged and older workers, i.e. through internal flexibility.

The early retirement policy has also put enormous pressure on the social insurance system, since expenses are increasing and revenues are declining. The state has already responded by codifying a new pension law which imposes most of the early retirement costs on employees and employers, making it worthwhile for both sides to look for other strategies. Moreover, Germany already faces a visible mismatch on the labor market for qualified workers today that will rise significantly within the next twenty years, as fewer and fewer younger people will enter the labor market. Relying on highly skilled workers from other EU-countries will not solve the problem, since many of these countries have to deal with the same issues raised by the aging of the workforce.

Given this combination of demographic and economic forces, continuing (further)[1] training will become much more important than it is today. Continuing vocational training is defined as every kind of training after initial vocational (apprenticeship) training or graduate trainee programs for new recruits. The applicability of skills attained during the period of initial vocational training always declines over the lifecycle, and faster technological change is now causing it to decline more rapidly than in the past (Blechinger and Pfeiffer 1996: 24). People will therefore have to update and expand their skills more than once in their working lives, which makes human capital investment through continuing training more profitable even for older workers. If the amortization period is short for everyone, the investment will be also worthwhile for older workers. As Mahnkopf (1989: 78) puts it: "Completed (initial) vocational training will become the prerequisite for stable employment to an increasing degree […], but the lasting willingness and ability to qualify will

---

1. The terms "continuing training" and "further training" are used interchangeably in this chapter, as are the terms "vocational" and "occupational."

become even more important." While initial and further vocational training have been often used as functional equivalents for skill creation in the past in different countries (see e.g., Regini 1997, Backes-Gellner 1996, Fischer 1995), this will be not sufficient for the quickly changing economies of the future.

Companies can prepare for this situation by developing and implementing schemes of lifelong learning for different groups of workers and long-term personnel planning. Preliminary research results of a survey we conducted with company personnel managers (see Schmähl and Gatter 1994, Gatter and Hartmann 1995) indicate that demographic challenges are not on their agenda. Looking more closely at the work of researchers in the field of personnel or human resource management in Germany, one has to conclude that this topic is not on their agenda either.

This chapter deals mainly with the long-term demographic challenge for German competitiveness and assesses to what extent the existing training institutions are capable of meeting the challenges of maintaining Germany's high-skill/high-wage economy without significantly widening inequality. After a short overview of demographic trends in Germany, the focus will be on the problems of skill creation and the role of institutions in overcoming these market failures. The final section will summarize the results and make some policy recommendations.

Germany's Demographic Time Bomb

The causes and extent of demographic changes in Germany have already been well documented (e.g., Roloff 1996, Sommer 1994, Deutscher Bundestag 1994). The information given here will concentrate on the key trends as a basis for understanding the main argument regarding demographics and skills. Germany is an aging society with a population that will shrink over the long term. This is mainly due to low fertility rates and the rising life expectancy of older people. Although projections[2] show that this trend will be somewhat mitigated through the influx of new immigration and the unification of the former two German states, it is unlikely to be reversed this way. The German population is expected to rise from 80.8 million people (1992) to more than 83 million people in 2002. Afterwards it is projected to decline to about 72.4 million in 2040 (see Sommer 1994: 500).[3] More importantly, as the population declines the age structure of the population will change dramatically. Figure 6.1 shows the anticipated development of the different age groups in the future.

Figure 6.1　Development of different age groups in the German population in the future

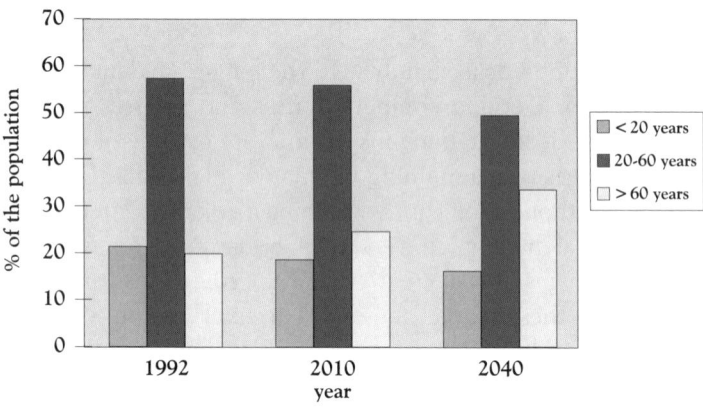

Source: Data from Sommer 1994: 501.

2. A good overview of several projections in given in Deutscher Bundestag 1994.
3. The cited figures are mainly drawn from the eighth coordinated population development projection *(8. koordinierte Bevölkerungsvorausberechnung)*. The population projection covers the period from 1993 to 2040 and shows how population number and structure will develop under different assumptions concerning (im)migration numbers. Here, for simplicity, we refer only to the medium projection. For more details see Sommer (1994).

The aging process began decades ago, but it will pick up speed in the future. The percentage of people sixty and older is predicted to increase from 20 percent in 1992 to 25 percent in 2010 and 33 percent in 2040, while the share of people under twenty is likely to decline from 22 percent in 1992 to 16 percent in 2040. The share of people of prime working age (twenty to sixty years) will likely decrease from 58 percent in 1992 to 56 percent in 2010, and to 50 percent in the year 2040 (Sommer 1994: 501, medium projection). The rising proportion of older people in the population – who often draw a pension from age sixty onwards – is a major source of concern for the viability of the German pension and health-care systems. For the international competitiveness of the German economy, the age structure of the working population itself is of at least equal importance.

Thon (1995) shows that the aging of the workforce has already begun, but the largest shifts still lie ahead of us: the share of new labor force entrants (fifteen to thirty year olds) is projected to decline from about 30 percent to 20 percent of all workers in the next fifteen years. The percentage of the thirty to forty-nine year-olds will first increase sharply (because of the last of the baby boomers now in this age bracket), which will create an increase of the fifty years and older category twenty years from now. From the year 2000 onwards, there will be more people over fifty than under thirty in the potential labor force. In reality not all people in the relevant age group are in or seeking gainful employment. Moreover these trends do not necessarily indicate that the actual workforce in companies is aging to the same extent. Figure 6.2 shows a comparison of the German population and the current workforce as of 1994.

The biggest change over time has occurred among younger and older men, who have much lower labor force participation rates than a generation ago, while at the same time the labor force participation rate of (married) women has been continually increasing, although it still lags behind the participation rates of men. The low labor force participation of younger people is

Figure 6.2 The German population and the current
workforce in 1994

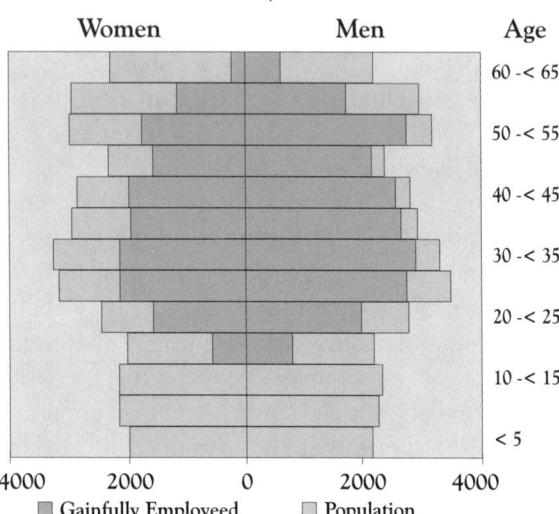

Source: Data from Statistisches Bundesamt (Federal Statistics Office), Fachserie 1:
Population and gainful employment 1994.

mainly due to the educational system's expansion: more young
people are staying in school until they get their *Abitur,* and then
going on to apprenticeships, higher education or both (see Wagner, Chapter 1). Thus the overall education level has increased
in the last twenty-five years. If one makes the conservative
assumption that at least the same proportion of every class
(*Jahrgang*) will go on to the *Abitur* or university as today, and that
labor force participation of older people will rise compared to
today, the aging of the workforce will be even more dramatic
than indicated above.

To avoid skill shortages leading to a rising skills mismatch
on the labor market and sustain the welfare state, three major
options are available for the society:

• keeping people in the workforce longer than today and
providing older workers with new skills;

- increasing the proportion of women in the workforce after they give birth to children; and
- bringing more immigrants into the workforce.[4]

The following will deal explicitly with the first and to some degree with the second option.

Obstacles to Skill Creation

Researchers dealing with training issues usually stress the problem of market failures in creating human capital and point to the importance of the institutional setting in which skill creation occurs (e.g., Soskice 1994, Backes-Gellner 1996, Finegold et al. 1993). This line of reasoning will be followed here as well, but with a slightly different emphasis.

Quantity – The Collective Goods Problem

Human capital is different from other capital because it is embodied in the people obtaining it and is therefore mobile. Without external pressure on firms to invest in human capital, whether or not firms provide training for their employees depends solely on the expected rate of return of the investment. The usual assumption is that, from an individual point of view, the new skills require an up-front investment that is then recovered over time. Skill updating or even creation for older people is therefore often seen as not profitable. The time period for return is too short to be worthwhile. This assumption is proved by many empirical studies finding the typical u-shaped wage profile over the lifecycle (Mincer 1994: 116f.).

Becker (1964) introduced the distinction between general and firm-specific skills. Because general skills are transferable to

---

4. A single firm's perspective may also include moving jobs abroad.

other jobs,[5] usually the firm is not willing to pay for this kind of training, so it must be paid for by the employee. With firm-specific skills, the workers are reluctant to invest in their own training because they bear the risk of a layoff. Firms are also reluctant to pay for specific skills training because they face the risk that the worker will quit after completing the training. Because the "hold-up"[6] problem exists for both sides, it seems reasonable that firms and employees share the costs of this sort of training since they share the returns afterwards. It is not easy to separate general and specific human capital acquired during a training period.[7] A working assumption is therefore usually made: all training acquired in firms contains some elements of firm-specific skills. General skills, on the other hand, have to, in theory, be acquired at the individual's expense. It is obvious that job-specific tasks determine continuing training needs. In this respect continuing training is merely the attempt to adapt the workforce to current or emerging requirements and is mainly targeted to facilitate firm-specific human capital. From a strategic perspective on competitiveness, investing only in currently needed skills is short-sighted. Polyvalent skills are the precondition for the ability of fast "retooling" to unpredictable market changes, therefore investment in general human capital should also be in firms' interest. However, without any market intervention we can expect a significant under-investment in polyvalent skills. Thus, the question here is whether the German further training system includes some elements to overcome this prisoner's dilemma.

5. The mediation of transferable skills faces the typical collective good problem of free-riding, referred to as poaching, of competitors. In sum, the trade-off between individual and collective rationality can lead to significant under-investment in transferable skills.
6. This neo-institutional term refers to ex-post enforcement problems of contracts due to relation-specific investments, i.e., sunk costs. For more details see Alchian and Woodward (1988).
7. Soskice (1994) offers an application for Germany's initial vocational (dual) training system.

Quantity and Quality – Training as an Experience Good

The quality standards of continuing training are a very important issue: not only the amount of training, but also its quality, are the key preconditions for a successful performance outcome. No one would deny the fact that the better training the more useful it will be for the person getting it.[8] How can someone assess in advance if the available training suits his needs? Here we face a typical situation of asymmetric information between supply and demand. Training has characteristics of experience and credence goods. Something is labeled an experience good when the buyer only knows after consumption whether the quality matched his expectations or needs or not. Credence goods are characterized by the fact that some quality aspects are hard to assess even after consumption. Health service is a typical example of a credence good. Even after treatment, the patient never can be exactly sure whether this was really the best treatment for his illness (Tirole 1988: 106). The same holds for training issues: no one will ever know whether he or she got the best quality of training available or not. For our purpose the experience good characteristic on its own is sufficient to produce market failures. For any demander, the transaction costs in checking out several training options by several providers are excessive, which gives providers a strategic advantage: if they offer a certain quality (satisficing) not many consumers would bear the risk of a double investment with another provider (Tirole 1988: 294f.). Thus, an opaque training market with many providers and non-standardized courses will probably lead to under-investment in skill creation.

Institutions – A Pivotal Role in the Skill Creation Process

Regulations on different levels can mitigate market failures to some degree. According to North (1990: 3), "Institutions are

8. From an economic point of view an investment is only profitable until the point where the marginal costs are equal to the marginal utility of the training.

the rules of the game in a society or, more formally, are the humanly devised constraints that shape human interaction." Putting it differently, institutions set certain property rights, which impose transaction costs for different actions, and set strong incentives to make particular choices. With the given technology, institutions determine the costs of the economy: transformation (production) costs and transaction costs (North 1990: 6).[9] Institutions are made up of formal constraints (rules, laws, and constitutions) and of informal constraints (e.g., norms of behavior, conventions, self-imposed codes of conduct) (North 1994a: 360).

Institutions are important for economic performance because they offer a structure for many everyday transactions. Especially in today's fast-changing economies, stable institutions can provide a high degree of reliability and reduce uncertainty about the future. Institutions reduce transaction costs, and provide credible commitments, prerequisites for long-term relationships. In this respect, institutions are closely linked to the economic performance and competitiveness of countries and their ability to adapt these institutions to new challenges. Hence, institutions should not be too rigid: they should be able to adapt and transform themselves according to needs in the environment.

Institutions can provide incentives or disincentives for human capital investments: e.g., the state can pay for the training, impose levies on firms that do not train, provide tax relief to firms or individuals for skill investment. Labor market regulations, like protection from dismissals, can facilitate individual investments in human capital, while deterring firms from hiring new employees. Likewise, state policies encourag-

---

9. Transaction costs are the costs tied to economic exchange, i.e., to specifying and enforcing the contracts that underlie exchange. One can distinguish search and information costs, bargaining and decision costs, monitoring, and enforcement costs. Transaction costs arise not only in markets, but also in firms, e.g., with regard to labor contracts (Richter, Furubotn 1996: 49ff.).

ing early retirement may deter firms from offering continuing training for older workers. Internal labor markets are important institutions, especially in larger German firms, and a very good example of how institutions create trust through long-term relationships, and thus reduce transaction costs. As Soskice (1994: 31) points out "the usual port of entry to skilled work in an internal labor market is via an apprenticeship." The possibility of permanently screening employees helps to avoid poor investments in firm-specific qualifications (Hardes and Schmitz 1991: 664).

For new hires there is a minimum level of qualification which has to be met by potential employees to "signal" that they are the sorts of people who might be able to enter the internal labor market. Before getting access to career advancement there is the screening process, started during initial vocational training followed by further training, a better job, further screening, and so forth. The long period one needs to advance in the firm hierarchy provides an opportunity to create mutual trust. Internal labor markets set incentives for employees to stay with a firm after receiving continuing training because of deferred compensation such as occupational pensions, later career advancement, and so forth (Osterman 1994b). Long-term relationships can also help to mitigate part of the experience good problem of training. In game theoretic terms: if the one-shot game which sets strong incentives for the training provider to offer low quality is replaced by a repeated game, the provider can build a reputation for offering good training which might attract other customers. Large companies also have the option of "making," rather than "buying" training but, i.e. to establish their own training center. Another option is to standardize training content through collective bargaining and then oblige training providers to meet these standards, which can be controlled using examinations by an independent agency; this is more or less how the German initial vocational training system works.

On the other hand, these trust relationships can lead to institutional inertia. Once established, policies set incentives "to act in ways that lock in a particular path of policy development." (Pierson 1993: 606). Certain patterns of decision-making that provided "satisficing solutions" in the past may hinder the establishment of new policies. Facing new problems individuals tend to apply the old routines. The search for more radical new solutions often occurs only after the failure of the old routines (March 1994: 29). Thus learning is adaptive, based more on past experience than on assumptions about the future. Seen in this way, institutional change is usually incremental and not revolutionary. Even when formal rules are changed, the informal rules often are not.[10]

Whereas this chapter focuses mainly on formal constraints, it is acknowledged that informal institutions are important complements to and not substitutes for the legal ones.[11] I am also not assessing how institutions change (see e.g., North 1990, 1993, 1994a, 1994b, Hall 1992, 1993, or Skocpol 1992 on that issue). My aim is different: I am focusing on existing institutions and asking whether the German set of institutions is equipped to overcome the two major hindrances to skill creation: the collective good problem of investing in general skills and the need to assure the quality of further training within firms.

Continuing Training in Light of the Relevant Institutions

Looking at advanced industrialized societies, the relevant institutions for high skill provision are not primarily private property

10. In this respect, the evolved institutions may not need to be the most efficient ones.
11. "[…] and it is the complex interaction of formal rules and informal constraints, together with the way they are enforced, that shapes our daily lives […]." (North 1990: 83).

rights, but instead labor market institutions.[12] Thus, I first describe the merits and shortcomings of German training institutions. I start with the initial vocational training system to show whether this system provides a solid basis for continuing training needs, and if it can serve as model for the organization of further training in Germany. Then I deal in more detail with the continuing training system itself (structure, incentives, empirical evidence). Afterwards I investigate to what extent the institutional framework given by social security and industrial relations provides incentives for firms to invest in continuing training for (older) workers.

The Vocational Training System as a Model for the Continuing Training System?

To date, Germany's high-skill equilibrium has mainly been based on the success of the German apprenticeship training: the dual system of initial vocational training. Since the dual system is described in detail by Wagner in Chapter 1, I focus on some of its shortcomings important for my purposes, i.e., the negotiation process for new and out-of-date curricula.

The training follows a codified curriculum *(Ausbildungsordnung)* for every occupation. Each curriculum sets minimum standards for the skills acquired through in-firm training, offers advice for structuring the training process, and provides information about the requirements of the final examination (Streeck et al. 1987). This system is highly standardized because the awarded certificates provide reliable information about the acquired qualifications (Allmendinger 1989b). In this respect the certificates have an important "signaling" function which allows firms to avoid the transaction costs of a thorough "screening" process and the training of newly hired people in firm-specific skills. For

---

12. In a wide definition labor market institutions comprise not only labor law (individual and collective), but also pension systems and training regulations.

the apprentices this standardization also lowers transaction costs by reducing the asymmetric information problem (the costly trial and error processes of finding the right provider), since people can rely on getting a certain level of training quality (see Hilbert et al. 1990, Soskice 1994).

New curricula or adjustments of older ones are discussed in the BIBB's main committee *(Hauptausschuß)*. Its members are delegates from the states, the unions, the employers' organizations and the federal state. This process is therefore a highly political one. Detailed work is done by sectoral experts which reduces conflicts, but also give these people a lot of power. New curricula are only enacted when all sides approve. According to Streeck et al. (1987: 17) it is usually a highly complicated and long process to create a new or revise an obsolete curriculum. The involvement of all the relevant actors facilitates long-term relationships and implementing the new training programs once agreement has been reached, but it can cause problems because of the long delays before qualifications are updated or new ones are created.

One example is the curriculum of the bank clerk *(Bankkaufmann)* which was finally revised in 1997,[13] but had not been adjusted since 1979, a time when computer knowledge and service orientation was rather low. After several years of negotiation with little progress, the Federal Minister of Education, Science, Research and Technology had to launch a special program in 1995 to create training regulations for new professions and to restructure obsolete regulations. More than eighty professions are affected.[14]

The consequences of the slow revision process are twofold: either apprentices acquire already obsolete qualifications when

13. Many other rather old-fashioned curricula are given in BMBW (1996a).
14. The main aim of this initiative is to speed up the revision of old and the creation of new curricula (see BMBW 1996a: 67f. and 99). Since the text of the agreement gives a lot of freedom for interpretation, it remains to be seen if the goal will be achieved.

trained according to curricula, or firms take curricula as minimum standards and use the leeway provided for facilitating
more or higher level skills. The latter seems to be true especially
for larger companies (Streeck et al. 1987).[15] In this respect, the
dual system loses its signaling function. Workers with the same
certification can no longer be assumed to have a uniform qualification level, since the company that provides the training
becomes more important than passing the standardized examination, which only ensures a minimum level of qualification.
These facts provoke questions about the ability of the dual system to meet the skill demands of the future.[16]

Despite these shortcomings, the dual system remains important as a basis for establishing lifelong learning schemes: in providing some basic occupational and transferable skills, and in
mediating an attitude to work (learning how to learn) for still a
high share of young people.[17]

15. Empirical studies in banks (e.g. Regini 1997) show that all of them use in-
firm training to a high degree to create skills of their apprentices according to their needs.
16. This is not the only reason why the dual system is currently under strain.
Another discussion is centered around the costs apprenticeships impose
on employers (e.g., Wagner, Chapter 1). The capacities for vocational
training have been cut by many companies during the last years. Combined with rising preferences for an academic education and other problems caused by the dual system (gender and ethnic segmentation) the
prospects of the dual system of vocational training has been a subject of
controversy during the last years (for an overview of the main arguments,
see Wagner, Chapter 1; Schmid 1992; or Timmermann 1990).
17. A study by the IAB (Institute for Employment and Occupational
Research) in Nuremberg estimates that the labor demand for unqualified
workers will drop from 20.2 percent of the workforce in 1991 to 10.1 percent in 2010, while the need for people with certified vocational training
will increase from 59.1 percent to about 63 percent in 2010 (Tessaring
1994: 12).

Continuing Occupational Training: Institutional Structure and Incentives

In contrast to the dual system, continuing occupational training in Germany is a very broad and ill-defined concept that can embrace nearly everything beyond initial training. Further vocational training can include learning processes at the workplace itself, reading special literature at home, attending in-firm or external courses, seminars, informational events, or an interruption of gainful employment to attend full-time courses, or training during periods of unemployment. A narrower definition comprises only organized forms of learning like attending seminars and courses.

REGULATIONS

The following list of regulations dealing with continuing occupational training is neither complete nor very detailed. This is due to the huge amount of existing regulations on several levels which constitute more a "jungle" than a "system" of continuing training.[18] The main sources of regulations are labor law, trade *(Gewerbe)* law, and educational laws like the Employment Promotion Act *(Arbeitsförderungsgesetz)*, the *Handwerksordnung*, and the Vocational Training Act *(Berufsbildungsgesetz)*. The Vocational Training Act is the legal basis for initial and further vocational training, while the Employment Promotion Act is relevant for publicly financed training. For other kinds of further school or university training, the Education Promotion Act *(Berufsausbildungsgesetz, Bafög)*, which was codified in 1971, is important.

The Employment Promotion Act of 1969 distinguishes between adaptive *(Anpassungs)*, and career advancement *(Aufstiegs)* continuing training (Streeck et al. 1987: 38). Whereas "adaptive continuing training" is usually short-term, does not lead to standardized examinations, and rarely yields certification

---

18. In 1994 the catalogue of acknowledged professions listed 2,250 rules for further vocational training (BMBW 1996a: 120).

of skills at all, career advancement continuing training is longer and usually leads to a recognized certificate. The best known example here is the master *(Meister)* training and its equivalent in the service sector, the *Fachwirt* training (Sadowski and Decker 1993: 87f; Finegold and Keltner 1997).

Ten states *(Länder)*, including North Rhine-Westphalia and Bremen, also have so-called training leave laws (Bildungs-urlaubsgesetze), which give every employee the right to receive up to five days of paid leave for general training courses per year *(Berichtssystem Weiterbildung VI 1996: 357, referred to hereafter as RSFT, for Report System on Further Training).

There are collective agreements on occupational further training that are relatively vague about the conditions under which an employee has access to certain kinds of training. Bahn-müller et al. (1991) show that even when continuing training questions are addressed in collective agreements,[19] there are problems of implementation and enforcement at the regional and firm levels. In sum, the formal rules for further occupational training are of only minor importance; the system is largely reg-ulated through informal agreements with a diversity of financial arrangements between employers and employees (Sadowski and Decker 1993: 188). Official statements by the government also stress the market orientation and the subsidiary role of the state in continuing training issues in Germany (Sadowski and Decker 1993: 36). The same is true for managers, who strenuously object to any proposed state intervention (Finegold and Keltner 1997).

FORMS AND PROVIDERS

Publicly financed continuing vocational training is mainly designed to reintegrate unemployed people into the labor market. It includes retraining *(Umschulung)* activities as well as continu-ing training courses for people who have already finished initial

---

19. They investigate the enforcement of the collective wage agreement *(Lohn- und Gehaltstarifvertrag)* for North-Württemberg-Northbaden from 1988.

vocational training successfully and need an update of skills (e.g., women after a long period of family leave). This kind of training is part of the so-called "active labor market policy" and is basically financed through contributions to unemployment insurance. There is a trade-off between unemployment benefits and active labor market policy: since the budget of the unemployment insurance is limited, and, in times of high unemployment, revenues drop while the claims for unemployment benefits increase, the funds available for active labor market policy are declining. Not surprisingly, the former head of the Institute for Employment Research (Institut für Arbeitsmarkt- und Berufsforschung), concludes that publicly financed continuing training has only a supplementary function in Germany (Buttler 1994).

Universities are usually not involved in occupational further training, although they provide courses in some professional areas, e.g. for physicians and teachers. Given the overcrowding in German universities that has resulted from large increases in student numbers and government funding cuts, a greater role for universities in this field is not on the agenda. Furthermore, the current regulations set major disincentives for universities, especially the professors, to engage in continuing occupational training (Finegold and Keltner 1997). Universities play a crucial role in providing initial vocational training for future German managers. But even here inappropriate government regulation is seen by company managers as a major hindrance for course innovation, since it results in a lack of involvement of universities in ongoing management development (Finegold and Keltner 1997). *Fachhochschulen* are more vocationally-oriented, education is shorter, and professors usually have some work-experience in the industry, which puts *Fachhochschulen* in a comparatively favorable light with regard to future demands in further training.

The most standardized career advancement training (*Aufstiegsweiterbildung*) is the *Meister* and the technician *(Techniker)* continuing training. The courses are overseen by the Chambers of Industry and Commerce, which also carry out the final examination. The regulations for the crafts *Meister* are very old, but in 1977 the regulations for the increasingly important industry *Meister* were added. Some *Meister* exams can only be taken in specific chamber districts (Streeck et al. 1987: 43). This system guarantees equivalent standards for all masters in a field. Usually courses are taken in the evenings and weekends, and are paid for by the individuals.[20]

Besides the *Meister*, there are several other forms of standardized career advancement training for people in business occupations, like accountants (Sadowski and Decker 1993: 87). People in these fields acquire a so-called *Fachwirtausbildung* or *Fachkaufmannausbildung,* whose conditions are quite similar to those of the *Meisterausbildung.*

The banking sector is very involved in further occupational training issues. One example is the public savings banks *(Sparkassen),* which run an inter-company training system, in which employees are prepared for a standardized examination that leads to the degree *Sparkassenbetriebswirt.* The full-time course lasts seven months, and is generally paid for by the employer. In addition, people can attend the central savings institution academy in Bonn. Graduates from these programs are treated like graduates from universities in the *Sparkassen* sector. The banking sector also runs a banking academy, which can be attended by employees on their own initiative in the evening (and weekends) and leads to an academic degree.

Nevertheless, in 1994 the most important providers for continuing occupational training were firms, accounting for 53 percent of all incidences of further occupational training and 35 percent of the total continuing training days, followed by private training providers with 10 and 19 percent respectively, and chambers with 6 and 9 percent respectively (RSFT 1996: 253).

20. Since 1996 the "Career Advancement Promotion Act" (*Aufstiegsfortbildungsförderungsgesetz, Meister-Bafög)* has been in effect, providing subsidies for fees and tuition as well as loans (see BMBW 1997: 173 for more details).

EMPIRICAL OUTCOMES OF CONTINUING TRAINING

This section will summarize results from empirical studies of German and international further occupational training. There are a large number of studies, each with a different focus and methodology, which makes direct comparisons difficult;[21] the data can thus only show some differences and tendencies, but are not precise accounts of further vocational training practices in different countries. Moreover, all training data are input-oriented and show only the level of time spent and the costs of continuing training activities. They are poor indicators of the "outcome," or performance, achieved, both on the macro and on the micro level (Auer 1992: 28). In fact, we know little about the quality of the training provided or its effectiveness using survey data (Auer 1992: 51). Evaluation of training activities is only available for publicly financed training in Germany.

THE QUANTITY OF CONTINUING OCCUPATIONAL TRAINING[22]

Overall, the estimates of the money spent on occupational further training in Germany per year (including opportunity costs) lie between 101.9 and 120.4 billion Marks in 1994, the last full

---

21. For Germany the most recent large scale studies from a firm perspective are the IW-survey (*Institut der Deutschen Wirtschaft*) with data from 1992 (Weiss 1994) and the European Training survey, initiated through the FORCE program, with data from 1993 (e.g., Grünewald and Moraal 1995). An overview and summary is given yearly by the Berufsbildungs-bericht. In the rest of this chapter, I cite these two surveys as (IW) and (Force), respectively. Smaller studies are documented in Knoll and Knoss (1995), Pawlowsky and Bäumer (1995), Sadowski and Decker (1993), Schömann and Becker (1992) for all groups or mid-level workers, and Keltner and Finegold (1996), who focus on manager training. Pawlowsky and Bäumer (1993) draw on surveys among individuals in longitudinal view. The most recent *Berichtssystem Weiterbildung VI* with data for 1994 (Report System Further Training, RSFT), and Auer (1992) deal with both the firm and the individual perspectives.

22. For more English information on further training in Germany, see Gatter 1997.

year available (RSFT VI 1996: 317). Publicly financed further training (through the Federal Labor Office) amounted to 21 billion Deutsche Marks, semi-public institutions (*Gebietskörperschaften*) spent about 10.3 billion, and individuals spent 45.9 billion (including 36.1 billion estimated opportunity costs for leisure time). According to the two large-scale studies of company-provided training (see Fn. 21), firms spent between 24.7 (Force) and 43.2 (IW) billion Marks.[23] Table 6.1 summarizes these numbers; it includes only real expenditures, not estimates.

Table 6.1   Overview of money spent on continuing training in 1994 (in billion DM)

Individuals	9.8
Public financed (FLO)	21
Firms	24.7*/36.5**
Sum	55.5/67.3

*Force Study (data from 1993)
**IW-Study
Source: RSFT 1996: 317.

This table shows clearly that companies spend much more than any other institution on further training. However, new data show that firms expenses per employee in the old *Länder* dropped from DM 1924 million in 1992 to DM 1670 million in 1995.[24] Training practices differ significantly by sector. The highest amount is spent in the banking and insurance business (e.g. Weiss 1994: 119). Banks for example have pretty similar human resource strategies with a heavy reliance on internal labor markets, whereas

23. This is mainly due to different definitions of "occupational further training" in the two large firm surveys and the reluctance of the Force-Study to use estimated numbers. Weiss also adds an estimated sum of 6.7 billion for the sectors (farming, liberal professions, etc.) not included in the IW-survey.
24. The overall expenses dropped from 36.6 billion to 33.9 billion DM (*Süddeutsche Zeitung* 30 October 1997).

policies in manufacturing are more diverse (Backes-Gellner et al. 1994: 44). According to the Force study, 59 percent of all firms in Germany offered further occupational training. A comparable survey for the United States, the National Employers Survey[25] with data from 1994, indicates that 81 percent of all establishments pay for or provide some type of formal training either on site or at a school or technical institute (EQW 1995: 9). This disparity is confirmed in an international comparisons of labor force survey data, indicating much higher rates of individual participation in formal initial and further training in the US (38 percent) than in Germany and France (27 percent), as shown in Table 6.2.

Table 6.2 Participation rates of employed people in formal initial and further occupational training in the 12 month period preceding the survey

Country	Year	Participation rate
France	1992	27%
United States	1991	38%
Germany	1991	27%

Source: OECD 1995: 160.

According to the RSFT (1996: 44) the participation rates for further vocational training alone was 21 percent in 1991 in Germany and 24 percent in 1994. The rates in the new *Länder* are higher than in the old ones (in 1994: 27 percent compared to 23 percent), where the training mainly consists of publicly financed upskilling or retraining courses instituted as part of the transformation process following unification. Since in France fewer activities are counted as further occupational training in the official statistics and the level of initial training is much lower, we can suppose that the participation rates in all forms of further training are significantly higher than in Germany. Results

25. Administered by the Bureau of Census in collaboration with EQW (National Center on the Educational Quality of the Workforce).

of a matched pair comparison for 1992 in Germany, France, and the United Kingdom confirm this assumption.[26]

Table 6.3   Participation rates of employed people in further training in different countries in 1992

Country	Participation rate
France	28.6 %
Germany	16.2 %
United Kingdom	15.2 %

Source: Backes-Gellner 1996: 266.

In particular, the difference between France and Germany is striking. It shows that continuing occupational training is often used as a substitute for initial vocational training in France. There is a French law according to which every firm has to spend at least 1.5 percent of the total wage bill for further training purposes. In fact, French firms on average have spent more than two percent of their payroll on continuing training since 1983. For larger firms the statutory rate serves more as a minimum; since the law's enactment in 1971 the gap between required and actual expenses has widened (Fischer 1995: 232). But for small firms the legally defined rate is an important yardstick, and induced many of them to engage in further vocational training for the first time (Fischer 1995: 233).

For our purposes, it is not only the overall participation rates that are important, but also the participation rates of different sociodemographic groups and the hours of training (further occupational training volume) that people receive. For Germany, all data show an increase in further training participation and spending over the last 20 years. Younger cohorts start out with a higher level of training and maintain a higher

---

26.   The sample comprises eighty-two companies in Germany, England, France and Luxembourg, for more details see Backes-Gellner et al. 1994 or Backes-Gellner 1996.

level over their working lives than older cohorts (e.g., Schö-mann, Becker 1992 or Pawlowsky and Bäumer 1993, both with longitudinal data). Still, we find some remarkable differences between groups shown in Table 6.4.

Table 6.4   Further occupational training for employed people by selected demographic characteristics in 1994

	Participation rates in %	Training volume (sum is 100%)
Sex		
Men	35	68
Women	31 (24 for part-time)	32
Age		
19-34 years	27	55
35-49 years	29	36
50-64 years	14	10
Occupational Training		
None	5	3
Apprenticeship	21	55
Master	36	12
University degree	43	19

Source: RSFT 1996.

As predicted, participation rates decline significantly for people over fifty years of age. The participation rates for people between the ages of thirty-five and forty-nine years are slightly higher than for the youngest age group. Looking more closely at the volume and the hours spent in continuing occupational training, it becomes even more evident that younger Germans get much more training than older ones. There are also striking differences between people in the new and the old *Länder*; in the former, upskilling is still the indispensable precondition for economic survival in the transformation process (Table 6.5).

Table 6.5 Hours spent by participants in further occupational training in the old and the new German Länder in 1994

	West	East
All interviewed people	117	220
Sex		
Men	131	188
Women	93	251
Age		
19-34 years	157	268
35-49 years	106	200
50-64 years	49	151
Occupational training		
None	61	134
Apprenticeship	131	278
Master	124	169
University degree	92	147
Labor force participation		
Employed	102	131
Not employed	259	490
Employed persons according to firm size		
1-99 employees	120	113
100-999 employees	91	153
> 1000 employees	90	95

Source: RSFT 1996: 73

While the German workforce as a whole receives less further training than in the countries with which Germany competes, women in particular receive less training, since many work part-time and the participation rates of part-time workers in training are much lower than for full-time workers. The long training hours in the east, especially for women, are mainly due to their high rates of participation in publicly financed training for those who would otherwise be unemployed (see Table 6.5).

Another interesting issue is to what extent participation cor-relates with educational attainment. Table 6.4 suggests that access to training is cumulative, since the better the educational back-ground, the higher are participation rates. Looking at the training volume and the training hours we find that people with com-pleted apprenticeships spend by far the most time in further voca-tional training. In 1992 roughly 22 percent of all employed persons in the west who had completed apprenticeships had a higher occupational attainment like a *Meister* or *Techniker* (BMBW 1996: 104). The very time-consuming courses explain the high volume of training for people with completed apprenticeships.[27]

A survey conducted by the Bureau of Labor Statistics in 1995 shows that 69.9 percent of all employed people in the United States received some form of further training in the year preced-ing the survey, part-time workers 56.1 percent, and full-time workers 71.7 percent (BLS 1997: Table 5). Table 6.6 gives infor-mation on participation according to different characteristics.

The results are not completely comparable with the German ones, because in the US only employed people were counted. Moreover most questions were asked for the six-month period pre-ceding the survey. Not surprisingly, the total hours of training are lower than in the German survey. However, we find that the dif-ferences between men and women are much smaller than they are in Germany, and the same is true looking at different age groups.

After this short overview it seems safe to conclude that Ger-many does not lead the field for further vocational training in the advanced industrial countries. While an increasing share of peo-ple invest in their human capital, the main emphasis is still given to initial vocational training provided either through the dual system (apprenticeships), or universities and *Fachhochschulen* for higher positions. When starting a job, newly employed people are usually expected to bring their certificates proving their abil-

---

27. Moreover people with completed apprenticeship get more publicly financed further training than any other group (RSFT 1996: 129).

Table 6.6   Hours of training per employees by selected
demographic characteristics in the US,
May-October 1995

| | Hours of training | | |
	Total	Formal	Informal
All employed*	44.5	13.4	31.1
Sex			
Men	47.6	12.2	35.4
Women	41.5	14.6	26.9
Age			
< 25 years	24.1	2.7	21.4
25-34 years	46.5	14.0	32.5
35-44 years	45.7	15.4	30.3
45-54 years	56.2	17.2	39.0
> 54 years	22.9	5.7	17.1
Establishment size			
50-99 employees	40.1	5.9	52.6
100-499 employees	48.0	13.5	34.5
> 499 employees	42.6	16.6	26.6

*   Employees working in establishments of 50 or more employees.

Source: BLS 1997 Table 4 and Table 8.

ity to handle the tasks. The access to further training in firms
is then mostly regulated through the immediate superior or
another person from the upper levels of the hierarchy. They will
only provide training to people from whom they expect a high
rate of return on the investment. In line with the basic assumptions of human capital theory, this explains the lower participation rates of part-time working women and older employees,
since they are expected to have lower rates of return than younger
persons and full-time employees.

Despite the fact that an increasing percentage of human
resource managers stress the pivotal role of further training for
competitiveness, they do not generally adopt a strategic approach,

as shown by several studies (Knoll and Knoss 1995, Pawlowsky and Bäumer 1995, Weber et al. 1994). Most companies have a highly reactive human resource policy. Skill formation needs are simply the result of new technical or organizational requirements and not of an increasing awareness of human resources as a key factor for the viability of a company.

Another relevant issue is the distribution of costs when creating general and firm-specific skills. My own research based on interviews with human resource managers in German insurance companies found about half of firms are not afraid of employees' quitting after successfully completing further training (Schmähl and Gatter 1994, Gatter and Hartmann 1995); this is confirmed by case studies cited in Sadowski, Decker (1993: 184). The reasons managers give for investing in training focus mainly on the attractiveness of the company to employees, ranging from, "we do a lot for our employees" to "internal career ladders."[28]

Most companies do not attempt to evaluate the effectiveness of further training, nor do they gather relevant data to do so. Thus, one does not know whether further training has any impact on productivity and if the rate of return for younger people and full-time workers is really higher than for other employees.

TRANSPARENCY AND STANDARDIZATION

Several initiatives and projects address the needs to adjust further occupational training to future requirements, in particular seeking solutions to the experience good problem by making training more transparent (see BMBW 1996a: 115ff.) Roughly 58 percent of all people between 19 and 64 in Germany consider themselves sufficiently informed about the further training market (BMBW 1996a: 109). Conversely stated, this means more than 42 percent are not pleased with the transparency of further

---

28. In the study by Knoll and Knoss (1995) the danger of employees' quitting after finishing their training is not acknowledged by more than two of three firms, as most of them have safeguards in the form of implicit or explicit contracts.

training. The lack of a further training system leads to the existence of a huge number of providers, and the opaque market makes it difficult to assess the quality of a single provider or seminar. Thus, a lot of people (especially when they have to pay as well as give up their spare time) are very reluctant to bear these high transaction costs. Several studies assess the quality of information in brochures, and the advice by providers. They show that most of them do not give sufficient information on content, target groups, financial and other conditions (RSFT 1996: 378f).

The standardized career advancement training programs, like the *Meister* or *Fachwirte* courses, seem to overcome the transparency problem, and therefore they lower transaction costs and attract a high share of people to these courses. The certificates serve as credentials and help to enhance mobility. But the courses usually take about two years to complete and concentrate mainly on enhancing *Fachkompetenz* (occupational skills) (BMBW 1996a: 115), which does not fit the redundancy needs of rapidly changing markets (cf. Regini 1997). Furthermore, the revision of outdated curricula needs to undergo a similar process as the curricula for initial vocational training, since the standardized career advancement programs are too inflexible to cope with the rapidly changing environment created by contemporary markets.

To get more transparency and standardization in the market, there are two trends in the quality-management field: the joining of further training suppliers to so-called consortia for quality assurance *(Gütesiegelverbünde)* and certification according to DIN EN ISO 9000 (Kuwan and Waschbüsch 1996: 12). The *Gütesiegel* associations differ considerably in terms of their size and form of organization, but what they usually have in common are functions and goals (Kuwan and Waschbüsch 1996: 13). The main goal of these consortia is to play a signaling role, particularly for companies,[29] by guaranteeing that the

---

29. Private/individual demanders of training do not pay so much attention to this.

association's members adhere to a minimum standard of quality. The point of the program is to create a greater market transparency, which will eventually eliminate low-quality providers (Kuwan and Waschbüsch 1996: 13ff.).

Reasons for certification are mainly the demand of customers for standardization, as well as efficiency gains, through the control of internal procedures (Kuwan and Waschbüsch 1996: 20). The quality definition in the two approaches differs considerably: while the *Gütesiegelverbünde* try to set the same quality standard for all members, certification according to ISO 9000ff. comprises the certification of self-defined criteria for internal processes, but not for products themselves, and therefore does not lead to any standardization of outcomes. Therefore the ISO-approach seems to be less appropriate for further training providers; or at the very least, it does not lower the transaction costs of finding the appropriate course. But as Finegold (1997: 2) points out, the certification process can lead to upskilling in some industry firms. To obtain an ISO-certificate companies have to prove that they have a set of standardized and clearly documented processes for different quality-management areas, and that their employees are able to repeat these process. In this respect, the ISO-certification may at least induce managers to rethink their training practices, and lead to some training for all employees and not only for certain groups. To retain the certificate the firms must pass an audit at least once every three years, which sets incentives for continual skill updating. However, small-scale surveys by Finegold and Wagner (1997) of thirty-six firms in Germany and the US, and Homburg and Becker (1996) of forty firms of different sizes and different industrial sectors in Germany, Austria, and Switzerland suggest the need for skepticism about the benefits of ISO certification. Only 30 percent of the companies noticed an increase in their product quality. It remains to be seen whether "certification euphoria" in Germany leads to more involvement in human capital creation or if it is just one more fashionable management method. According to Kuwan and Waschbüsch (1996: 79f.) the *Gütesiegel*-approach has some shortcomings as well. *Gütesiegelverbünde* can provide some minimum standards, at least on the regional level, but they lack a continual evaluation.

Industrial Relations and Social Security: Germany's Institution of Early Retirement

Industrial relations and social security regulations are not directly connected with the provision of initial or further vocational training. But since they can set strong incentives either for an early exit or for remaining in the workforce, they are of great importance for the expected rates of return on investments in human capital. In Germany, institutions like the pension regulations and the Employment Promotion Act *(Arbeitsförderungsgesetz)* have provided major incentives for early retirement.[30] There is only space here to present some core features of the system on different institutional levels.

The statutory pension system *(Gesetzliche Rentenversicherung)* exists nationwide for most employed people.[31] People pay contributions according to their income. The pension they draw later mainly depends on their former income level and the number of years during which they paid into the system.[32] Hence, the German statutory pension system preserves former income positions

30. Like educational systems, social security regulations structure life courses, but mostly at a later point in an individual's life (Allmendinger and Hinz 1997). For a thorough treatment on the history of the early retirement regulations see Gatter and Hartmann (1995) or Rosenow and Naschold (1994). Abridged English information is given in Schmähl and Gatter (1994) or Naschold et al. (1994). A complete overview would also have to take into account family law, because current institutions set strong incentives for women to exit the labor force after giving birth to children.
31. Above a certain level of income and weekly hours worked. Civil servants have their own pension system which is financed through tax revenues.
32. For some differences with the American pension system, which seems quite similar on first sight, see Hinrichs (1993).

to a high degree. This work-centered system therefore provides a predictable and relatively high level of pensions for people with a long working life (compared to many other countries).

The reference retirement age is sixty-five years, but there are several exemptions from this rule. Up to 1997 it was possible to claim a pension[33] at sixty-three (for long-term employed men) or at sixty (for the unemployed, and most women). People with an occupational disability or a general inability to work are eligible for a pension at any age,[34] if certain minimum conditions regarding contribution payments are met.

In times of high unemployment these rules were adapted to relieve the labor market while not sending older workers into an uncertain autumn of life *(Lebensabend)*. To give an example: those eligible for an occupational disability pension are obliged to work part-time. Because most of these people cannot compete with healthy people in the present labor market, the Federal Constitutional Court *(Bundesverfassungsgericht)* decided that these people can draw a pension designed for people who are unable to work in general. This court ruling replaced property rights set by law and became a very important institution itself.

One governmental attempt to alleviate the unemployment problem was the Early Retirement Act, which was in force from 1984 to 1988. It enabled workers from the age of fifty-eight onwards to withdraw from the labor market and bridged the period until the earliest possible receipt of a retirement pension with payments from their employer. The law had to be implemented at the sectoral level through collective agreements. The negotiated agreements covered only one-third of the potentially eligible workforce, because most of the financial burden had to

33. Without actuarial deductions for the longer period of drawing the pension (longitudinal view).
34. Nota bene, the risk of becoming occupationally or generally disabled before the age of 60, increases disproportionally from the age 50 onwards, reaching a peak between the ages of 55 and 60 (Hoffmann 1993: 314).

be carried by the employers.[35] However, in the sectors covered through collective agreement, about 70 percent of those who were entitled to take early retirement did so. Collective agreements on early retirement were still enforced through the mid-1990s, with the most recent being in the insurance sector.[36]

Cheaper for companies, and therefore more often used, is the pension for the unemployed, in connection with the so-called "59 rule": the maximum period of drawing unemployment insurance benefit has been extended for older people up to two years and eight months. Especially in companies which had to carry out staff cuts, older people were dismissed[37] at the ages of fifty-seven or fifty-eight, and their unemployment insurance benefit was supplemented by the employer. This was a very elegant way of getting rid of older workers in a socially acceptable manner. During the early transition period in the former GDR, several similar institutions were established to alleviate at least some of the huge effects of restructuring.

However, many older workers themselves wanted (and still want) an early exit from the labor force. As Kohli (1985) puts it: in Germany, retirement has become an established period of life, an institution. Codetermination on the sectoral and firm level (dual system of workers representation) played a decisive role in institutionalizing early retirement for older workers. The long-established system of codetermination[38] provided the needed cred-

---

35. The Federal Labor Office gave subsidies when certain conditions were met.
36. In 1995 the collective agreement was prolonged until the end of 1997. The unions were strongly in favor of the agreement, whereas the employers did not want to prolong it because of its high cost. The bargaining result was the prolongation of pre-retirement, but a flexibilization of weekly working hours (downwards and upwards to more than 40 hours) for all employees.
37. Usually, mutual agreements to end the labor contract were signed, because in most sectors the shedding of older workers is nearly impossible, due to dismissal protection for people with longer tenure.
38. It is codified in the "Co-Determination Law" (*Mitbestimmungsgesetz*) from 1976 (for the *Montan*-industries there is an older law from 1951).

ible commitment and trust for the bargaining processes between employers and employees. The "dismissal protection law" in combination with collective agreements in several sectors usually makes it impossible to dismiss older workers. Unions and works councils, who are often in favor of early retirement because of high unemployment rates, used this leverage in negotiations about early retirement to get high severance packages for the older workers.

The first serious governmental attempt to reverse the early retirement trend on social security expenses was the Pension Reform Act of 1992. The main aim of this reform was to enhance the viability of the pension insurance system in anticipation of the demographic changes to come. Thus, the "Pension Reform Act of 1992" introduced a partial pension for elderly people to induce them to postpone retirement and scheduled a rise in the minimum age a person could draw a pension without actuarial deductions[39] from 2001 onwards. Because of serious financial problems due to increasing unemployment rates in Germany, recent legislation moved forward this raising of the age at which one could claim a pension without deductions in 1997, and complemented the highly unsuccessful partial pension scheme by the "Old Age Part-Time Work Law" *(Altersteilzeitgesetz)* which has been in force since August 1996. The partial pension scheme has not been able to stop the trend to an early and abrupt retirement: it still is very complicated (thus, imposed high transaction costs), the minimum age of eligibility is too high, older men are reluctant to work part-time, and so forth (see Oswald et al. 1996: 345, for more details). These new laws will provide a wider range of retirement options by combining part-time work with drawing part of the pension or getting subsidies from the Federal Labor Office (see Bäcker and Naegele 1996).

The codetermination on firm level is strictly regulated in the by the "Workplace Labor Relations Law" *(Betriebsverfassungsgesetz)*.

39. Of 3.6 percent for every year drawing the pension before the age of sixty-five.

In sum, we can conclude that until recently, labor regulations set strong incentives for an early exit from the workforce, and thus correspondingly strong disincentives for human capital investment in older workers. Recent legislation has substantially changed these formal rules (especially retirement regulations).[40] The pull factors from the retirement side have vanished. Someone who wants to take early retirement now has to face severe financial deductions, because it is highly unlikely that companies will completely fill the income gap. The former success of unions and works councils in negotiating high severance payments for their clients could become a severe problem in the future, since many workers now see early retirement (with enough income) as an entitlement due to them for a long work-life. Hence, as already pointed out, institutional change is a slow process, especially when informal rules play a major role in the success of formal ones.

Companies are already making innovative use of the recently changed pre-retirement options. To avoid part-time work of older workers, several sectors[41] reached collective agreements and/or works agreements using the new old-age part-time law in a creative way: officially, older workers between fifty-five and sixty years work half-time, but in reality they will work full-time for 2.5 years and then stop working entirely. Furthermore, most of the agreements subsidize the income of the older workers beyond the statutory level.[42] In the metal sector people are getting 82 percent of their former full net income for all five years. Firms also pay 95

---

40. The necessary reform of the pensions for occupational disabled persons is still under review.
41. E.g., the chemical, the metal, and the banking sectors.
42. The employer is obliged to supplement pay by at least 20 percent of the previous net income and also has to pay the difference in pension insurance contributions between the actual part-time payment and 90 percent of the former level. If an unemployed person or a former apprentice is hired to fill the job, the employer gets reimbursed by the Federal Labor Office.

percent of the contributions to the pension system until the age of sixty. This seems a generous arrangement on first sight, but as pointed out earlier, those who draw pensions from the age of sixty onwards will face severe financial deductions from now on.

Conclusion

Empirical findings suggest that both formal and informal institutions matter a great deal in the process of skill formation. Appropriate and tight regulation in the initial vocational training system sets incentives to provide basic qualifications for a broad range of young people. The institutions of the dual system solve the collective and experience good problems of general skill creation, but they have difficulty coping with rapid technological change. The highly fragmented German further occupational training system, on the other hand, is built in such a way as to be able to cope with rapid change. But because of high transaction costs and the unsolved experience good problem in this unstandardized market, Germany bears the risk of under-investment in future skills and a rising mismatch on the labor market. In addition, the current arrangements for further training produce several types of discrimination that will probably lead to a stronger stratification of the workforce in the future.

German firms seems to be trapped in the vicious circle of short-term and long-term problems: even as Germany continues to face enormous unemployment rates, short-term profit considerations lead to cost-cutting programs for further vocational training in firms. A better labor market integration of older workers and part-time working women is not in sight. The externalization of older workers still seems to be the profit maximizing strategy, but this strategy will worsen the demographic problem, and in turn undermine competitiveness, in the long-run.

The further training efforts in other countries like France, which were established simply because of necessity (to remedy the defects in the initial vocational training system), could become a competitive advantage for these countries in the future (Backes-Gellner 1996: 315). This is not to say that Germany should simply copy the French or any other model of further occupational training. Any successful market intervention has to fit into the institutional context of a country; thus, quite different institutions can serve as functional alternatives in different countries.

For the further training system, there are three major obstacles to optimal performance: the lack of transparency in the further training market, uneven access of different sociodemographic groups to further training, and the quality on offer. These market failures could be the starting-point for regulations which might be based on already existing institutions, particularly on those at the regional level. To enhance the transparency of the further training market, publicly financed local consulting agencies could be established (Mahnkopf and Maier 1991: 243). The main task of these offices would be twofold: first, to give an overview of all measures on offer, and second, to provide advice to individuals or firms to find the right training for their purpose. According to the BMBW (1996a: 122f.) these agencies can already be found in some of the new *Länder*. The existing agencies are targeted more toward diffusing information about publicly financed further vocational training.

To solve the discriminatory effect of the actual access of different groups, it is worth considering giving out vouchers for part-time working people to attend further training courses in their leisure time and to offer child-care facilities. Search costs would decline considerably if the local agencies helped to find the appropriate training measure. This might seem highly speculative, but in the new *Länder* the main customers of these agencies are women. Hence, the combination of vouchers and public agencies could help to lower the entry costs of taking part in further training for groups that face discrimination in the training market. Quality could be improved too, since quality evaluation (e.g., in collaboration with the *Gütesiegelverbünde*) would go along with more transparency, and help to sort out the "lemons" among the further training providers.

Yet successful institutional change also requires the adjustment of informal institutions. A closer investigation of this interplay between different types of institutions and their possible outcomes remains a fruitful area for future research.

Part III

INTERNATIONAL EXPERIMENTS WITH IN-FIRM TRAINING

Chapter 7

INDIVIDUAL CHOICE, COLLECTIVE ACTION, AND THE PROBLEM OF TRAINING REFORM

Insights from France and Eastern Germany[*]

Pepper D. Culpepper

Introduction

This chapter assesses the ongoing reforms of the systems of vocational education and training in France and in eastern Germany. The two cases are geographically separated by the object that unites their training reforms: western Germany. The new institutions and practices of the dual vocational training system constitute just one of the many institutional transfers

* I presented an earlier version of this chapter at the Bosch Seminar on Comparative Public Policy and Institutions at the American Institute for Contemporary German Studies in May 1997. Thanks to Peter Berg, David Finegold, Peter Hall, Steven Silvia, and Karin Wagner for comments that have contributed to improvements in this version.

from western Germany that followed German unification in 1990. The French reform effort, of slightly older vintage, was hardly less overt in taking the celebrated German dual system of apprenticeship training as its benchmark when overhauling the system of in-firm initial training in France, beginning with the reforms of 1984 and culminating in the five-year law of 1993.

The comparison may strike some readers as odd. And in what follows, I shall not try to obscure the different nature of the challenges the two countries face. The reforms converge, though, in a common goal: to establish a system of in-firm training through which private companies in a market environment make substantial investments in the development of skilled labor. Divergent historical and cultural paths of development, different levels of overall investment and industrial moderniza-tion, radically different experiences with the market – all these and more affect the exact challenges facing the reform of voca-tional training in France and in the states of the former German Democratic Republic (Culpepper 1998b). Yet the fact that both tried over the last decade to increase in-firm youth training leading to certifiable skills provides a quasi-experimental design, imperfect though its controls may be, for examining the causal factors that lead to success or failure in institutional reform. In each case, governments have tried to increase the level and quality of in-firm vocational training, but the success of the reforms depended ultimately not on a government's ability to pass laws, but on its ability to convince private actors (compa-nies and workers) to cooperate with each other.

The German Democratic Republic had an established prac-tice of industrial apprenticeship and shared with western Ger-many the historical roots of craft training in Germany. Unlike in France, therefore, the primary challenge was not to convince companies and personnel managers that apprenticeship was an attractive way to train highly skilled workers, nor was it to con-vince youths and their families that apprenticeship training was a viable port of entry to a respected and well-remunerated position in society. These factors, so difficult to put in place in France, were already part of eastern Germany's historical heritage, a heritage not fundamentally altered by the nature of unification.[1] What was radically new in eastern German apprenticeship training after 1989, as in many other aspects of life in eastern Germany, was the primacy of the market in the making of company decisions. As discussed in more detail in Chapter 1, the introduction of the market economy has dramatically reduced industrial employment in the new federal states, and thus, the need for future skilled labor. Many industrial companies in eastern Germany find themselves placed in severe market competition, a situation in which the guarantee of future skilled labor through apprenticeship may seem an unaffordable luxury.

In France, too, the challenge of in-firm training is to convince a large number of firms to invest in the development of the skills of their workforce through initial in-firm training. In-firm training has occupied a much less significant place in the French than in the German political economy: at the end of 1996 the number of students enrolled in purely school-based professional training still exceeded the number of apprentices and the number of qualification contracts combined (Roullin-Lefebvre 1997, DARES 1997). The challenge in France is not therefore to convince companies to invest in a market context, which is nothing new to French companies, but rather to convince them to provide both quantitatively and qualitatively

1. There are important practical differences between training as it existed in the GDR and in the Federal Republic: notable among these are the duration of apprenticeship (three years in FRG, two in GDR); the distribution of apprenticeships among different types of professions (in the GDR, industrial training was dominant and *Handwerk* training practically non-existent); and the fact that schools were located in plants in the GDR, as opposed to being maintained separately by the *Länder* in the Federal Republic. See Wagner (this volume) and Anweiler et al. (1990) for a discussion of some of the differences between East and West German training before the *Wende*.

improved in-firm training (cf. Maurice et al. 1986). Quantitatively, governments introduced three reform waves of initial training (1984, 1987, and 1993) in an effort to increase company use of in-firm training in the battle against France's very high youth unemployment (Chamard 1994); in particular, the government wanted to increase the meager participation of large companies in apprenticeship training.[2] Qualitatively, they hoped to increase the supply of skilled workers with recognized occupational qualifications available to French companies, a constant complaint of those companies over the past two decades (Goasguen 1994). Thus, the goal of recent training reforms in France is to convince firms to move from a model in which apprentices occupy a low social and economic position – and do not develop broad, transferable skills – to a pattern in which the companies take on a greater number of trainees than in the past and train them in broader skills than they have done before.

This fundamental problem is thus similar between the French and the eastern German cases: to convince firms to invest in sustainable, high-level youth training. The western German apprenticeship system overcomes this problem by persuading companies to invest in the provision of these skills and by convincing apprentices to accept low wages in return for learning a craft. If all companies invest in the provision of these skills, then all benefit from the pool of skilled labor that has allowed German firms to capture export markets for high value-added goods by relying on the comparative skill advantage of their work-

---

2. In 1992, for example, 50 percent of the youths in in-firm training contracts in France were employed in companies of fewer than ten employees. Only 6 percent were in firms with more than 500 employees (Chamard 1994: 3). The weak involvement of large companies in apprenticeship training and similar measures is a common observation in comparisons of the French and German training systems: "[t]he major difference between the two systems rests on the fact that large firms [in France] remain markedly at the margins on these measures of training" (Géhin and Méhaut 1993: 50).

force. Yet individual companies in such a system face the temptation not to invest, and instead to free ride on the investments of other companies by poaching their newly minted skilled workers; or they may choose to train only with low-cost methods that abuse the trust of their trainees, who are expecting to learn a craft that increases their long-term returns. If there are no costs to abusing this cooperation, it pays for the individual company to adopt a non-cooperative strategy.

The following analysis relies on interviews conducted with personnel and training managers from companies in France and eastern Germany in 1995-96. The sample used in this chapter includes fifty-two companies in the metal and electronics industries, all of which are members of the chambers of industry and commerce in their respective countries.[3] The information was collected through interviews conducted on plant premises; supplementary information was frequently gathered through follow-up phone calls or documentation supplied by the company. The companies presented in this chapter were drawn from the French regions of Rhône-Alpes, Picardy, and Alsace and from the eastern German states *(Länder)* of Saxony and Saxony-Anhalt. These data allow me to compare training practices of companies in the most important industrial sector in both France and eastern Germany with the benchmark they both seek to emulate: western German apprenticeship training.

In the next section of this chapter, I argue that two features of the political economy – the predominant organization of pro-

---

3. The sample comprises almost entirely single-plant companies. Four of the largest companies (two in eastern Germany, two in France) have multiple plants for which personnel/training decisions are handled by a single office, and for these cases the data refer to total company employment managed through the single office. One French concern I visited was managed as two independent plants, producing for different sectors and with different strategies of human capital development. These two plants are treated as two discrete companies in my sample. Legally separate subsidiaries are not included in the data.

duction and the exit options created by the existing educational system – structure differently the decisions facing companies trying to acquire skilled workers in the two cases. The third section summarizes the criteria of western German training that will be used to assess these reforms. In the fourth and fifth sections of the chapter, I present the firm-level training data to demonstrate how companies of different sizes in eastern Germany and in France are responding to government attempts to change the training system; while there are other meaningful ways to divide the interests of firms, the size-based distinction turns out to be especially relevant in both the political economies discussed here. The sixth section nuances the argument about the importance of exit options and of pre-existing product market strategies by considering the political factors that may help companies that face seemingly difficult collective action problems to overcome them. Finally, in the conclusion I develop the implications of the preceding analysis for policy-makers interested in effecting thoroughgoing reforms of a training system in the advanced industrial countries today.

The Training Game

Because the central conceptual problem of the two training reforms is to convince individual firms to invest in the provision of transferable skills, we need to focus on the interests of these companies to understand their choices with respect to apprenticeship training. While the reforms analyzed here were pushed by governments, the principal peak associations of employers in both countries also actively pursued the greater collective implication of private companies in youth training. Yet what business wants collectively does not always equate to what individual firms want. This axiom of collective action allows us to add a new twist to the analysis of Becker (1964) and others, which posits that the amount of skills provided by the market will likely be socially suboptimal because of problems of poaching and of adverse selection.

I argue that the structure of the stylized collective action problem facing companies differs according to their (historically developed) product market strategies and the educational systems through which they can procure skilled workers.[4] The strategy of "diversified quality production," on which western German companies have built their export competitiveness, demands the broad skills associated with the German dual system (Streeck 1991).[5] To the extent that eastern German companies adopt DQP-style methods of production – which is certainly not an automatic product of German unification – we would *ceteris paribus* expect them to be even more likely to invest in the provision of broad skills for their workforce. French large firms have not, historically, had access to the dual system, and partly as a result have developed strategies based on different skill requirements than those of their German counterparts

4. The two variables are interdependent, in that companies develop product market strategies under the constraint of what skills are provided by the social system in which they are situated. Likewise, the educational system produces future workers, and it therefore faces more or less pressure to respond to the needs of companies in the private economy, which must rely on these workers. A prolonged mismatch between the skills produced by the system and the product market strategies of companies will put pressure on one or the other to change. However, there is no reason to think that the outcome of these pressures will be the most efficient possible combination of the two variables.

5. When talking about systems of production, like DQP, with reference to a whole economy, the claim is obviously not that every firm in the economy organizes production exactly this way. Instead, production regimes are heuristics that underline in ideal-typical form the differences in production between an average group of firms in one society with those in another.

There is an ongoing debate about how the organizational innovations associated with lean production are affected by the traditional dual system model. See Herrigel and Sabel, Chapter 2, and Finegold and Wagner, Chapter 3.

(Maurice et al. 1986, Géhin and Méhaut 1993). As opposed to DQP, large French firms have continued to cling to the tenets of Fordist production and trying to compete on the basis of price (Boyer 1995). Such a system of "flexible mass production" puts the onus of flexible responses to changes in demand less on a broadly skilled manual workforce and more on technicians and mid-level management (Regini 1995, Hancké and Soskice 1996). As we will see in the empirical sections, the historical development of these ideal typical product market strategies has influenced the way that large firms in the two countries respond to the current training reforms.

The other structuring difference between the two countries is the existing system of vocational education and training, and in particular the options for in-firm initial training. The German dual system has only apprenticeship regulations, whose procedures for updating and changing qualifications are standardized. If a company wants to train, it must do so under an approved qualification, and be certified by the relevant chamber (e.g., industry and commerce) to dispense training in that profession. France gives companies the choice of apprenticeship qualifications or professional qualifications through the qualification contract.[6] Each of the French programs has associated procedures for changing qualifications and for ensuring that companies have the capacity to deliver that training. Yet these procedures differ from those in Germany in ways that can be important for training behavior.

To institute a change to the German metal-working professions – either to update an existing certification or to introduce

---

6. French companies can also hire graduates of the (numerically predominant) school-based vocational training system, although they have long expressed their disdain for the school-based track as being far-removed from the needs of production. The existence of the school-based track only exacerbates the problems recounted above by giving companies yet another exit option from high investments devoted to in-firm training contracts.

an entirely new one – requires approval by a board of experts nominated in equal numbers by the IG Metall union and by the peak association of engineering employers, Gesamtmetall.[7] A representative of the employers' association characterizes the typical lines of divergence between the two in the following way: the union wants to ensure maximal breadth of the skill qualification (transferability), whereas the employers want to ensure the maximal specificity of the skill qualification for that particular profession. This process is laborious and is sometimes decried by firms as being too slow to adjust to new methods or areas of production.[8] However, there is no large-scale alternative mode of initial qualification to which individual firms in Germany firms can turn. The work of Albert Hirschman (1970) reminds us that, lacking the realistic possibility of exit from the system, the German company may of course use voice by lobbying for changes in the professions. But the bottom line is, if a firm in Germany wants to train apprentices, it must train them in one of the approved professions.

A French firm that wants to train in an in-firm youth training contract can choose between the apprenticeship and the qualification contracts.[9] An actor that is much less present in the

---

7. The procedure is similar for all other professions, but in the metal professions the degree of autonomy enjoyed by Gesamtmetall and the IG Metall within their respective federations gives them *de facto* the ability to push changes through without the input of the umbrella federations (the BDA and DGB, respectively).

8. Firms are of course free to tailor their courses to *more demanding* standards (e.g., some of the European or TÜV standards). However, they must meet the minimal breadth and depth requirements laid down by the formal training regulations.

9. There are "pay-or-play" taxes for apprenticeship and the alternating contracts in France, which could be interpreted as one way of blocking the use of the exit option. However, the apprenticeship tax and its collection has created much opportunity for graft without efficiently increasing the use of apprenticeship training (Chamard 1994). With respect to the payroll charge that supports alternating training, most large firms exceed the

federalist German system dominates French apprenticeship: the national ministry of education. Attached to the ministry of education are parity boards (CPCs) which bring together sectoral representatives of the professional world *in a consultative role only* (d'Iribarne and Lemaître 1987). Unlike in Germany, these groups have no decision-making power. Thus, whereas in Germany the content of apprenticeship qualifications is determined by negotiations between employers and employees, and consequently depends on debates among experts on the qualifications for the *Facharbeiter*, the role of the professions in French apprenticeship is far more limited (Jobert and Tallard 1995; Interview, Education Ministry). The dominant voice in French apprenticeship is an education ministry which, historically, has been more concerned with the functions of the general education of French citizens than with their training as skilled workers.

The lack of real power accorded to the French social partners in decision-making about apprenticeship was one of the factors that led to the development of the youth *alternance* contracts in the early 1980s, most notably the qualification contract (*contrat de qualification*, or CQ). In the metal and electronics sector, the definition of the content of the qualifications awarded at the end of the process, the CQPM (*certificat de qualification professionnelle de la métallurgie*), is dominated from start to finish by the metal employers' association, the UIMM.[10] The CQPM qualifications

---

minimum with their continuing training budget in any case, and so are not affected by it; many small firms do not meet the minimum and prefer to pay rather than to train (Bertrand 1996: 27). These taxes are not a credible constraint on firm training behavior, and the apprenticeship tax certainly does not prohibit firms from using the exit option of the CQ.

10. CQ refers to the general qualification contract, which is available to all French industries; CQPM refers to the certifications awarded at the end of the CQ in the metal-working industry. There are three possible ways of determining a validation of training received by means of a qualification contract. Above I discuss only the method widely used in the metal and electronics branch, as that is the relevant one for this chapter. See Charraud (1995) for a comparative discussion of the three approaches.

are designed by companies and technical experts associated with the UIMM, sometimes in (informal) consultation with local representatives of the educational ministry. There is no set duration to the CQPM; it may last from six months to two years. In theory, the CQPM must be ratified by a collective agreement signed by at least one of the representative unions, but "in practice this negotiation is not systematically understood by all the sectors as a procedure to be realized simultaneously with the construction of the *référent* [qualification]. This [delay of the approval by collective agreement] can sometimes *take up to several years*" (Charraud 1995: 124; emphasis added). Rather than being a product of arduous negotiations between the experts of the unions and the employers' associations, the CQPM is usually a product of experts primarily associated with the employers, which is only later presented to the unions for ratification.

The CQ system has proved to be more amenable to control by the French social partners, and is obviously much closer to the "economic world" than is the apprenticeship system, dominated by the French education ministry. It also confers on firms with good access to the employers' association a flexibility and rapidity of innovation in qualifications that is absent from the German system. However, the balance of power between employers and unions in the definition of the CQPM is quite likely to result in a firm-specific training qualification, without a much wider transferability of those skills (cf. Charraud et al. 1996).[11] The existence of CQs thus gives some French firms a legitimate, credible exit option from apprenticeship when considering the possibilities for youth in-firm training.

To summarize this difference, recall Becker's distinction between general and firm-specific human capital (1964): the German system of apprenticeship combines these characteris-

---

11. For this reason, some firms in my French sample reported that the use of qualification contracts was distrusted by their workforce, seen as a source for replacing workers rather than for legitimately training future workers.

tics in a skilled-worker qualification, such that firms must invest in some of the costs of general training in order to get the specific qualifications they need; in France, the twin system of in-firm youth training contracts does not marry the relevance of qualifications (for employers) with the breadth of skills acquired (by the trainees).

These differences have direct implications for the training decisions facing individual companies. If we take an "average" French industrial company, the odds are that the company has aimed itself at product market niches where a "flexibly Fordist" production strategy will be competitive. If we assume that the company is using increasingly sophisticated machinery, and so has greater technical needs than in the past, or that the company is implementing more team-based production methods, thereby calling for a higher "social competence" of the worker than in the past, then the company may be pushing the employers' association to increase the availability of highly skilled workers. However, this does not automatically imply that the company will itself utilize the new training measures, which are actively supported by its own association. The company may have a political interest in improving the general supply of skilled workers, but it will not automatically train young people using the new system if doing so would not be in line with the immediate interests of the company.

If the arguments I have made in this section are right, then the collective action problem of training will be more difficult to solve in France than in eastern Germany.[12] However, under-

---

12. Alternatively, we could say that the game facing German companies is more likely to resemble an assurance game – in which the highest individual and social payoffs accrue to cooperation – whereas the game facing French companies looks more like a prisoner's dilemma, in which social and individual rationality do not coincide (cf. Heckathorn 1996).

   But the argument laid out in this section is only valid to the extent that eastern German companies adopt diversified quality production methods *and* insofar as the rigidity of the dual system constrains employers

standing the interests of firms represents only the first step in explaining the outcome of training reforms in the two countries. Training reforms are political projects, and the outcome of such reforms – which require the cooperation of private actors with each other – cannot be inferred solely from the distribution of interests among those actors. The interest distribution of firms only yields a prediction about the difficulty of reform; to explain success or failure in these reforms, we have to take into account two political actors: employers' associations and governments (Culpepper 1998a). The distribution of interests relative to high-skill training only tells us something about the "raw material" these political actors have to work with. Political actors that face an adverse distribution of interests are, *ceteris paribus*, less likely to be able to facilitate successful transition to a high-skill equilibrium; but failure is not inevitable in the face of such an adverse interest distribution. The theoretical purpose of this chapter is to illuminate that the organization of production and the exit options available through the existing educational system are variables that allow us to better understand the interest distribution of firms with respect to high-skill training. But the argument made here raises two empirical questions: first, do eastern German firms indeed benefit from such a favorable distribution of interests? And second, has the more favorable distribution of interests led to greater progress on the road to high skill than in France? To answer these questions, we need to establish a metric of success, and it is to that task that I turn now.

---

from pursuing alternative methods of finding skilled workers. Having a labor market flooded with lots of skilled workers made redundant by the closing of their old companies would certainly provide one way to get around the latter problem, and the propensity to follow a DQP profile is not automatically one that will be chosen by eastern German companies. These are empirical questions, and we return to them below.

High Skill Training as a Measurement Problem[13]

I take as central to the success of reform of both systems the key characteristic of the dual system in the former West Germany: that firms themselves are willing to bear a significant share of the costs of training. Methodologically, it is quite difficult to assess the net investment that employers make in training, but scholars have made fairly sophisticated estimates of training costs and benefits in western Germany. Two of the results of this research are especially relevant for the problem of measurement in assessing training reforms: first, that the net costs to the company of training in the crafts sector are negligible; and second, that small companies on average invest a much lower amount per trainee than do large firms (see von Bardeleben et al. 1995 and Wagner, Chapter 1, for a more complete discussion). Since craft (*Handwerk*) firms are on average smaller than industrial (IHK) firms, there is a great deal of multicollinearity between the effects of firm size and the effects of being an industry or crafts firm.[14] While the exact contributions of the two factors remain unclear, both seem to make a significant difference to the net costs of training to firms.

In effect, as argued in Soskice (1994), there are two sectors in the German training system: one comprising craft firms and one made up of industrial firms.[15] For many craft firms there is no reason to worry about losing money by investing in the training of a worker who then absconds with her newly acquired skills to a competing firm; the net investment of the firm is often

13. This section draws on Culpepper (1996b and 1998b).
14. IHK is the abbreviation for the German chambers of industry and commerce, *Industrie- und Handelskammern*.
15. David Soskice has influenced my thinking on this point, and the above paragraph relies largely on the account developed in Soskice 1994. In the real world, there is obviously a much less clean bifurcation of types of firm training: there are small firms in the *Handwerk* sector where training is expensive and thorough and larger industrial firms where the level of training is quite low.

very close to zero. Industrial firms pay a lot more per apprentice than do craft firms, and it is logical that they will therefore maintain a lower proportion of apprentices than will the latter; the data in Table 1-9 (in Chapter 1) provide empirical confirmation of this logic. Industrial firms will also be likely to retain a much higher percentage of those they train. They want to hire almost all the trainees in whom they have invested, and they do not want to make this substantial investment in someone whom they are not planning to hire. *Handwerk* firms, on the other hand, lose little if anything in hiring apprentices; they will therefore maintain higher ratios of apprentices in relation to their total employment than will the industrial firms, and will have lower rates of post-apprenticeship retention.

It is relatively unproblematic for a government to implement a new system of training regulations when that system costs firms very little. The problems of cooperation associated with the wholesale reform of a training system will be most severe for the industrial firms that have to invest heavily in the development of their workforce, but these investments can also be the most fruitful. It is in the training patterns of industrial firms that we can observe the ideal-typical game in which the firm has to be willing to make the uncovered investment in the training of a skilled worker in order for both to reap the payoff of the "high-skill equilibrium."[16]

I use two measures to assess the degree to which eastern German and French training practices approximate the stylized model of western German training: the ratio of apprentices to the

16. Because industrial company data are those most important for trying to establish that firms are investing in in-firm initial training, I concentrated on firms in this sector in structuring the comparison between France and eastern Germany. However, my firm sample in Germany, east and west, did include several *Handwerk* companies, whose training practices were very much in line with the two-sector discussion presented above. This chapter presents data only from firms currently belonging to the chambers of industry and commerce in France and in eastern Germany.

total workforce and the rate of retention of apprentices after their training. In western Germany, the ratio considered by firms and by training experts in the metal and electronics industry as necessary to maintain the level of skilled workers is about six percent. That is, on average these firms need to train six apprentices per 100 total skilled workers to fill the gaps left by skilled workers moving on (to other firms), moving up (to management positions), or moving out (to retirement).[17] The 6 percent figure is obviously approximate, so I use a margin of error of ± 2 percent in defining the target range (4-8 percent) in which I classify training in the metal industries in eastern Germany as conforming to western German training patterns. Those firms training above this level, unless they are growing at a very rapid rate, are training more workers than they will need to replace their workforce; those training below this level are shrinking or are not investing at a sufficiently high level to be able to replace the skilled workers lost to natural attrition. Either case represents a divergence of training patterns from those which maintain the dual system in western Germany. Because it is widely available and easy to calculate, this ratio represents the best single measure of training practices in companies in the metal and electronics industries.

17. This figure was cited to me by several people familiar with training in the German metal and electronics industry (in the employers' associations, in the chambers of industry and trade, and in firms themselves). The former head of training for the French metal employers says the association would eventually like to see a ratio of apprentices/workforce of 4-5 percent, indicating that the German target range corresponds to the goals of French employers for high-level training.

In Chapter 1, Wagner presents data from firms in all sectors, which show that the average training ratio for western German companies fell from 7.0 percent in 1990 to 5.5 percent in 1995. Her data confirm moreover that larger firms maintain lower training ratios than smaller firms, as expected from the two-sector model. While the data are not limited to the metal and electronics sector, the figures lend further credence to the training range of 4-8 percent as being a reliable indicator of the training practices of the (West) German model.

Does France aspire to having its firms perform in the same range? Certainly the French government has encouraged its companies to mimic the use of in-company training contracts in western Germany. Yet French companies are also able to rely on general educational institutions and a further training system that has advantages over the German institutions (Regini 1995, 1997). We can expect that French companies will continue to rely on this comparative advantage by hiring more highly skilled graduates of the general technical education system than do German companies, even as they increase the use of in-firm training contracts – or in many cases, they will try to combine the two (e.g., by developing higher level apprenticeship contracts). Is it reasonable to use the western German standard to assess the training practices of French companies? It would seem so: in an interview with the author, the former head of training for the French metal employers said the association would eventually like to see a ratio of apprentices/workforce of between 4 and 5 percent, slightly below that enunciated in western Germany. If that is so, then the equivalent target range of French metal companies should be ± 2 percent around 4.5 percent: so the target range I use for French companies is 2.5 percent-6.5 percent, based on the statements of their own representative.

Do these two different target ranges capture the same, or analogous, phenomena? If the baseline is to be the idealized western German practice of high investment per trainee, it is helpful to adduce an additional criterion for the French companies, which should not vary from the western German standard. This criterion – the retention rate – also has its basis in the presumed investment of companies in the training of their apprentices. Companies that invest a lot in apprenticeship training want to secure the return on their investment by hiring the apprentice after training. As suggested by the differential training costs of large and small companies, the retention rate of western German small firms is much lower than that of larger firms, in which the firm invests significantly more in training per worker: the retention rate of all western German firms with less than fifty workers is around .62, while the retention rate of firms having more than 500 workers is about .85 (Büchtemann 1989 cited in Soskice 1994: 37).[18] More recent (1995) data on western German companies from an IAB panel show an average retention rate across all industrial firms of .68 (Pfeiffer 1997: 15).[19] Rates of post-apprenticeship retention offer a second good measure of firm investment in youth training, and I take the .68 figure as a benchmark retention rate characteristic of western Germany. I am thus able to use this retention rate as a second indicator of firm investment in trainees in the French case. French apprenticeship ratios may be lower, because of the greater relative role of the two-year technical college track (*bac* + 2), but there is no reason that French companies should retain fewer of those trainees they do train through in-firm contracts if they have incorporated in-firm training contracts as an enduring part of their strategies of human capital development.

18. The data from Büchtemann are somewhat dated, but I have not found more recent figures on retention rates for firms in different size categories. Results of a large IAB panel survey of companies in 1995 confirm that the retention rate continues to increase with firm size, without giving actual numbers (Pfeiffer 1997: 15). Thus the trend observed in Büchtemann's data appears to hold true today.

    The retention rate refers only to the period immediately following the successful completion of the apprenticeship and does not imply that skilled workers in Germany never move from their original training company, or that such immobility is a prerequisite of a high-skill training equilibrium. Harhoff and Kane (1996: 12) present data from 1992 showing that, even in western German industrial firms with more than 1000 workers, "50 percent of those completing apprenticeships leave the firm where they were trained within 5 years." Successful establishment of the high-skill equilibrium in fact depends on companies being able to draw on deep occupational labor markets to replace their skilled workers who occasionally leave the company; but the predominant track of training must be apprenticeship.

19. Retention rate is the percentage of apprentices hired into a contract after successful (passing) completion of their apprenticeship exams.

The problem with using retention as a measure for eastern Germany is that if no apprentices finished in the last year, there is no retention rate. A large number of eastern German companies, which had only very recently started training again when I conducted my interviews in 1995-96, had no data on retention. Moreover, many of the eastern German companies that did train during the early 1990s allowed their current apprentices to finish their training, in spite of large reductions in other parts of their workforce that reduced the availability of jobs for the apprentices after their training. Thus, some of the retention data that is available for 1995 reflects the decimation of employment several years earlier.

In the next two sections I use these criteria to analyze the training behavior of individual firms, with the objective of understanding where progress is being made in the French and eastern German political economies in their attempted moves to a high-skill equilibrium. The criteria are imperfect indicators of high-skill training, but they comprise a useful standard that can discipline the comparison I make among firms in different contexts. I supplement these data on apprenticeship ratio and retention rate with detailed information gathered from interviews with company representatives, which provide an additional window into firm decision-making relative to youth training. The evidence I have gathered suggests that the training policies of firms in similar size-categories in the two political economies share some common features, and so the next two sections present the empirical material relevant to firms according to company size. The world looks similar to firms of different sizes, but it is nevertheless true that some of the most interesting variation in my sample is observed between firms of similar sizes; this is notably true of small French firms and medium-sized eastern German firms. To understand the dynamics of a training reform aimed at moving a political economy to a high-skill equilibrium, I need to be able to explain both the commonalities within size categories and this variation; it is to this task that I turn now.

Eastern Germany: Large Firms in the Lead, Subsidies in the *Mittelstand*

The standards of the dual system have been transferred inflexibly to the new federal states of eastern Germany. The evidence from my sample of twenty-three industrial companies in eastern Germany demonstrates that how company training practices have responded to these changes differs according the size of the firm in question. The rigidity and breadth of the qualifications associated with the dual system presents many companies with challenges in using the apprenticeship system to meet their needs. Large companies, relying on their ownership links to parent corporations in western Germany, have led the push toward a high-skill equilibrium in eastern Germany. Companies in the *Mittelstand* depend on subsidies to underwrite their training activities, as they find the breadth of demands imposed by the training regulations in the metal and electronics industry to be a heavy burden. The small companies, too, feel the pinch of these regulations; because of their relative lack of resources, they are the ones least likely to be able to take on apprentices and train them to western German standards.[20]

---

20. No one would disagree that a firm with 2000 employees operates on a very different scale than one with 75 employees, but the problem with size categories is how to establish the boundaries between them. At the margins, conceptual categories depend on prior theoretical considerations, and my size categories in this chapter correspond roughly to my perceptions of the character of "bigness" in a company. The point is mostly presentational, and I present enough of the data that skeptical readers will be able to consider how, if at all, a different choice of size categories would affect the evidence. I use the same categories for both political economies: large firms are those employing 500 or more people; medium-sized firms are those with employment between 150 and 500 people; and small firms are all those having 150 or fewer employees. When I refer to the eastern German *Mittelstand*, I mean only medium-sized companies, not small companies.

Large Firms

The five companies in my sample with more than 500 employees all maintain a ratio of apprentices to the total workforce well above the floor of the western German target range for sustainable training (see Table 7.1). One of the companies actually trains above the western German target range, with an apprenticeship/ employment proportion of 12 percent (company LG5 in Table 7.1). This company is part of a well-known western German conglomerate that is one of the paragons of virtuous dual training in the west. Between 1992 and 1995, after calculating its own 'need' for apprentices, the company hired 100 *extra* apprentices (that is, above the calculated need for replacing their skilled workers) per year in its eastern German plants, because of the lack of in-firm training places available to eastern German youth.[21] Without these extra (politically motivated) places, then, this firm would also be training in the target range.

The three largest firms in the eastern German sample train for different markets – engineering, consumer electronics, machinery – but all train and retain their apprentices at high levels. As with company LG5, another member of this elite group (LG2) also said that it had taken on extra apprentices in 1992 at the behest of the local IHK, when the crisis of the local labor market was particularly acute. As a result, the firm only retained 69 percent of its trainees in 1995 (when those who entered in 1992 finished), although all passed the final tests. However, a company representative noted that this outcome was unusual, saying the company normally retained all its trainees who had finished, and that the company tried not to take on more

---

21. As one of the most prominent German corporations, it is safe to conclude that the company faced very intense political pressure to take extra apprentices in the gutted eastern German youth labor market. The company certainly derives a public relations windfall from the extra training, and it makes this extra commitment very public in company literature about its training program.

Table 7-1   Eastern German firms, employment>=500

Firm	Training ratio	Ownership
LG1	7.0%	th
LG2	4.6%	w
LG3	5.4%	w
LG4	8.0%	w
LG5	12.0%	w
AVG	7.4%	

Ownership key for both eastern German and French tables:

w: owned by a western German firm or conglomerate;
th: owned by the Treuhand's successor organization;
c: owned by a non-German firm or conglomerate;
i: independently owned eastern German firm or French firm;
h: a former Handwerk cooperative, with cooperative private ownership.

Notes: All companies are members of the chambers of industry and commerce. For eastern German firms, the training ratio equals apprentices as a proportion of total employment. For French firms, the training ratio equals the sum of youth with apprenticeship or qualification contracts as a proportion of total employment. Firms are sorted by ownership category.

Source: interviews conducted in 1995 and 1996 in France and Germany.

apprentices than it would need.[22] For these three companies, apprenticeship training is an investment in future skilled workers, and only in exceptional cases are trainees who pass the final exam of the IHK not retained. In cases where the companies do train beyond their own projected skills needs, it is as a political action to respond to weaknesses in the local labor market.

Moreover, all three of these companies train in partnership with smaller companies that lack the machinery and/or personnel to train their own apprentices according to the broad requirements of the IHK training regulations. None receives subsidy support for its own training program, nor does any of the

22.   The local IHK representative in fact lamented that company LG2, which has a high profile in its local economy, did not regularly train above need.

three receive direct public support to participate in partnership training schemes (although they are reimbursed for administrative costs).[23] These three companies, owned by western German conglomerates, are model citizens of the new market world of eastern German training.

The other two large firms, which also train in the target range, both claim to be training at least somewhat beyond their need for future skilled labor. Both are involved in steel production, although with different levels of product differentiation. One of these companies (LG4) retained only 64 percent of its finishing apprentices in 1995, and the chief of apprenticeship there noted that training slightly above need increases pressure on apprentices to work hard, since all are not likely to be hired. What is interesting about this company, in comparison with the French firms examined below, is that apprenticeship nevertheless remains the overwhelming qualification path in the firm: 82 percent of the people working in the firm received their apprenticeship training there. Even for an eastern German firm not at the leading edge of industrial technology, apprenticeship is the dominant mode of skill acquisition.

The other steel firm (LG1), which is the only one not owned by a western German parent corporation, was still owned by the successor to the *Treuhand* in 1995. This company was in fact training far above its own future need for workers and was doing so only because its training was subsidized and encouraged by the *Treuhand*. It hired none of its apprentices who finished their training in 1995 and voiced no plans to retain any of its younger apprentices when they finished their training. Anticipating further lay-offs in order to make the company an attractive privatization candidate, the appearance of company LG1 in the

---

23. Large companies were eligible for a one-time subsidy program in 1993 aimed at modernizing their training facilities. This modernization subsidy increased the attractiveness of large firms as poles around which training partnerships with smaller firms could be constructed (Culpepper 1998a and 1998b).

target range is a spurious reading on the high-investment metric: the firm is neither investing itself in the training of apprentices nor planning to use them as future workers.

The headline finding in this size category is that large firms in the eastern German sample that are owned by western German corporations do in fact train at levels associated with the high-skill equilibrium. Ownership by a western German company may entail certain attributes, which make these firms more likely than others to train. As argued by Carlin and Mayer (1995), the collateral and reputational effects that east German firms gain by having western ownership structure can greatly ease their access to long-term finance. The importance of such access to finance would certainly conform to arguments about the importance of long-term finance in sustaining the "high-skill equilibrium" (Soskice 1990b, 1994, Finegold and Soskice 1988). Of equal significance may be the access of these companies to the rich internal networks of information exchange of the large western German conglomerates; these networks are a resource for eastern German managers who may be skeptical of western German training practices, but who can draw on these informational resources both to increase their knowledge of the system and to increase their confidence in its functioning. The relative roles of these two factors in explaining the link of western German ownership to virtuous training practices are difficult to disentangle, given the limits of this evidence; clearly, though, the strong association between ownership and high-skill training merits further study.

Medium-Sized Firms

Eight of the ten companies in the sample with between 150 and 500 employees receive subsidies to train apprentices. Despite this aid, these companies still maintain a lower training ratio than large firms in eastern Germany. As it turns out, some subsidies seem better able than others to respond to the needs of firms in this size bracket that want to offer apprenticeships. Direct subsidies, though, are anathema to the principle of firm responsibility for the in-firm costs of training that is dominant in the west, and their widespread use in eastern Germany could potentially dilute the extent to which firms invest in the development of human capital through apprenticeship. I return to this theme below.

Table 7.2 demonstrates that only one of the seven privately-owned *Mittelstand* companies is training in the western German target range (MG9).[24] For two more, 1995 was the first year in which they had begun training again since the *Wende*. If they reach a full complement of apprentices (that is, having trainees in the first through fourth years) – and both planned to take on new trainees in the upcoming years – they will be at or even above the target western German range. Two firms, which were already training below the target range, planned to further reduce or phase out apprenticeship entirely. Representatives of one of these companies, now owned by a British corporation, claimed that the management of the company had decided that apprenticeship no longer fit the skill production strategy of the firm. The other, smaller company was owned by a western German firm, and was located in a labor market characterized by unusually high official unemployment (over 20 percent). This company reported that it found sufficient skilled workers on the local labor market, because so many trained people in the metal professions were unemployed (Culpepper 1996b).[25]

24. Company MG10 in Table 7-2 has a training ratio of 46.5 percent, meaning that almost one of two employees of this company is an apprentice. This bizarre case is heavily subsidized, and the situation results from the break-up of a much larger former *Kombinat* into several different companies. The one company depicted here took on all the former apprentices still under contract at the old *Kombinat* and received direct EU and state government to support the cost of this training until these apprentices finish their training. Since the case is so unusual, I exclude it from the average calculated for the rest of the companies in this size range.

25. In the two years prior to the interview in the fall of 1995, this firm had hired forty workers directly off the labor market but only retained three

Table 7.2 Eastern German firms, employment > 150 and < 500

Firm	Training ratio	Ownership
MG1	2.3%	th
MG2	14.0%	th
MG3	14.0%	th
MG4	2.2%	c
MG5	1.5%	w
MG6	1.6%	w
MG7	2.2%	w
MG8	2.9%	w
MG9	6.2%	w
MG10	46.5%	i
AVG*	5.2%	

* This average excludes MG10,which has an abnormally high training ratio. The situation results from the break-up of a much larger former *Kombinat* into several different companies; company MG10 took on all the former apprentices still under contract at all the companies of the old *Kombinat* and lobbied for direct EU and regional aid to support the cost of this training.

Turning to the publicly-owned companies, the high training ratios of two of the three *Treuhand* firms are eye-catching (MG2 and MG3). Company MG2 received from the successor to the *Treuhand* 25,000 DM per apprentice per year for more than half of its apprentices (guaranteed for three years). This aid, which is by far the most generous subsidy of which I am aware for in-firm apprenticeship training in eastern Germany, is used to finance the hiring of apprentices beyond the "need" of the company – a need that, given the uncertainty of the company's ownership status, is currently difficult to estimate. The second firm training at an excess level (by western German standards) claimed to be training to need and had not therefore taken the available aid for extra places; this company had retained 78 percent of those

of its own apprentices. A large industrial *Kombinat* in the area closed down in 1994, accounting for much of the glut on the labor market.

apprentices who finished their training in 1995.[26] Knowledge of these subsidies is not widespread; in fact, the personnel chief at the third *Treuhand* firm in the size range (MG1) claimed to have no knowledge of the existence of *Treuhand* aid, lamenting the firm's inability to train more. Because the future ownership situation of these firms was unclear at the time of interview, my interlocutors at the companies did not portray this subsidized training as part of any long-term strategy to guarantee future skilled labor.

Although the federal government refuses to provide direct subsidies for in-firm training places,[27] governments in the new *Länder*, regardless of their political complexion, have not felt constrained by this principle. All five of the new *Land* governments and that of Berlin have developed subsidy programs for in-firm training places: in 1995, almost 60,000 in-firm apprenticeship places in eastern Germany – which is more than half the total in-firm places in the new federal states – were supported by some of this public money (BMBW 1996: 6). Yet devoting all that money to in-firm training has not led to good results everywhere: many firms continue to train not at all or at levels below those characteristic of the west. The results presented in this section suggest that only privately owned *Mittelstand* firms in Saxony – not *Treuhand* firms, and not *Mittelstand* firms in Saxony-Anhalt – have used subsidies to begin training at levels consistent with the high-skill equilibrium in western Germany.

The reason lies in the different design of subsidies in Saxony (for a fuller discussion of the Saxon policy and its development,

26. While this firm took no *Treuhand* aid, it had been able to get 170,000 DM in subsidies from the state government of Saxony-Anhalt for "equipment," subsidies which are tied to the number of trainees. This works out to over 6000 DM per apprentice trained.

27. The *Treuhand* aid described above could be construed as an exception to the policy of the federal government not to pay directly for the costs of in-firm training. Leaving aside the important technicality the THA and its successors are independent agencies, aid funneled through the THA is opaque and not easily monitored by the federal government.

see Culpepper 1996a and 1998a). The Saxon government in 1995 introduced a program for sponsoring training alliances among companies that lack the "organizational and technical prerequisites" necessary to hire an apprentice in a so-called *Ausbildungsverbund* (SSWA 1995).[28] This policy recognizes that the broad standards set by German training regulations, particularly in the first year of an apprenticeship in the metal professions, require access to machinery that many smaller companies do not possess. While in the states of western Germany, many IHKs provide out-of-firm training centers that give smaller firms access to a broader range of machinery than they themselves possess, such a network of out-of-firm technical centers has not yet developed fully in eastern Germany. The *Verbund* mimics this function by giving companies in the *Mittelstand* access to the machinery and use of other (larger) company trainers that can help them to fulfill those IHK requirements. In so doing, the policy not only allows these firms to meet these material requirements; it also establishes information linkages between these and other training companies, information that gives them more confidence that they can use the training system effectively and that provides them with demonstration-effects of the benefits of training at other companies.

The amount of money given by the subsidy does not explain the success of the *Verbund* program. The aid supplied by the program is certainly generous, but it is equal to less than one-sixth of the amount given to the THA firm discussed above (MG2 in Table 7.2). Likewise, the government of Saxony-Anhalt spends more per capita on the subsidization of apprenticeship, and subsidizes more places per capita, than does the Saxon government

28. The program aims to help the smaller companies that are most likely to need help to be able to meet the requirements of German training regulations, and it thus limits aid to companies with less than 500 employees. Larger companies can participate as the training center for the partnership, but they are only reimbursed for the organizational costs entailed in this role.

(BMBW 1997: 226). Rather than depending on the amount of the subsidy, the success of the *Verbund* appears to lie partly in the fact that it lowers the barriers confronting smaller firms wanting to train apprentices without exempting them from the rigorous breadth of the skill requirements demanded by the training regulations of the dual system.[29] I return below to the question of why the *Verbund* policy in Saxony seems to have accomplished the goal particularly effectively.

It remains to be seen whether the subsidies given to eastern German companies will indeed be withdrawn as the economic situation there improves, or whether instead a mentality of subsidy-dependence is developing. The dependence of companies in the eastern German *Mittelstand* on subsidies to support apprenticeship represents a sharp contrast with western German practice and a break with the foundation of the dual system: company responsibility for the costs of in-firm training. Among these subsidies, though, the *Verbund* policy of Saxony alone had spurred companies in my sample to begin training in a manner consistent with western German training practice.

Small Firms

The bleakness of the apprenticeship market in eastern Germany is especially apparent in Table 7.3, which shows the situation of firms in my sample having 150 employees or fewer. Only one-fifth of these companies are training apprentices at all. The obstacles that hinder firms in the *Mittelstand* from training are more daunting still to small industrial companies in the new federal states of eastern Germany. The non-training small firms cite two principal reasons for not training apprentices. First, five of six report an abundant supply of the skills they need on the external labor market as the reason they chose not to train

29. A BiBB survey finds that one-third of companies currently training across eastern Germany name training in a *Verbund* as a condition that would allow them to increase their level of training (BMBW 1996a: 10).

apprentices. Second, three of the six cited lack of a qualified trainer, or inability to spare a worker to supervise an apprentice, as the reason they had not trained.[30] Moreover, all answered that there was no subsidy program which could convince them to train, suggesting that cost is not the principal obstacle to training for firms in this size range.

Table 7.3   Eastern German firms, employment < = 150

Firm	Training ratio	Ownership
SG1	15.1%	h
SG2	0.0%	th
SG3	0.0%	i
SG4	0.0%	i
SG5	0.0%	i
SG6	1.6%	c
SG7	0.0%	w
SG8	0.0%	w
AVG	2.1%	

The two exceptional cases in this size bracket – firms that do train – underscore the probable inability of subsidies to solve the problems of eastern German small firms: neither of these companies receives any subsidies to train apprentices. The one company (SG1) that maintains a high ratio of apprentices/workers (over fifteen percent) in 1995 retained none of its trainees. This firm, which in the GDR fell under the *Handwerk* property law,

30. In an earlier, larger survey of non-training firms in the new federal states, von Bardeleben (1993: 49) found availability of skilled labor as the most frequently cited reason for not training, chosen by one-third of firms. In a later round of the panel (1993-94), the non-training companies citing easy supply of skilled labor was cut in half, named by only 17 percent as their ground for not training (von Bardeleben 1995: 84-85). These findings are consistent with the proposition that the number of skilled or easily trainable workers has dropped significantly since unification, and that therefore firms demanding skilled workers in eastern Germany will find it increasingly difficult to meet their future personnel requirements without training their own workers. Only time will tell if this hypothesis is accurate.

conforms more closely to the artisanal model discussed earlier, in which firms train at a higher proportion of workforce, retain a much lower proportion of their trainees, and have very low or zero net training costs.[31] The second training company among the small firms was growing and had invested substantially in the development of new plant. Owned by an international parent company and producing goods for export to the advanced industrial countries, the only reason this company's training does not land in the target range is, ironically, because it has been unable to find the qualified apprentices it seeks.[32] This company paradoxically behaves more like the large companies in the sample, with its ownership links to a parent company permitting substantial investment in new machinery; difficulties in attracting skilled labor also characterize the large eastern German companies. While an attractive model, this company has little in common with the other eastern German small firms.

Surveys by the German Federal Institute for Vocational Training, while not specific to the metal and electronics industry, confirm that small companies in eastern Germany find it especially difficult to train apprentices according to western German standards (von Bardeleben 1995). These surveys yield some contradictory results with respect to why these companies do not train, and whether subsidies can solve those problems. Von Bardeleben's 1993-94 survey of non-training firms found that only sixteen percent gave "apprenticeship too expensive"

31. There were several *Handwerk* firms in my eastern German sample, which I exclude from this presentation for the sake of direct comparability with the French firms in my sample (all of which belong to the chambers of commerce and industry). However, the *Handwerk* firms in the German sample have training ratios which conform to the predictions of the Soskice model: those which trained had an average training ratio of 14.5 percent. The newly declared IHK firm discussed above thus fits squarely in the *Handwerk* training pattern.

32. Located in a small town near the border with the Czech Republic, the company's manager put down his problems to attracting skilled workers to the location's distance from the large cities.

as their reason for not training, an answer given less frequently than "inability to fulfill training regulations" or "no time" (1995: 84-85). However, two-thirds of them named "financial aid" as the measure most likely to entice them to train more.[33] Certainly, the experience of small firms in this sample rejects the idea that the mere introduction of indiscriminate subsidies would suffice to enable them to train apprentices in ways characteristic of a high-skill equilibrium.

France and the Possibility
of New Cooperation in Training

This section lays out the broad patterns of in-firm youth training in French companies, categorizing them according to the same size brackets used in the previous section. One of the prime objectives stated in debates around the French reforms was to increase the use of the youth training contracts by large firms. While, quantitatively, the number of apprenticeship and qualification contracts in companies of more than ten people is creeping upwards (DARES 1996), the data I gathered from twenty-nine industrial companies in France suggests the reform has in this respect failed, at least thus far. Large companies in France do not carry the same training load as their eastern German counterparts and retain few of those they train. Medium-sized French firms do somewhat better in terms of training ratios, but their rates of retention are far below those we would expect for firms making a high net investment in youth training. Small firms, though, are as a group relatively more involved in using in-firm youth training contracts than is true of their counter-

---

33. Von Bardeleben himself questions the validity of this result, saying that "it shows only that many firms in the new federal states, as a result of their lack of economic experience with in-firm training and the lack of a longer-term apprenticeship culture, do not at all see the middle- and long-term advantages of apprenticeship training" (1995: 86).

parts in eastern Germany. Even more striking are both the level and quality of training in small firms producing for the bar-turning industry in the Valley of the Arve, which represents one of the few bright spots on the in-firm training landscape in France. If we can understand how successful cooperation was created in the Arve, we gain significant analytic purchase on the question of how high-skill training patterns can be created from scratch.

Large Firms

Table 7.4 depicts the training practices of the nine French companies in the sample that have employment of at least 500. Only one of these companies trains in the German target range, and that firm in 1996 retained *none* of its apprentices who finished their training that year. In eight of the nine companies, some young people had finished their training contracts in 1996, but only half of these hired even one of these trainees into permanent contracts. While most of these companies have used the policy tools available for youth training in a deliberate strategy to maintain or upgrade the skill base of their workforce, the ways in which they have done so bear little resemblance to the practices of the largest eastern German companies and to the practices of the dual system in western Germany.

Table 7.4   French firms, employment > = 500

Firm	Training ratio	1996 retention	Ownership
LF1	3.2%	0.00	i
LF2	0.4%	0.96	c
LF3	0.7%	0.00	c
LF4	1.0%	0.00	c
LF5	3.0%	0.60	c
LF6	3.0%	0.57	c
LF7	6.4%	0.00	c
LF8	0.2%	na	w
LF9	1.7%	0.67	w
AVG	2.2%	0.35	

Three of the firms – LF2, LF5, and LF6 – produce complex mechanical goods, and youth training at these firms demonstrates some common characteristics of the largest, most technologically advanced manufacturing companies in my French sample. All three report having developed specific strategies of youth training to cope with new product development and consequently increased skill demands, or in order to replace the know-how of existing workers nearing retirement. Yet the training measures used in these firms were generally special initiatives to replace or create new workers of a certain skill level, rather than sustained programs of bringing in young workers to replace the old on a continuous basis. Two of the firms (LF5 and LF6) had a training ratio equal to about 3 percent of their workforce and retained roughly 60 percent of those who completed their training program in 1995 and/or 1996. These ratios are at the low end of the target range for France, but they are at least in the target range. However, their retention rates bespeak a low net investment in human capital through in-firm training contracts: they retain their trainees at a rate more characteristic of small craft firms in Germany.

Such low retention rates would be irrational if these firms had a heavy net investment in youth training; but they do not. Instead, given the level of state subsidies available for youth training, they are probably breaking even or better from their youth training. Only one firm in my sample reported conducting a systematic analysis of the costs of youth training, including estimates for the productivity of the youth in the firm (but excluding the factors shown by von Bardeleben et al. (1995) to reduce the net cost of apprenticeship training). To the surprise of the personnel director, these calculations show that the firm in 1995-96 was making a slight profit from the training program, thanks to generous government subsidies. This firm and the other, slightly larger mechanical firm training at a rate of roughly 3 percent of its workforce, indicated that they might reduce their training in the absence of government subsidies.

The third large mechanical goods firm, the largest single plant in the sample (LF2 in Table 7.4), has a higher retention rate than any other plant in the large or in the medium-sized range. However, the experience of company LF2 is not indicative of a long-term, high investment in initial youth training. Instead, the training program developed there was targeted very narrowly at meeting a minimal level for the company's skill requirements over a short time period. In conjunction with the development of a new product line, the company embarked on the training program because the existing local labor market would not be able to meet its needs for skilled labor. Whereas the firm had previously hired production workers with no qualifications and had not engaged in any programs for training young people, the new technology and production methods required the company to impose a minimum of CAP qualification for production workers, with a long-term goal of establishing the *bac* (the final secondary-school qualification) as the minimum level of hiring for workers in production. But the decision to train was a stop-gap measure, rather than a durable change in the way the company does business.

Cognizant that such qualifications were not available in sufficient quantity on the local labor market, the company entered negotiations with regional government and public education officials to develop a qualification program which met the company's need for math, technology, and industrial design qualifications. After a year, the firm broke off the negotiations, unable to agree with education officials on a diploma-granting program.[34] The firm turned to the UIMM, the French sectoral employers' association for the metalworking industries, which succeeded in negotiating a CQPM with the regional *direction du travail* that

---

34. The central point of disagreement was the content of the program. Officials of the company wanted only technical subjects relevant for production, while education ministry officials insisted on including broader training requirements; the broader requirements also would have required that the trainees spend more time in a training center.

concentrated training requirements in only the technical skills demanded by the firm.

Between 1991 and 1996 company LF2 trained over 250 youth through the CQ program, hiring all who succeeded in passing the final test (the plant almost doubled its total employment during this time; roughly one-fourth of the new hires came by way of the youth training program). However, the final group of trainees finished this program in 1996, and the company has discontinued its training program at the level of the qualification contract, while continuing to take a small number of apprentices each year. "[Now] we hire fewer and fewer [trainees], it is easier to find people with diplomas […]. if in 1997 we need 37 workers, we would find them on the labor market; we will not do any more qualification contracts." In 1995, while the company was still actively engaged in this youth training initiative, the proportion of young trainees there represented just over 2 percent of the total workforce; and this, at the peak of their extra-ordinary training initiatives. At the time of interview in 1996, the ratio of trainees to total employment had returned to its normal level of only 0.4 percent. The company's training director is quite satisfied with the training program and the flexibility afforded by the qualification contracts. The company does train in apprenticeship, but in numbers that are tiny by comparison to its German counterparts; for this firm, as for the other two very large firms discussed above, routine youth training plays a subsidiary role in strategies of recruitment.

The remaining six companies in the large-size category all have lower skill demands than the companies just discussed. While a heterogeneous bunch, these companies as a group tend to have few youths in training contracts and to retain few of those they do train. Those that train the most retain the least. Illustrative of the general trends in this group are the practices of two firms (LF4 and LF7) that occupy similar product markets, in which the skill demands put on the workforce are extremely low. Both characterize their training as more of a "social" mission than one that fills an economic need for future skilled labor. A personnel director at one of the firms notes that "for us, by contrast to [the practice in] other firms, training is a question of [creating] the necessary qualifications, but also of managing the evolution of [the careers of] the other personnel here; of these people, maybe one in ten will be trained for promotion [...]. Thus, the fact is that we have to manage this frustration." Both these firms retained none of the youths they trained over the past year.[35]

These cases are exemplary of the behavior of many French large companies, for which training is more often considered a cost than an investment. For those firms with higher skill demands (the minority in my sample), in-firm youth training contracts have on occasion been used to bridge current or predicted shortages of skilled labor. Yet these programs are generally temporary and do not fit into any larger pattern of skill development in the companies. Moreover, the existence of the CQPM has allowed several companies to tailor qualifications

35. One of the two firms (company LF7 in Table 7-4) has constructed a special training school for apprentices, as a result of a deal with the unions signed in 1995. The firm agreed to take on a group of apprentices from disadvantaged neighborhoods in exchange for an agreement that gives management flexibility as to when the apprentices attend training; demand in the industry is highly seasonal. Trainees forego training in the winter months of peak demand and spend more time in the training center during summer periods of slack demand. The firm's personnel director notes that the program was begun with an eye towards the retirement of some older workers; the firm wants to replace them with younger workers at a minimum level of CAP (the lowest level French vocational certificate). However, he makes clear that the purpose of the program is not to retain trainees at a high rate: "we will not necessarily [hire them after apprenticeship], but at least they will have the diplomas, and would do better on the labor market [than without any training]." Asked if the firm would train in the absence of state subsidies for training, the personnel director answered, "no, because that [training] costs money, and the firm cannot support that cost. We don't do it [train] *because* of the money, but *without* public money we would not be able to do it."

very specifically to their own needs, without requiring them to bear the costs of conferring broader, more portable skills on trainees. And, even when investing in youth training contracts like these, French large firms train a lower proportion of workers, invest a lower amount per youth trainee, and retain a lower proportion of young people trained in such programs, than do their counterparts in Germany.

Medium-Sized Firms

The next size group, including six firms with between 150 and 500 employees, maintains a higher average training ratio than the large companies in the sample, and two-thirds of these companies maintain a training ratio within the target range between 2.5 and 6.5 percent of total workforce (see Table 7.5). Because they are in such different markets, it is hard to generalize about these firms. However, using the criteria of the training ratio and retention, it is helpful to distinguish the larger two companies (MF2 and MF3) from the smaller four. Eighty-six percent of the trainees at the larger two companies are in qualification contracts, the majority at the CAP (i.e., the lowest possible) level. Company MF3 has many workers nearing retirement and finds itself in a position analogous to that of company LF2 (discussed in the previous section), which used the qualification contract as a flexible tool capable of being rapidly structured to the needs of the firm at low cost.[36]

The four smaller firms in this group, all of which have between 200 and 250 employees, show a greater resemblance to patterns of German training. Three of the four train within the target range, and each of the firms trains at a variety of different levels of certification (BEP, *bac*, and DUT). Yet their retention

36. Both LF2 and MF3 are located in Alsace, and thus are far more likely than other French companies to suffer from tight labor markets. Unemployment in Alsace was about 8 percent at the time this research was conducted, compared with a national unemployment rate close to 13 percent.

Table 7.5   French firms, employment > 150 and < 500

Firm	Training ratio	1996 retention	Ownership
MF1	2.9%	0.80	i
MF2	1.0%	0.00	c
MF3	2.7%	0.64	c
MF4	6.5%	0.25	c
MF5	7.0%	0.67	c
MF6	3.8%	0.18	w
AVG	4.0%	0.42	

rates are lower than one might expect to see from firms making a heavy net investment in youth training. The average retention rate of the four firms is .48, meaning that less than half of youth trainees are hired by these companies after the end of their training contracts.

For one of the four, a high-end mechanical goods producer (company MF6), low retention is partly a product of the difference between training for office jobs and for production jobs. "If we train somebody in the workshop, we do it to hire them. In the offices, our policy is different: he [the trainee] can give us a little help, it's nice to have young person to lend a hand […]. [At the end of the training period] we would rather take another young trainee than to hire somebody […]. On the shop floor, we keep them because we need them; in the office, we are not looking to increase the number of office workers." For this firm, at least, technically trained apprentices are valuable and are retained; but those who pursue office qualifications are principally a source of cheap labor.

The training patterns of French firms in this size range are heterogeneous. Most interesting is the division between the two larger and the four smaller companies in their use of the CQ and the apprenticeship contracts. At the two largest companies, most of the contracts are CQs; in the four smaller companies, three-fourths of the youths in training contracts are in apprenticeship contracts, with qualification levels running the gamut from lowest to highest. As the discussion below explores more thoroughly, larger companies are more likely to be able to use the CQ for the development of narrowly defined firm-specific skills. Medium-sized companies like these, lacking both the personnel and the political resources to develop firm-specific qualifications, are less able to use the "exit option" presented by the CQ, and thus more likely to rely on apprenticeship. Even so, these companies still retain their apprentices at a rate that suggests that their net investment in training is low, and that in-firm youth training is not their primary means of attracting skilled workers.

Small Firms

It is only among some of the small enterprises, those with fewer than 150 employees, that we find firms in the French sample that frequently train and retain their trainees at very high levels. The firms that tend to exhibit high-skill training characteristics are located in the Arve valley and produce for the bar-turning industry. 60 percent of the production of the French bar-turning industry is concentrated in the valley of the Arve river, on the border with Switzerland, with production dominated by small firms; bar-turning refers to the mechanical production of large or small cylindrical components for use in larger, more complex mechanical goods. These firms are typically suppliers to larger producers, especially in the automobile industry. Over the past decade, despite high average youth unemployment, bar-turning and many other mechanical industries in France have experienced a shortage of skilled labor. Representatives of the firms in this industry whom I interviewed repeatedly mentioned conditions under which they competed with other firms for labor and feared the poaching of their own skilled workers by other companies. Yet the bar-turning firms in the Arve have, despite the acknowledged threat of poaching, been able to invest collectively in the use of the in-firm skill contracts as a way to train their own future skilled workers.

As shown in Tables 7.6a and 7.6b, small firms in the valley of the Arve maintain a substantially higher ratio of trainees as a total proportion of the workforce (5.6 percent), and retain a higher proportion of their apprenticeship graduates (.88), than do small firms in other metal-working sectors in France. The sorts of figures that we see among firms in the Arve are characteristic of western German firms making a substantial investment in youth training. Attitudes towards subsidies, and whether a firm would train less in the absence of subsidies, further support this finding. Four of the small firms not located in the valley of the Arve – including one company producing for the bar-turn-

Table 7.6a   French firms, employment < = 150, outside the Arve

Firm	Training ratio	1996 retention	Ownership
SF1	0.0%	na	i
SF2	0.0%	na	i
SF3	0.9%	0.50	i
SF4	1.1%	1.00	i
SF5	1.9%	na	i
SF6	3.4%	1.00	i
SF7	4.0%	1.00	i
SF8	5.0%	0.67	i
SF9	9.1%	0.50	i
AVG	2.8%	0.78	

Table 7.6b   French firms, employment < = 150, Valley of the Arve

Firm	Training ratio	1996 retention	Ownership
SFA1	0.0%	na	i
SFA2	2.9%	1.00	i
SFA3	3.0%	1.00	i
SFA4	8.7%	0.50	i
SFA5	13.3%	1.00	i
AVG	5.6%	0.88	

ing industry but not located in the Arve valley – would train fewer or no young people in the absence of state subsidies; none of the training firms in the valley would take on fewer young trainees in the absence of public subsidies to training.

Moreover, the companies in the Arve use the available skill contracts, particularly the CQ, to attract trainees of higher educational qualifications than do other small firms in France. The companies in the Arve valley have used the qualification contract to create skill categories at high levels – *bac* and *bac*+2 – which prove more satisfactory than apprenticeship to these firms, while also providing them with more highly skilled workers. Among companies in the bar-turning industry in the sample, 60 percent of the youth training contracts are CQs; in the non bar-turning industries, only 24 percent of contracts are CQs, equal to the percentage for the overall French firm sample. Also notable is the fact that almost all the CQs in bar-turning are in technical fields, whereas the majority of CQs in other small firms are in service qualifications. Most importantly, the bar-turning firms in the Arve valley use the CQ to attract trainees of much stronger educational background than is the norm in small firms in other parts of France: 70 percent of the trainees in Arve valley firms possessed a qualification at least at the level of the *bac*, and over half of those had two additional years after the *bac*; in the small firms in the rest of France, 75 percent of trainees had qualifications below the *bac* level.

All the firms in the Arve that train cite one of two connected reasons for their heavy reliance on the CQ. First, the qualification has a professional skill content: as noted at one firm, "apprenticeship is more general, the diploma [it gives] is scholastic […] while the content of the qualification contract is completely professional." But this difference in content is not unique to either the bar-turning industry or the Arve valley, and it could indeed serve as a blanket description of the distinction between the two qualifications for all industries. The second element that attracts firms is the level of training equipment available at local training center located in the Arve. "Personally," said one manager, "I prefer the qualification contract because the [training center] is much more technically advanced than the [vocational] high school, much more up to date." The combination of degrees appropriate to firm demands and high level machinery and instruction available through the local training center has made the qualification contract a preferred measure for companies in this small corner of France. To understand the way in which the CQ has come to be widely used in the companies in the Arve valley, we will in the next section examine more closely the role of the bar-turning trade association, whose offices are located in the valley, in lobbying for the development of qualifications considered relevant and useful for firms in this industry and in putting at their disposal training facilities whose technical endowments the companies appreciate (Culpepper 1998a).

Before analyzing why the companies in the Arve valley have largely succeeded in moving to high-level training practices, a word about the firms which choose not to train at all in youth training contracts. As in the sample from eastern Germany, it is among the small firms that we find a concentration of firms that have no trainees. Three firms in my sample, ranging in size from 40 to 107 employees (and including one located in the Arve valley), did not have any young people in training contracts. While all three noted that they did not have much turnover in their personnel, each had hired production-level workers on the external labor market in 1995 and 1996. All three cited the amount of time required to train young people, namely the time devoted by other workers to supervise and assist the trainees, as the principal reason they did not have youth training contracts. As one noted about youth training, "we lack time. Our people in charge no longer want to train [in youth contracts], it is a heavy burden." Unlike in eastern Germany, none of these firms cited the abundance of skilled labor available on the labor market as reasons they chose not to train.

Exit Options and Firm Choices

The differences observed between the patterns of training in companies of different size-categories in France and eastern Germany are striking, but so too are those within the eastern German *Mittelstand* and small firms in France. In this section, we return first to the explanatory axes of the organization of production and the structure of the educational system to try to make sense of the inter-category differences. In the second part of the section we then consider the elements of policy design that allow some firms to overcome the collective action problems involved in training reform more easily than others, holding these variables constant. The two dimensions of variation create an easier collective action problem for large firms in eastern Germany than for those in France; yet the rigid framework of the dual system, which is what has made cooperation for eastern German large firms easier, also makes it difficult for smaller companies in the new federal states of eastern Germany to use apprenticeship to procure skilled labor. In the second part of the section, I analyze how the Saxon *Verbund* policy helps companies overcomes these difficulties by crafting aid in such a way that companies using it cooperate with other companies while gaining confidence in the functioning of the training system. In fact, these are exactly the conditions of subsidized aid that the bar-turning trade association has been able to create in the French valley of the Arve, which has enabled firms in the valley to overcome the collective action problems that bedevil the training reforms in most other parts of France.

Training Systems and the Possibility of Exit

The contrast between the training behavior of large companies in eastern Germany and in France aptly illustrates the way in which the nature of the educational system, along with the existing product market strategies of companies, structures firm preferences for training. The largest firms are numerically in the minority in the overall apprenticeship training populations of both France and Germany, but they constitute the most powerful members of the employers' associations and thus occupy a central political role for the outcome of training reforms. Because large, western German-owned firms have played a leading role in apprenticeship training in the eastern German economy and because the broad skill requirements of the dual system suit their existing product market strategies, there has been no significant political pressure for loosening the requirements of the German training regulations. For these companies, with deep pockets and excellent access to information through the training networks of their parent corporations, the qualifications supervised by the IHK are a baseline on top of which they are able to develop their own firm-specific specialization of training standards. This allows them to compete in product markets where their skill resources give them comparative advantage by facilitating incremental product customization (Streeck 1992, Carlin and Soskice 1997). Given their dominant voices in the employers' association and the IHKs, these companies are well-placed to press for new professions (or changes in old ones) that respond to their new requirements.

Large firms in France, as represented in my sample, mostly remain indifferent to reforms encouraging them to train more apprentices. This choice stems from the options available to them through the bifurcated structure of the French initial in-firm training system and from their implication in a given organization of production.[37] The existence within the French system of the CQ, which allows large firms in pressing need to pursue extremely firm-specific upskilling, provides an exit option should the apprenticeship system, dominated by the national education ministry, prove insufficiently pliable to firm demands for new skills. In addition, the CQ provides firms of all sizes with a means to hire workers with

---

37. The availability of the technical and professional *bac* and *bac+2* degrees in France further amplifies the number of alternative training options available to French companies.

a sound foundation of general skills at the *bac+2* level, and to give them firm-specific training while paying a fairly low wage. In some cases the CQ serves as a two-year probationary period for workers who, once permanently employed, entail high wages and social charges on the company's payroll.

Developing a tailor-made qualification requires extensive aid from the employers' association (Charraud et al. 1996). This aid is much less likely to be available to individual small firms than to large conglomerates, as the former pay much lower membership fees than the latter. Two relatively large firms (with employment of 400 and 700) employed the large majority of the CQs training in technical professions from my entire sample. They each trained their workers at the lowest level (CAP) and retained only two-thirds of them. The personnel manager from one of the firms derided the skill level of the participating youths as "quite lamentable." For each of these firms, the training adopted was a low-level, firm-specific qualification: the lowest-cost way to acquire the workers necessary for semi-skilled jobs. As in the case of company LF2, these firms were able to use the qualification contract to tailor their "training" as specifically as possible to the firm's needs.

The addition of the CQ has increased the ability of French large firms to have more input over the construction of relevant qualifications without surrendering a significant voice to French unions. Eastern German firms, in contrast, have not only the carrot of incentive, but also the stick of constraint. The most notable of these is the legally enforced presence of labor representatives at every level of standards development and certification through the dual system. Their role in defining national standards, in concert with the representatives of the employers' association, is paramount, but it is supplemented by parity representation in the training committee of the IHKs, which supervise all elements of regional training regulation, and in the *Land* committees that advise regional governments on training policy and problems. Finally, the works council has the authority to challenge abusive apprenticeship practices observed or reported at the firm-level. While works councils in eastern Germany have proved less confrontational than their western counterparts (cf. Hyman 1996), they nevertheless retain a shopfloor capacity for intervention that sets up one more obstacle to the exploitation of trainees.

In France, without the acquisition of relevant working qualifications being tied to the requirement that those qualifications be broad, the innovation of the CQ becomes either a source of cheap labor or a stop-gap measure for meeting temporary labor shortages. In the absence of a union movement able and willing to push for broad qualifications, large French firms have developed a strategy that makes best use of the qualities passed on through the school-based technical training system. These skills are supplemented by mandatory further training expenditures, which allow companies to impart firm-specific skills to their workforces on continual basis (Géhin and Méhaut 1993, Regini 1997). The existing educational system and the exit options it creates for large French firms do not entice, nor do they force, those firms to move away from their equilibrium strategy of reliance on "flexible Fordist" production strategies that do not require a broadly skilled workforce (Boyer 1995).

Because their ownership links to western German companies have allowed them to pursue DQP strategies, large firms in eastern Germany that have been incorporated into German conglomerates have very little to gain by defection in the training game: they do not have a credible alternative means of attracting skilled labor to produce the sort of good they would like. The fruits of defection are lower than the returns to cooperation, which means that training for them is an assurance game. They do not want to train if no other firm does, but if they are assured that others will train, they prefer the payoffs of the cooperative outcome. If they have an effective mechanism for information circulation – which, through eastern German employers' associations, they do – the hurdles on the path to cooperative training are low. By contrast, as long as large French firms face a system in which a majority of firms view their productive advantage as lying in competition along flexible Fordist lines, then it pays not to invest in high-level in-firm training, even if other companies are cooperating. To get the skills that they need for this sort of production, neither the structure of the educational system nor the power of the unions in France is enough to force them to provide broad skills at the same time they provide firm-specific training. This is the problem facing French policy-makers.

Public Policy and Collective Action

Yet the German alternative – a rigid system with no credible prospect for exit – is not without risks. Small and medium-sized companies in eastern Germany find the qualifications imposed by this system quite onerous; and as a result, they either do not train (small firms) or require subsidy assistance to do so (*Mittelstand*). As the availability of unemployed, well-qualified skilled labor decreases in eastern Germany, the small and medium-sized firms that want to train young workers will face increasing pressure to take on apprentices through the dual system. The Saxon *Verbund* policy was deftly designed in that it focused public money on the specific problems of firms in the *Mittelstand*: meeting the broad IHK requirements for the metal professions during (especially) the first year of training. What is clever about the design of the Saxon policy is the fact that it channels this aid to medium-sized companies in a format that brings them into close cooperation with other training companies. Thus, not only do they benefit from the subsidy in overcoming technical obstacles to training, but they build links with other training companies that serve to lengthen their time horizons (by opening up the future possibility of cooperation) and that reinforce their confidence in the functioning of the German skill provision system. The *Verbund* works because it lowers costs by increasing cooperation, not by lowering standards.

If the argument I have made about the prisoner's dilemma of French training is right, then how have small companies overcome this problem in the valley of the Arve? As we would expect from the theoretical discussion above, they are nudged towards cooperation by their product market strategies in combination with how the educational system looks to them. As an industry of suppliers dependent on orders from larger producers in the automotive and other mechanical industries, the bar-turning firms of the Arve have been forced to maintain their technological edge in order to remain internationally competitive. Companies in this industry manufacture for a wide variety of markets, and in varying production runs. What all share is a reliance on families of CNC machinery that are at the center of bar-turning work. Since the 1980s, the trade association of the industry has sought numerous ways to meet the demand for highly skilled technical labor to run these machines.

The organization of production in bar-turning should not be confused with the breadth of skill requirements associated with the large DQP firms in Germany. However, the need to stay abreast of technically sophisticated methods of production in order to compete in world markets helps to make cooperation a more attractive proposition to bar-turning companies (raising the payoffs to cooperation and lowering the payoffs to defection). Moreover, the bar-turning industry in the Arve valley is dominated by small units of production (SESSI 1996),[38] to which the educational system appears very different than to large firms. While large companies in France may tailor a CQ to their exact specifications, no firm in the bar-turning industry holds this kind of sway with the general metal employers' association (UIMM), which helps design and authorize CQs. This density of firms with similar needs for basic and advanced technical skills (from the

---

38. Firms with over 100 employees account for only 10 percent of total employment in the French bar-turning sector, and three-quarters of companies in the industry have fewer than twenty employees.

lowest level, CAP, to the *bac+2*), has led even small firms to develop a close relationship with the national trade association for bar-turning, whose offices are located in the heart of the Arve valley. With a multitude of small firms, each using different manufacturing techniques and strategies, the CQs produced under trade association pressure lack the firm-specific traits of the CQs negotiated by larger companies. The certifications, to be sure, are very specific to bar-turning industry; they do not contain the broad initial year's training of German metal-working apprenticeships. But the balance of many competing small firms has produced unusually transferable qualifications from the routinely firm-specific CQ in France.

Thus, both the organization of production and the way the educational system looks to small firms move the bar-turning firms in the valley of the Arve towards an assurance game and away from the prisoner's dilemma. The acute labor shortage in the companies in the valley, which was the reason for which the association aggressively pursued the elaboration of the CQ, also mimics the constraint function played by unions in Germany. These companies may not have strong works councils to watch over firm-level training, but they have competitors who are also in search of labor, which strengthens the hand of the trainee worried about getting low-quality training: he can always find another bar-turning firm down the road that will hire him. In these structural respects, then, the bar-turning industry in the Arve valley has some of the features that ease collective action among German firms in the area of training. However, the Arve valley is not alone in having tight labor markets – indeed, labor markets in Alsace are tighter than in any other part of France, but firms in Alsace (as represented in my sample) have shown little evidence of cooperative training practices.[39]

39. A reviewer of this chapter suggested that the proximity of the Arve to Switzerland, which also has a German-style dual system, might explain how companies in the Arve succeeded in achieving cooperation where other firms in France failed. Yet the almost total failure of firms in Alsace

The distinctiveness of the Arve case lies in the role played by the local association of bar-turning companies and its affiliated technical center. The association decided in the in the 1980s that the technical center (called the CTDEC) should take on the role of training center for local companies in response to the chronic shortage of skilled workers and technicians in the bar-turning industry. The CTDEC made a massive investment in machinery that is specific to the industry, financed by member firm contributions. Access to these high-level machines and the trainers of this center are one prominent reason why smaller companies in the Arve valley opt to train through the qualification contract. They are also willing to train using the qualification contract because the association devised qualifications that responded to their needs for production, which required that the association have the capacity to gather information from a broad spectrum of companies and deliberate effectively about the most suitable skills to include in these certifications (Culpepper 1998a). Then, the CTDEC makes available to small firms in the Arve the gamut of machinery used in the industry.

Having developed appropriate qualifications and a well-functioning training center, the association of bar-turners in the Arve is able to lobby members to use national subsidy money to begin investing more heavily than they have before in high-skill training practices. These national subsidies, which are available to almost all firms in France, have thus been joined through a mechanism of employer coordination to a training center that has identified the problems of companies and that tries to respond to them. Like the *Verbund* aid in the state of Saxony, the existence of such a training center gives smaller companies access to a broad range of machinery that they could not afford

---

to move towards high-skill training practices – when Alsace sits on the German border and even retains many legal vestiges of the German training system from its days under German rule – certainly calls into question any sort of argument about cooperation based solely on proximity to a dual system.

to provide on their own, which in turn allows them to train in broader qualifications than what is strictly necessary for their own firm.[40] And as in the Saxon case, this material aid is provided in the context (a joint training center) in which firms witness other firms training; in the assurance game, this assurance that other actors will also cooperate is the key to reaching the cooperation that is the most desired outcome for all parties. Thus have the bar-turning companies in the valley of the Arve been able to escape the sub-optimal outcomes characteristic of training reform in many other parts of the French political economy.

Conclusion

The evidence in this chapter buttresses the argument that the predominant organization of production and the exit options offered by the existing educational and training system structure firm choices about the use of in-firm training contracts. In this respect, large, privately owned eastern German firms face a less difficult collective action problem than do their French counterparts in trying to adopt the practices of the high-skill equilibrium. However, the evidence also documents that many eastern German firms do not train at high levels, and that some French firms do. These two broad variables thus determine the stylized payoffs to cooperative training patterns, but they do not determine the choices of companies. Some companies are able to overcome the obstacles to cooperative training in order to reap the rewards of a high-skill strategy, despite the perceived threat of opportunism by other firms that could poach their skilled workers.

Large companies in eastern Germany have engaged themselves at high rates in the dual system, accepting the rigidity of

40. Lest this "functional equivalence" of *Verbund* aid and the bar-turning technical center seem an overly stretched parallel, recall that *Verbund* aid fills a gap left by the absence of IHK out-of-firm centers in eastern Germany.

German apprenticeship qualifications there rather than using the new context to bargain this rigidity downward. Smaller eastern German industrial firms have encountered greater difficulties in using this system of broad qualifications, because of the machinery and personnel demands it makes on them. The *Verbund* policy has been one state-level solution for making entry into dual training practices less onerous for the companies of the *Mittelstand*, combining subsidy assistance in a package that encourages newly training companies to cooperate with other training companies.

In France, successive measures to make in-firm youth training contracts a more attractive tool for skill provision have failed to have a major impact on the training strategies of large companies. The use of broad, higher-level degrees is almost as marginal in 1998 as it was when the 1993 reform law was passed. Large companies have used the CQ to their advantage, but not as the measures of broad skill acquisition that its proponents intended when the contracts were originally introduced. In the bar-turning industry in the valley of the Arve, however, the inability of companies to use the CQ as a purely firm-specific training tool and the need for skilled workers have facilitated the push by the bar-turning association to convince companies to train and to retain their trainees at high levels. French policymakers could draw from this evidence the inference that subsidies and tax relief alone will not persuade companies to begin engaging in patterns of high-skill training. These enticements have been the primary element of French policy thus far. On the one hand, my analysis suggests that, so long as companies perceive their competitive advantage to lie in the Fordist organization of production and so long as they face an educational system that presents them with easy exit options for acquiring the skills they need, it will be difficult to extend the success observed in the valley of the Arve to other parts of the French political economy. On the other hand, the story of the Arve suggests that policies designed in consultation with employers' associations may be better able to attract potential new training firms than are the indiscriminate subsidies that France currently offers to any firm to take on apprentices.

Governments in the advanced capitalist democracies that want to persuade companies to increase their investment in the development of intermediate skills have a problem: how to convince companies to take the cooperative step in a potentially one-period game, leaving them open to defection. If a government is to solve this problem, it needs to make the first cooperative step less costly for companies. In all the cases of success discussed in this chapter, employer associations attempted to mobilize public money (national or regional) to facilitate the training decisions of private companies. For the eastern German large companies, the aid came early on, through one-time federal subsidies that allowed them to update their machinery and training facilities (Culpepper 1998a). The Saxon *Verbund* policy built on this success by procuring state money to enable medium-sized companies to have access to modern technology and experienced trainers. The small bar-turning firms in the valley of the Arve had access to the general subsidies of the national government to lower the costs of their training. This investment was abetted by their development of a training center with the latest equipment and qualified trainers, giving these small firms access to training expertise that would not have otherwise been available to them.

Based on the success of the large, western-German owned companies in eastern Germany, it seems that the establishment of a network of large companies training at high levels may facilitate the move to the high-skill equilibrium. There are at least three reasons supporting this hypothesis: first, a network of large companies can circulate information and make possible access to machinery that can enable other, smaller companies to make the decision to invest. Second, large companies among themselves, by virtue of their large size and small numbers, face lower obstacles to collective action in the absence of strong existing institutions of employer coordination. Thus, in political econo-mies like the United States that are largely bereft of strong employer coordinating capacity, consortia of large companies may be able to jump-start mini-experiments in high-level voca-tional training.[41] And third, establishing a critical mass of large companies making the sorts of skill investments required for a regime of diversified quality production may provide both a demonstration effect (of the merits of DQP skills investment) and the establishment of inter-firm networks that facilitate cooperation on questions like vocational training in western Germany. For this reason, Carlin and Soskice (1997: 70-74) rightly note that the paucity of large firms in eastern Germany presents an obstacle to the wider diffusion of the high-skill equi-librium model to the new federal states, as a critical mass of large companies has not emerged there to serve as the corner-stone of high-level training.

Even if large companies do establish themselves in greater numbers in eastern Germany, we must remember that large firms in Germany provide only about 10 percent of the total appren-ticeship places; the *Mittelstand* customarily provides the bulk of the total places. In order to achieve a successful overall transfor-mation of the eastern German training system, then, small and medium-sized companies are going to have to carry a larger pro-portion of trainees than they have done up to now. The capabil-ity of employers' association to circulate information to, from, and across companies will be an asset for these companies in the formulation of their individual training strategies. As shown by the Saxon example, the problem is not just one of getting money from the state, although that matters; in addition, the form of the subsidy must be well-crafted, so as to meet the demands of the companies that are most likely to want to engage in high-

41. Some of the most promising experiments with vocational training reform in the US have grown out of employer-run consortia of this sort. See the chapter by Parker and Rogers in this volume and Osterman (1994c) for examples of consortia-led experiments in vocational training.

skill-training (Culpepper 1998a). In eastern Germany, smaller companies need access to the broad range of machinery required for training in all metal qualifications, especially in the first year. The Saxon employers' association recognized this need and pushed for specially targeted aid, which not only lowered the net cost of training, but did so while giving companies a way to meet the rigorous requirements of the German qualifications.

Yet the Saxon *Verbund* policy, despite its apparent success, nevertheless undercuts the central pillar of the German dual system: that employers pay the full costs of in-firm apprenticeship training. Although cleverly crafted, it remains unknown whether the policy will succeed in establishing a pattern of high-level training that can survive the withdrawal of subsidy support, as the precarious situation of eastern German companies improves. While the subsidy program is a success in relation to other programs, it remains to be seen whether the trend established under subsidy will continue in the absence of government assistance. The success achieved in the valley of the Arve, although partly subsidized, seems less likely to create subsidy dependence because most firms there deny that the absence of the subsidy would change their training behavior. The problem of replicating the Arve's success across France is not so much a function of the particularity of the bar-turning industry as it is the weakness of French employers' associations (Bunel 1995, Levy 1999). The organizational splintering of French unions does not compel employers' organizations to move from the provision of specific goods to the provision of collective goods. Nor do the existing product market strategies of many French companies lead them to push actively for the provision of such goods. While the government can exert little direct influence on the product market strategies that dictate the demand for labor, it can intervene in the facility with which firms can use the CQ as an exit option from apprenticeship. However, recent attempts in this direction (most recently in 1993) have failed (Culpepper 1996a), and the area of education and training has proved notoriously treacherous for reform-minded French governments of any political stripe.

The general, sober lesson to be drawn from these cases is that the best way to overcome collective action problems like the prisoners' dilemma is to turn them into more easily soluble assurance games. Given the path-dependence of the structures necessary to change the payoff matrix of employers, this counsel may be cold comfort for would-be reformers. It is important to recognize, though, that the successful cases of training reform are impressive, especially given the high unemployment currently bedeviling both the eastern German and French political economies. We can summarize two general lessons from these cases. First, to encourage employers to make substantial, uncovered investments in skill provision demands that the employer have some confidence that he or she will be able to exert influence over the nature of certifiable skills. Well-functioning institutions of employer coordination appear to provide the best practical form of this assurance. Second, lowering the costs of a company's initial investment can be most effectively achieved through judicious public intervention, developed in close collaboration with these employers' associations. Neither national nor state governments are likely to possess detailed knowledge of the needs of struggling companies in transitional economies; this information circulates best through private networks of coordination. In the game of training reform, these two elements offer the best possibility of generating the cooperative behavior on which the successful transition to a high-skill equilibrium ultimately depends.

Chapter 8

SECTORAL TRAINING INITIATIVES
IN THE US

Building Blocks of a
New Workforce Preparation System?

∽◯◯◯

Eric Parker and Joel Rogers

Introduction

The United States continues to lead the world in labor productivity and recent performance on employment has become the envy of the OECD. But over the past quarter century, US labor markets have generated enormous income inequality and absolute declines in income for large segments of the workforce. Despite recent improvements in manufacturing, the economy-wide secular rate of annual productivity growth over the same period has remained stuck at a disappointing one percent.

In response to both the income and productivity concerns, much recent policy reform has focused on enhancing the skill sets of workers, with special attention to delivering training to "frontline" production and non-supervisory workers. Whatever the long-run promise of such strategies in relieving income and inequality problems,[1] however, they are almost immediately frustrated by uncertain signals from the demand side of the training equation. Only a minority of employers are embarked on "high-road" (quality-centered, continuously improving) competitive strategies of the sort that require substantial ongoing training of such workers. Even those that are engaged in such training remain generally disorganized, without the capacity to solve common collective action problems in the provision of training or to declare convergent training needs and thus realize economies of scale in their satisfaction. The same variation in firm competitive strategy and disorganization among the "high-roaders" limits the achievement of productivity gains among enough firms within a sector to affect the dynamics of regional labor markets as well as industry aggregates.[2]

1. For a skeptical view, which we generally endorse, see Heckman (1994). Assuming a 10 percent return on investment in skills, Heckman estimated that it would take $426 billion (in 1989 dollars) to reverse the decline of wages for high school-educated workers during the 1980s. That figure is more than 47 times the current federal budget of $9 billion for adult basic education, job training, job search, skills standards, school-to-work, and welfare-to-work combined.
2. For an analysis of why markets tolerate unproductive manufacturing in the United States, see Luria (1996). Using an unusually detailed data set on industrial practice and firm performance among small to medium-sized manufacturers in the Midwest, Luria documents three clusters of alternative competitive strategies adopted by sweatshops, lean producers, and high-roaders. The lean producers combine the low-wage, low-skill strategy of sweatshops with modern inventory and quality-control systems to produce commodity goods, while high-wage, high-skill firms feature the greatest utilization of advanced technology on the workfloor. These high-roaders are struggling to maintain a sufficient edge in productivity to compensate for the wage premium they pay in a more heavily unionized urban environment. Consistent with this analysis, a longitudinal study of the adoption of advanced manufacturing technology among a representative sample of large firms in the durable goods sector finds that high-tech usage is greater among higher wage firms (Doms, Dunne, and Troske 1997).

In response to these and allied problems, many communities in the United States have begun experimenting with a more deliberate organization of employers, typically on a sectoral basis, around training, modernization, and other aspects of the "high-road." In this chapter, after reviewing the general performance of the "American Model" of labor market governance and recent efforts at its reform, we examine a range of such experiments, focusing in some detail on one of them – the Wisconsin Regional Training Partnership (WRTP) – that we take to be exemplary of their problems and general promise. We then speculate on the conditions for replicating such training partnerships, and the role they might play in administering a more devolved, but organized, workforce preparation system.

The "American Model" of Labor Market Regulation

More than any other advanced capitalist economy, the United States relies on competitive labor markets to determine pay, employment, and other aspects of worker welfare.[3] Outside the public sector, only 10 percent of workers belong to unions. Their collective bargaining agreements generally cover individual firms or establishments, rather than entire industries or regions, and are not extended to non-union employers. Public regulation of labor markets is also minimal. The minimum wage applies to a relatively small number of workers, has no obvious spill-over on the overall level of wages, and recently fell to its lowest level in forty years before triggering a modest raise by Congress. Unemployment insurance is more time-limited than in other countries. Outside a cluster of means-tested programs directed to the very poor, the welfare state is largely limited to old-age pensions and insurance. Exclusive of occupational health and

---

3. The following comparison of US and European labor market outcomes is drawn from Freeman and Rogers (1996). For lengthier treatments, see Freeman (1994) and Freeman and Katz (1995).

safety regulation and equal employment opportunity laws pro-tecting groups from discrimination, the federal government has few national policies safeguarding workers. Job security, training, and provision of medical insurance are generally determined at the workplace – through collective negotiations for a small num-ber and through employer policy and individual negotiations for the vast majority. The bottom line is that for most Americans, how one fares in the economy depends overwhelmingly on how one fares in the labor market and thus upon the employer.

For more than two decades now, this market-driven system has led the developed world in job creation. Since 1983, the US unemployment rate has always been at least 3-4 percentage points lower than that of the European OECD. More recently, as US unemployment rates have reached quarter-century lows, the gap has widened further. Of course, unemployment rates are relative – to the population regularly having or seeking employment. But noting this only places US success in job-gen-eration into starker relief. From 1974 to the present, the US employment/population ratio has grown from 65 to 71 percent, while OECD Europe's has fallen from 65 to 60 percent. Com-pared to Europeans, US workers also put in about 200 more hours at their jobs annually – a difference that itself widened during the period – further underscoring relative US success in generating work. Given their tax weariness and long-term unem-ployment problems, many European policy-makers find the US example powerfully instructive. If only they were to "liberalize" their economic governance, the thought goes, both problems could be solved.

The spectacular US success in generating work, however, has not been matched by success in improving job quality, or the distribution of the benefits of economic cooperation. Inequality has risen, and wages have stagnated for much of the population.

Given a secular shift in labor demand toward more-skilled workers compared to the supply of those workers, flexibility in wage determination assures rising inequality. In the United

States the college/high-school wage differential nearly doubled in the 1980s, rising from a 34 percent advantage for college graduates in 1979 to a 57 percent one in 1993; over the same period, the white-collar/blue-collar premium grew by more than 50 percent; and the pay of CEOs skyrocketed relative to that of other employees.[4] But inequality has also increased within educational and occupational strata – suggesting the increased importance of sheer luck in labor market outcomes. Over the same 1979-93 period, for example, the ratio of earnings of male high school graduates in the 90th percentile to those in the 10th increased 25 percent. Similar changes are found within detailed occupations.

As inequality has risen, wages have stagnated or declined for much of the working population. Real hourly wages of men with fewer than twelve years of schooling dropped 27 percent over 1979-93; wages of high school graduates fell 20 percent; even male college graduates suffered absolute wage declines. Income erosion was especially severe among the young, with the wages of male high school graduates with one-to-five years of work experience, for example, falling 30 percent over the period. Even more troubling, fewer workers experienced lifecycle wage improvement – that is, earning more as they aged and advanced in their careers, gained skills, and attained seniority. In the 1970s the ratio of such life-cycle winners to losers was 4:1. In the 1980s it was halved to 2:1, meaning that one-third of workers actually lost ground as their job experience increased.

4. On the demand side of the labor market, educational and occupational upgrading attributable to "skills-biased technological change" accelerated in the 1970s and has decelerated since then, especially in the 1990s. On the supply side of the labor market, the massive cohort of college-educated baby boomers swamped the demand for a more highly educated workforce in the 1970s. Thus, the college-wage premium only materialized in the 1980s when the "baby bust" pressed wage effect into relief. The plateau in returns to education during the 1990s reflects the boom-let on the supply side and the deceleration of skills-biased technological change on the demand side. See Autor et al. (1997).

Nothing even approximating this result is found in Germany, or any other developed nation (see Hinz, Chapter 4).

These adverse labor market outcomes are most dramatic, of course, for those at the bottom of the earnings distribution. The bottom decile of US workers earn only 38 percent of the US median wage; by contrast, the bottom decile of OECD European workers earn 68 percent of the European median. And in absolute terms, using a purchasing power parity measure, bottom decile US workers earn just 69 percent of what bottom decile European workers earn. Compared to their colleagues in Germany, they earn just 45 percent.

Very low earnings at the bottom of the wage distribution, and the difficulty of making even normal gains in income over the life-cycle, contribute to the growth of an "underclass" in the United States – concentrated in our cities, sometimes violently criminal. Lacking any social or economic policies to prevent or remedy this problem, US policy increasingly deals with the underclass through physical incarceration. The US prison population, already a higher share of the general population than any other nation, has been growing since the early 1980s at 7 percent annually. As of 1993, the population directly supervised by the criminal justice system – either in prison, or on supervised probation or parole – equaled 7 percent of the total workforce. At present rates of incarceration, by 2000, 3 percent of male Americans of working age will be in prison – roughly comparable to long-term joblessness among the same population in OECD Europe.

Even given the dimensions of these social costs of liberal labor market (non)regulation for those at the lower end of the wage distribution, they might be thought bearable if downward wage flexibility had a meaningful positive relation to employment. But apparently it does not. Massive drops in the real wages of less skilled American men did not improve their employment prospects absolutely, or relative to high-skill workers. Comparing male high school and college graduates in 1980 and 1993, for example, shows lower employment rates for both groups over time, but a sharper drop among the less-skilled. Annual weeks of joblessness in the bottom decile of male workers increased by eight and a half weeks over the late 1960s to late 1980s while remaining unchanged among those in the top four deciles. In the 1990s, for those in the bottom decile, the fall in hours has continued, while for those in the top decile hours have increased. Studies of the declining real value of the mandated minimum wage also show no positive employment effect among classes of workers earning it.

The Conventional US Policy Response

Concern about stagnating wages and rising inequality has led US policy-makers to focus on improving workforce quality – most obviously through increased training, as well as more efficient delivery of other sorts of labor market assistance and support.[5] And, indeed, there are welcome signs of movement to improve the quality of the US labor market system.

Many states have moved to integrate the delivery of various labor market services, offering prospective "customers" income support, job search assistance, and job training assistance at "one-stop" jobs centers. In some of the most developed cases, including Wisconsin, these centers are linked to provide a more integrated state system of labor market service access, with a common menu of services for employers and job-seekers, and effective integration of policy and service delivery. Responding to the long-standing problem of fragmented labor market services, the trend towards one-stop jobs centers is gaining momentum from federal welfare reform. The latter has underscored the need, especially for the millions of disadvantaged workers who

5. Criticism of that system is a minor cottage industry. For an overview, see OTA (1990). On the inherited employment and training policy, see Osterman (1988). On the traditional role of community colleges, see Brint and Karabel (1989).

are being forced into the labor market, to integrate social services with more specific training and other labor market supports. Federal funds to operate these social and training supports will likely become "block-granted" to the states and, to achieve greater functionality in regional labor market administration, it is widely anticipated that human resource investment boards will take on the task of integrating workforce development systems on a regional basis. In some states, such boards have already been established.

Partly as a result of integration of social supports with training and job services, and partly because resource constraints have required reorganization, the role of *technical and community colleges* has been changing rapidly as well. Major community colleges have pledged themselves to a more integral role in the community and are working to strengthen their connections both to potential students and firms. In order to be more responsive to community residents and incumbent workers, they are generally offering shorter courses, more computer-based and self-paced learning packages, and more convenient hours and locations for courses. In order to be more responsive to the needs of firms, they are also developing more flexible training for high-growth, high-wage industries; working on customized, short-term courses to improve training in specific workplaces; designing basic skills courses which emphasize "soft skills" such as teamwork and communication; and developing improved evaluation procedures to monitor their successes and prepare for future needs. In an education and training system geared most heavily toward those attending four-year colleges such reform of the two-year community/technical college system probably offers the best hope for a significantly improved public sector presence in more vocational training.[6]

6. There are obvious dangers along with opportunities in this innovation that are broadly described by the tradeoffs between short-term vs. long-term, customized vs. standardized, and off-the-job vs. on-the-job training. The balance of evidence suggests that short-term, firm-specific

The US School-to-Work Opportunities Act was passed in 1994, and is currently funded at about $400 million on an annual basis, with the money earmarked for providing career education and development in the public schools and for creating work-based learning components. Substantially inspired by US admiration for German apprenticeships, the broad goal of the program is to link schools to the workplace much more tightly and to make school work more relevant to the world of employment. The Act emphasized local partnerships between schools, employers, labor, community organizations and parents.

---

training, whether provided on the job or off, provides some positive short-term productivity effects for firms. However, these gains are not sustained, longer-term ones, and this sort of training does little for workers interested in the portability of their training credentials. A community college system that gets ever "closer to its customer" in providing such, then, is a community college system not serving public ends. A labor force equipped with longer-term, more formal and standardized training, on the other hand, provides the desired productivity and portability effects, but is difficult to apply without a firm-based, on-the-job link that is itself hard to provide without clear payoffs to employers. We await the balance struck between community college interest in customization and interest in standardized programs, but suspect the correct balancing lies in demarcating broad career paths and training complements, entry into which could be provided either to new entrants or, for incumbent workers, through customized and on-the-job training. The general goal – to increase the opportunities for workers to feed into some system, itself described in its mid-range by standardized training and its upper range by functionally equivalent performance requirements – is clear enough. The realities of variation in firm and individual worker circumstance also seem clearly to recommend a higher degree of modularization in the demarcation and delivery of skill sets. The key role of sectoral organization of employers in keeping such a system in place, and (as a condition of that) in touch with the reality of changing skill needs, should become evident from what we argue below. For a review of the payoffs to alternative forms of training for employers and individuals, see Lynch (1994). For evidence from the latest employer survey, see Lynch and Black (1997). On the impact of long-term training from two-year schools, see Grubb (1993), Kane and Rouse (1995), and Leigh and Gill (1997).

Access to career information and counseling should lead students to select a "career major" no later than the eleventh grade. Workplace mentoring is supposed to be provided along with instruction in competencies required in the workplace. The goal is to provide students with two "portable and validated" credentials – a high school diploma and a skills certificate – recognized by area employers.

The issue of portable and validated credentials for the incumbent workforce has been recently revived through a program to create *national skill standards*. The development of skill standards is proceeding on a sectoral basis, although some basic standards, such as literacy and numeracy, may hold across sectors. In banking, for example, the California Business Roundtable and the California Department of Education have developed skill standards for many positions throughout the California banking industry. These standards are divided into foundation standards (for all positions) and occupational standards for data and item processing, loan processing, and sales and services. Generally, the standards are geared towards employees with flexibility and good basic skills, as well as skills that are specific to one of the three occupational areas listed above. Many of these skills are specific to the work process in banking, and clearly would be most efficiently acquired on the job.

The Barriers to Effective Reform

Such efforts at reform, however, face a number of problems that have thus far severely qualified their effectiveness. The one-stop job centers capture only a tiny portion of the actual employment flow in most labor markets, and welfare reform threatens to marginalize them as places of interest only to the truly needy. School-to-work initiatives are not reaching scale, since they generally lack serious employer commitment to training their young participants and offering them challenging jobs. Com-

munity/technical college interest in getting "close to their customer" has most commonly taken the form of tailoring programs
to the needs of particular firms – without providing workers
with broader and more portable occupational skills. And the
national skills standards program, while successfully piloted in a
few industries, is nowhere near providing authoritative labor
market signals to labor market entrants or incumbent workers.
In most major sectors, particularly among the larger firms, there
simply is no interest in buying into job or occupational standards
not set by the employers themselves. A common complaint
heard across these policy areas is the need for constantly renew-
ing personal relationships and inspiring management goodwill
or civic-mindedness.

The common problem here is the lack of organized, collective involvement of those on the "demand" side of the labor
market – the firms that are actually going to be employing
workers – in the administration of our labor market system.
More particularly, there is a lack of organized involvement by
firms committed to "high-road" production and service delivery
of the sort needed to improve wages, and persuade business
itself of the value of well-trained workers.

On the demand side of the training equation, while US
labor markets have shown, since the late 1970s, a strong secular increase in the relative demand for skilled as against
unskilled labor, overall employer demand for skilled labor
remains relatively weak. As measured by occupational trends,
business demand for more educated workers is actually projected to slow over the next decade, not increase.[7] Such occupational measures are limited by their inattention to within-

7. The college-wage premium has leveled off somewhat over the last decade
   as wage stagnation has climbed up the skills distribution. The technology-
   related shift in relative demand for college-educated workers has decelerated since the 1970s and returned to the level of the 1960s (see
   footnote 4). On trends in the occupational composition of the workforce,
   see Howell and Wolff (1991) and Mishel and Teixeira (1991).

occupation changes in desired skill, but more nuanced investigations of such changes – themselves driven by changes in work organization and technology use – are not particularly comforting. Particularly among smaller firms employing fewer than 250 workers, rates of investment in new technology are flat. And only a minority of firms – on no estimate accounting for more than 20 percent of overall employment – are making the broad changes in work organization that drive increased skill demand.

Much of the present US labor market, instead, appears to approximate a "low-wage, low-skill" equilibrium.[8] Given a low-skill environment, and little rigidity in wages, even firms operating under increased competitive pressure have continued with low-skill forms of work organization that require little more than obedience and a good work attitude from direct production or service workers. Having chosen such a strategy, however, the skill demands of these firms are low. While they may wish to remedy deficiencies in very basic worker skills, or provide training to a few in the application of expensive new technology, they generally do not demand or promote broad and continuous skill upgrading among their frontline workforce. Such low-skill, low-wage strategies of course lower overall living standards, but that makes them no less profitable or attractive to firms, and their adoption weakens the political thrust for a stronger training effort.

On the supply side of training provision, meanwhile, most efforts suffer from a series of collective action problems – again centered on employers – that inhibit the effective linkage of workers to jobs and the provision of adequate private sector training. These include simple coordination problems – for example, in matching public training efforts to private firm needs; these also include mixed motive problems – for example,

---

8. For an examination of the characteristics of such an equilibrium point, and the dynamics of a system inclined toward it, see Finegold and Soskice (1988).

in getting agreement on industry-wide standards on skill credentialling. Most famously, however, they include a deep cooperation problem in private firm training investments. Even firms anxious to improve the skills of their workforce face the threat of competitors free-riding on their training efforts. Unless the training employers provide is so narrow that it is only useful in their own firm, it will be tempting for other firms to hire away these newly trained individuals; one firm's trainee may thus become another firm's asset, with the second firm advantaged by the benefits of training but not burdened by its costs. This threat of free-riders leads firms not to train much at all, or to train very narrowly, in ways that are not useful for workers on the external labor market, and that may not be useful for the dynamic efficiency of the firms themselves. In classic "prisoner's dilemma" fashion, individually rational action does not aggregate to socially rational choice. While the economy as a whole would benefit from a better and broadly trained workforce, no individual firm may have the incentive to start providing it.[9]

As a highly liberal political economy, the United States generally lacks mechanisms of association among firms and worker organizations, or working relations between the private and public sectors, that could address the various collective action problems just noted. US governance tends still to be exhausted by "live free or die" choices between command and control regulation and market exchange. Secondary associations performing economic functions are generally weak, and in any case they are rarely integrated explicitly into public governance. As a consequence, virtually all regulation of the kind involved in the training case – i.e., involving the achievement of goals within diverse, dispersed, and numerous sites of economic activity – suffers from severe monitoring and enforce-

9. For an elegant statement on the poaching problem and its solution, see Streeck (1989). For a formal treatment, see Stevens (1994).

ment problems, the expectation of which makes initial goal specification itself more difficult. In the United States, we are very far from the sorts of dense associations that drive the German training system, and that permit, for example, skills standard setting and training enforcement to be a publicly supported and ratified, but essentially privately driven process. And we are far even from the level of private-sector organization, reach, and linkage to public governance relied on in most of the more publicly-driven training systems.[10]

At the same time, the very lack of overarching regulation in the United States and the weakness of encompassing private-sector organization permits experimentation with different sorts of training systems at the regional labor market level. And the highly federated character of the US polity, soon to be underscored with the "devolution" of federal training programs, provides clear incentives for such experimentation while providing it with a material base. Just as "welfare reform" has motivated states to experiment with different programs to move welfare recipients into gainful employment, impending "training reform" will push decision-making about the design of training programs closer to where the "action" really is: into specific regional labor markets dominated by different industry clusters.

Sectoral Consortia to the Rescue?

It is here that a growing number of experiments with sectoral training initiatives offer an interesting base for broader systemic reform.[11] These initiatives organize groups of firms within regional

10. On the institutional and policy supports of Germany's apprenticeship system, see Streeck (1993) and Soskice (1994). On the failings of recent reforms in Britain, see Cappelli (1996) and Wood, Chapter 9.
11. The emphasis here is on the commonalities of sectoral projects to highlight their advantages over common practice. They generally achieve scale, scope, and network economies despite differences arising from the business environment, bargaining power, and policy support. For a

labor markets rather than along national product lines. The firms may compete in the same local market, or operate in entirely separate industries, or form customer-supplier relationships with one another. But what they have in common with one another in each case is the convergence of their work systems and/or skills sets. Firms are brought together by a variety of independent worker organizations responding to the unique challenges encountered by the local parties in a rapidly changing business environment. The projects are designed to advance the living standards of workers by addressing the emerging skill requirements of employers beyond the boundaries of individual firms in the sector.

A sectoral project focused on the shared labor force needs of multiple firms thrives on three key efficiencies. The first has to do with economies of scale obtained by expanding the breadth of employer participation within a regional labor market. Unlike modernization, workforce development, or job connection activities that adopt a narrowly customized firm-by-firm approach, a sectoral approach makes it possible to benchmark public and private sector efforts to advanced industry practices. An information-sharing and standard-setting process across organizations that account for a significant share of the market enables the participants to share the cost of replenishing the skilled labor pool. With enough market share, they have the capacity to secure the accountability of modernization and training institutions to high-road production or service delivery. Instead of reinventing the wheel in one workplace after another, scaling up new programs spreads out the cost of their development and delivery.

Second, sectoral initiatives achieve economies of scope by extending the range of policy areas responsive to the shared needs of organized firms. The development of a diversified pro-

---

comparison of sectoral projects based on their differences in programmatic focus and scope, see Dresser and Rogers (1997a; 1997b) and Bernhardt and Bailey (1998).

gram aligns modernization, training, and related labor market services to the most advanced practices in the sector. Just as the scale of the initiative can capture the accumulated wisdom of learning across firms to augment common elements of curriculum and training routines, the scope of the project achieves efficiencies in program development across policy areas defined by the segment of the workforce they are intended to serve, such as unemployed adults and youth. The same set of core competencies apply whether the individual is employed, unemployed, under-employed, disadvantaged, still in school, or returning to the paid labor force. The alignment of institutional and public policy supports for skill upgrading with a progression of proficiency standards enables workers to build on what they already know to get to where they want to go throughout their careers.

Third, a successful sectoral initiative develops positive network externalities as a growing number of employers, unions, public-sector and community-based partners come together and find ways to solve recurrent problems and meet convergent needs. By sharing information, identifying models, conducting experiments, defining curricula, and building toolkits, the participants are able to sustain and diffuse high-road production or service delivery. The legitimation and dissemination of advanced practices among a growing share of firms in sector facilitates joint investments made by all the stakeholders in the formation of a skilled and committed workforce. As the sector becomes more competitive relative to the low-road, the high-road firms within it may become more tied into the regional economy. With the institutional and public policy supports knitted together by a successful intermediary in the regional labor market, the sector contributes to job opportunity and career security within the region.

Summarizing across these economies of scale and scope and positive network externalities, successful sectoral initiatives create a "win-win" situation for firms, workers, and new labor market entrants from the community. Such initiatives may increase demand for a skilled and committed workforce; enhance learning across business, labor, and community organizations; facilitate benchmarking and standard setting across them; enable related firms to pool their investments in human capital; establish the accountability of public institutions to the high-road; realize efficiencies in the delivery of supports and services; build the capacity of a wider range of players in the labor market; clarify entry-level skill requirements and advancement opportunities; and improve the employment relations climate in the area.

A Proliferation of Examples

There are many examples of sectoral initiatives that advance most of these goals and effects. Their diversity reflects the particular circumstances of their beginnings which vary in terms of the business environment of each sector, the bargaining power of workers within them, and the public-policy supports in their regions. Despite their differences, however, these projects all share important commonalties. Clusters of employers with shared skill needs are brought together through some form of independent worker representation to achieve gains for the local parties.

Industrial Unions

Until quite recently, the most prominent training initiatives of industrial unions were company-wide training funds negotiated at the national level (for example, in aerospace, auto, steel, and telecommunications). But the regional structures of national unions may facilitate the development of sectoral initiatives among firms engaged in different product markets or market segments. These jointly governed projects are part of a more comprehensive strategy for unions to retain and expand the organized share of their respective sectors.

The Labor-Management Council for Economic Renewal was formed in 1990 by the United Auto Workers to assist independent parts suppliers in the Detroit area (Baugh and Hilton 1997). The council supports the development of joint processes for employee involvement and worker training to raise productivity, improve quality, and achieve supplier qualification. With the combined weight of thirty-nine union shops, the project negotiates a lower price for various modernization and training services for its members. A variety of workshops and task forces provides opportunities for managers and labor leaders to share information and learn from one another's experience. The results include the diffusion of electronic-data interchange, quality assurance certification, and computer-based curricula. The council supports the participation of local unions in the reorganization of work for high-road production, while the regional office coordinates the education and mobilization of members to participate in the organization of low-road, non-union competitors.

The Garment Industry Development Corporation (GIDC) was founded back in 1984 by a precursor to UNITE, the textile and apparel union, to support union jobs in New York (Seigel and Kwass 1995). In conjunction with an anti-sweatshop campaign and immigrant worker rights center, the union's partnership with industry associations and public-sector agencies brings about a degree of order in a highly fragmented and competitive industry. The GIDC delivers a wide range of modernization and training services, including export promotion, management and engineering assistance, technology-transfer services, and worker training systems. It also operates a centralized training center and job referral service for employers, workers, and new labor market entrants. The project helps dozens of firms modernize each year (electronic-data interchange, modular work systems, statistical process control, etc.), and train 300 workers off-site and hundreds more in the workplace. The export promotion campaign has generated over $20 million in sales over the last three years.

Multi-Employer and Union Partnership Funds

In service industries where competition in product markets and labor markets coincides at the regional level, unions have occasionally established wage norms through multi-employer agreements. The bargaining arrangements represent something of a hybrid between industrial and craft union models of organization in that most workers are regular employees of a single establishment, yet their employers contribute to industry-wide training funds. In a handful of cities, these funds have become an integral part of comprehensive strategies of bargaining, organizing, and public policy in the health care and hospitality industries.

The largest health-care union in New York, Local 1199, has negotiated multi-employer training funds to support mobility within and between facilities (Cimini and Muhl 1994). Under the terms of the current agreement with fifty-five private hospitals and nursing homes, for example, employers contribute 0.75 percent of payroll to a common fund. The progression of proficiency standards and certification requirements for care-giving and technician occupations provide clear pathways for workers to advance their careers. Large health-care facilities have traditionally provided diverse urban residents with entry-level jobs which can become stepping stones to further training and career development. The fund has supported training for thousands of workers over the years, and, more recently, the fund has become a key part of adjustment to a new environment brought about by managed care and fiscal austerity. Through on-site committees in each facility, the union is able to participate in the reorganization of service delivery, including the redesign of work on the inside and the creation of outplacement centers on the outside, in exchange for a commitment to employment security for most of the workforce. Those who lose their jobs have the right to additional training, income maintenance, and transfer rights to other facilities under the contract. The relocation and redefinition of diagnostic, care-giving, and other service work elevates the strategic importance of training for the union to build solidarity and the capacity to shape the future direction of restructuring in the sector.

The San Francisco Hotels Partnership Project was formed by unions and employers in 1994 to upgrade customer service and job quality in the hospitality industry (Moy 1997). A joint steering committee sets up working groups of managers and local union leaders to develop strategies for achieving objectives such as an industry-wide curriculum for core skills, cross-classification procedures for combining flexibility in staffing with stability in working hours, and the revival of a hiring hall to dispatch workers to special events. Strategies are adapted to the needs of each workplace by joint problem-solving teams that deal with training, work redesign, workload, job security, and related issues. These teams are now engaged in the development of work site procedures for quickly resolving disputes at the lowest possible level within their respective organizations. The first major project is to deliver the core curriculum to more than 1,600 of the 5,000 union members covered by the partnership. More than 100 hours of on-the-job and classroom training, including courses in team-building and English as a Second Language for a diverse workforce, provide the foundation to enhance flexibility for managers and stability for workers through rotations, transfers, reclassifications, and promotions. Additional training is tailored to the main job clusters in the industry, such as the culinary and housekeeping occupations. Resources come from a combination of the state's employment and training fund and the multi-employer fund negotiated by the unions.

Craft Unions

Most multi-employer bargaining agreements are found in the construction industry where the apprenticeships and hiring halls of craft unions have helped employers bring about greater stability in a volatile environment. But union density has declined sharply over the last two decades, particularly in the residential segment of the market. The America Works Partnership was formed with federal support in 1995 to rebuild central city neighborhoods and provide training, stable employment, and union wages and benefits to their residents (America Works 1996). The building trades leverage a variety of resources, such as pension funds, joint apprenticeship funds, and economic development resources, to forge local partnerships with contractors, public sector agencies, and non-profit groups. Local partnerships develop comprehensive strategies to meet the credit, employment, and business development needs of urban neighborhoods. In addition to chapters in Detroit, San Francisco, and Buffalo, America Works has projects started in more than twenty other cities. During the first year in St. Louis, for example, the local project provided pre-apprenticeship training to twenty-five residents with 19 of them going on to an apprenticeship. The aim is to build capacity in numerous cities to recruit, train, and employ hundreds of local low-income people per year. America Works has already achieved a national reputation for being able to train former welfare recipients for living-wage jobs.

Contingent Workers

Emerging models for organizing the new contingent workforce resembles the way that construction has traditionally been organized for generations. The union provides training, employment stability, and continuous benefits for workers who move from job to job. In effect, the union functions very much like a non-profit temp agency that redistributes the surplus to its members.

The Communication Workers of America (CWA) recently formed three employment centers in Cleveland, Seattle, and Southern California to supply skilled workers for high-tech jobs (Carre and Joshi 1997). The union uses its bargaining relationships with the phone companies to convince the companies to establish agreements with contractors to hire qualified workers from its centers, and then the union negotiates an agreement with the contractors or their agents to contribute to common benefit funds. Although the union has some degree of leverage, the prohibition of pre-hire agreements outside the building trades means that the centers must ultimately compete on the open market based on the quality of their workforce. CWA has developed a newly recognized apprenticeship program to qualify dislocated workers, disadvantaged workers, and youth for various kinds of technical work in a rapidly growing field, such as the installation of fiber-optic cable networks. The hope is that a modular design of skill delivery will enable workers to build on what they already know to acquire the skills they need for new jobs in the future.

Some sense of the promise of this approach is available from the Cleveland site, where 200 workers have moved through the employment center thus far. The center matches workers to a variety of jobs based on their qualifications and preferences, such as working part-time to supplement early retirement benefits, stringing together a series of jobs into full-time, year-round employment, or obtaining permanent jobs with client firms. In Seattle, the CWA center recently launched an apprenticeship program with forty participants and developed a school-to-work program to qualify youth for the program. It is also building relationships with community and faith-based organizations to attract unemployed adults to emerging careers in the sector.

Working Partnerships USA, the non-profit arm of the South Bay Labor Council in San Jose CA, is developing a strategy to organize the large contingent workforce in Silicon Valley. Building on its assistance with the development of joint labor-management processes to improve public services, the organization is piloting a training and referral system for limited-term jobs in government agencies (Working Partnerships USA 1997). One promising strategy for scaling this up is to reach similar agreements with a growing number of unionized employers to use the training and referral system for their temporary workers. A critical mass of agreements with employers would enable members to increase their work hours, earnings, and benefits, and seek permanent employment when available.

Non-Union Models

Alternative models of worker organization have emerged as traditional unions have declined. One model is the formation of a network of employee-owned enterprises providing child-care. Childspace Cooperative Development in Philadelphia assists with the development of child-care centers in urban areas which can then be replicated to expand market share (CCD 1997). Two centers employ about 35 workers to care for 235 low and middle income kids. They provide a high level of training, pay a 25 percent premium over the average wage, and offer good benefits by industry standards. The combination of employee voice and superior compensation reduces turnover by half, enabling the centers to recoup their investment in training and improve the continuity and quality of care. In an emerging strategy, the employee-owned centers serve as the hub for a network of organizing, coalition-building, and lobbying to upgrade the quality of care and the quality of jobs in regionally defined markets.

Another model is based on community and faith-based organizations with a strong enough community base to secure public resources for their low-income residents to secure good jobs in target sectors. The San Antonio-based Project QUEST, for example, was sponsored by one of the strongest local affiliates of the Industrial Areas Foundation. Project Quest is based on commitments of substantial resources to fund an integrated program of employment-linked training and support for hundreds of low-income community residents (Clark and Dawson 1995). Area employers in lead sectors, including finance and health care, agree to source living wage entry level to residents who demonstrate specified skills. Community organizations and area technical colleges then work together to identify candidates for the reserved positions, train them to the required competencies, and support them during the training period with integrated income and other supports.

None of these initiatives is identical to any of the others. But while their sizes vary in both absolute and relative terms, they all strive to achieve certain scale economies. Their programmatic reach ranges in scope, but they all leverage public and private resources for skill upgrading. And they generally provide, formally or not, a forum for employers, workers and their organizations, and public training-providers to learn from one another on an ongoing basis.

Wisconsin Regional Training Partnership

One of the most important such sectoral initiatives, exhibiting innovation across the range of modernization and training policy on a large and growing scale, is the Wisconsin Regional Training Partnership (WRTP). We examine it in a bit more detail.

The WRTP was formed in 1992 by employers and unions to support the development of high-performance workplaces providing family-supporting jobs in the durable goods sector of Milwaukee metro area. Working with local Workforce Investment Boards, community/technical colleges, high schools, extension centers, community-based organizations, and other organizations, the WRTP seeks to develop and deliver advanced modernization and training services to both the incumbent and "future" (displaced or pre-entry) workforce. In the manufacturing sector of the region, its activities support an emerging norm of industrial governance in which firms engage in dynamic benchmarking of their training efforts, increasingly conform their external hiring and internal promotion to demonstrated worker competencies, and administer their growing investments in human capital budgets (as a proportion of their payrolls) through joint labor-management committees.

The WRTP now includes more than forty firms, collectively employing more than 40,000 workers in the Milwaukee metro area, or about twenty-five percent of that area's industrial workforce. Firm membership is varied, but concentrated among larger manufacturers and first-tier suppliers. With a range in site size from 100 employees at a tool and die shop to 3,000 at an industrial controls plant, about half of the members have fewer than 500 employees. Despite various differences in products, processes, and technologies, the firms share core design, engineering, and manufacturing competencies in machining, electronics, and/or plastics.

The sector is also still highly unionized in the region, at least by US standards, with roughly one-quarter of the non-supervisory workforce organized on an industry basis, and well above that proportion among larger employers. The production and skilled trades workforce is typically represented by one or more industrial union: e.g., Auto Workers, Electrical Workers, Machinists, Paperworkers, Steelworkers, etc. A few bargaining units are covered by national contracts, but most bargaining agreements are locally negotiated.

Origins of the WRTP

The WRTP emerged at a time when the civilian durable goods sector of the Midwest was still recovering from the deep crisis of the 1980s. Most major employers in the area either relocated, outsourced, or otherwise downsized their operations between 1979 and 1987, and in that period alone Milwaukee County lost almost one-third of its industrial job base. But as a shrunken employment base stabilized in the late 1980s, and exchange rate and national economic conditions turned more favorable, two sharply divergent paths of restructuring became evident: a "low-road" strategy focused principally on reducing production costs for low-end industrial commodities or standardized products (commonly using residual strengths in marketing and distribution acquired during earlier periods of growth to maintain market position); and a "high-road" strategy focused on more diversified quality production. Viewed as a decision about labor-management relations, the choice of strategy was "sweat" (reduce wages and benefits for the existing workforce, outsource as much production as possible to low-wage havens, etc.) or "invest" (in products, processes, technologies, skills, and cooperative labor-management relations). Although some employers continued to pursue a low-wage strategy that exacerbated conflicts with unions, others improved their relations with unions to compete on quality, productivity, and innovation.

The mixed response of unions reflected the difficulty of resisting concessions and preserving jobs amidst the crisis. A few major locals embarked upon a new relationship with employers to turn around troubled companies, such as A.O. Smith and Harley-Davidson, while others became embroiled in protracted conflicts persisting to this day, or went out of existence along with the bankruptcy of a major company like Allis-Chalmers. As the dollar began to fall against other major currencies and the decline in manufacturing bottomed out in the mid-1980s, a growing number of employers and unions began to cooperate on training to facilitate the reorganization of work. This process was aided by the Wisconsin AFL-CIO, which built on its experience with the development of a one-stop assistance center for dislocated workers. Within a few years, the center's director assisted nearly two dozen employers, unions, and their local technical college to establish workplace learning centers. Many of these firms would later become charter members of the partnership.

In this context, a major study of the industry conducted by the Center on Wisconsin Strategy and submitted to industry leaders, unions, and the training establishment for evaluation in 1990 provided the occasion for high-level deliberations about what might be done to support coordination and cooperation among them (Rogers and Streeck 1991). The recommendation that industry and union leaders form a consortium on modernization and training was conditionally accepted, pending further discussion of all-important details on joint governance, programmatic focus, and the like.

From the start of negotiations over consortium structure and program, however, the basic argument for joint industry action was clear. A consortium would provide a forum for cross-firm learning in the development of advanced practices, benchmarking skill requirements on a sector-wide basis, mapping out career paths with respect to the emerging skills set, and securing public and private resources to move people through it. And with a critical mass of members, the consortium could spread the costs of developing a highly skilled and committed workforce for employers (effectively eliminating the poaching problem), and enhance mobility and security for employees both within and between work sites. A local industry leader who chaired a state commission on workforce development and the president of the state labor federation agreed to co-chair the nascent effort, beginning with what turned out to be a prolonged series of meetings, separately at first and then jointly, on the mission and governance of the consortium (for a detailed chronology, see Neuenfeldt and Parker 1996).

The underlying conditions giving rise to the WRTP involved the changing business environment of charter member firms, the remaining strength of industrial unions in the region, and the availability of public policy support for the effort. By design, most of the charter member firms were large or medium-sized firms with a union-represented workforce, experienced in the negotiation of workplace change and skill development. A combination of product market position, worker representation, and previous experience conferred on them interest and the resources to act collectively. Their combined weight in the labor market would reduce the barriers for smaller firms to join later, perhaps with encouragement from their customers who already belonged. The collective deliberations necessary for getting the initiative off the ground benefited from the leadership, social capital, and political clout evident on both sides of the table, and the confidence of key players in the facilitation and technical assistance received throughout the process.[12]

Governance and Growth

The WRTP is jointly governed by a steering committee composed of top business, labor, and public-sector representatives who define the goals and objectives of the consortium. The strategies for achieving them, however, come from managers and local union leaders on the frontline of workplace change. They participate in a series of working groups respectively dedicated to incumbent worker education and skills standards, future workforce needs, and modernization. These taskforces provide an ongoing forum for members to share their stories, identify advanced practices, develop pilot projects, benchmark skill requirements, create new tools, and advocate public policies to be pursued on a consortium-wide basis. Within member firms, meanwhile, managers and unions form joint steering committees and peer adviser networks to implement these general policies in ways attentive to their distinctive production systems, organizational cultures, and bargaining agreements.

The participatory process in which managers, union leaders, and their partners in education, government, and the community learn from one another is key to expanding the scale and scope of the consortium. What generally happens is that members of a working group identify a recurrent problem like the

12. For example, the management representatives recruited business associates to participate in the discussions, while the state labor federation provided a forum for affiliates with members in different industries. By forming a joint steering committee, the parties were confident that they could obtain bipartisan political support for their proposed initiative at both the state and local levels. They both enjoyed various relationships with local government agencies and educational institutions which would assist with implementation, including private industry councils, local technical colleges, and public-school districts.

inconsistency of on-the-job training or a common objective such as the development of a youth apprenticeship program, and then develop a strategy for addressing the issue. The project is presented to the board and any member interested in working on it is invited to attend subsequent meetings and focus groups where they can participate, for example, in the development of a train-the-trainer guide or the standard for youth apprentices. Firms represented in these meetings may become pilot sites where labor-management issues are thrashed out, and the tool or curriculum is tested. Managers and union leaders involved in these projects report on the results to the board and share their experiences with the membership as a whole, by hosting site visits, conducting workshops, and the like. These models are presented at an annual conference which is attended by current and prospective members to expand the partnership and its programs.

INCUMBENT WORKING TRAINING

Members of the WRTP generally have or plan to develop an on-site or multi-work site learning center for everything from basic skills to process improvement to technical skills, such as parts programming. Much of the training and related services, such as assessment, counseling, and confidential testing, are provided by a third party, such as one of the local technical colleges. In Milwaukee County, where about half the learning centers are located, employers invested roughly $1.5 million in 1996. Almost 2,000 workers enroll in learning center programs on an annual basis with more than 500 participants taking part in any given month. Reflecting the demographic composition of the workforce, two-fifths are women and one-quarter are people of color. These figures do not include the additional resources invested by most employers in customized training courses and/or tuition reimbursement programs. Production workers thus have greater opportunities to qualify for apprenticeship or obtain further education from a local technical college or university.

Furthermore, employers and unions increasingly focus on building their own in-house capacity for learning and training on the shopfloor. Many firms have participated in the development of a new peer adviser training manual and one-on-one training guide. They have also defined the objectives for the development of toolkits to upgrade orientation training programs and create training coordinator positions. About three-fourths of the membership has also begun to revive their traditional apprenticeship programs under the revised state standards that members helped upgrade. The skilled trades have customarily required the combination of training on and off the job, but this is now more the norm and less the exception for production workers as well. Skills weigh more heavily in promotion and compensation when the proficiency standards are mutually agreed upon and workers gain universal access to the necessary training through their learning centers and local educational institutions.

FUTURE WORKFORCE PREPARATION

Preparation of the future workforce is an increasingly critical issue now that significant numbers of jobs are being created once again, and an age-compressed workforce is retiring in huge numbers. These trends raise serious concerns about the quality of entry workers for both labor and management. Unions also identify other reasons for taking an active role in solutions to the future workforce problem, such as passing their history on to the next generation, becoming more involved with local schools, orienting new members to their organizations, supporting cultural diversity within their ranks, establishing goodwill in their communities, and showcasing alternatives to punitive welfare reforms and temporary work agencies.

The WRTP piloted the development of the state's youth apprenticeship program in manufacturing three years ago.[13]

13. Wisconsin has developed youth apprenticeship programs in financial services, printing, and other sectors by convening a focus group with employers in the target sector. The metalworking sector has the highest

Members set high occupational standards for the state (taking the first level of voluntary national standards as their starting point), collaborated with a local technical college on the school-based curriculum, negotiated model contract language, piloted a model mentoring program, initiated take-the-teacher-to-work days, and provided technical assistance to the schools. The first graduates qualified for entry-level production jobs, adult apprenticeships in surrounding job shops, advanced standing in technical colleges, and admission into the university system. More than one-third of the member firms have taken on youth apprentices and related school-to-work efforts within the first year since the pilot projects were completed.

The WRTP also developed a model for entry-worker training that provides jobs to successful graduates of pre-employment programs. Members identify the basic skills requirements for major occupations, approve the assessment and curriculum, and assure the participants of a living-wage job. They also work together to improve hiring, mentoring, peer advising, orientation, and further training to retain and develop new workers. This "employment-linked" training model has since become the general approach adopted by the Milwaukee Jobs Initiative. This is a major community development effort funded by national and local foundations to support the expansion of pilot projects in manufacturing (with a goal of 100 entry-level workers in the first year) and the development of additional sectoral

---

level of ongoing employer coordination and employee involvement due to coordination between state officials, educational institutions, and the WRTP. The Milwaukee Graphic Arts Institute, funded by a multi-employer bargaining agreement in the printing industry, encourages firms to participate in youth apprenticeship. Fearing that an officially recognized youth apprenticeship program available to union and non-union contractors would dilute traditional apprenticeship standards, the Milwaukee Building Trades Council recently adopted an alternative school-to-work program (developed by the carpenters) as a model for the construction industry.

initiatives first in construction and printing, and then in other sectors in the future. The jobs initiative mobilizes substantial public and private resources for a central-city workers center founded by the Campaign for a Sustainable Milwaukee to recruit low-income residents for the projects.

MODERNIZATION

The third (and most recent) focus of the WRTP is on the development of the state's new manufacturing extension program for small firms. Most bargaining units are in smaller shops even though the majority of union members are in larger plants. The emergence of largely unorganized supplier networks erodes standards within union suppliers and major hub firms alike. And the poor performance of non-union shops might also erode the competitiveness of final products on world markets. The supplier network is a critical problem without an easy, one-size-fits-all solution in a labor-management environment.

Members of the partnership are currently preparing to launch pilot projects on supplier network development. Unions will have to decide for themselves whether to participate in these types of projects based on the contract provisions they obtain on sourcing, which range from decision-bargaining (where the union receives advance notice and access to information to prepare an alternative plan for in-house production) to joint decision-making (where the company and union co-determine strategic decisions about the core competencies of the enterprise). Some locals may obtain a union preference where, everything else being equal, work is kept or brought back in-house, or is shifted from non-union to union shops.

Whatever the case may be, the pilot projects should showcase models for employers and unions to upgrade their core competencies and optimize their supply chains, and lead to the development of new policy guidelines for extension centers to follow in the future. Should these work out, the overlapping supplier networks of larger manufacturers and first-tier suppliers would become a powerful lever for extending wage norms and skills standards to hundreds of additional shops throughout the region.

Policy Implications of Sectoral Initiatives

While still in their infancy, we believe that regional/sectoral partnerships like the WRTP show considerable promise as the foundation for an alternative to the traditional "American model" of training. In effect, they provide at the regional level what is not provided nationally: a genuine infrastructure of employer and union collaboration that both drives industries toward more advanced skill demands and provides the flow of information, and assurances against free-riding, needed to meet them. Given pressures for devolution in policy, moreover, there is no reason why such efforts could not become more effectively integrated into public labor market administration. There are 46 metropolitan areas in the United States with union densities above 15 percent, including 32 with higher densities than Milwaukee (Hirsch and Macpherson 1996). Their sectoral profiles, labor movements, and local politics obviously vary, but these areas each have the potential to replicate several of the initiatives presented above or develop new ones of their own.

Effective reform of the US workforce development system has generally been frustrated by the absence of organized employer demand for high-road production or service delivery. This has muddied labor market signals to workers and the public sector, encouraged a highly stratified public training system (in which credentials matter more than competencies, and response to new industry practices and demands is slow and uneven), and generally failed to provide critical mass for high-road production as an industry norm. At least in regional labor markets, consortial efforts like the WRTP appear to be making considerable progress in addressing these problems. They provide much clearer industry signals to workers and the public sector; scale and scope in the provision of training directed to competencies and advancement; and sufficient critical mass and shared planning capacity to underwrite strategic choice for the high-road.

Building on this experience, we can imagine a new workforce development system in many regional labor markets where such consortia could provide the natural ballast and direction for program administration. Whatever the many confusions of US training reform at present, it is fairly clear that block grants are coming, and that the structure for their administration will be some descendant of the Private Industry Councils first mandated under the Job Training Partnership Act (JTPA) with jurisdictions carved on regional labor market terms. Various states, Wisconsin included, have already established "Workforce Development Boards" along these lines, with an essentially private governance (with a majority of seats assigned to business) broadly mimicking that of the original PICs. Were sectoral consortia more widely developed, their leaders would provide a natural source of such business (and union and community) representation, with the effect of tying the public system much more closely to the real local economy. Consolidation of labor market services, moreover, might be naturally extended to include elements of the fledgling manufacturing modernization infrastructure the Clinton administration has been at pains to preserve and develop. This federally supported, state-based system for assisting small and medium-sized manufacturers is now capable of reaching thousands of firms annually. Operating at some $300 million annually, it is the most significant US program acting directly on the demand side of the skills equation.

The result would be, in effect, a series of regional labor market boards, with financial resources to apply considerable leverage within a more organized private sector. How incentives for movement to such a system might be provided without mandating such industry organization would also be relatively straightforward. Participation in it could reasonably be offered as a condition for discounts on public training and modernization assistance based on the rationale that public dollars are best spent where private leverage and representativeness is demonstrated. Such boards could be charged as well with local implementation of the national skills standards, providing some baseline coordination of their activities. And the process of organizing regional industry and labor, which is not a desperately hard thing to do based on the experience in Wisconsin and elsewhere, could be supported through demonstration grants and a minimal national technical assistance infrastructure. The demonstration effect and constituency arising from these initial efforts would create the impetus for the further development of supports at the federal and state levels.

Of course, whether this really happens, or happens fast enough to capture the energies now unleashed by reform-mindedness and devolution, is not something we can confidently predict. But it is certainly a development worth watching, and for Europeans the fact that it is already happening unselfconsciously, without almost any explicit public support, may carry some interesting lessons. Based on the experience in the most liberal of polities, with the greatest hostility to government, with the weakest associational structures in business and the most decimated labor movement, it appears that there is at least a plausible way to develop functional, flexible, and politically supported labor market administration on a regional/sectoral basis. That level of administration appears to capture the operative efficiencies of associational action, while being sufficiently informed by local experience, and allowing a speed and flexibility in government response, to allow the requisite organization of employers and labor. The process of building broader institutional and public policy supports in the United States may come to resemble the process of accelerating the adaptation of such supports in Germany to a changing environment.[14]

14. For a comparison of meso-level innovations designed to reduce unemployment without eroding social standards in Germany and to support

What is less clear is the feasibility of such organization where labor, or some other encompassing organization with real presence and clout in the community of workers, is weak. Milwaukee, while hardly the "union town" it once was, still has a significant union presence. San Antonio, while never a union town, still has COPS (Communities Organized for Public Service). Where such non-business organization does not exist, the spontaneous organization and maintenance of sectoral initiatives is a more remote prospect. Even if employers succeed in organizing themselves, they would not have the capacity to represent worker interests. But it is possible to imagine incentives for the development of independent worker organization, and certainly the evolution of new structures of representation, such as networks of employee-owned enterprises, community-sponsored worker associations, and community-based hiring halls. Doing that through explicit policy supports would of course require deeper political commitment to the promise of sectorally based initiatives than currently exists. In moving that policy agenda, however, the demonstration effect of even modest support for current or emerging initiatives, in more "naturally" favorable sites, should not be slighted.

Nor should the appeal, in an era of "downsized" government, devolution, and "public-private partnership" rhetoric, of harnessing private industry power to public purpose. The real boost to workforce development capacity provided by sectoral initiatives comes not from increased public spending, but from more disciplined (by collective industry voice) targeting of public training resources, and increased firm commitment (itself occasioned by resolution of the collective action problems noted) to investing in the technology and training needed to underwrite the high-road. What is most needed at the moment is simply public recognition of the potential contribution of such regional

---

wage norms and skill standards in the United States, see Parker and Wever (1997).

partnerships, which is essentially costless, and clearly in the interest of a public sector under sustained attack. The devolution of some labor market administration to sectoral consortia, and the development of routines on the delivery of training, modernization assistance, and other public labor market supports more closely coordinated with those consortia, provides a natural way to "reinvent" government in ways more fruitful than its simple defunding or haphazard privatization.

Chapter 9

BUILDING A GOVERNANCE
STRUCTURE FOR TRAINING?

Employers, Government and the
TEC Experiment in Britain[*]

Stewart Wood

Introduction

In the British government's own words, "there is nothing quite like a TEC" (DfEE 1995: paragraph 1.2). Born out of New Right and New Public Management paradigms, Training and Enterprise Councils (TECs), and their Scottish equivalents, Local Enterprise Councils (LECs), sit on the boundaries between the public and private spheres. Though formally commercial entities, they are charged with a range of local economic development tasks, and implement an array of government programs. Their central task, however, has been "to plan and deliver train-

[*] I am grateful to Pepper Culpepper and David Finegold for very helpful comments on an earlier version of this chapter, as well as to Gary Herrigel, Desmond King, Joel Rogers, and Karin Wagner for their suggestions.

ing" (Department of Employment 1988: 40); and in this respect TECs, though a novel institutional innovation, represent the latest in a catalogue of public policy efforts to address Britain's longstanding failure to produce skilled labor (Finegold 1992, Finegold and Soskice 1988). In the 1960s, Industrial Training Boards were established with statutory powers to impose a levy on all firms within a sector in order to finance increased training activity (Wood 1997, Sheldrake and Vickerstaff 1987). In the 1970s, intervention was centralized under the aegis of the Manpower Services Commission, a tripartite body which orchestrated manpower policy until the mid-1980s (Worcester 1990, Dale 1989).

The creation of TECs marked an explicit rejection of these collectivist and interventionist principles. Underlying TECs was the belief that the coordination among employers required for the collective provision of skilled labor would be best achieved by a *decentralized, employer-led* governance structure. The comparison with the German case is illuminating because of Germany's clear success in maintaining a continuing supply of marketable skills over time. Employers in Germany have "inherited" an enduring network of institutions, practices and incentive structures that supports a "high-skill equilibrium" (Soskice 1994, Streeck et al. 1987). Occupying a central place in this network are the much-vaunted *Industrie- und Handelskammern*, or chambers of industry and commerce, legally and functionally central to the governance of in-firm training in German companies. In Britain, however, as in a number of other countries, such coordination has historically been absent. These countries therefore face the policy problem of stimulating employer involvement and collective action in order to create a set of intermediate skills. The TEC experiment is from this perspective a case study of an attempt to move away from a "low-skill equilibrium" by *creating* institutions of private governance (Williamson 1985).

This chapter evaluates the success of this attempt over the past decade. Its conclusions are pessimistic about the transformative capacity of TECs, however. Competitive rather than cooperative relationships between firms remain fundamental obstacles to TECs' ability to overcome collective action problems among employers. Nevertheless, many of the weaknesses of TECs can be argued to stem from problems of "constitutional design," and could be mitigated by institutional reform. In addition, more successful programs (notably the recently introduced "Modern Apprenticeship" scheme) offer hopeful signs for future public policy regarding British vocational training.

There are deep ambiguities about the mission of TECs which are ingrained into their constitution and practices. At least five fundamental "constitutional" tensions can be identified at the outset:

(a) *Control vs. autonomy*: TECs were intended to be autonomous bodies and are encouraged to develop their own strategies for mobilizing the employer community in their area. However, the government has proven reluctant in practice to allow TECs such latitude. Rather, it has chosen to introduce a plethora of budget controls and performance requirements whose incentives divert TECs from the task of fostering skill creation.

(b) *Local vs. central*: Although TECs were designed to exemplify the virtues of a local approach to local economic needs, led by prominent local businessmen, most of their work consists of administering national government programs. In addition, concerns about variations between TECs, and problems of coordination between TECs, have led government and its "monitoring agents" to centralize control to an even greater degree.

(c) *Public vs. private*: The clear intention behind TECs was that they should be private-sector entities, operating on general commercial principles, and run

by leading businessmen in an entrepreneurial way. However, TECs are dominated by former public sector employees, and, more generally, by the fiscal pressures and bureaucracy of the public sector.

(d) Coordination vs. competition: One of the core rationales for TECs was that they would act as catalysts for the coordination of employers, helping to bring together the various employer organizations, and to overcome fragmentation within the local employer community (Fowler 1989). In contrast, employers and employer organizations see TECs as competitors for increasingly scarce government funds. TEC funding to employers is explicitly based upon competitive principles, rather than being structured in ways that encourage cooperation and collective action.

(e) Skills vs. employment: TECs were intended to increase the skill levels of the local workforce. However, the training and employment programs they administer have primarily been used as a form of temporary alleviation of unemployment. As employers have adjusted to this shift in emphasis, it has become increasingly difficult for TECs to engage employers in collective action oriented toward "upskilling."

The chapter is divided into six parts. Section 1 illustrates the nature of the training and education problem in Britain, and sketches out the strategic incapacities of British business that make its solution so difficult. Section 2 provides some background on the origin and structure of TECs. Section 3 examines the internal organization of TECs, while section 4 turns toward the relationship between TECs and government, the area in which TECs have (justifiably) been criticized most vociferously. In section 5, the relationship between TECs and employers is analyzed, as well as their interaction with a host of other groups and actors involved in the provision of training. Lastly, reforms and developments since 1993 (some encouraging) are outlined in section 6. The conclusion provides some suggestions about reforming the TEC apparatus.

A preliminary note about the emphasis of this chapter. The focus here is the nexus between TECs and training in order to facilitate comparison with the role of employer organizations in the German dual system. This does not provide an exhaustive overview of TEC functions. TECs are engaged in four broad areas of local economic activity – training, education, enterprise, and economic development. Though the training function was initially prioritized, and remains the central task of TECs, their involvement in these other activities is far from insignificant. Indeed, from 1993 onwards the Conservative Government attempted to increase the role of TECs in local economic development, and established new institutions and funding to this end. Furthermore the Scottish version of TECs, LECs, are considerably more involved in economic and community development than their English and Welsh counterparts – in 1994 approximately twenty percent of their budgets was allocated to this area, while TECs had no budget allocation for local economic development whatsoever (Bennett et al. 1994: 261). Many of the problems of employer coordination are replicated across these various functions, and to that extent much of the analysis here is applicable across the gamut of TEC activities, although they do not receive explicit attention here.

The Problem of Training in Britain

In spite of a considerable increase in recent years, participation in further and higher education (FE and HE) remains relatively low in Britain (Mason 1996). Staying-on rates after compulsory schooling ends are poor in international comparison – in 1992, 70 percent of 16-18 year-olds were in full-time education and training in the UK, compared to 81 percent in the US and 92 percent in Germany (FEFC 1992). By 1996 the English figure had risen to 75.4 percent, though it has been virtually unchanged since 1993 (DfEE 1997b). Nevertheless, the number of eighteen-year-olds in full-time enrolment in Britain is still under 50 percent, compared to over 90 percent in the Netherlands, Belgium, Japan and Germany (CERI 1995). Britain also lags behind in terms of attainment and qualifications. In 1991 only 27 percent of English sixteen- year-olds reached GCSE grades A-C in math, their national language and one science, trailing 62 percent of German and 66 percent of French students in equivalent exams. In the same year the number of eighteen-year olds obtaining an upper secondary school qualification or equivalent was 68 percent in Germany, 80 percent in Japan, but a mere 29 percent in England (Green and Steedman 1993). Drop-out rates in British further education (FE) are also very high – between 30 and 40 percent of sixteen-to-nineteen year olds leave schools and colleges without achieving the qualifications connected to the courses for which they enrolled (OFSTED/ Audit Commission 1993, Hillman 1996). Relatively low educational attainment among school-leavers is manifested in a shortage of basic skills upon entry into the workforce. In one recent survey nearly one in four employers reported that applicants' basic skills were only just adequate or worse (Atkinson and Spilsbury 1993). The Adult Literacy and Basic Skills Unit has estimated that there are around ten million adults in Britain who are "functionally illiterate" (Education 1994).

With regard to vocational qualifications the position is bleaker still. At the time of the TECs' inauguration in 1990, 63 percent of British workers had no vocational qualifications at all, compared to 26 percent of the German workforce. Intermediate vocational qualifications had been earned by 56 percent of German workers, but by only 20 percent of British workers (Prais and Beadle 1991). In 1986 a new type of qualification, the National Vocational Qualification (NVQ), was introduced. In principle this marked a welcome innovation. The policy introduced a *national* and comprehensive certification system for the first time, with standards for each industry's scheme defined by sectoral industry organizations. It was also a genuine attempt to correct the traditional emphasis on "time served" as a criterion for vocational qualifications, i.e. a "standards-based, not time-constrained" qualification (Saunders et al. 1997). But NVQs have suffered from criticisms that their low entry-level standards, and their rewarding of discrete rather than flexible tasks, have in effect merely legitimized the low-skill status quo (Cleveland 1993, Steedman 1990). More generally a number of studies have demonstrated a persistent and sizeable gap in the skill levels of British workers compared to their occupational equivalents in other West European countries (Prais 1995, Steedman, Mason and Wagner 1991). Equally worrying is the evidence of a parallel gap in the *demand* for skills between British and European firms (Finegold 1993).

The failure of British firms and schools to deliver a workforce equipped with flexible, marketable skills has been at the forefront of the public policy agenda for more than forty years. Yet despite a barrage of policy initiatives since the Carr Report of 1957, the problem has remained severe. Finegold and Soskice (1988) have persuasively argued that this resistance of the political economy to policy stimuli can be explained by the concept of a "low-skill equilibrium." Low levels of industrial training, they argue, are rooted in a network of supply-side institutional incentives that underpin a distinctive set of product market and innovation strategies characteristic of British firms. The problem of training cannot, therefore, be taken in isolation from other "subsystems" of the political economy. Efforts to increase the supply of or demand for skilled labor run up against the barriers of conflicting incentives and constraints within these subsystems. Managers dependent upon short term capital, for example, face short-term strategic planning horizons that militate against investment in human capital. These horizons are reinforced by the absence of trained trainers within firms, and the prevalence of traditional accounting techniques (Finegold 1993). The ease of hire-and-fire within firms prevents the creation of strong, protected internal labor markets within firms, while the low pay differential between skilled and unskilled workers acts as a further disincentive to workers to invest in their own training (Tan and Peterson 1993). Employers are also faced by an educational system that rewards academic high-flyers, offering few incentives for vocationally oriented students to stay on in school. Lastly, employers themselves enjoy weak mechanisms of coordination, whether in the form of industrial districts, strong employer organizations, or looser forms of employer networks (Wood 1997).

The result of this package of incentives is a low capacity for organizing training collectively, *coupled with a low demand for skilled labor* in general. The second of these features follows on logically from the first. Where collective action to solve the problem of providing skilled labor is either absent or ineffective, surviving firms will become progressively less reliant on product market strategies that rely on such skills. Those firms that do conduct in-firm training emphasize firm-specific training (i.e. skills that are not transferable, and skilled workers who are less "poachable") rather than general training resulting in marketable skills (Becker 1964, Groot 1996).

The question of the weak demand for skills raises a crucial question for training policy. For if employers are simply uninterested in employing skilled workers, policy measures designed to increase the supply of marketable skills will be unfeasible, irrelevant or both (Wood 1997, Keep and Mayhew 1996). Weak demand for skills is certainly at the root of many of the problems faced by TECs in the local economy, and in many ways there is little that TECs, or tinkering with their institutional design, can do to overcome this problem. Nevertheless, sectoral skills shortages persist, suggesting a continuing role for public policy oriented toward the supply of marketable skills. In addition there is some evidence that the supply-shock of increased numbers of graduates entering the workforce from the mid-1980s onwards has had knock-on effects in increasing employers' demand for skills (Mason 1996). Thus, while expectations of TECs should perhaps be kept reasonably low, their potential contribution to the improvement of Britain's training record is not insignificant.

The Origin and Establishment of TECs

The task that prompted the launch of TECs was to stimulate training by creating an institution that would be a "catalyst for change in its local community" (Training Agency 1989: 1) by mobilizing employers into increasing and coordinating their activities. Undoubtedly the example of the *Kammern* in West Germany was influential in this respect. However the specific model for TECs was based on Private Industry Councils (PICs) in the US, established in 1978 under the Job Training Partnership Act (Bailey 1993). Though the remit of PICs was far more circumscribed (to training and employment services for the disadvantaged) than that of their British counterparts,[1] PICs and TECs are centered around four common organizational principles. First, they are private-sector bodies, run by a board of private-sector employees acting in a private rather than a representative capacity. Second, TECs are organized locally, at the helm of the local economy, and recruited from the ranks of local businessmen. The hope was that employers would thereby "be given a sense of *ownership* of the system of training and enterprise creation" (Industry Department, Scotland 1988: 9). Third, the management of TECs was to be run according to the principles of an "enterprise organization," "capable of driving radical reform …. born of the enterprise culture, with a bold vision that stretches beyond existing programs, institutions, and traditional

---

1. The Department of Employment enlisted the help of Cay Stratton, an aide of Michael Dukakis and expert on PICs, in the drawing-up of blueprints for TECs.

methods of delivery" (Training Agency 1989: 8). Lastly, TECs were intended to make the educational and training systems more coherent, with an accent on implementing rewards and penalties based on carefully measured *performance* of different training providers.

In short, TECs are government-created but privately run regional organizations, charged with the tasks of administering the various government schemes that subsidize employers to undertake different forms of training activity, and more broadly of being a local-level stimulant to economic development and enterprise. TECs thus truly straddle the conventional divide between public and private spheres. In terms of objectives, TECs can be said to be the local deliverers of national public policy, as well as catalysts for more coherent and systematic cooperation between companies and other economic actors. In terms of structure and activities, however, TECs are clearly private sector organizations, run by leading local employers with (in theory at least) considerable decisional latitude.

TECs thus embodied a number of different strands of New Right thinking (King 1987). Advancing the interests of employers was justified on economic grounds – TECs were designed to emulate the virtues of a private-sector company in the pursuit of public goals. Private-sector dominance of TECs would increase their prestige and credibility. Furthermore, employers were considered best placed to estimate skill needs in the short and medium term (Training Agency 1989: 222), and to bring more efficient administration to the operation of government programs (Stratton 1989). Government White Papers talked of "[giving] leadership of the training system to *employers*, where it belongs" (Department of Employment 1988: 43). The timing of the introduction of TECs – in 1989-90 – coincided with a mini economic boom and a tight labor market, which, it was hoped, would get employers behind the TECs and eager to work together on training.

Behind this justification, however, lay a political motivation to marginalize the role of trade unions, and to a lesser extent that of professional organizations and local authorities, in training policy (King 1993). By 1988 the government had become exasperated with the perceived obstructionism of TUC members of the Manpower Services Commission and its successor, the Training Agency, reaching its peak in the call for the abolition of the Employment Training program at the TUC Congress that year (Evans 1992). Clearly TECs have also served to distance government from the day-to-day management of unemployment and labor market policy. TECs have also been seen as part of a consistent philosophy of privatizing government functions, and specifically the culmination of the retreat of government from training that had gathered momentum throughout the 1980s (Farnham and Lupton 1994). Lastly, the management ethos of TECs – based on contracts, targets and "purchaser-provider" relationships between the state and private actors – conforms to the principle of "new public administration" that governed the restructuring of the health service, the state education sector, and the civil service in the 1980s (Deakin 1996). Underlying this paradigm of "government through sub-contracting" is a view of the virtues of markets over state regulation; in the words of Michael Heseltine, the President of the Board of Trade, "if you want really accountable units, you want them as far removed from the disciplines of the classic public sector arrangements as possible."[2]

TECs were introduced with a flurry of White Papers and publicity between December 1988 and April 1990. By October

2. It is far from clear that the constitution and "modus operandi" of TECs are consonant with all of these New Right objectives. Certainly trade unions remain marginalized in TECs, as do local authorities. But the state has retained an active, interventionist role in manpower policy. In the name of enforcing performance targets and improving monitoring capacity the government has become a dominant influence over TECs. The TEC experiment thus illustrates a more general feature of Conservative government policy after 1979, namely the tension that exists between principles of state and market, withdrawal and interventionism (Gamble 1988, King 1987).

1991, 82 TECs had been established in England and Wales, and a further 22 LECs in Scotland. Organized as not-for-profit limited companies, TECs were to be run by Boards of Directors of no more than 15 members, two-thirds of which had to consist of "chairmen, chief executives or top operational managers at the local level of major companies" (Training Agency 1989: 4). TEC staff initially comprised civil servants on secondment who were workers previously employed in the regional and local Manpower Services Commission offices. Individual TECs, however, were established by a process of "bidding-up" – the Training Agency of the Department of Employment issued guideline criteria for the size, budget, and staffing levels of TECs, and invited bids from locally organized groups to set up a TEC in their area. Budgets, on the other hand, were (and remain) strictly controlled by the administering department. In 1994 each TEC received an average of £20m from the Department for Education and Employment (DfEE), 74 percent of which went toward government employment and training programs (38 percent of LECs budget). Of these by far the two biggest are Youth Training (YT) and Training for Work (TfW, formerly Employment Training or ET) programs. TECs' role in these programs is to arrange for training providers in their area (meaning firms, colleges, voluntary organizations, chambers of commerce, and professional training companies) to take on trainees under these schemes, and to provide government funding from the DfEE. Since 1995 TECs have also administered a new program entitled Modern Apprenticeship (MA), a scheme that has expanded with remarkable and perhaps surprising speed (see below). The remainder of the budget is devoted toward a variety of enterprise, education and development programs (Bennett et al. 1994: 3-7).

The task of evaluating TECs brings with it the problem of finding an appropriate yardstick. Perhaps the sternest test is to measure them against the standard provided by German chambers of commerce. Although, as noted earlier, TECs were not created in imitation of the German *Kammern*, both are employer-led bodies based in the local economy to coordinate employer activities (including, but not limited to, company training). Yet TECs share few structural features with German chambers of commerce other than their location in the local economy. Basic differences in "constitutional" features can account for much of the inability of TECs to emulate the coordinating functions exercised by the *Kammern* in Germany. First is the question of size. TECs' jurisdictions average about 250,000 working people, considerably smaller than German chambers. Their staffing level is about half that of the chambers, while their core budget is about one-tenth the size (Bennett et al. 1993). Second, whereas chambers have a long-standing organizational identity, rooted in public law and integrated into local economies, TECs are institutional upstarts that have inevitably been viewed as competitors by other local actors. Routine collaboration between German chambers and employers associations over a range of training policy and administration issues, for example, is a far cry from the mutual suspicion still in evidence between TECs and sectoral employers organizations (Streeck et al. 1987). In addition, apprentice wage levels are part of collective agreements in Germany negotiated by unions and employer associations, who in turn have strong links with and representation within chambers of commerce. In Britain there are virtually no parallel links between training and other structural features of the employer-employee relationship. Consequently, the range of supporting incentives and constraints that promotes in-firm training in Germany is absent in the British case.

But the most important contrast concerns the role of the state in the two systems. German *Kammern* are statutory bodies, protected by public law from government intervention. TECs, on the other hand, are not statutorily protected. Consequently they are victims not merely of repeated government intervention – in turn leading to problems of long-term planning and inconsistency of mission – but also of low expectations of their long-term survival. This has made it hard for TECs to earn credibility among the groups that they are intended to bring together. The (well-founded) suspicion that TECs are more the creatures of a Government Department than of business itself contrasts sharply with chambers of commerce, which are quite clearly institutions of private governance. Independence from government is *functionally* crucial to chambers of commerce, particularly in their efforts to solicit accurate information from firms about future manpower needs and training practices. On the other hand, TECs have great difficulty in obtaining the cooperation of firms in supplying information. Differences in the funding regimes between the two systems are equally important. TECs are almost totally dependent on central government funding, and their autonomy is strongly constrained by the terms upon which they are required to administer government programs. German chambers of commerce receive compulsory membership dues from all firms in the region over which they have jurisdiction, and consequently escape the vagaries of public expenditure rounds, fiscal cutbacks and switches of government priorities that have bedeviled TECs. Finally, whereas German chambers embody a long-standing and cross-partisan commitment to consensual regulation involving both trade union and employer representatives, TECs were explicitly founded on a rejection of such corporatist principles (King and Wood 1998).

The weakness of TECs relative to German *Kammern* should not prejudice the question of TECs' performance, however. Most TECs have now been in operation for over six years, and there exists a wide range of research evaluating their structure, activities and relationship with other bodies. A more realistic evaluation of TECs should assess their contribution in the light of the weak institutions and governance structures that they inherited. TECs were launched to help coordinate the disparate activities of a variety of actors at the national, sectoral and local level. Thus the remainder of this chapter examines three aspects of TECs' *governance*: the "internal" question of TEC organization; the "vertical" relationship between TECs and government; and the "horizontal" relationship between individual TECs, employers and other groups.

The Internal Organization of TECs

Clearly TECs were designed to be managed by "movers and shakers" from the business world (HCEC 1996: paragraph 29). To some extent TECs have lived up to this aspiration – surveys of the composition of TEC boards of directors suggest that over 80 percent come from large or medium-sized companies in the private sector (Vaughan 1993). However, TEC Boards have fallen short of the objective that they "adequately reflect a mix of company size, sector and geographical location" (TEC National Council 1995: paragraph 32). In particular the eligibility criteria for Board membership tend to exclude members from the numerous small businesses, and from subsidiary sites of large companies, in particular of national chain-stores (HCEC 1996: paragraph 32). General Managers of national companies thus find themselves excluded from TEC Boards whereas Chief Executives of smaller firms dominate. Aside from the problems of representing the diversity of the business community, one consequence of this gap has been that relations between TECs and the largest companies (also, in many cases, the largest trainers) have suffered considerably.[3] There also appears to be a sectoral bias toward manufacturing and extractive industries on TEC boards – over 68 percent of directors in an early cross-sectional survey came from these sectors, which account for under a third of overall employment in the national economy (Bennett et al. 1994: 55).

Surveys of TEC Boards reveal that Directors are overstretched, and vary widely in their commitment to TEC work

3. The collapse of South Thames TEC in 1994 was partially attributed by its Chairman to the fact that the major employers in the area – Sainsburys, Shell and the *Financial Times* – were excluded from participation under the rules governing Board composition.

(Houghton et al. 1995). Directors are not paid for their service, yet over 25 percent reported working over six hours per week. Perhaps unsurprisingly, about 17 percent of private sector directors do not attend Board meetings regularly (Financial Times 1992, 1993), and annual turnover rates are high (Bennett et al. 1994: 53, Vaughan 1993). TEC Chairmen work for the TEC for about 40 hours per month; Directors work for approximately 23 hours per month (HCEC 1996: paragraph 31). Paradoxically, however (in the light of the government's desire for TECs to epitomize the entrepreneurialism of the private sector), over 70 percent of the first wave of TEC Chief Executives came from the *public* sector, in no small part because it was government policy, as stated in the TEC Operating Manual for 1989, that "TECs should first consider appointing the Training Agency area manager."

TEC personnel were recruited largely from former Training Agency Area and Regional Offices when these were wound up in 1990. Many did not go voluntarily, yet TECs were faced with little alternative because government guidelines issued by TEED (the Training Education and Employment Directorate which manages TECs for the DfEE) severely constrained autonomous personnel policies. Bennett et al. (1994), in their authoritative study of TECs, go so far as to call this "the most crucial design-failure of the TECs" (Bennett et al. 1994: 59). Employers have expressed concerns about the quality of TEC staff, particularly that they have little experience in dealing with employers rather than with fellow bureaucrats (Crowley-Bainton 1993). Studies of individual TEC organization also reveal that staff efficiency suffers from a variety of organizational problems, such as excessive bureaucratic tiers and insufficient devolution of tasks.

TEC-Government Relations

One of the central complaints about TECs is that individual boards do not have sufficient discretion to pursue autonomous local training and enterprise strategies. Some of the contributory factors lie in internal constraints stemming from the personnel rigidities highlighted above. More central, however, are constraints imposed by government: a general lack of financial resources; restrictions on the deployment of budgets outside allocated areas; the necessity of hitting nationally defined targets of performance in order to receive monies; and the constant (many would also say increasing) intrusion of TEED and the Treasury into TEC activities.

Individual TECs are supervised directly by government departments. In England, the "master" of the TECs is the Department for Education and Employment (combined from the separate Employment and Education Departments in July 1995), whereas in Scotland and Wales LECs and TECs report to the Scottish and Welsh Offices respectively. (Within England, the TEED within the DfEE handles most TEC-related business, and after 1993 much of the Department's administration was devolved to the newly established regional offices of government.) Until 1994 TECs and the departments to which they are linked negotiated annual operating contracts. Each TEC agreed to specific objectives with the Department for a twelve-month period, based upon aims expressed in a three-year corporate plan. Money was allocated to each objective, although TECs were expected to obtain supplementary finance from other sources. In 1994, however, this system was modified after repeated complaints that the short time-horizon of the one-year contract system was hampering long-term planning and effective cooperation with employers. A new three-year licensing system was introduced, replacing the annual contracts. To obtain a license, TECs must achieve a certain minimal standard over a range of criteria (including meeting national targets on program delivery, management of Youth Training Guarantees, and demonstrating financial viability and auditing practices). Introducing the license was thus partially designed as a signal of confidence to local employers that their TEC was a "quality organization." The outgoing Conservative Government made it clear that after 1997 it would only deal with licensed TECs, thus establishing a form of preferred supplier relationship. By February 1997 all 74 English TECs had been awarded three-year licenses (DfEE 1997d). In order to monitor the terms of the contract, the government imposed an array of financial control and auditing requirements on TECs. Audits are conducted by the Department, the National Audits Office, the European Commission and the Regional Offices of government. Furthermore, TECs are required to monitor the delivery of government programs by training providers at regular intervals.

This system of contractual obligations and monitoring is the primary source of conflict within the TEC constitution. Contracts are routinely "excruciatingly detailed," even compared to other public-sector contracts, making it almost a certainty that TECs will not "deliver" on all terms, and undermining the ability of TECs to act as flexible institutions in their locality. Furthermore, the contracts are specified with reference primarily to *national* blueprints. After contracts are concluded TECs are further constrained by the demarcation of individual budgets for each program – most TECs receive over 20 different budgets. Each program is managed and audited separately, leading to high management costs and mind-boggling paper chasing. The TEED at the apex of this bureaucracy has in consequence been described with some justification as a "colonial-style administration (with) 1000 civil servants issuing documents trammeling local boards" (Bennett, from HCEC 1996: paragraphs 11-12).

Rationalization since 1993 has ameliorated the excesses of this system to a small degree. Regional Offices of TEED have taken over administrative responsibilities from TEED's headquarters at Moorfoot to allow for greater variations between localities, and organize TECs into regional bids for EU funding.[4]

4. The development of TEED Regional Offices was a response to the 1992 Styles Report, which examined the tension identified here between

Since 1993, responsibility for TECs has been shared by the DfEE with the Department for Trade and Industry (DTI), with the latter monitoring business support and enterprise programs. Nevertheless, the problem of excessive interventionism and centralization in the name of ensuring accountability and adequate performance remains acute. Restructuring the national representation of TECs has been particularly problematic. In October 1992 the National Training Task Force, set up two years earlier as a para-public body to influence TEED policy, was wound up. The government chose instead to communicate with TECs through the "G10," a self-appointed group of TEC directors that was widely resented by other TEC boards. From mid-1993 onwards the TEC National Council was established, but like its predecessors it suffers from the perception, if not the reality, of domination by the TEED.

The system of financial control received its greatest criticism in 1994 after the collapse of South Thames TEC. According to the Comptroller and Auditor General, "the board of the TEC went for four or five months without receiving any financial advice at all, any accounts at all" (Public Accounts Committee 1996: 108). Once South Thames TEC realized the seriousness of its financial condition, however, the Department of Employment refused to modify its standard accounting procedures, a decision which effectively drove the TEC to bankruptcy. A review by the Public Accounts Committee laid the blame for the collapse on the hybrid nature of TECs, neither Government department nor executive agency, but something quite different with ill-specified chains of responsibilities and no internal auditing mechanisms.

While financial controls inside TECs may be patchy, *external* financial control of TECs by TEED is remarkably stringent.

---

accountability and local flexibility. It also marked a recognition of the growing importance of strong regional organization within the European Union – see NTTF 1992.

Unlike German chambers of commerce, TECs receive 95 percent of their funding from government sources (HCEC 1996: paragraph 77), a system which puts them at the mercy of government policy and public expenditure rounds. Allocations to programs have been accompanied by constant threats of cuts, and, after 1993, a prohibition on "virement" (the movement of funds from one program to another). Furthermore, in the past 2-3 years the government has increased the proportion of TEC budgets that depends upon "results." "Output-related funding" (ORF) is now used to distribute 75 percent of TEC budgets for the Training for Work (TfW) program – payment for the training is only fully provided if the course has led to a "successful outcome" (a job, full-time education or a recognized qualification). The problem with ORF is not the principle of conditioning funding upon results, but rather the way in which these results are set and measured. One central effect of ORF has been to tie TEC budgets more than ever to achieving targets on national *unemployment* programs, making the pursuit of local *upskilling* strategies a low priority.

But ORF is not merely a distraction from the task of training; there is evidence that it reduces the amount, quality, and equality of distribution of training. Certainly there are now strong incentives for training providers to "cream" the lower-risk groups, as taking on more needy trainees involves the not insignificant risk of their failing to obtain a qualification, and therefore non-payment to the firm. A Coopers and Lybrand report on the ORF pilot schemes observed that firms also trained to a lower level to avoid this danger, or placed people in less demanding jobs merely to register a "successful outcome." Job placements are emphasized by ORF irrespective of the training that is required to equip trainees for the tasks involved. Meanwhile training in skill areas that are too demanding has been cut back. In other words, the net effect of ORF is to reinforce rather than overcome the problem of poor skill production by constructing incentive structures to move individuals into low-skill employment as rapidly as possible (Coopers and Lybrand 1995). ORF is a system that serves the interests of the Treasury far more than those of British employers and their workforce, perpetuating rather than overcoming the low-skill equilibrium (Finegold 1992: 242).[5]

One response of TECs to excessive dependency on shrinking government funds has been to hoard money and squeeze the amount paid to training providers. In recent years TEC reserves have increased, perhaps as a form of insurance against financial uncertainty in the future. Government has spoken repeatedly of the need for TECs to seek private finance, but some recent exceptions involving matching funds for enterprise programs (DfEE 1996d) notwithstanding, they have had little success in raising other money. Without additional funding, TECs are excessively reliant upon money received for administering the government's *unemployment* programs – Youth Training, Training for Work, and more recently Community Action and Workstart. Funding for programs such as YT is weighted toward the local employment situation rather than any measure of skill needs. With funds derived disproportionately from stop-gap unemployment schemes, small wonder that TECs have been widely criticized for concentrating more on feeding the demand for low skilled employment rather than initiating an increase in the supply of marketable skills. Despite the rhetoric of leading a new training system for employers, TECs have responsibility for only 3.7 percent of all training expenditure in Britain (Bennett et al. 1994). In such a situation it is difficult to see how TECs can be the prime movers in a shift away from the low-skill equilibrium.

5. Performance-related funding (PRF), on the other hand, is an award scheme for the best performing TECs – in 1996-7 £21m was distributed to TECs based upon their scores on five different indicators (DfEE 1996a). The fund is, however, too negligible to offer incentives to TECs, while the cost of administration involved in submitting scores is not.

TECs at the Local Level – Relations with the Training Community

Many of the problems that TECs experience with employers are knock-on effects of government controls over TECs. A classic example of this spillover is evidenced in the contract negotiations between TECs and training providers. Prior to the introduction of three-year licenses, TECs were bound by contracts with TEED that were renegotiated each year. Given this constraint and the omnipresence of budgetary uncertainty, it was extremely difficult to make long-term commitments to local-level training providers, or to plan any coordinated training strategy. Haughton et al. (1995a) found this problem to be one of the most pressing facing TECs in their attempts to construct good relations with employers:

> [W]here, for instance, Task Forces and City Challenge projects can plan over a five year time horizon, TECs can not work their budgets in this way. In consequence, neither can their contractors [...]. [W]e entered many training premises where all staff had just been handed their redundancy notices, just in case contracts with the TEC were not renewed. In some cases this had happened every year since the TECs were launched, with redundancy notice withdrawn if, as usually happened, the contract was renewed at the last minute.

Similarly, the onerous level of detail in TEC contracts with TEED is passed on to training providers in the form of equally long and overly specified contracts to provide training. As part of their duty to monitor training provision, TECs are forced into highly intrusive scrutiny of firm practices and, more importantly, of commercially confidential firm accounts. If anything this scrutiny has been tightened in recent years because of a number of problems concerning fraudulent, incorrect and duplicated payments to firms. Furthermore, since performance is measured in terms of NVQ attainment rather than training *per se*, strong accountability is justified by a legitimate concern to ensure the proper use of public money. This degree of intervention by a body so closely tied to government has excited considerable resentment – as one TEC Chairman exclaimed, "[it] smacks of public intervention down to the level of the employer's own commitment to training. What right have these civil servants got to tramp around in these areas?" (Bennett et al. 1994: 123). Faced with decreasing margins, overbearing monitoring and increasing uncertainty, many employers have dropped out of participation in government training schemes altogether. TECs and LECs have in turn increasingly resorted to dealing with public-sector providers (mainly colleges of further education) or groups that were already involved in providing training (such as chambers of commerce and voluntary organizations). Both TECs and firms thus seem to be trapped in a vicious circle of low trust – in the name of exercising accountability over the use of public money, central control of TECs, and thus indirectly intervention in management, has risen; this in turn leads to a weakening of trust, accusations of excessive bureaucracy, and partial exit from the system. As a result the very links with employers that TECs were built to foster have suffered severely, and TECs have to a significant extent retreated into linking government programs with *other* parts of the public sector rather than making inroads into the private sector.

Relations with employers have also been affected by another development in government policy – the "targets revolution." NVQs were developed in 1986 in an attempt to generate a recognized, universal certification scheme for vocational skills. From 1988 onwards the government became increasingly preoccupied with measuring performance of training in terms of the attainment of NVQs, and after 1992 this objective was concretized in the form of National Education and Training Targets (NETTs) – e.g., that by 1997 at least 80 percent of sixteen-to-nineteen year-olds should have obtained an NVQ level 2 in their foundation year of training. The scheme enjoyed long-standing support from the Confederation of British Industry (CBI 1988, 1991), but was developed outside the TEC framework. After 1992, however, the TEC framework was reconstructed in order to make TECs instrumental in the pursuit of targets. The Employment Department's TEED was split into two branches – an Operating Division, and a new National Council for Education and Training Targets (NACETT). NACETT's ostensible task was to report back to ministers informing them of progress in meeting the national targets. Very quickly, however, it became clear that the government would incorporate the attainment of targets as a condition of TECs receiving portions of their budgets.

As discussed above, the need to perform in terms of national targets is a strong constraint on TEC independence and strategic capacity. But there are also widespread concerns about whether the target system is contributing anything to producing marketable skills. NACETT monitoring of company activities is, in the view of Bennett et al. (1994), appalling, suffering from poor sampling and even poorer response rates. Over a third of TECs expressed the opinion that the NETT information collected by the TEED's Regional Offices was poor, and almost a quarter said that the information they were required by TEED to assemble themselves was not useful (Vaughan 1993). About a third of TECs have contracted out the task of information gathering altogether, while others obtain data from local authorities and Job Centres. Problems of managing the system probably underlie the doubts that persist among employers about the value of state-sponsored accreditation schemes in general. The "Investors in People" program (IiP) illustrates these doubts. Designed as a "kitemark" scheme for firms that have made provision for the long-term training of their employees, the "IiP stamp" is issued to firms and subsequently required for eligibility for certain discretionary portions of TEC budgets. A key problem is that most firms see IiP as burdensome and irrelevant, particularly small firms. Given the fact that firms use their own assessment schemes for personnel planning, IiP standards are arbitrary and inconsistent. Certainly IiP accreditation is now widespread – 70 percent of all firms employing over 200 workers, and 38 percent employing over fifty, have been recognized by July 1997 (DfEE 1997a). Yet its take-up is more the product of budget carrots dangled by the DfEE which require companies to have obtained accreditation, than it is indicative of an upsurge in training activity. One London TEC chief executive commented scathingly, "IiP could make TECs the laughing-stock of the business community" (Bennett et al. 1994: 163).

The domination of performance criteria, and the dependence of funding upon such "outputs," magnifies the general problem of TECs' "leverage" over firms and their training. Influencing firms' activities is difficult enough in the context of programs that are oriented toward unemployment rather than training, and given the small proportion of total training handled through these programs. Unlike German chambers of commerce, TECs do not enjoy the benefits of compulsory membership of companies in the locality, and therefore suffer from relatively weak representational legitimacy. An additional problem generated by the focus on targets and qualification-oriented definitions of performance is that the measurement of "hoop-jumping" takes the place of the development of effective links with employers. To some extent a focus on outcomes rather than training processes has the considerable advantage of being administratively simpler. On the other hand, much of TECs' energy is devoted toward satisfying performance review by NACETT rather than assessing and addressing training needs in their area. This short-fall in good quality contacts is reflected in employers' views on the work being done by TECs. In 1993 it was estimated that only around 50 percent of employers were aware of the existence of TECs. Those that do know about TECs know little of what they do, generally perceiving TECs as "just a delivery mechanism [for government programs] with another name" (Crowley-Bainton 1993: 28). Many companies have deliberately remained outside the TEC network – foreign companies reluctant to share their skills base with competitors; firms who saw TECs as intermediaries in the delivery of unemployment relief programs; and firms whose managers were reluctant to commit time and energy to the paper-trails that accompany TECs (Bennett et al.1994: 39). The heavy hand of the DfEE has rubbed off onto firms' perceptions of TECs as too public-sector oriented, and too little in the hands of business, "a cocktail concocted at TEED…. distant from the realities of their everyday needs" (Bennett et al. 1994: 68). More generally, TECs seem to be victims of the short life-span of training policy experiments that preceded them – they enjoy low credibility in their ability to survive changes of government and favor. As one employer put it:

> There was the Manpower Services Commission and all the different bodies that the government have set up – as soon as a new government comes into power, you're left with a defunct body, which you might be quite a long way down the road with. You're left holding the baby and the Government say, "We're not using that one any more. We're going to start a new one now." (Crowley-Bainton 1993: 27)

Regularized contact with firms varies greatly between TECs. Many have established "sub-board structures" to facilitate contact. Most also have membership schemes, though this ranges from cases of highly organized "local constitutions" (e.g., SOLOTEC in South London) to mere mailing lists. Nevertheless, TECs' attempts to solicit membership has brought them into conflict with other employer organizations, giving the appearance of competition rather than collaboration. Chambers of commerce have been particularly concerned that TECs are attempting to oust them from the position of local representatives of business. Given the fact that TECs are the main intermediaries between government and firms in the administration of state programs, this is hardly surprising. It is an impression that persists despite the government's repeated insistence that

TECs should be "a driving force in bringing local players together to work as partners to a common goal" rather than "the direct deliverers of business support service" (DE/DTI, 1994: 5). Chambers can also claim a large efficiency advantage in the delivery of business support and training service – Bennett et al. estimate that costs per comparable unit of service output are on average 70 percent higher for TECs than for chambers, and in some cases are up to 800 percent higher (1994: 272)! Nonetheless, one sign that relations between chambers and TECs are improving is the fact that in five areas the two bodies had merged by 1996, with fourteen more potential mergers being discussed (ABCC 1996). Although these moves have worried trade unions, as well as those within the DfEE concerned to keep the roles of TECs and training providers such as chambers distinct, they do suggest an improvement on the turf-wars of the early 1990s.

Sectoral industry associations generally remain hostile, however. The Engineering Employers Federation (EEF) has expressed frustration at the inconsistent treatment of member firms by different TECs (HCEC 1996: 27). Industry training associations have been particularly critical of TECs, emphasizing their comparative advantage over TECs in addressing *national* needs in a consistent and thorough way. The two biggest training industries – engineering and construction – have statutory national bodies with levy-raising powers and responsibility for sectoral training nationwide (remnants of the Training Board structure set up in 1964). The Engineering Construction Industry Training Board (ECITB) complained that TECs were ill-suited to dealing with "nomadic" industries such as theirs in which locations change rapidly, and where workforces follow work (ECITB 1995, paragraph 1). Cooperation between the Board and TECs has been hampered by perennial uncertainty about the value of contracts with particular TECs. More direct criticism has been provided by the Construction Industry Training Board (CITB). In their view, TECs have focused unduly on Government initiatives, rather than private-sector training *per se*. The local orientation of TECs suggests to the CITB "no evidence of co-ordination to ensure national cost effectiveness" (HCEC 1996: 35). TECs are also accused of aiming "at the relatively soft target of medium- to large-sized companies, and do not address the large audience of relatively small companies" which constitute the bulk of the construction industry. It is a mark of the immensity of the coordinating task confronting TECs that the two Training Boards from the pivotal training industries regard them with such suspicion.[6]

Problems of inter-TEC coordination to which national employer organizations point stem from the "bottom-up" way in which TECs came into being. The process of creating a nation-wide map of TECs took only two years to complete, but the lack of any national blueprint was quickly evident. The Department did not attempt to establish criteria for desirable size. Many smaller areas found themselves wedged between two TECs, leading to "residual TECs" and irrational boundaries (the so-called "Swiss cheese effect"). Boundary problems were acute in London, where collections of boroughs carved up the city into numerous small units. Employers in London are forced to deal with up to eight separate TECs. Many of these problems resulted from an over-eagerness on the part of the Department of Employment to accept the bids. In consequence, half of the TECs that had emerged by 1992 did not meet the minimum budget criterion stipulated by the Department. In rural areas such as Sussex and Lincolnshire the Department had problems finding businessmen to take the lead on TECs at all. These and the later TECs to be established have tended to receive less support from

6. The future of these ITBs has recently been thrown into doubt. In late June 1997 Kim Howells, the new Labour Education and Employment Minister, invited employers into consultation over the future arrangements for training in the engineering and construction industries, with particular reference to the possible reform or abolition of the two Industrial Training Boards still in existence.

local business organizations (Bennett et al. 1994: 42-4). Overall, the way in which TECs emerged has led to important diseconomies of scale – too small in urban areas to plan for and integrate the area's economy, and too large in rural areas because of a dearth of interest (HCEC 1996: paragraph 67). By 1995-6, even though some reorganization and amalgamation had taken place, the largest TEC still had a budget over 18 times the size of the smallest.[7] Thus, while the activities of TECs have been excessively "nationalized" by an interventionist Department for Employment, huge variations in the size of individual TECs have made consistency and strategic planning extremely difficult to achieve. Meanwhile the costs to industry of dealing with multiple TECs whose policies, audit procedures and management styles vary so widely is a cause of great concern (CBI 1993).

One exception to this pattern – the Scottish case – suggests an alternative model for TECs. The 22 LECs in Scotland are linked to the Scottish Office rather than the DfEE. But in between LECs and their Department lies a layer of intermediary bodies: Scottish Enterprise (SE) and Highlands and Islands Enterprise (HIE). SE and HIE are regional planning bodies, coordinating TECs and ensuring consistency across their boundaries. In contrast to the TECs in England, the distribution of LECs was planned in advance by civil servants in consultation with the Scottish CBI. The functions of LECs also differ from those of TECs, reflecting the very different economic needs of dispersed, rural economies. Whereas only 16 percent of TEC budgets go toward enterprise programs and no proportion toward economic and community development, LECs devote 27 percent and 19.6 percent of their budgets toward these two categories of expenditure. Scottish LECs are therefore more explicitly regional planning bodies than their English counterparts (as their name suggests) and are constituted in a way that

---

7. The largest TEC in terms of budget is Merseyside TEC (£38.35m), while the smallest is Wight Training and Enterprise (£2.13m) – see Agenda 1996: 5.

is more consistent with these aims. This gives LECs particular advantages in linking with the regional development programs administered by the European Union.

TEC contacts with non-employer organizations involved in training and economic development do not seem to have flourished since 1990. Local authorities, perhaps correctly, have seen the funneling of government economic and training programs through TECs as a continuation of the Conservatives' attempts in the 1980s to bypass locally elected officials. Their response has been to accuse TECs of being undemocratic, unduly secretive, and unaccountable (LAA 1996).[8] In a survey of the relations between TECs and their "non-employer stakeholders" in 1994, the most common problem reported by TEC chief executives was relations with voluntary organizations – both the sheer number of them (one TEC reported over 2000 in its area!), and the culture clash between the voluntary sector and the commercial incentives associated with TECs (Haughton et al. 1995a).

Trade union representation on TEC boards exists, though it is minimal (5.4 percent of directors in 1991), but there is little evidence of regular contact between TECs and unions in most parts of Britain. As noted earlier, the distancing of unions from the governance of training marks one of the biggest breaks with British corporatist policies of the 1960s and 1970s. However it is also one of the strongest points of contrast between the operation of *Kammern* in Germany and TECs (Streeck et al. 1987). The costs of excluding unions from TEC activities are not merely a loss of legitimacy, but also a significant strategic handicap in securing consent for TEC programs among workers and trainees. The German example also shows how trade unions can be constructive rather than obstructive actors in the modernization of training curricula, as well as in the introduction of new forms of work organization.

---

8. For some "showcases" of constructive collaboration between TECs and local authorities, see Local Government Management Board 1994.

But perhaps the most surprising "missing link" with the training community is in the field of education. TECs deal frequently with schools and colleges of further education in administering training contracts leading to NVQs and other qualifications. Yet their influence over the curricula offered has been minimal. Formally TECs have only 2 percent of their annual budget allocated to developing education. Programs such as the now-defunct TVEI (Training and Vocational Education Initiative) and NVQs were developed by the Department rather than by TECs, while links to universities remain virtually non-existent. The Modern Apprenticeship program hints at a more formative role for TECs in developing training schedules (see below). TECs are also now responsible for handling "compacts" and "education-business partnerships" between local business groups and education authorities aiming to raise educational standards (Richardson 1993). But involvement of TECs in educational programs outside the *delivery* of contracts for government schemes remains small (Huddleston 1993), even though many boards include representatives from schools and local education authorities. Rather than help break down the barriers between education and in-firm training, TECs have been constrained by the resilience of their separation.

TEC Performance and the "Silver Lining" of the Modern Apprenticeship Scheme

One of the central ironies of the "targets and outputs" orientation of TEC service delivery is the consensus on the unreliability of performance data. Both the data gathered from TECs on contracts with training providers (represented in the Inter-Tec tables) and the surveys of program participants (in *Labour Market Trends*) are extremely questionable (HCEC 1996: paragraphs 111-19). Variations in record-keeping and the absence of consistent measures of outputs across TECs "make it extremely difficult to make any firm conclusions about the success of TECs, either individually or as a whole" (HCEC 1996: paragraph 120). For example, the TEC National Council has estimated that over-recording of the number of starters and leavers from the YT program can lead to understatements of TEC performance of up to 40 percent. Nevertheless, this does not stop the DfEE from claiming great progress in the past six years. Cost per "output" (a completion of the course) on both Youth Training and Training for Work programs has been descending year-on-year (*Labour Market Trends* 1995: 402-3; Agenda 1996). In addition, differences between best and worst performers in terms of the NETTs has narrowed in both 1994-5 and 1995-6.

Irrespective of the questionable accuracy of this data, and setting aside the problem that "lower cost per trainee" is not equivalent to more skills and better training, the downward trend in take-up of the two main training programs (YT and TfW) remains conspicuous. In 1996-7 starts on YT dipped by 7 percent, while in the period March-May YT starts were 17 percent lower in comparison with the previous year. The TfW program has suffered from a massive exodus in the past three years. In March 1997, the total number currently in training on TfW was 60,800 in England and Wales, compared to 133,100 in March 1994 (DfEE 1997c). Dwindling popularity of TfW and YT seem to confirm the hypothesis that TEC performance mirrors the economic cycle. When demand falls – as between 1989 and 1991 – the number of participants placed in work after completion of TEC-administered programs ("positive outcomes") falls, and the number of starts in government programs increases. When the economy is buoyant, however, the number of "positive outcomes" increases, and program participants (or potential participants) leave (or decline to start) in favor of "genuine" employment. Furthermore, it should be remembered from the discussion of the incentives associated with targets that TECs and training providers are under pressure to place workers in jobs irrespective of the skill level involved. Many employers, meanwhile, continue to treat these programs as cheap sources of constantly renewable labor (NACAB 1994). Indeed, the introduction of "Project Work" by the outgoing Conservative Government – a scheme explicitly oriented toward subsidizing employers to take on low-skilled workers – seemed to mark a recognition and acceptance of this practice.

In the midst of these trends the Conservative government signaled a declining commitment to the training functions of TECs. The training-led approach of TECs was downgraded in 1993, when the Department of Trade and Industry joined the (then) Department of Employment as coordinators of TEC activity. Business enterprise programs were put at the center of TEC activities, while, as we have seen, training programs were increasingly incorporated into education policy and meeting qualifications targets.[9] Integrating training with other local development functions has the potential to increase the supply of those skills most in demand – to date, however, this integration has not been achieved. Most damagingly of all, the November 1994 budget saw a sizeable cutback in the funds available for the main training programs, and a declaration of intent to reduce participation periods in the programs. All this hardly bodes well for the government's commitment to TECs as leaders of Britain's skills revolution.

However, lessons have been learned and some progress made in rectifying these problems. Rarely have public bodies been subject to the welter of reviews, audits and academic critiques that have barraged the DfEE and TECs. In 1993, TEED was restructured, regional offices were set up to provide greater coordination among TECs, and operating contracts were lengthened to allow for better planning with training providers. Three years

---

9. The then Education and Employment Secretary, Gillian Shepherd, set out the challenge for TECs in the next century as: "To lead local Task Forces that set and meet demanding local targets in order to achieve the National Targets for Education and Training" (DfEE 1996b).

later, in the wake of the critical House of Commons Employment Committee review, a number of smaller revisions were made to TEC programs – for example, consultations were launched to introduce a new quality inspectorate to assess standards of TEC-funded training provision; and a £50m Discretionary Fund was established for local economic development projects involving private-sector finance.

Perhaps the brightest prospect for TECs lies with the newly inaugurated "Modern Apprenticeship" (MA) program, hailed by the responsible Minister as "the most important development in industrial training for a decade or more" (Ian Paice, 2 September 1996). As with many other countries in the 1990s, Britain seems intent on rediscovering its apprenticeship system. During the 1980s and early 1990s there seemed to be a direct competition between government training schemes and the ailing apprenticeship system (Crouch 1992). In the mid-1990s, however, a new scheme was launched which attempted to integrate the NVQ system with a revitalized apprenticeship scheme.

Under the Modern Apprenticeship scheme, employers and trainees sign a "pledge" specifying rights and obligations, underwritten by the local TEC – should the employer be unable to fulfil his responsibilities to the trainee, the TEC is obliged to find her alternative training. Significantly, and in a marked departure from traditional youth training programs, nearly all apprentices under the MA scheme are *employed* by the firm. Apprenticeships normally last three years, and involve a mixture of formal vocational education and in-firm training. The target age-group was initially the 16-17 year old cohort, although some slightly older school-leavers have also been incorporated into an accelerated version of the scheme. After three years, all apprentices are required to have attained NVQ level 3 – i.e., a skilled worker/technician qualification. Modern Apprenticeships are noteworthy partly because of the collaboration between sectoral associations involved in the development of curricula. For example, the Engineering Training Authority, the Engineering Employers

Federation and the Confederation of Shipbuilding and Engineering Unions jointly developed an Engineering MA. By July 1996 about sixty sectors had drawn up MA programs.

MAs combine broad "foundation" skills (such as communication, use of information technology and working in teams – usually taught "off-the-job") with more specialized vocational skills in the second and third years. The scheme therefore marks a response to the charge of inconsistency between government programs, but also represents a genuinely industry-led training scheme. Nowhere is the paradigm of TEC coordination of employer organizations and other training providers realized more clearly than in the early phases of the MA program. Most encouraging of all for the government and industry has been the take-up rates in the first 30 months of its operation. At the end of 1995, 784 young trainees had entered Modern Apprenticeships – by March 1997 it is estimated that 80,000 individuals had embarked on the course (Lister 1997). Though employers were expected to bear the brunt of the costs under the program, some government money was also made available through the TECs. Government funding has come via the Youth (or Training) Credit scheme, consisting of vouchers enabling students to buy training from providers.[10] TECs' budgets have also been boosted to meet the costs of the scheme, though details of funding vary TEC-by-TEC depending on locally negotiated arrangements.

It is of course too early to evaluate the contribution of MAs to Britain's skills performance, but the reaction of employers to the scheme has on the whole been very positive – over two-thirds

10. The introduction of Youth Credits aimed at injecting market imperatives into the training system. Consistently poor training providers would, it was hoped, either be stimulated by low demand into improving their services, or face extinction at the hands of superior competitors attracting more trainees. Early studies of the Youth Credits pilot scheme, however, revealed that the quality of training provision remained poor, suggesting that the resilience of the low-skill equilibrium cannot be overcome merely by expanding consumer choice. See Hodkinson and Hodkinson 1995.

of participating employers said that they were willing to take on more modern apprentices and to recommend the scheme to other firms (Ernst and Young 1995). The criticism that pay rates for MA apprentices were too high to encourage employer take-up (Marsden and Ryan 1995) has not been borne out by the early popularity of the scheme. While most Modern Apprentices are located in traditional apprenticeship sectors (engineering, construction, electrical contracting, etc.), the scheme has flourished in some large *service* sectors such as business administration, retailing, and hotel and catering. It is a welcome sign of the viability of service-sector apprenticeships that firms such as Sainsburys, the largest supermarket chain, are using the scheme as a way of facilitating promotion to management positions. Modern Apprentices are a clear improvement on conventional apprenticeships' emphasis on informal, uncertified, and largely untransferable upgrading. The standardization of sectoral training required by the MA program may thus increase the supply of marketable skills within and across related sectors. It may also make it harder for firms to exploit trainees by using them as cheap labor substitutes.

However, several notes of caution should be sounded. First, in contrast to German apprenticeships where wage rates are controlled by sectoral agreements, British employers are free to pay wages to modern apprentices at the level they choose (and in some cases have requested that TECs pay a substantial portion of the wage bill). Second, some commentators have reminded the government that the apprenticeships of the past often institutionalized outmoded practices and skills, serving to hinder rather than advance the cause of upskilling (Unwin 1996). Third, while Modern Apprenticeships are expected to raise the percentage of sixteen-to-nineteen year olds obtaining intermediate-level qualifications via a work-based route from 4 percent to 8-9 percent, the figure is still extremely low in comparative terms (Richardson et al. 1995: 25). MAs are also premised on an acceptance of the education-work divide after compulsory schooling finishes at age sixteen, and it is difficult to see how they will avoid the problem of low prestige that plagued their vocational predecessors. Lastly, and perhaps of most concern, many firms are merely substituting Modern Apprentices for training positions that they would otherwise have provided themselves. Indeed, some firms have simply renamed existing schemes to qualify as a certified "MA program." If this results in no net rise in the *total* number of apprentices produced, the spread of the MA scheme may be quite misleading.

Despite these problems, there is little doubt that the Modern Apprenticeship scheme is a promising development in training policy. Its initial success shows the possibilities for state-sponsored but employer-run schemes, with the potential for raising both training standards and transferability of skills.

Conclusion and Possible Reforms

It is difficult to avoid the conclusion that TECs were founded on a mistaken view of the impediments to training in Britain. The philosophy underlying TECs of the need to "return" training to employers, and to liberate them from interference by bureaucrats and trade unions, was premised on a view that the low level of skill production was primarily a function of *external impediments*. But as a sarcastic editorial before the birth of TECs pointed out, "(t)he truth is that in regard to training, it is free enterprise which has failed over many decades to deliver the goods. Why should we expect it not to do so now?" (TES 1988). The paucity of training is rooted in product market strategies that keep the demand for skilled labor low, and is reinforced by a number of related supply-side incentive structures. Constructing TECs as private sector bodies has not been sufficient to induce them into reversing this track record, particularly as their constitution and relationship with government requires them (in typically British fashion) to opt for cost-minimizing over quality-improving strategies. On top of this the task of mobilizing local employers to improve the quantity and quality of their training has been undermined by the nature of the programs TECs administer, which continue to offer firms opportunities to use "trainees" as cheap labor. The current Labour government's "welfare-to-work" scheme, which offers employment subsidies to firms to take on the unemployed, is one example of the way in which the ambition to raise employers' commitment to youth training remains frustrated by the conflicting incentives of different government policies.

But criticism of the general performance of TECs should not translate too directly into pessimism about their future. TEC cooperation with sectoral associations such as the Industry Training Organizations has been more successful in the development of Modern Apprenticeships. Where TECs can enlist the support of employers organizations to construct defined training schedules that meet the actual needs of local companies, their prospects are clearly much brighter, as the case of the Modern Apprenticeship scheme suggests. It is encouraging that sectoral organizations see the MA program as a way of modernizing and standardizing training schedules, and particularly encouraging that the program is being used in some service sectors to provide a previously non-existent framework for career promotion. The interest that industrial associations and employers have shown in the scheme is a sign that the demand for more and better marketable skills is not as pitiful in the mid-1990s as was suspected in the early 1980s. Without this exogenous shift in the demand for skills, TECs or analogous local-level coordinators can only have a limited effect at best; with it, however, the prospects for making inroads into the classic collective action dilemmas of British industry are at the very least improving.

But, as this chapter has shown, in order to take advantage of these developments TECs will need to be reformed in significant ways. First, the internal and external auditing processes require attention. Recent scandals exposing serious fraud in as many as twenty TECs, involving about £17m paid to companies to teach non-existent trainees, will almost certainly accelerate this process (*Financial Times* 1997). While financial controls are in need of tightening, however, this should not be at the expense of TEC autonomy over local agreements with training providers. Rather than implement rigorously defined national programs, TECs must be allowed to set their own program agendas, and then negotiate with national funders for the resources required. This would allow TECs to adopt in turn a more flexible approach to performance targets, which should be reformulated to encourage upskilling that is in firms' interests rather than to require "outputs" that often have little to do with genuine training. A crucial role for TECs in this regard could be to develop a system for certification for NVQ training, whose quality has been in serious doubt since its inception. In this way TECs could develop analogous functions to those exercised by the examination committees of the German Chambers of Commerce (Streeck 1987).

Another lesson from the *Kammern* in Germany, as well as from the LECs in Scotland, is that broader local development functions should be integrated with training activities. This would give TECs the opportunities to influence the broader set of institutions and incentives that shape company strategies, of which training is a vital component. Organizational reform of TECs should also promote their role as representatives of local interests. To this end it is crucial to encourage greater links between education authorities, trade unions and TECs, perhaps aiming for the sort of regional partnerships that have achieved some success in Wisconsin in the United States' similarly hostile institutional environment (see Parker and Rogers, Chapter 8). The trend toward mergers with chambers of commerce is clearly important in this regard, and will increase the legitimacy of TECs among employers. Newly merged "TEC-chambers" will of course be both funders and deliverers of training, and thus further institutional restructuring may be necessary to avoid conflicts of interest. Reconstitution of TECs must also address the problem of size. Mergers between TECs should be used to engineer TEC boundaries that coincide with those of the new regional administrative units created by the last government. Coherently structured and more autonomous TECs are also more likely to be effective advocates of regional business interests at the national and EU levels. German chambers have representation in the peak-level committee coordinating the interests of business on training policy, the Joint Committee of German Business for Vocational Training (KWB). An analogous national forum in Britain would offer a way of integrating employers (particularly those of large national chains) who do not fit easily into the present TEC structure.

In terms of programs the central focus must be on expanding and improving the Modern Apprenticeship scheme. Previous training schemes have always "appear[ed] … more as a new means for government to manage its unemployment commitments … than as a means of shaking Britain from its low skills equilibrium" (Bennett et al. 1994: 282). With the advent of MA, a policy has finally been developed which shows signs of avoiding the stigma of being merely a substitute form of unemployment, and which is focused on skill creation rather than providing cheap and temporary work (King 1995). The contribution of TECs in the coming years will hinge on the success of this program more than any other.

Conclusion

THE FUTURE OF THE
GERMAN SKILL-CREATION SYSTEM
Conclusions and Policy Options

David Finegold

The German apprenticeship system, long the envy of other countries, was considered by many to be in a state of crisis by the mid-1990s (Schmidt 1996). While reforms of the system are needed (and in many cases already underway), a central conclusion of the research in this volume is that apprenticeships will remain a vital part of the German education and training system and the wider German economic model for the foreseeable future. This concluding chapter will deal first with main strengths and areas for improvement in the dual system in comparative perspective and then examine the changes that are needed in other elements of the German skill-creation system

The dual system, despite its deep roots in the pre-industrial era, continues to be a potential competitive advantage for Germany in an increasingly knowledge-based global economy. To provide sustainable competitive advantage, a resource must produce an edge over rivals (e.g., by making possible superior productivity or quality) and be *distinctive* – a feature that is difficult for competitors to replicate (Porter 1990). The dual system meets these criteria, as the failed efforts of many other nations to replicate it attest, because of the complex set of institutional mechanisms that are necessary for it to function effectively. What this set of institutions provides is a means of solving the difficult collective action problem of insuring high-quality, firm-based training in transferable skills at a time when this form of skill provision is of increasing importance to all advanced industrial economies (Crouch et al. 1999, Stevens 1996, Streeck 1989).

The dual system has been able to maintain its crucial place in German society, despite the significant changes in the economy and accompanying skill requirements, through a process of gradual adaptation within the same basic institutional framework. Although the process of consensual change among the key organized interest groups (employers, trade unions, and education and training providers) has drawn considerable criticism for failing to respond quickly enough to the rapidly shifting competitive environment, it helps insure that once changes are introduced, they have the support of all the relevant actors. Among the significant, closely related changes that have taken place in the dual system in the last two decades that appear likely to continue are

- the older average age but improved basic qualifications of trainees, as young people complete more years of general education prior to entering apprenticeships;
- the ongoing consolidation of apprenticeships in many sectors to create fewer, broader courses that avoid overly narrow, early specialization;
- the addition of new apprenticeships in the expanding sectors of the economy: services and high technology;
- the increased combination of apprenticeships and higher education, as young people recognize that career

advancement will increasingly depend on obtaining a
degree or some form of higher education qualification
to complement the more applied training offered
through the dual system; and,

- an expansion of alternative education routes (e.g.,
private training consortia, Fachhochschulen sandwich
courses, full-time technician courses) that will continue
to erode apprenticeship's monopoly position in the
provision of initial vocational and technical skills.

In the midst of these changes, there appear to be some fairly
constant, long-standing, and powerful impacts of the dual system on individuals and firms. The dual system has been very
successful in comparative perspective in creating clear paths for
individuals from school to the workplace, with the result that
the absolute levels of youth unemployment and the ratio of
youth to adult unemployment remain much lower in Germany
than in other advanced industrial countries, despite the sharp
rise in overall joblessness. The apprenticeship system has also
been a vital ingredient in Germany's long-term success in global
markets for specialized, medium-technology goods (such as
industrial machinery), which require high levels of workforce
skill (O'Mahony 1997). In the process of building these skills,
the dual system also instills a strong occupational identity in
individuals, which has caused some concern that apprenticeships may be counterproductive for organizations seeking to
build effective, multi-functional work teams (Herrigel and
Sabel, Chapter 2; Finegold and Wagner, Chapter 3). Despite
these concerns, the aggregate economic effects of the dual system appear to have been and remain, on balance, positive.

The dual system also has important distributional consequences, exercising a powerful influence on the career paths and
subsequent life chances of different groups of individuals. Hinz
(Chapter 4) shows that, relative to less standardized systems,
the dual system acts as a powerful brake on class mobility, shield-

ing qualified individuals from a loss of earnings and status but also providing few opportunities for upward career progression, with particularly severe consequences for individuals who fail to obtain a qualification. He projects that the opportunities for upward mobility for skilled workers will become more limited as the number of higher education graduates continues to expand. The vocational education and training system also limits the career prospects of women in the German economy. Young women are discriminated against within the dual system, where, despite the fact they have better academic qualifications, they find it difficult to secure some of the more prestigious and better paying apprenticeships; women are also significantly over-represented in the full-time school-based courses within the post-secondary vocational training system whose graduates, whether male or female, find it more difficult to find a job than do their peers trained in the dual system (Krüger, Chapter 5). The shift toward greater participation in higher education and the growth in service-sector occupations, both areas where women have been more successful, should help to improve labor market outcomes for women, but there remains a need to reduce inequalities between the two paths of the vocational training system.

Responding to the Challenges to the Dual System

Maintain Fair Sharing of Costs

One of the great strengths of the German dual system has traditionally been its capacity to distribute the costs of training fairly among the relevant actors. This has generally enabled the system to maintain a sufficient supply of firms with training placements to accommodate all young people who want an apprenticeship without resorting to a training tax, that can, as in France, have a distorting effect on employer behavior (see Culpepper, Chapter 7). The balancing of costs and benefits occurs at two levels: first, for each apprenticeship, the training firm pays the trainee's wage and costs of on-the-job training in return for the apprentice's productive labor and the other benefits that Wagner enumerates (see Chapter 1). And second, for the system as a whole, costs are shared among employers. Those firms not offering apprenticeships (but often making use of the skilled workers produced through the dual system) subsidize some of the costs of operating the system through the compulsory membership fees they pay to the chambers of industry and commerce; these fees help fund all of their activities, including monitoring the quality of training and administering the examinations to apprentices. In addition, the costs of each training place vary significantly among employers, which enables the system to share the costs of training over the business cycle. During high-growth periods, when the supply of places typically exceeds the demand, trainees will naturally gravitate toward the high-prestige, high-cost apprenticeships in the larger companies. During recessions, the number of these places is reduced significantly, and the *Handwerk* sector of craft enterprises, where there is little or no net cost to the firm from employing an apprentice, takes up the slack (Soskice 1994).

As Wagner (Chapter 1) notes, however, the combination of expanding the off-the-job component of training and the major increase in the real level of trainee allowances has upset the delicate balance of training costs, creating disincentives for employers to offer apprenticeships. This is a particular problem at a time when German companies are struggling to reduce costs and actively seeking to relocate investment to lower wage nations in order to remain competitive. There is thus a significant need to, at a minimum, freeze the current level of trainee allowances (causing them to fall in real terms), if not actually to take the politically more difficult step of reducing the trainee allowance, at least in the initial two years of an apprenticeship. This would still offer youth trainees significantly higher income than their counterparts in full-time education, either in Germany or other countries. The relative financial incentive to undertake apprenticeships could be further enhanced by introducing student fees for higher education (see below).

Encourage Employer Training Consortia

The issue of reducing the youth training costs for employers is most acute in eastern Germany, where the dual system relies heavily on state subsidies in order to attract employers (other than subsidiaries of large western German firms) to participate. As Culpepper demonstrates (see Chapter 7), the way in which the subsidies for employer training are crafted can have an important impact on the success of the policy. Rather than directly subsidizing individual employers, the eastern *Länder* may want to follow Saxony's example and use their funds to support local employer consortia that provide small and medium-sized enterprises with both the training experts and capital equipment that they lack to deliver quality apprenticeships.

Similar types of consortia arrangements are also increasingly important in western Germany to enable small companies to meet the broader requirements of reformed apprenticeships (see Wagner, Chapter 1; Finegold and Wagner, Chapter 3). In some cases the alliance takes place directly between companies, as apprentices rotate through the different requirements across several firms; in others, the chamber provides the coordination through a training center that offers equipment not available to some smaller enterprises. These partnerships can have the added benefit of encouraging the transfer of best practices and other expertise among companies, particularly if the consortia bring together large, internationally competitive firms with their suppliers and customers.

Modernize Apprenticeship Content and Delivery

The need to update the apprenticeship system to keep pace with the rapidly changing economy has been widely recognized in Germany, with all of the main actors agreeing, in principle, to a set of reform proposals (Schmidt 1996). The research presented in this volume suggests a number of the changes that need to take place.

1. FACILITATE THE UPDATING OF QUALIFICATIONS

Expediting the process of updating qualifications and creating new ones has been a long-standing problem in the dual system. As Wagner documents (Chapter 1), some improvements have been made, with apprenticeships in twenty-six new occupations created in 1996, including a popular new set of qualifications in information technology, and another fifty occupations updated. These processes, however, still take too long to complete; in the fast-food industry, for example, the social partners began work on defining an apprenticeship that would train managers for the sector in 1991, but a new qualification was not issued until the end of 1997. The lapse could prove costly as some of the leading employers in the sector, who were tired of waiting, developed their own, in-house training programs and may now be reluctant to take part in the apprenticeship system. Likewise, it took eight years for the banking industry to revise its apprenticeship qualifications, during which time some banks left the system altogether.

The primary obstacle to more rapidly updating apprenticeships or to developing new ones does not appear to be technical; many of the revised apprenticeships introduced in 1996 were updated in less than two years. And in the case of the fast-food industry, virtually all of the content needed for the qualification was already part of existing qualifications. Rather, the problem is gaining agreement among the social partners, or in some cases, among different types of employers in the same sector. This problem might be mitigated if the parties were given a clear deadline at the start of the process – e.g., they must agree to complete the process within two years. Any issues unresolved by that deadline could be submitted to an independent arbitrator for resolution.

2. BROADEN THE CONTENT OF EXISTING QUALIFICATIONS

The long-term trend has been away from a plethora of narrowly defined occupations toward fewer and more broadly defined apprenticeships. The number of recognized apprenticeship qualifications has declined from 606 in 1971 to 364 in 1996, despite the introduction of dozens of new qualifications. The large number of different occupations still covered by apprenticeships is somewhat misleading, since most young people are concentrated in relatively few fields; the twenty most popular apprenticeships for males account for 62 percent of all male trainees, while women are even more concentrated, with 74 percent in just twenty occupational areas.

There are at least two crucial reasons to broaden apprenticeship content. First, as noted above, more and more global leaders in manufacturing and services are organizing the work process around multi-functional teams (Womack and Jones 1996); if Germany is to compete successfully, it is important to give individuals a common grounding in areas such as business strategy, customer service, quality processes, problem-solving and interpersonal skills, rather than fostering a narrow occupational focus (Herrigel 1996a; Herrigel and Sabel, Chapter 2); the most recent reforms of the metalworking and electrical apprenticeships attempted to strengthen these areas, and similar content is being added to other apprenticeships as they are updated. In some respects, apprenticeships have always offered a broad educational foundation for a global economy – e.g., emphasizing good reading, numeracy and communication skills, including requiring a second language of all trainees. If apprenticeships are to promote, rather than hinder, high performance workplaces, then additional emphasis could be placed on transferable skills and less on specific technical competencies.

Second, a broader initial preparation, particularly if common modules are defined across large families of apprenticeships, enables young people to keep their occupational choices open and to remain more flexible as technology changes, and with it the occupational structure. It is important to recognize, however, that broadening apprenticeships will have important cost implications for firms and make it difficult for some small companies to participate on their own (see above on the need for employer consortia). After a common foundation year it is useful to allow individuals to develop an area of specialized expertise, as occurs in the updated metalworking apprenticeships.

3. IMPROVE THE SCHOOL-BASED COMPONENT OF APPRENTICESHIPS

The school-based portion of apprenticeships has always been intended to focus on more theoretical subjects in contrast to more applied firm-based training. While apprenticeships need to provide individuals with a set of general skills, the traditional lecture format in which much of this content is delivered in the *Berufsschulen* is often not the most effective way for individuals to learn these vital skills. The shortcomings of this form of instruction are likely to become even starker as more companies transform themselves into *learning organizations,* where the ongoing improvement of individual and firm capabilities is consciously built into the work processes (Mohrman and Mohrman 1995). Research from the US suggests that some of the same elements that make learning effective in the work place – increasing the relevance of the material, making the learning more active and group-based, and giving the learner more ownership and control over the process – can also be used to improve the teaching of generic skills in schools (e.g., Bailey 1993). These changes could be fostered by ensuring that the faculty in schools continue to remain up to date with the latest changes in the workplace by doing regular placements in industry; by using this knowledge to update their curriculum more frequently, rather than waiting for official changes in the standards; and by making greater use of information technology to provide real-time linkages between firms and educational institutions.

Build Links between Apprenticeship and Higher Education

Currently one of the most glaring weaknesses of the German skill-creation system is the lack of a clear pathway from the dual system into higher education. Completing an apprenticeship generally does not provide young people with access to higher education. Those skilled workers who, after several years of work experience, may want to obtain a degree in order to make the transition to a managerial track, must first go back to school to obtain an *Abitur*, a step many adults are loath to take. They can obtain a *Meister*-level qualification without completing additional academic prerequisites; but these qualifications generally provide access to only the first tier of management jobs, and as Finegold and Wagner (Chapter 3) have shown, these supervisory positions are increasingly rare, although the qualification is useful in a variety of technically demanding, and equally prestigious, occupations.

If the dual system is to retain its high status, and avoid the ghettoization that has plagued vocational training in countries like France and the US, where the vocational path is generally still seen as a last resort for those who have failed in the education system, then it is vital that apprenticeships provide a stepping stone to higher education for those individuals that desire it, rather than serving as the educational endpoint for most individuals. This is particularly important because more and more young people are passing the *Abitur* and qualifying for higher education, a trend that is likely to continue as an increasing percentage of the youth cohort has at least one parent who attended higher education. With a growing percentage of the brightest young people attending higher education, there is a risk that firms will change their career structures, limiting access to technical and managerial positions to those who have a degree and thus making apprenticeships a less attractive option.

The way to avoid this outcome is to have apprenticeships complement, rather than substitute, for higher education. There are encouraging signs that this is already occurring. The proportion of young people with the *Abitur* who undertake apprenticeships and of apprentices who then go on to higher education have both been increasing in the last decade; between 1985 and 1995, the percentage of West German higher education students who had already completed an apprenticeship more than doubled from 15 percent to 33 percent.[1] Further integration between apprenticeships and higher education would be beneficial, however. An example of what such arrangements might look like is provided by the banking sector, which contains the occupations where it is most common for individuals to combine apprenticeships and higher education; nearly two-thirds of banking apprentices pass the *Abitur* (up from 55 percent in 1985) before securing one of these highly competitive training places. One of the newest Fachhochschulen, Fachhochschule Westküste (West Coast), has begun a pilot program in conjunction with local vocational schools and banks. Students who qualify undertake the bank-clerk apprenticeship and their degree course simultaneously. By consolidating some of the course content and shifting the apprenticeship to a block release format (six five-week periods of full-time study), students are able to save one and a half to two years over the time required to do the courses separately. This alternative higher education route addresses two of employers' most common complaints with the universities: the high average age and the lack of work experience of most graduates. At the same time, the completion of the much-delayed updating of the bank apprenticeship has helped address employers' concerns that the old standards were failing to keep pace with the changes in technology and work organization within banks. Students typically continue working for the same firm throughout the course, thus avoiding another central problem facing banks under existing apprenticeship arrangements – unlike other sectors, which use apprentices to screen applicants, banks typically

1. The percentage of university students with an apprentice certification grew from 14 percent to 22 percent, while the percentage in Fachhochschule grew from 24 percent to 63 percent.

lose many of their best trainees, after a substantial investment, to university courses. The launch of the program was a response by the apprenticeship and the *Fachhochschule* programs to the students they were losing to the *Berufsakademien,* the state-run institutions that are particularly popular in Baden-Württemberg, which offer three-year diploma courses to individuals who have passed the *Abitur.* The pilot program has proved very popular with students as well, attracting five applicants for each one of the twenty places, despite the demanding study-hour requirements of this accelerated course. Similar experiments in banking and other sectors are underway in most of the *Länder*, perhaps most prominently in Bavaria and North Rhine-Westphalia; most experiments are still small-scale, however, and there is no clear national coordination of the different efforts.

Ending Time-Served Apprenticeships?

While all of the above changes would represent relatively incremental adaptations of the dual system, a more radical and controversial reform would be to do away with the time-served element of apprenticeships. Currently, young people must spend three to three and a half years in most apprenticeships, unless they have completed the *Abitur*, which exempts them from one year of training.[2] Rather than specifying the precise length of the apprenticeship, including all of the hours that a trainee must spend in on- and off-the-job training, the BiBB could define, as it does already, what a skilled worker in a given occupation needs to be able to do and the underlying knowledge required. Such a radical change would move Germany closer to the outcome- or competency-based qualifications systems that have been introduced in the UK and Australia (Keltner et al. 1996).

---

2. It is possible for the brightest young people, either with or without an *Abitur,* to reduce the length of an apprenticeship by an additional six months through mutual agreement with the training firm.

There are several advantages to a competency-based system. By specifying the desired outcome, rather than the one "best" way to attain it, the system would have the inherent advantage of performance over design standards, encouraging rather than stifling innovation among education and training providers (Tucker 1995). This characteristic of competency-based systems is particularly important at a time when new information technologies (such as interactive video and distance learning over the internet) are making possible much more efficient, self-paced instruction. In addition, a move toward a competency-based system would broaden access to skilled-worker status, and the greater earnings this provides, for adult workers who failed to obtain or complete an apprenticeship when they left school, but who could subsequently learn the required competencies through a combination of work experience and additional courses. This option is already available to semi-skilled workers who have worked for at least twice the duration of the apprenticeship in their occupation, a group that now accounts for 8 percent of all individuals taking the apprentice exam. This figure could be increased if the time-served requirement were removed. This reform would also acknowledge that young people are entering the apprenticeship system with more years of general education, and may thus require less time in off-the-job courses on basic language and numeracy skills; young people who have passed the *Abitur* are already able to conduct an abbreviated, two-year apprenticeship, but this option still has a specific time requirement. In addition, removing the formal classroom training requirements could significantly reduce the costs of training for high-performance work organizations that are able to design the work process and in-company learning opportunities so that individuals are able to learn all the necessary general competencies without spending one-to-two days per week in a formal classroom setting. For some of the more theoretical subjects, most companies would probably still choose to use the vocational schools, where it costs them nothing.

The most powerful objection to a competency-based system is that it risks reducing the quality and breadth of the nationally recognized apprenticeship qualifications, by encouraging individuals and their firms to focus just on the specific competencies which are tested, with insufficient attention to the underlying knowledge, general skills, and work socialization process needed to prepare individuals who are flexible enough to adapt to the changing economy (e.g., Streeck 1996, Bailey and Merritt 1995). This is the problem that has bedeviled the British and Australian efforts to create national systems of competency-based skill standards (see Wood, Chapter 9; Keltner et al. 1996). The German system, however, already has a powerful set of institutions in place, which are lacking in these other systems, to safeguard quality. The chambers of commerce could continue to test whether individuals can meet the required national standard through a combination of written exams and practical demonstrations. The trained trainers *(Meisters)* and works councils within firms could continue to monitor the quality of training provided to insure that trainees are not being exploited as cheap labor. And by continuing to specify the broad set of competencies required for a skilled worker, rather than specifying separate modules of competence, the German system could avoid the problem of overly narrow training that has characterized the US and UK systems. These standards could continue to include general subjects, such as two languages, math, and writing, which have helped give the German qualifications high status and to prepare individuals for life, and not just a narrow first job.

Another, potentially more serious objection to the reform proposal is that removing the time-served requirement would end up increasing the net costs of apprenticeships for employers. The net costs of training are typically highest at the start of the training period, when individuals spend most of their time learning and do little if any productive work; employers then recoup some or all of this investment in the latter stages of the apprenticeship, when individuals have mastered most of the required competencies and spend a high percentage of their time adding value in the workplace, but are still paid a trainee allowance that is less than half of the skilled worker's wage. Enabling trainees to become qualified as soon as they have the necessary competencies would shorten or eliminate this latter phase, and hence reduce the incentive for employers to take part in the system. This disincentive could be offset by two changes to the system that have already been mentioned: first, reducing the real level of the trainee allowance and second, decreasing the time spent in formal classroom training for some of the most able young people.

Even if the move toward a competency-based apprentice-ships would produce a more innovative and flexible training system that would benefit German young people, it is unlikely ever to be introduced because it runs counter to the powerful interests who run the existing system. Most trade unions are likely to see it as a watering down of training requirements and as providing employers with too much control over the forms of training; the state schools that currently provide the off-the-job training are likely to object because it would introduce new competitors and potentially eliminate the need for formal classroom training in some cases; and some employers, particularly the *Handwerk* firms that are currently making a profit on each apprentice, are likely to resist because of the cost argument outlined above.

Reforming the Wider German Model

Reform of Higher Education

The reform of the German higher education sector is beyond the scope of this volume, but there are some specific changes closely related to the dual system suggested by our analyses.[3] The most

---

3. See Ash (1997) for a full discussion of the German HE system and pro-posals for reforming it.

relevant has already been covered – improving access to higher education for those with apprenticeships but without the *Abitur*. Other reforms that would help broaden access to higher education are already under discussion in Germany, most notably the splitting of the German first degree, to enable individuals to leave with a bachelor's degree after 3-4 years, rather than the current system that requires university students to obtain a master's degree by passing a single, comprehensive examination at the end of five or more years of study or receive no qualification at all. This two-step degree process would make university far more attractive to older workers, help reduce the dropout rate from higher education, and would make the German system far more comparable to the tertiary systems in other European countries and the US, an important consideration with the moves toward European integration and the growing internationalization of higher education. Simply splitting the degree into bachelor's and master's, however, is unlikely to broaden access significantly, unless universities are also given incentives to become more responsive to student needs, e.g., by offering courses during vacations, weekends, and evening, when part-timers can enroll.

Germany has already dramatically expanded its higher education sector in the last two decades. This expansion, however, has come at a high cost – in the quality of the education provided to students (as measured, for example, by student:teacher ratios), the time required to complete a degree, and the time and resources available for research. If Germany is to continue to expand its HE system, given the likely tight constraints on government spending, it may need to consider the introduction of tuition fees. This has long been the case in mass higher education systems like the US and Japan and has been common in formerly tuition-free systems that have recently undertaken major expansion – such as the UK and Australia. Such a reform would help put higher education on a more equal footing with other forms of further education, e.g., *Meister* and some full-time vocational courses that already charge fees, albeit fairly low ones. It would increase resources at a time when government funding is very limited. And it would also discourage individuals who treat higher education as solely a consumption good, while increasing the pressure that the customers (students) place on universities to enable them to complete their courses in a timely fashion.

Enhance Labor Market Flexibility

Arguably the greatest challenge facing apprenticeships is external and hence more difficult for the actors in the dual system to address – the broad array of labor market regulations, corporate taxation, and other institutional features of the economy that make Germany one of the most expensive and least attractive places for new corporate investment. A series of changes in the last decade have combined to undermine the competitiveness of Germany's export-driven economy: allowing real hourly labor costs to rise more quickly than productivity;[4] the growing importance of high-technology sectors, which require greater acceptance of risk and inherently more labor market instability; the costs of reunification; and the emergence or resurgence of new lower cost and less regulated competitors both within the European Union (the UK, Spain and Portugal) and in the wider global economy (Eastern Europe, Asia, and the US in particular). Germany's multinational corporations and the *Mittelstand* have begun the process of restructuring to restore profitability, increasing the use of global sourcing, and moving more of their internal operations outside of Germany, but these solutions reduce investment in new job creation in Germany and with it the demand for apprentices.

The problem facing Germany, and the rest of Northern Europe, is often posed as a stark choice between "good jobs" and "many jobs" (OECD 1994). According to this argument, Ger-

---

4. This was caused more by a reduction in working hours than a large increase in real wages.

many can maintain the employment protections that have helped its workers receive the highest pay for the fewest hours worked in the developed world, but which have also contributed to unemployment of over four million people in 1998, or it can pursue the Anglo-American path of labor market deregulation that has helped create millions of new jobs, while giving rise to large increases in income inequality. There is a great deal of enthusiasm for the deregulationist option among German companies, but this path also carries the risk of undermining the institutions for collective employer action that have been such a vital part of the dual system.

The challenge for decision-makers in the German political economy, in government as well as in employer organizations and unions, is whether they can shape an alternative course: making the German economy more flexible and competitive without undermining the basic guarantees of a living wage and some measure of employment (if not job) security. Finegold and Wagner (Chapter 3) discuss one component of this "third way" – the increasingly common annual hours contracts that have enabled metalworking firms to compensate for the loss of competitiveness that occurred with the move to a 35-hour work week by adjusting labor supply to meet changes in demand, while providing workers with more flexible working time and greater income stability. Another policy that might be considered would reduce the high costs and regulatory burden on firms that lay people off (one of the significant disincentives for new hiring in Germany, particularly in turbulent high-technology sectors), while maintaining the requirement for early notification of downsizing and ensuring that high-quality, publicly subsidized retraining options are available for individuals who are displaced. At the same time, it is also important for Germany to continue to push for a high level of basic employment rights within the European Union through the social charter, since this will help maintain a more level playing field in the market that accounts for 70 percent of all German exports.

While policy-makers focus on unemployment – the most pressing problem currently facing the German economy – there is a very real danger that the solutions they are pursuing will exacerbate a longer-term, yet equally daunting problem: the aging of the German population and the accompanying pension burden this is creating (see Gatter, Chapter 6). Politically, the most palatable way to combat unemployment is to reduce the size of the workforce. This can be done most easily by shortening working lives – encouraging young people to remain in full-time education for more years before entering the labor force and creating incentives for older workers to take early retirement. It can also be achieved by discouraging the groups that have traditionally been marginalized in the German job market – women and immigrants – from participating in the labor force. The problem is that these solutions perpetuate a vicious circle – attacking unemployment by reducing the size of the labor force only increases the proportionate cost burden on firms and the remaining workforce, further undermining competitiveness and reducing the incentive for companies to create new jobs.

The government has taken the first steps toward addressing this problem with successive reform of pension schemes to decrease the incentives for early retirement, but significant additional reforms are needed to encourage more flexible work arrangements that can entice more women with children and individuals over sixty to remain in the labor force and shorten the average time required to complete a university degree. As older individuals are remaining healthy and potentially productive for longer periods, Germany may need to consider raising the retirement age and/or reducing the state support for younger retirees. As Gatter points out, however, this will be very difficult politically, since a generous and relatively early retirement has become an accepted right, painstakingly negotiated by the social partners.

The much-publicized example of the Netherlands demonstrates clearly that it possible for corporatist European economies

to tackle the twin problems of high unemployment and an insup-
portable retirement system without adopting the Anglo-American free market model (Visser and Hemerijck 1997, Schmid
1997).[5] The Netherlands entered the 1980s in far worse shape
than Germany, with an unemployment rate of nearly 10 percent
in 1983, and the lowest labor force participation rate – just 52
percent – in the OECD (69 percent for men and 35 percent for
women versus 77 percent for men and 48 percent for women in
Germany in 1983) (OECD 1997). Between 1983 and 1996, it
created new jobs at the rate of 1.8 percent per year (versus an EU
average of 0.4 percent), matching the US "job machine" without
a similar growth in earnings inequality (ibid.). It achieved this
dramatic turn around through a set of incremental changes,
negotiated by the social partners, in three related policy realms:
welfare, social security, and active labor market policy.

At the core of the change was a shift in the policy approach
from failed attempts to reduce unemployment, by encouraging
early retirement and other measures to discourage labor-force
participation, to a recognition that the only way to support the
existing standard of living, including a very generous welfare
state, was to have the maximum number of people in employment. To create new jobs, the Dutch recognized they had to
make the Netherlands a more attractive place to invest, which
meant cutting real labor costs through wage moderation by
unions and reductions in the statutory minimum wage; as a
consequence, unit labor costs in manufacturing were held constant in real terms between 1983 and 1995 in the Netherlands,
compared to a 2.6 percent annual increase in Germany – a
huge swing in wage competitiveness. Yet this did not translate
into a loss in the Dutch family incomes relative to Germany, as
the Netherlands shifted from a norm of single family bread-
winner to 1.5 earners per family by the mid 1990s. The explo-
sion in employment opportunities was in turn facilitated by a

---

5. This account of the Netherlands is drawn from Visser and Hemerijck (1997).

series of reforms designed to make the labor market more flexible for both firms and individuals that could be applicable to the German model:

- Removing constraints on working hours where agreed to by employee and employer
- Individualizing social security, tax, and pension law
- Encouraging pro rata wages and benefits for part-timers to remove disincentives for this form of employment
- Decreasing the regulations governing dismissals
- Shifting from constraints on temporary employment agencies to using them as a primary vehicle for retraining displaced workers to find new jobs

Enhanced Further Training

While Germany is an acknowledged leader in the initial training of its skilled workforce, it fares much less well in international comparisons of levels of further training (Finegold and Keltner 1997, Finegold and Wagner 1998). Most further training within German firms goes to a relatively small cadre of managers, and the ongoing firm-based training of the frontline workforce tends to be limited to short updates on new machinery provided by equipment vendors. In part, this reflects the fact that by the time they have completed their apprenticeships, German workers have already been socialized to the workplace and built a broad base of technical skills, tasks which are accomplished through further training in many other countries. But it is also a sign of real competitive weakness during a period of rapid technological and organizational change. The dramatic aging of the German population creates an additional dual imperative for raising the level and profile of further training (Gatter, Chapter 6). First, as a higher percentage of the German workforce is accounted for by older workers who received their initial training prior to many of the changes in the workplace, German firms will need to devote more attention to ongoing training if they are to improve inter-nal flexibility, adopt more team-based organizations, and increase competitiveness. Second, in order to support the growing retired population, Germany will need to attract more women and immigrants into highly skilled positions that will require sub-stantial further training. These are in addition to the already extensive retraining initiatives underway for the large number of unemployed workers, particularly in the eastern states, to try to equip them with new sets of skills.

Given the current focus on deregulating labor market insti-tutions, particularly among employers, it seems unlikely that the tripartite governance model for the dual system will be extended to further training, as some have proposed (Blossfeld 1992). What is required, however, is putting mechanisms in place that will allow the market for further training to operate more effi-ciently. This could include better information on the quality of existing education and training providers, providing more open access to short courses for individuals at all skill levels, reliably certifying the transferable skills individuals have acquired in these courses or within the workplace, and increasing the tax incentives for firms and individuals to invest in further training.

One area of strength within the German system has tradi-tionally been the *Meister* courses that skilled workers take in their own time in order to become qualified to advance into supervi-sory positions. This type of qualification has been extended to a growing array of service-sector occupations, and up to 20 percent of skilled workers are pursuing this further training route at some point in their careers (Finegold et al. 1994). As the number of traditional supervisors and foremen continue to decline in more empowered organizations characterized by flatter managerial hierarchies, it is vital that the content of these qualifications con-tinue to be updated to reflect the new roles that *Meisters* and their counterparts in other sectors are being asked to play in coaching and leading teams, improving quality processes, etc. (Finegold and Wagner, Chapter 3).

Support Development of New Enterprises

Another sign of the lack of flexibility in the German model and a cause for concern about its future viability is the difficulty Germany has had in creating new enterprises (Casper and Vitols 1997; Herrigel and Sabel, Chapter 2). With some notable exceptions – such as the rapidly growing software giant SAP – Germany has been much less successful in developing high-technology or global service firms than the US and UK. Some have blamed a shortage of capital, citing the reluctance of German banks to make high-risk loans and the lack of a domestic venture-capital industry (Deeg 1997). This is unlikely to be the primary source of the problem, however; commercial banks in the US and UK are equally reluctant to make loans to high-risk start-ups (Keltner and Finegold 1996), and there is sufficient venture capital in the US and UK seeking global investment opportunities that finance could be obtained if entrepreneurs with viable products and business plans were being produced. Rather, the problem appears to lie in the wider regulatory environment. Rules that make it more difficult and costly to take a company public or reduce the number of employees are even more hostile to new businesses in highly uncertain sectors than they are to more mature corporations.

In addition, the German culture does not appear to reward risk-taking (cf. Streeck 1996); for example, dropping out of university to start a business is a common, often glorified route to success in the US computer industry, even if the initial company fails. In Germany, such a step would be viewed as career suicide. This attitude is reinforced by the educational system. The civil-service status of professors and the heavy regulation of universities discourage entrepreneurial behavior among faculty, another common source of business start-ups in the US (Finegold and Keltner 1997). Likewise, the gradual pace at which apprenticeships are changed is often out of sync with the rapidly changing skill needs of high-technology entrepreneurs. Traditional apprenticeships and *Meister*-level qualifications do provide a broad foundation of skills that help many individuals, in sectors ranging from hotels and catering to machine shops, to start their own business. Even in these cases, however, the preparation for entrepreneurs might be enhanced by emulating some of the most successful work-preparation programs in the US and UK, where young people learn by starting their own small business (Stern et al. 1995).

Cross-National Lessons

New approaches to build entrepreneurial skills are just one of many potential lessons from other countries for the German skill-creation system suggested by the research in this volume. Summarizing some of the other key cross-national lessons that German policy-makers may want to consider:

- Experimenting with more competency-based approaches to certifying skills, while retaining strong external quality control, as a way to open the system more to those who fail to obtain an initial apprenticeship and encouraging more certification of further training;
- Continuing to reform the content and delivery of apprenticeships to foster team-working and a broad understanding of the enterprise, rather than a specialized, functional identity and skill set;
- Broadening the finance for universities to include individual contributions as a way to raise the quality of provision and create a more equal playing field with other forms of post-secondary education and training;
- Extending part-time work and other forms of labor flexibility to foster greater employment growth, particularly among women.

While Germany may benefit from applying these comparative lessons to its own system, a number of other countries have sought to learn from the time-tested model of the German dual system as a way to successfully link employers and educational institutions to deliver high-quality, transferable skills. All advanced industrial countries have now recognized that if they are to maintain their standard of living and compete effectively in the global economy, they need to equip not just their academic elite, but the vast majority of their workforce with a high-quality general education and a foundation of occupational skills. There is also growing acceptance that the workplace, if organized for learning, can be an effective, if not indispensable, part of the skill development process. But the experiences of France, Britain, and the US – reviewed in Part III of this volume – suggest that it is difficult to translate Germany's success in creating intermediate skills to other national contexts. The principal barrier to such policy transfer is the set of institutions in which apprenticeships are embedded that make the dual system operate effectively. Among these institutions are:

- An educational system that ensures that individuals entering apprenticeships have sound basic knowledge and skills from which to build more work-related competencies.
- A network of chambers of commerce, with compulsory membership of all local companies, which administer the apprenticeship exams and help ensure that the content of the system remains relevant to employers' needs.
- A highly regulated youth labor market, in which few alternative jobs exist to attract teenagers and push up wages.
- Skill standards that safeguard the quality of the training provided and ensure that apprentices in a given occupation are learning the same skills throughout the country. Individuals must complete their certification in order to work in many occupations, thus giving qualifications a high status and financial reward.

- An ample supply of trained trainers *(Meisters)*. *Meisters* oversee the quality of on-the-job training and link it to the latest changes in the production process. They also provide a career path for trainees, who can aspire to becoming a *Meister* after acquiring the necessary years of work experience and returning to education part-time to obtain additional qualifications.
- An industrial relations system that includes:
  - Unions that cooperate with firms to promote the flexible work organization needed to make full use of the latest technologies.
  - Works Councils that oversee the quality of training and protect trainees' interests within companies.
- A partnership of government, business, and organized labor that can build, albeit slowly, the consensus needed to change occupational standards and training in response to new skill demands. The highly regulated and consensual nature of the German system means that it is slow to adapt to changes in technology and work organization; however, when changes do occur, they have the support of all the main actors in the system (Casey 1990).
- Perhaps most importantly, a large pool of employers who have developed product and service markets and organized the work process in a way that utilizes the skills that apprentices acquire.

While it is unlikely, and probably undesirable, for other countries to attempt to emulate this set of deeply embedded German institutions, it is possible to try to create functional equivalents tailored to each country's own institutional and cultural context (Finegold et al. 1993). By creating mechanisms to bring employer, employee, and educational representatives together to define common skill requirements, to assure the quality and transferability of the training on offer within firms, and to share the costs of training equitably among the principal actors, it is possible to build an effective system for initial training. Perhaps the most difficult task many countries face is convincing a critical mass of employers to adopt work and job designs that demand high levels of skills from frontline workers. The recent, although still small-scale experiments in the US with regional employer training consortia (Parker and Rogers, Chapter 8) and in the UK with modern apprenticeships (Wood, Chapter 9) offer some encouragement. They suggest that a growing number of employers are recognizing the benefit of this skill investment, even in the highly mobile Anglo-American labor markets. The creation of forums for collective action can, at least in the US case, not only satisfy the demand for skills, but also help employers reorganize to adopt high-performance work organizations.

In most countries, apprenticeships, even if they become established, are likely to remain simply one of several routes to acquiring vocational qualifications, alongside full-time schooling options. In contrast, apprenticeships are likely to continue to cater for a majority of all German young people into the next generation, although more will be combining this vocational training with further post-secondary studies. To this extent, there may be some degree of convergence between Germany and other nations, as the number of educational options open to German young people (from privately run training centers to the full-time, applied courses in the *Berufsakademien* and *Fachhochschulen*) continues to expand.

Conclusions

The German dual system and the wider economic model of which it is an essential part face arguably the most severe and multi-layered set of challenges in the postwar period. Nearing the year 2000, Germany confronts major short-term pressures –

a sharp cyclical downturn in the early 1990s from which it is still recovering, the large, ongoing cost burden of reunification, and the fiscal constraints that were imposed by the requirements for entering the European Monetary Union. At the same time it must deal with the impact of significant, interlinked, structural problems: declining competitiveness, high levels of long-term unemployment, and the cost of supporting a rapidly aging population. These forces combine to create strong disincentives for firms to invest in new jobs in Germany that are vital if apprenticeship places are to be maintained.

While not minimizing the magnitude of these challenges, the research presented in this book provides some reasons for optimism. The Dutch experience suggests it is possible, given sufficient political will, to tackle the problems of unemployment, the pension system, and competitiveness without abandoning the corporatist model. And the German model is worth saving. The complex web of institutions that supports the dual system continues to achieve what many other countries desire, but have been unable to obtain – providing the majority of the population with relevant, high-status, transferable skills. We have identified a set of clear needs for reform, but it appears possible to address these issues without abandoning the core elements that have made the dual system such a long-term success: cooperation among employers, organized labor, and the state to insure a fair sharing of training costs and to certify the quality of training provided within firms.

BIBLIOGRAPHY

Abraham, K. and Houseman, S. 1992. *Job Security in America. Lessons from Germany.* Washington DC: Brookings.

Adler, P. and Borys, B. 1996. "Two Types of Bureaucracy: Enabling and Coercive." *Administrative Science Quarterly*, 41.

Agenda 1996. "Inter-TEC Tables." September 1995-96.

Alchian, A., and Woodward, S. 1988. "The Firm is Dead; Long Live the Firm – A Review of Oliver E. Williamson's *The Economic Institutions of Capitalism.*" *Journal of Economic Literature*, 26:1, pp. 65-79.

Alex, L., A. Menk, and M. Schiemann. 1997. "Vorzeitige Lösung von Ausbildungsverträgen." *Berufsbildung in Wissenschaft und Praxis* (BWP), 26:4.

Alex, L. and Stooß, F. 1996. *Berufsreport. Daten, Fakten, Prognosen zu allen wichtigen Berufen. Der Arbeitsmarkt in Deutschland – das aktuelle Handbuch.* Berlin: Argon Verlag.

Allmendinger, J. 1989a. *Career Mobility Dynamics. A Comparative Analysis of the United States, Norway, and West Germany.* Studien und Berichte 49. Berlin: Max-Planck-Institut für Bildungsforschung.

Allmendinger, J. 1989b. Educational Systems and Labour Market Outcomes. *European Sociological Review* 5: 3, pp. 231-250.

Allmendinger, J. 1994. *Lebensverlauf und Sozialpolitik.* Frankfurt a. M.: Campus.

Allmendinger, J. and Hinz, T. 1997. Mobilität und Lebensverlauf. In S. Hradil and S. Immerfall, eds., *Die westeuropäischen Gesellschaften im Vergleich.* Opladen: Leske and Budrich, pp. 247-285.

Althoff, H. 1994. "Die Ausbildungsbeteiligung der Jugendlichen – Argumente wider die behauptete Krise des dualen Systems." *Berufsbildung in Wissenschaft und Praxis* (BWP), No. 23.

America Works Partnership. 1996. "Working Together for Jobs: Profile of the America Works Partnership." Washington, DC: America Works Partnership.

Andresen, B. 1992. "Bildungsaktivitäten des Daimler-Benz-Konzerns in den neuen Bundesländern." In W. Schlaffke and R. Zedler, eds. *Wirtschaftlicher Wandel im neuen Bundesgebiet und Strategien der Qualifizierung*, Cologne: Deutscher Instituts-Verlag.

Anweiler, A., et al. 1990. *Vergleich von Bildung und Erziehung in der Bundesrepublik Deutschland und in der Deutschen Demokratischen Republik*. Cologne: Verlag Wissenschaft und Politik.

Aoki, M. 1988. *Information, Incentives and Bargaining in the Japanese Economy*. New York: Cambridge University Press.

Applebaum, E. and Batt, R. 1994. *The New American Workplace: Transforming Work Systems in the US*. Ithaca, NY: ILR Press.

Arum, R. and Shavit, Y. 1995. "Secondary Vocational Education and the Transition from School to Work." *Sociology of Education* 68: 187-204.

Ash, M., ed. 1997. *German Universities Past and Future*. New York: Berghahn Books.

Ashton, D. 1993. "Understanding change in youth labor markets: A conceptual framework." *British Journal of Education and Work*, 6, 5-12.

Association of British Chambers of Commerce (ABCC). 1996. "Memorandum submitted to the House of Commons Employment Committee on Mergers of chambers of commerce and Industry and TECs."

Atkinson, J. and Spilsbury, M. 1993. *Basic Skills and Jobs*. London: ALBSU.

Audit Commission. 1989. *Urban Regeneration and Economic Development: The Local Government Dimension*, London: HMSO.

Auer, P. 1992. "Further Education and Training for the Employees (FETE): European Diversity." Discussion Paper FS I 92-3. Berlin: Wissenschaftszentrum für Sozialforschung.

Autor, D., L. Katz, and A. Krueger. 1997. "Computing Inequality: Have Computers Changed the Labor Market." NBER Working Paper No. 5956. Cambridge, MA: National Bureau of Economic Research.

Axhausen, S. 1992. "Auswirkungen der Vereinbarkeitsproblematik eines Zusammenlebens mit Kindern und kontinuierlicher Berufstätigkeit für Frauen." In H. Krüger, ed., *Frauen und Bildung. Wege der Aneignung und Verwertung von Qualifikationen in weiblichen Erwerbsbiographien*. Bielefeld: KT-Verlag, 35-86.

Bach, H.-U., T. Jung-Hammon, and M. Otto. 1996. "Aktuelle Daten vom Arbeitsmarkt, Stand November 1996." *Institut für Arbeitsmarkt- und Berufsforschung der Bundesanstalt für Arbeit*, 11:1.

Backes-Gellner, U. 1996. *Betriebliche Bildungs- und Wettbewerbsstrategien im deutsch-britischen Vergleich.* München und Mering: Rainer Hampp.

Backes-Gellner, U., et al. 1994. "Quinter Studie zur Praxis der Personalpolitik in Europa (QUIPPE): Konzeption und erste Befunde." Quint-Essenzen Nr. 41. Trier.

Bäcker, G., and Naegele, G. 1996. "Altersteilzeit statt Frühverrentung: Gelingt der Durchbruch zu einem flexiblen und späteren Austritt aus dem Berufsleben?" *Zeitschrift für Gerontologie*, pp. 348-351.

Bahnmüller, R., R. Bispinck, and W. Schmidt. 1991. "Weiterbildung durch Tarifvertrag." *WSI-Mitteilungen* 44:3, pp. 171-180.

Bailey, T. 1993, "The Mission of TECs and Private Sector Involvement in Training: Lessons from Private Industry Councils." In Finegold et al. 1993.

Bailey, T. and Merritt, D. 1995. *Making-Sense of Industry-Based Skill Standards*. Berkeley, CA: NCRVE Report, December.

Bash, L. and A. Green eds. 1995, *1995 World Yearbook of Education*, London: Kogan Page.

Baugh, B., and Hilton, M. 1997. "Economic Development: A Union Guide to the High Road." Manuscript. Washington, DC: AFL-CIO Human Resources Development Institute.

Bausch T. 1997. "Beruflicher Erfolg von erwerbstätigen Abiturienten mit Lehrabschluß." *Berufsbildung in Wissenschaft und Praxis* 26:4.

Beck, U. 1986. *Risikogesellschaft. Auf dem Weg in eine andere Moderne*. Frankfurt a.M.: Suhrkamp.

Beck, U. and Brater, M., eds. 1977. *Die soziale Konstitution der Berufe*. Frankfurt: Campus.

Becker, G. 1964, *Human Capital: a Theoretical and Empirical Analysis, with Special Reference to Education*, New York: Columbia University Press.

Becker, W. and Meifort, B. 1994. *Pflege als Beruf – ein Berufsfeld in der Entwicklung; Berufe in der Gesundheits- und Sozialpflege: Ausbildung, Qualifikationen, berufliche Anforderungen.* Berichte zur beruflichen Bildung, H. 169. Berlin: Bundesinstitut für Berufsbildung.

Bednarz-Braun, I. 1983. *Arbeiterinnen in der Elektroindustrie*. München: DJI.

Behringer, F. and Ulrich, J. 1997. "Attraktivitätsverslust der dualen Ausbildung: Tatsache oder Fehldeutung der Statistik?" *Berufsbildung in Wissenschaft und Praxis* 26:4.

Bennett, R. and Krebs, G. 1993, "Chambers of commerce and the Challenges of a Single Market." In R. Bennett et al. 1993.

Bennett, R., A. McCoshan and P. Sellgren eds. 1989, *Training and Enterprise Councils (TECs) and Vocational Education in Training (VET): Papers on Practical Requirements*, Department of Geography, LSE, July.

Bennett, R., G. Krebs and H. Zimmerman 1993. *Chambers of commerce in Britain and Germany and the Single European Market*, London: Anglo-German Foundation.

Bennett, R., P. Wicks, and A. McCoshan 1994. *Local Empowerment and Business Services: Britain's Experiment with TECs*, London: UCL Press.

Berichtssystem Weiterbildung VI 1996. Bundesministerium für Bildung, Wissenschaft, Forschung und Technologie, ed. Bonn.

Bernhardt, A. and Bailey, T. 1998. "Making Careers out of Jobs: Policies for a New Employment Relationship." Manuscript. New York: Columbia University.

Bertrand, O. 1996. "Financial and Fiscal Devices to Encourage the Development of Training: A Case Study of France." Paper prepared for the European Institute of Education and Social Policy.

Best, M. 1990. *The New Competition: Institutions of Industrial Restructuring.* Cambridge, England: Polity Press.

Bird, E. and West, J. 1987. "Interrupted lives: a study of women returners." In P. Allatt et al., eds. , *Women and the life cycle. Transitions and turning points*. Houndsmills/Basingstoke/Hampshire/London: Macmillan Press, 178-191.

Bishop, J. 1996. "What we know about employer-provided training: a review of the literature." Working Paper 96-09, Center for Advanced Human Resource Studies, Cornell University.

Blanchard, O. and Summers, L. 1986. "Hysteresis and the European Unemployment Problem." *NBER Macroeconomics Annual*: Cambridge, MA: MIT Press.

Blechinger, D., and Pfeiffer, F. 1996. "Technological Change and Skill Obsolescence: the Case of German Apprenticeship Training." ZEW-Discussion Paper No. 96-15. Mannheim: Zentrum für Europäische Wirtschaftsforschung.

Blossfeld, H. 1987. "Entry into the labor market and occupational career in the Federal Republic – a comparison with American studies." *International Journal of Sociology*, 17: 86-115.

Blossfeld, H. 1989. *Kohortendifferenzierung und Karriereprozeß – eine Längs-schnittstudie über die Veränderung der Bildungs- und Erwerbschancen im Lebenslauf.* Frankfurt/New York: Campus.

Blossfeld, H. 1990. "Changes in Educational Careers in the Federal Republic of Germany." *Sociology of Education,* 63, 165-177.

Blossfeld, H. and Mayer, K. 1988. "Arbeitsmarktsegmentation in der Bundesrepublik Deutschland. Eine empirische Überprüfung von Segmentationstheorien aus der Perspektive des Lebenslaufs." *Kölner Zeitschrift für Soziologie und Sozialpsychologie* 40, 245-261.

BLS 1997. "1995 Survey of Employer-Provided Training – Employer Results." News Release. Washington: Bureau of Labor Statistics.

Bluethmann, H. 1992. "Ueberholt und abgehaengt. Erstmals baut BMW mehr Autos als Mercedes." *Die Zeit* Nr. 14, April 3, 1992, 9-10.

Born, C. 1989. *Wie sich die Bilder gleichen … Zur Situation weiblicher Lehrlinge nach Kriegsende bis heute.* Arbeitspapier Nr.2. Reihe Sfb 186. Bremen: Universität.

Born, C. 1993. "Abhängigkeiten zwischen ehepartnerlichen Erwerbsver-läufen in der BRD – Dilemmata und Dissonanzen zwischen Struktur und Norm." In C. Born and H. Krüger eds., *Erwerbsverläufe von Ehepartnern und die Modernisierung weiblicher Lebensführung.* Weinheim: Deutscher Studien Verlag, 71-88.

Born, C. , H. Krüger, and D. Lorenz-Meyer. 1996. *Der unentdeckte Wandel. Annäherung an das Verhältnis von Struktur und Norm im weiblichen Lebenslauf.* Berlin: edition sigma.

Robert-Bosch-Stiftung, ed., 1992. *Pflege braucht Eliten.* Denkschrift der Kommission zur Hochschulausbildung für Lehr- und Leitungskräfte in der Pflege. Beitrage zur Gesundheitsökonomie Bd.28. Gerlingen: Bleicher.

Robert-Bosch-Stiftung , ed., 1996. *Pflegewissenschaft: Grundlegung für Lehre, Forschung und Praxis.* Denkschrift. Materialien und Berichte Bd. 46. Gerlingen: Bleicher.

Boyer, R. 1986. *La théorie de la régulation : une analyse critique.* Paris: La Découverte.

Boyer, R. 1995. "Wage Austerity and/or an Education Push: The French dilemma." *Labour* Special Issue.

Boyer, R and Mistral, J. 1978. *Accumulation, Inflation, Crises.* Paris: PUF.

Braun, F. and Gravalas, B. 1980. *Die Benachteiligung junger Frauen in Ausbildung und Erwerbstätigkeit.* München.

Braun, H. and Jung, D. ed. 1997. *Globale Gerechtigkeit? Feministische Debatte zur Krise des Sozialstaats*. Hamburg: Konkret Literatur Verlag.

Brinker-Gabler, G. ed. 1979. *Frauenarbeit und Beruf. Die Frau in der Gesellschaft*. Frühe Texte. Frankfurt: Suhrkamp.

Brint, S. and Karabel, J. 1989. *The Diverted Dream: Community Colleges and the Promise of Educational Opportunity in America, 1900-1985*. New York: Oxford University Press.

Broadberry, S. and Wagner, K. 1996. "Human Capital and Productivity in Manufacturing During the Twentieth Century: Britain, Germany and the United States," in B. van Ark and N. Crafts eds., *Quantitative Aspects of Post-War European Economic GrowT*. Cambridge: Cambridge University Press.

Broedner, P. 1990. "Technocratic – Anthropocentric Approaches: Towards Skill-Based Manufacturing," in M. Warner, W. Wobbe and P. Broedner eds., *New Technology and Manufacturing Management*. Chichester: Wiley.

Brusco, S. 1982. "The Emilian Model: Productive Decentralisation and Social Integration." *Cambridge Journal of Economics* 6.

Büchtemann, Ch., J. Schupp, and D. Soloff. 1994. "From School to Work: Patterns in Germany and the United States." In Schwarze, J., Buttler, Fr. and Wagner, G. eds., *Labour Market Dynamics in Present Day Germany*. Frankfurt/Boulder Co.: Campus/Westview. 112-141.

Bundesministerium für Bildung und Wissenschaft (BMBW), ed. *Berufsbildungsbericht*, various years. Bonn.

Bundesministerium für Bildung und Wissenschaft., ed. *Grund- und Strukturdaten* (various years).

Bundesministerium für Bildung, Wissenschaft, Forschung und Technologie (BMBW), ed. 1996a. *Berufsbildungsbericht 1996*. Rheinback: Druckpartner Moser.

Bundesministerium für Bildung, Wissenschaft, Forschung und Technologie (BMBW), ed. 1996b. "Zukunftsbündnis Lehrstellen." Press Release, 24 April 1996.

Bunel, J. 1995. *La Transformation de la représentation patronale en France: CNPF et CGPME*. Paris: Commissariat Général du Plan.

Buttler, F. 1994. "Berufliche Weiterbildung als öffentliche Aufgabe." *Mitteilungen aus der Arbeitsmarkt- und Berufsforschung*, pp. 33-42.

Buttler, F., and Tessaring, M 1993: "Humankapital als Standortfaktor – Argumente zur Bildungsdiskussion aus arbeitsmarktpolitischer

Sicht." *Mitteilungen aus der Arbeitsmarkt- und Berufsforschung,* pp. 467-476.

Cappelli, P. 1996. "Youth Apprenticeship in Britain: Lessons for the United States." *Industrial Relations* 35:1-31.

Cappelli, P. and Crocker-Hefter, A. 1996. "Distinctive Human Resources Are Firms' Core Competencies." *Organizational Dynamics,* Winter, 7-21.

Capelli, P., D. Shapiro, and N. Shumanis. 1998. "Employer Participation in School-to-Work Programs." *Annals of the American Academy of Political and Social Science* 559, September.

Carlin, W. and Mayer, C. 1995. "Structure and Ownership of East German Enterprises." WZB Working Paper, FS I 95-305.

Carlin, W. and Soskice, D. 1997. "Shocks to the System: the German Political Economy under Stress." *National Institute Economic Review* 159, 1/97, p. 57-76.

Carlin, W., A. Glyn, and J.van Reenen. 1997. "Quantifying a Dangerous Obsession? Competitiveness and Export Performance in an OECD Panel of Industries." CEPR Discussion Paper 1628.

Carre, F. and P. Joshi. 1997. "Building Stability for Transient Workforces: Exploring the Possibilities of Intermediary Institutions Helping Workers Cope with Labor Market Instability." Working Paper No. 1. Cambridge, MA. Radcliffe Public Policy Institute.

Carroll, Gl. R, Haveman, H. and Swaminathan 1990. "Karrieren in Organisationen." In K. Mayer, eds. *Lebensverläufe und sozialer Wandel.* Opladen: Westdeutscher Verlag. 146-178.

Casey, B. 1990. *Recent Developments in West Germany's Apprenticeship Training System.* London: PSI Policy Papers, No. 1, 1990.

Casper, S. and Vitols, S. 1997. "The German model in the 1990's." *Industry and Innovation*, Vol. 4, No. 1.

Cattero, B., ed. Forthcoming. *Modell Deutschland, Modell Europa – Probleme, Perspektive.* Berlin: Leske and Budrich.

CCD (Childspace Cooperative Development). 1997. "Childspace: Innovations in Child Care." Philadelphia, PA: Childspace Cooperative Development.

CEDEFOP (Europäisches Zentrum für die Förderung der Berufsbildung) 1997. "Wirtschaft und Gewerkschaften stellen gemeinsam neue Weichen für Karrierechancen." CEDEFOP Info, No.2. Thessaloniki.

Centre for Educational Research and Innovation (CERI). 1995, *Education at a Glance*, Paris: OECD.

Chamard, Y. (rapporteur). 1994. Parliamentary Report on Apprenticeship, published as "Extraits du rapport Chamard." Documentation
Française.

Charraud, A. 1995. "Reconnaissance de la qualification: Contrats
de qualification et évolution des règles." *Formation Emploi* 52, Oct-
Dec 1995.

Charraud, A., Personnaz, E. and Venau, P. 1996. "Les certificats de
qualification professionnelle: de la construction des référents à leur
mise en oeuvre." Manuscript, CEREQ.

Cimini, Michael H. and Charles J. Muhl. 1994. "Job Security for Hospital
Workers." *Monthly Labor Review* 117(12):57.

Clark, Peggy and Steven Dawson. 1995. *Jobs and the Urban Poor: Privately
Initiated Sectoral Strategies*. Washington, DC: The Aspen Institute.

Cleveland, S. 1993, "Youth Training for the New International Economy."
In D. Finegold et al. 1993.

"Codewort Pretoria." 1993. *Manager Magazine*, May, 1993.

Coffield, F. 1992. "Training and Enterprise Councils: The Last Throw of
Voluntarism?." *Policy Studies*, vol. 13 (4).

Confederation of British Industry (CBI) 1988. *Toward a Skills Revolution*,
London: CBI Publications.

Confederation of British Industry (CBI), 1991. *World Class Targets:
A Joint Initiative to Achieve Britain's Skills Revolution*, London: CBI
Publications.

Confederation of British Industry (CBI), 1993. *Making Labour Markets
Work: CBI Policy Review of the Role of TECs and LECs*, London: CBI
Publications.

Coopers and Lybrand 1995. *Evaluation of Training for Work Pilots*, Report
to Employment Department, March.

Cornelsen, C. 1993. "Beruf und Tätigkeitsmerkmale der Erwerbstätigen."
Wirtschaft und Statistik, 1, 233-240.

Cramer, G. and K. Müller. 1994. "Nutzen der betrieblichen Berufsausbildung". *Beiträge des Instituts der deutschen Wirtschaft und Gesell-
schafts- und Bildungspolitik*, No. 19. Cologne.

Crouch, C. 1992. "The Dilemmas of Vocational Training Policy: Some
Comparative Lessons." *Policy Studies*, 13: 4.

Crouch, C., D. Finegold, and M. Sako. 1999. *Are Skills the Answer? The
Political Economy of Skill Creation in Advanced Industrial Countries*.
Oxford: Oxford University Press.

Crowley-Bainton, T. 1993. *TECs and Employers: Developing Effective Links – Part 2, TEC-Employer Links in Six TEC Areas*, Sheffield: DfEE, Research Series No. 13, AuguS.

Culpepper, P. 1996a. "Employers' Organizations and the Politics of Vocational Training in France and Germany." Paper presented at the 1996 Annual Meeting of the American Political Science Association, San Francisco, August 29-September 1, 1996.

Culpepper, P. 1996b. "Problems on the Road to 'High-Skill': A sectoral lesson from the transfer of the dual system to eastern Germany." WZB Working Paper, FS I 96-317.

Culpepper, P. 1998a. "Employers' Associations, Public Policy, and The Politics of Decentralized Cooperation." In P. Hall and D. Soskice, *Varieties of Capitalism: The Institutional Foundation of Comparative Institutional Advantage*, forthcoming.

Culpepper, P. 1998b. "Rethinking Reform: The Politics of Decentralized Cooperation in France and Germany." Ph.D. Dissertation, Department of Government, Harvard University.

D'Iribarne, A. and Lemaître, A. 1987. *Le role des partenaires sociaux dans la formation professionnelle en France*. Brussels: CEDEFOP.

Dale, R. 1989. *The State and Education Policy*, Milton Keynes: Open University.

Daly, A., Hitchens, D. and Wagner, K. 1985. "Productivity, Machinery and Skills in a Sample of British and German Manufacturing Plants." *National Institute Economic Review*, 111, 48-61.

DARES. 1996. "Apprentissage et contrat de qualification en 1995." *Premières synthèses* 96-09-36-1.

DARES. 1997. *Tableau de bord des politiques d'emploi*. No. 44, April.

Davies, R. B. , Elias, P. and Penn, R. 1992. "The relationship between a husband's unemployment and his wife's participation in the labor market." *Oxford Bulletin of Economics and Statistics*, 54, 145-171.

Davis, S. J., Haltiwanger, J. C. and Schuh, Sc. 1996. *Job Creation and Destruction*. Cambridge: MIT Press.

Deakin, B. 1996. *The Youth Labour Market in Britain: The Role of Intervention*. Cambridge: Cambridge University Press.

Deeg, R. 1997. "Banks and Industrial Finance in the 1990s," *Industry and Innovation*, Vol. 4, No. 1.

Degen, U., ed. 1993. *Berufsbildung im Übergang*. BiBB, Heft 18.

Degen, U. 1995. "Ausbildungsbeteiligung und -probleme der Betriebe und Praxen sowie Maßnahmen zur Förderung der betrieblichen

Berufsausbildung in den neuen Bundesländern." In Friedrich-Ebert-Stiftung, ed. 1995. *Berufsausbildung in den neuen Bundesländern*. Gesprächskreis Arbeit und Soziales, Nr. 42.

Degen, U. and Walden, G. 1995. "Ausbildungsbeteiligung der Betriebe." In Degen, U., G. Walden, and K. Berger, eds. 1995. *Berufsausbildung in den neuen Bundesländern: Daten, Analysen, Perspektiven*. BiBB, Heft 180.

Degen, U. and Walden, G. 1997. "Sicherung der Leistungs- und Zukunftsqualität des dualen Systems der Berufsausbildung durch hohe Ausbildungsqualität." *Berufsbildung in Wissenschaft und Praxis*, No. 5.

Department for Education and Employment (DfEE) 1995. *Efficiency Scrutiny: The TEC Contract and Management Fee*, London: HMSO.

Department for Education and Employment (DfEE) 1996a. *High Performance TECs Win £21 Million Bonus*, DfEE Press Release 367/96, 31 October.

Department for Education and Employment (DfEE) 1996b. *Shephard Drives TECs Forward to Success in the 21ˢᵗ Century*, DfEE Press Release 397/96, 21 November.

Department for Education and Employment (DfEE) 1996c. *TECs: Beyond 2000*, London: HMSO.

Department for Education and Employment (DfEE) 1996d. *TECs Win £55 Million Local Training and Business Package*, DfEE Press Release, 4 September.

Department for Education and Employment (DfEE) 1997a. *"Be Trailblazers for Investors in People": Kim Howells Tells Top UK Companies*, DfEE Press Release 153/97, 24 June.

Department for Education and Employment (DfEE) 1997b. *Participation in Education and Training by 16-18 Year Olds in England, 1986-1996*, DfEE Press Release 159/97, 26 June.

Department for Education and Employment (DfEE) 1997c. *Statistical Bulletin* (No. 4/97), 14 May.

Department for Education and Employment (DfEE) 1997d. *TECs Come of Age: Paice*, DfEE Press Release 25/97, 5 February.

Department of Employment 1988. *Employment for the 1990s*, Cm. 540, December.

Department of Employment/ Department for Trade and Industry 1994. *The Strategy for Skills and Enterprise 1993-1994: Guidance for the Secretary of State for Employment and the President of the Board of Trade*, London: DE and DTI.

Deutscher Bundestag 1994. *Enquête-Kommission Demographischer Wandel Zwischenbericht*. Bundestagsdrucksache 12/7876 (14 June 1994).

Dietz, G. -U., Mariak, V., Matt. , E., Seus, L. and Schumann, K. F. 1997. *Lehre tut viel … .* Münster: Votum.

DiPrete, T. A. and McManus. P. A. 1996. Institutions, Technical Change, and Diverging Life Chances: Earnings Mobility in the US and Germany. *American Journal of Sociology* (101). 34-109.

DIW (Deutsches Institut für Wirtschaftsforschung).1996. "Weiterhin steigender Lehrstellenbedarf in der Bundesrepublik Deutschland." *Wochenbericht* No. 41.

Doms, M., T. Dunne, and K. R. Troske. 1997. "Workers, Wages, and Technology." *Quarterly Journal of Economics* 112(1):253-90.

Dore, R. 1986. *Flexible rigidities : industrial policy and structural adjustment in the Japanese economy, 1970-80.* London: Atholone Press.

Dorn, C. and Rozema, A. 1992. "Analyse unterschiedlicher Entwicklungen hin zu den Dienstleistungsbereichen und die Auswirkungen auf Frauen und Männer." In Krüger, H. ed., *Frauen und Bildung. Wege der Aneignung und Verwertung von Qualifikationen in weiblichen Erwerbsbiographien*. Bielefeld: KT-Verlag, 225-271.

Drechsel, R., Görs, D. u.a., ed. 1988. *Berufspolitik und Gewerkschaften. Gewerkschaftliches Berufsverständnis und Entwicklung der Lohnarbeit*. Universität Bremen.

Dresser, L. and Rogers, J. 1997a. "Rebuilding Job Access and Career Advancement Systems in the New Economy." Manuscript. Madison, WI: Center on Wisconsin Strategy.

Dresser, L. and Rogers, J. 1997b. "Sectoral Strategies of Labor Market Reform: Emerging Evidence from the U.S." Manuscript. Madison, WI: Center on Wisconsin Strategies.

Drexel, I. 1993. *Das Ende des Facharbeiteraufstiegs? Neue mittlere Bildungs- und Karrierewege in Deutschland und Frankreich*. Frankfurt und New York: Campus Verlag.

Drexel, I. 1995. "The implications of different continuing training systems for corporate work organisation and personnel management policy – a Franco-German comparison." In Koch, R, and Reuling, J. eds. *The European Dimension in Vocational Training: Experiences and Tasks of Vocational Training Policy in the Member States of the European Union*, Bielefeld: Bertelsmann.

DSTE. 1993. *Bilan Statistique de la Formation Professionnelle en 1993.*

Dybowski, G. , H. Pütz, E. Sauter, H. Schmidt. 1994. "Ein Weg aus der Sackgasse – Plädoyer für ein eigenständiges und gleichwertiges Berufs-bildungssystem." *Berufsbildung in Wissenschaft und Praxis*, No. 23.

Education 1994. "The Right to Read has become a Family Matter." 25 March.

Edding, F. 1963. *Ökonomie des Bildungswesens – Lehren und Lernen als Haushalt und Investititon.*, Freiburg: Verlag Rombach.

Engineering Construction Industry Training Board (ECITB) 1995. *Memorandum submitted to the House of Commons Employment Committee on TECs.*

Enquête-Kommission des Deutschen Bundestages 1990. *Zukünftige Bildungspolitik – Bildung 2000.* Schlußbericht. Drucksache 11/7820. Bonn.

EQW 1995: "First Findings from the EQW National Employer survey." Philadelphia: National Center on the Educational Quality of the Workforce.

Ernst and Young 1995. *The Evaluation of the Modern Apprenticeship Prototypes*, London: Ernst and Young, October.

Erzberger, C. 1993. *Erwerbsarbeit im Eheleben. Männlicher und weiblicher Erwerbsverlauf zwischen Dependenzen und Unabhängigkeit.* Arbeits-papier Nr. 16. Reihe Sfb 186. Bremen: Universität.

Esping-Andersen, G. 1990. *The Three Worlds of Welfare Capitalism.* Princeton, NJ: Princeton University Press.

Esping-Andersen, G. 1996. "Welfare States without Work." In Esping-Andersen, ed. *Welfare States in Transition.* New York: Sage.

Evans, B. 1992. *The Politics of the Training Market: From Manpower Services Commission to Training and Enterprise Councils*, London: Routledge.

Falk, R. 1982. "Bildungskosten in der privaten Wirtschaft. Eine Synopse von Untersuchungen in den siebziger Jahren." In Göbel, U. and Schlaffke, W. eds. *Berichte zur Bildungspolitik 1982/83 des Instituts der deutschen Wirtschaft*, Köln.

Farnham, D., and C. Lupton 1994. "Employment Relations and Training Policy." In S. Savage et al. 1994.

Fels, G., ed. 1989. "Beruf und Arbeitswelt im EG-Binnenmarkt." In *Beiträge zur Gesellschafts- und Bildungspolitik 147.* Köln.

Financial Times 1992. TEC Directors survey, 25 March.

Financial Times 1993. TEC Directors survey, 10 May.

Financial Times 1997. "Move to Close TEC Over £1m Fraud Inquiry." 1-2 November.

Finegold, D. 1992. "The Low-Skill Equilibrium: An Institutional Analysis of Britain's Education and Training Failure." D.Phil. Dissertation, Oxford University.

Finegold, D. 1993. "The Changing International Economy and its Impact on Education and Training." In Finegold et al. 1993.

Finegold, D. 1997. "Creating World-Class Standards: A Process for Relating US Skill Standards to International Quality and Skill Standards." Report prepared for the National Skills Standards Board, US Department of Labor, June, 1997.

Finegold, D., K. Brendley, R. Lempert, D. Henry, P. Cannon, B. Boulting-house, and M. Nelson. 1994. *The Decline of the U.S. Machine-Tool Industry and Prospects for Its Sustainable Recovery*. Santa Monica, CA: RAND.

Finegold, D., and Keltner, B. 1997. "Institutional Effects on Skill Creation: A Comparison of Management Development in the U.S. and Germany." In K. Wever, ed. *Political Competition: An Institutional Comparison of Germany and the US.* Book manuscript.

Finegold, D., L. McFarland, and W. Richardson eds. 1993. *Something Borrowed, Something Learned? The Transatlantic Market in Education and Training Reform*. Washington D.C.: Brookings.

Finegold, D. and Soskice, D. 1988. "The Failure of Training in Britain : Analysis and Prescription." *Oxford Review of Economic Policy* 4 (3), Autumn, 1988, 21-53.

Finegold, D., and Wagner, K., 1997. "When Lean Production Meets the German Model: Innovation Responses in the US and German Pump Industries." *Industry and Innovation,* 4:2, December.

Finegold, D. and Wagner, K. 1998. "The Search for Flexibility: Skills and Workplace Innovation in the German Pump Industry." *British Journal of Industrial Relations* 36:3, pp. 469-87, September.

Fischer, J. 1995. "Weiterbildung im Spannungsfeld von öffentlicher Regulierung und betrieblicher Autonomie." In K. Semlinger and B. Frick, eds. *Betriebliche Modernisierung in personeller Erneuerung.* Berlin: edition sigma, pp. 229-244.

Flaake, K. and King, V., eds. 1992. *Weibliche Adoleszenz. Zur Sozialisation junger Frauen*. Frankfurt/New York: Campus.

Fowler, N. 1989. speech at 'Business in the Cities' conference, 6 December.

Frackmann, M. and Schild, H. 1988. *Schulische Berufsausbildung. Bilanz und Perspektiven.* Gutachten für die Max-Träger-Stiftung. MTS-Skript 1, Frankfurt/Main: Blümlein.

Franz, W. and Soskice, D. 1995. "The German apprenticeship system." Buttler,F. , Franz, W. , Schettkat, R. , and Soskice, D. eds. *Institutional Frameworks and Labour Market Performance,* London: Routledge.

Franz, W. and Zimmermann, V. 1996. "Das duale System der Berufs-ausbildung: Noch ein deutscher Standortvorteil?" *Wirtschaftsdienst,* Zeitschrift für Wirtschaftspolitik, No. 8.

Freeman, R. 1994. "How Labor Fares in Advanced Economies." In *Working Under Different Rules*, ed. Richard B. Freeman. New York, NY: Russell Sage Foundation.

Freeman, R. and Rogers, J. 1996. "Die Quintessenz: Der Inneramerikan-ischen Debate." *Mitbestimmung* (July-August):12-17.

Freeman, R. and . Katz, L. 1995. "Introduction and Summary." In *Differences and Changes in Wage Structures*. Chicago, IL: Chicago University Press.

Fricke, E. and Schuchardt, W. 1987. "Dienstleistungen im Zeichen technologie-orientierter Rationalisierungstendenzen: Kann das soziale Konzept 'Beruf' überleben?" In A. Weymann, Bildung und Beschäftigung. *Soziale Welt Sonderband 5.* Göttingen.

Fujimoto, T. "Reinterpreting the Resource-Capability View of the Firm," University of Tokyo, Faculty of Economics Discussion Paper, 94-F-20, May, 1994.

Fukuyama, F. 1996. *Trust. The Social Virtues and the Creation of Prosperity.* New York: Free Press.

Further Education Funding Council (FEFC) 1992. *Funding Learning,* Coventry: FEFC.

Gamble, A. 1988. *The Free Economy and the Strong State: The Politics of Thatcherism*, Hampshire: Duke University Press.

Garrett, G. 1997. *Partisan Politics in the Global Economy.* New York: Cambridge University Press.

Garrett, G. and Lange, P. 1991. "Political Responses to Interdependence: What's Left for the Left?" *International Organization* 45:4.

Gatter, J. 1997. "Continuing Training in an Aging German Economy." Policy Papers No. 4, AICGS, Wasington, DC.

Gatter, J., and Hartmann, B.K. 1995. "Betriebliche Verrentungspraktiken zwischen arbeitsmarkt- und rentenpolitischen Interessen." *Mitteilungen aus der Arbeitsmarkt- und Berufsforschung,* pp. 412-424.

Geer, R. and W. Hirschbrunn. 1994. "Zukunftsperspektiven von Fach-kräften in der Industrie." *Beiträge zur Gesellschafts- und Bildungs-politik des Instituts der deutschen Wirtschaft*, No. 194, Cologne.

Géhin, J.-P., and Méhaut, P. 1993. *Apprentissage ou Formation Continue?: Stratégies éducatives des entreprises en Allemagne et en France*. Paris: Éditions l'Harmattan.

Geissler, B. and Oechsle, M. 1996. *Lebensplanung junger Frauen. Zur widersprüchlichen Modernisierung weiblicher Lebensläufe*. Weinheim: Deutscher Studien Verlag.

Gerwin, D. 1987. "Manufacturing Flexibility in the CAM Era," University of Wisconsin-Milwaukee, School of Business Administration working paper, February.

Gewerkschaft Erziehung und Wissenschaft ed. 1988. "Arbeitsbedingungen und Arbeitsbelastungen in sozialpädagogischen Berufen. Ergebnisse einer Untersuchung des Instituts für Medienforschung und Urbanistik (IMU)." Frankfurt/München, Mimeo.

Giddens, A. 1984. *The constitution of society. Outline of a theory of structuration*. Cambridge: Polity Press.

Goasguen, C. (rapporteur). 1994. "Rapport de la Commission d'Enquête sur l'utlisation des fonds affectés à la formation professionnelle." Rapport no. 1041, Assemblée nationale, 2 vols.

Goldmann, M. and Müller, U. 1986. *Junge Frauen im Verkaufsberuf*. Stuttgart: Enke

Goldstein, J. and Keohane, R. 1993. *Ideas and Foreign Policy*. Ithaca, NY: Cornell University Press.

Görres, S., D. Koch-Zadi, H. van Maanen, and M. Schöller-Schmidt, eds. 1996. *Pflegewissenschaft in der Bundesrepublik Deutschland*. Bremen: Altera.

Gourevitch, P. 1996. "The Macropolitics of Microinstitutional Differ-ences in the Analysis of Comparative Capitalism." In S. Berger and R. Dore, eds. *National Diversity and Global Capitalism*. Ithaca, NY: Cornell University Press.

Green, A. and H. Steedman 1993. *Educational Provision, Educational Attainment and the Needs of Industry: a Review of Research for Germany, France, Japan, the USA and Britain*, London: NIESR.

Groot, W. 1996. "On-the-Job Training, Job Mobility and Wages in Britain." mimeo, Tinbergen Institute, Rotterdam.

Grubb, N. 1993. "The Varied Economic Returns to Post-Secondary Education." *Journal of Human Resources* 28(2):356-82.

Grünert, H. and Lutz, B. 1995: "East German labour market in transition: segmentation and increasing disparity." *Industrial Relations Journal*, No. 1.

Grünewald, U., and Moraal D. 1995. *Kosten der betrieblichen Weiterbildung in Deutschland*. Berlin: Bundesinstitut für Berufsbildung.

Grund- und Strukturdaten (various years). Bundesministerium für Bildung und Wissenschaft, Bonn.

Hall, P. 1986. *Governing the Economy*. Oxford: Oxford University Press.

Hall, P. 1992. "The movement from Keynesianism to Monetarism: Institutional analysis and British economic policy in the 1970s." In Steinmo et al. 1992.

Hall, P. 1993. "Policy Paradigms, Social Learning, and the State." *Comparative Politics*, 25, pp. 275-296.

Hall, P. 1997. "The Role of Interests, Institutions, and Ideas in the Comparative Political Economy of the Industrialized Nations." In M. Lichbach and A. Zuckerman, eds., *Comparative Politics: Rationality, Culture, and Structure*, New York: Cambridge University Press.

Hall, P. 1998a. "Organized Market Economies and Unemployment in Europe: Is it Finally Time to Accept Liberal Orthodoxy?" Paper presented to the 11th Annual Conference of Europeanists, Baltimore, MD, February 26-28, 1998.

Hall, P. 1998b. "The Political Economy of Europe in an Era of Interdependence." In Kitschelt et al. 1998.

Hall, P and Soskice, D., eds. Forthcoming. *Varieties of Capitalism: The Foundation of Comparative Institutional Advantage*. Book manuscript.

Halpern, D., S. Wood, S. White and G. Cameron eds. 1996. *Options for Britain: A Strategic Policy Review*, Aldershot: Dartmouth Press.

Hamilton, S. 1990. *Apprenticeship for Adulthood*. New York: Free Press.

Hamilton, S. and Hurrelmann, K. 1993. "Auf der Suche nach dem besten Modell für den Übergang von der Schule in den Beruf – ein amerikanisch-deutscher Vergleich." *Zeitschrift für Sozialisationsforschung*, 13, 194-207.

Hamilton, S. and Hurrelmann, K. 1994. "The school-to-career transition in Germany and the United States." *Teachers College Record*, 96 : 2, 329-44.

Hancké, B. 1997. *Reconfiguring the German Production System: Crisis and Adjustment in the Automobile Industry*. Paper presented at the workshop on Modell Deutschland in the 1990s, WZB 27-28, June, 1997.

Hancké, B., and Soskice, D. 1996. "Coordination and Restructuring in Large French Firms." WZB Working Paper, FS1, 96-303.

Hardes, H.-D., and Schmitz, F. 1991. "Tarifverträge zur betrieblichen Weiterbildung – Darstellung und Analyse aus arbeitsökonomischer Sicht." *Mitteilungen aus der Arbeitsmarkt- und Berufsforschung*, pp. 658-672.

Harhoff, D. and Kane, T. 1996. "Is the German Apprenticeship System a Panacea for the US Labour Market?" CEPR Discussion Paper 1311.

Harrison, B., with M. Weiss, and J. Grant. 1994. *Building Bridges: Community Development Corporations and the World of Employment Training*. New York, NY: Ford Foundation.

Hartmann, W., Steilmann, C., and Toepper, S. 1994. *Lean-Production in der Konfektionsindustrie*. Berlin: Wilke.

Houghton, G., J. Peck, T. Hart, I. Strange, A. Tickell, and C. Williams 1995. *TECs and their Boards*, Sheffield: DfEE, Research Series no. 64, October.

Houghton, G., T. Hart, I. Strange, K. Thomas, and J. Peck 1995. *TECs and their Non-Employer Stakeholders*, Sheffield: DfEE, Research Series No. 46, February.

Hausen, K. 1978. "Die Polarisierung der Geschlechtscharaktere." In Rosenbaum, H. (ed.), *Seminar Familien- und Gesellschaftsstruktur*. Frankfurt a. M.: suhrkamp, 15-38.

Häußermann, H. and Siebel, W. 1995. *Dienstleistungsgesellschaften*. Frankfurt a.M.: edition suhrkamp.

Heckathorn, D. 1996. "The Dynamics and Dilemmas of Collective Action." *American Sociological Review* 61, April.

Heckman, J. 1994. "Is Job Training Oversold?" *Public Interest* 115: 91-115.

Heinz, W. 1995. *Arbeit, Beruf und Lebenslauf. Eine Einführung in die berufliche Sozialisation*. Grundlagentexte der Soziologie. Weinheim/München: Juventa.

Heinz, W. 1996. "Youth Transitions in Cross-Cultural Perspective: School-to-Work in Germany." In B. Gallaway and J. Hudson, eds., *Youth in Transition. Perspectives on Research and Policy*. Toronto: Thompson Educational Publishing, Inc., 2-13.

Heinz, W. R., Krüger, H., Rettke, U., Wachtveitl, E. and Witzel, A. 1985. *Hauptsache eine Lehrstelle. Jugendliche vor den Hürden des Arbeitsmarktes*. Weinheim/Basel: Beltz (Second Edition 1987).

Heintze, R. G., J. Schmidt, and C. Strünck. 1997. "Zur politischen Ökonomie der sozialen Dienstleistungsproduktion." *Kölner Zeitschrift für
Soziologie und Sozialpsychologie*, 49:2, 242-271.

Herrigel, G. 1989. "Industrial Order and the Politics of Industrial Change."
In P. Katzenstein, ed., *Industry and Politics in West Germany*, Ithaca,
NY: Cornell University Press.

Herrigel, G. 1993a. "Large Firms, Small Firms and the Governance of
Flexible Specialization: Baden-Württemberg and the Socialization
of Risk." In B. Kogut, ed., *Country Competitiveness: Technology and
the Organizing of Work*, New York: Oxford University Press.

Herrigel, G. 1993b. "Power in Industrial Districts." In G. Grabher, ed.,
The Embedded Firm, London: Routledge.

Herrigel, G. 1996a. "Crisis in German Decentralized Production."
European Urban and Regional Studies, 3 (1), 1996, 33-52.

Herrigel, G. 1996b. *Industrial Constructions: The Sources of German
Industrial Power*. New York: Cambridge University Press.

Hilbert, J. et al. 1990. *Berufsbildungspolitik*. Opladen: Leske + Budrich.

Hillman, J. 1996, "Education and Training." In D. Halpern et al. 1996.

Himmelreich, F.-H.1996. "Das duale Bildungssystem ist kontinuierlich
veränderungsbedürftig." In *Wirtschaftsdienst*, Zeitschrift für Wirtschaftspolitik, No. 8.

Hinrichs, K. 1993. "Public Pensions and Demographic Change: Genera-
tional Equity in the United States and Germany." ZeS-Working
Paper 16/93. Bremen: Centre for Social Policy Research.

Hirsch, B. and Macpherson, D. 1996. *Union Membership and Earnings
Data Book 1996*. Washington, DC: Bureau of National Affairs.

Hirschman, A. 1970. *Exit, voice, and loyalty: responses to decline in firms,
organizations, and states*. Cambridge, MA: Harvard University Press.

HIS Hochschul-Informations-System GmbH. 1991. *Bildungswege von
Frauen: vom Abitur bis zum Berufseintritt.* Hannover: HIS-GmbH.

Hitchens, D., K. Wagner, and E. Birnie.1991. "Improving Productivity
through International Exchange Visits." OMEGA 19:5.

Hitchens, D., K. Wagner, and E. Birnie. 1993. *East German Productivity
and the Transition to the Market Economy*, Aldershot: Avebury.

Hodkinson, J., and Hodkinson, H. 1995. "Markets, Outcomes and the
Quality of Vocational Education and Training: Some Lessons from a
Youth Credits Pilot Scheme." *Vocational Education and Training*, 47: 3.

Hoffmann, E. 1993. "Zur Beschäftigung älterer Arbeitnehmer in West-deutschland – Qualitative und quantitative Aspekte." *Mitteilungen aus der Arbeitsmarkt- und Berufsforschung,* 26:3, pp. 313-327.

Hofstede, G. 1980. *Culture's Consequences.* Bevery Hills, CA: Sage Publications.

Hollingsworth, J. 1997. "Continuities and Changes in Social Systems of Production: The Cases of Japan, Germany, and the United States." In Hollingsworth and Boyer 1997.

Hollingsworth, J. and Boyer, R., eds. 1997. *Contemporary Capitalism: The Embeddedness of Institutions.* New York: Cambridge University Press.

Homburg, C., and Becker, J. 1996. "Zertifizierung von Qualitätssicherungs-systemen nach den Qualitätssicherungsnormen DIN ISO 9000ff." *WiSt No 9,* pp. 444-450.

House of Commons Employment Committee (HCEC) 1996, *First Report: The Work of TECs,* London: HMSO, February.

Howell, David R. and Edward N. Wolff. 1991. "Trends in the Growth and Distribution of Skills in the U.S. Workforce, 1960-1985." *Industrial and Labor Relations Review* 44:486-502.

Huddleston, P. 1993. "Developing the new 16-19 Curriculum in Further Education Colleges." In W. Richardson et al. 1993.

Hutton, W. 1995. The State We're In. London: Vintage.

Hyman, R. 1996. "Institutional Transfer: Industrial Relations in Eastern Germany." WZB Working Paper, FS-I 96-305.

Industrie- und Handelskammern in Nordrhein-Westfalen. ed. 1992. *Karriere mit Lehre, Ergebnisse der Ausbildung-Nachfrage,* no year, no city.

Industry Department, Scotland 1988. *Scottish Enterprise: A New Approach to Training and Enterprise Creation,* Edinburgh: HMSO, Cm. S34.

Iversen, T. 1997. "The Dynamics of Welfare State Expansion: Trade Openness, De-Industrialization, and Partisan Politics." Paper prepared for the Workshop on the New Politics of the Welfare State, Center for European Studies, Harvard University, December.

Iversen, T. and Wren, A. 1998. "Equality, Employment, and Budgetary Restraint: The Trilemma of the Service Economy." *World Politics* 50:4, July.

iwd (Informationsdienst des Instituts der deutschen Wirtschaft). 1997. *Flexible Lösungen sind gefragt,* No. 30.

Jessop, B. ed. 1991. *The Politics of Flexibility. Restructuring State and Industry in Britain, Germany and Scandinavia.* Aldershot: Edward Elgar.

Jobert, A. and Tallard, M. 1995. "Diplômes et Certification des branches dans les conventions collectives." *Formation Emploi* 52, Oct-Dec 1995.

Jürgens, U. 1997. "Rolling Back Cycle Times: The Renaissance of the Classic Assembly Line in Final Assembly," in K. Shimokawa, U. Jürgens, and T. Fujimoto, eds., *Transforming Automobile Assembly*. Berlin: Springer-Verlag.

Kane, T. and Rouse, C. 1995. "Labor-Market Returns to Two- and Four-Year College." *American Economic Review* 85(3):600-14.

Kappelhoff, P. and Teckenberg, W. 1987. Intergenerational and Career Mobility in the Federal Republic and the United States. In Teckenberg, W., ed., *Comparative Studies of Social Structure. Recent Research on France, the United States and the Federal Republic of Germany*. New York: Sharpe. 3-47.

Katzenstein, P., ed. 1989. *Industry and Politics in West Germany. Toward a Third Republic*. Ithaca, NY: Cornell University Press.

Katzenstein, P.J. 1985. *Small States in World Markets*. Ithaca, NY: Cornell University Press.

Katzenstein, P.J. 1987. *Policy and Politics in West Germany: Towards the Growth of a Semi-Sovereign State*. Philadelphia, PA: Temple University Press.

Keep, E. and K. Mayhew 1996. "Toward a Learning Society – Definition and Measurement." *Policy Studies*, 17: 3.

Keltner, B. and Finegold, D. 1996. "Adding Value in Banking: An Innovative Human Resource Strategy," *Sloan Management Review*, 38: 1, Fall 1996, 57-68.

Keltner, B., D. Finegold, and C. Pager. 1996. *Institutional Supports for a High-Performing Skill Standards System: Evidence from Germany, the UK and Australia,* Santa Monica, CA: RAND DRU-1548-NCRVE/UCB, November.

Kerckhoff, A. C. 1995. "Institutional Arrangements and Stratification Processes in Industrial Societies." *Annual Review of Sociology* (15). 323-347.

Kern, H. 1996. "German Captitalism: How competitive will it be in the Future?" Paper presented at the Conference "The Restructuring of the Economic and Political System in Japan and Europe: Past Legacy and Present Issues," Milan, May 15.

Kern, H., and Schumann, M. 1984. *Das Ende der Arbeitsteilung?*, München: Beck Verlag.

Kern, H. and Schumann, M. 1997. "Kontinunität oder Pfadwechsel? Das deutsche Produktionsmodell am Scheideweg." *SOFI Mitteilungen*, Number 26, 1997.

Kerschensteiner, G. 1901. *Staatsbürgerliche Erziehung der deutschen Jugend.* Gekrönte Preisschrift: Erfurt.

King, D. 1987, *The New Right: Politics, Market and Citizenship*, Basingstoke: Macmillan.

King, D. 1993. "The Conservatives and Training Policy 1979-1992: From a Tripartite to a Neoliberal Regime." *Political Studies*, 41.

King, D. 1995. *Actively Seeking Work? The Politics of Unemployment and Welfare Policy in the United States and Great Britain*, London: University of Chicago Press.

King, D. 1997. "Employers, Training Policy and the Tenacity of Voluntarism in Britain." *Twentieth Century British History*, 8 forthcoming.

King, D. and S. Wood 1998. "The Politics of Neoliberalism: Britain and the United States in the 1980s." In Kitschelt et al. 1998.

Kitschelt, H., P. Lange, G. Marks, and J. Stephens, eds. 1998. *Continuity and Change in Contemporary Capitalism*. New York: Cambridge University Press.

Kleinau, E. and Mayer, Ch., eds., 1996. *Erziehung und Bildung des weiblichen Geschlechts. Eine kommentierte Quellensammlung zur Bildungs- und Berufsbildungsgeschichte von Mädchen und Frauen.* Weinheim: Deutscher Studien Verlag.

Kloas, P.-W. et al. 1988. "Lernen nach der Lehre: die ersten Berufsjahre als Qualifizierungsphase." In *Bundesinstitut für Berufsbildung*, Berlin, Bonn.

Knight, J. 1992. *Institutions and Social Change*. NY: Cambridge University Press.

Knoll, L., and Knoss, B. 1995.: "Spezifisches Humankapital: Ökonomische Theorie und betriebliche Praxis." *Zeitschrift für Personalforschung No. 4*, pp. 401-415.

Kogut, B. 1991. "Country Capabilities and the Permeability of Borders," *Strategic Management Journal,* 12, pp. 33-47.

Kohli, M. 1985. "Die Institutionalisierung des Lebenslaufs." *Kölner Zeitschrift für Soziologie und Sozialpsychologie*, 37, pp. 1-29.

Krahn, H. 1991. "The school-to-work transition in Canada: New risks and uncertainties." In W. Heinz, ed., *The life course and social change*: *Comparative perspectives*. Weinheim: Deutscher Studien Verlag.

Krahn, H. 1996. *School-Work Transitions. Changing Patterns and Research Needs*. Discussion Paper prepared for Applied Research Grant. Human Resources Development, Canada. University of Alberta.

Krüger, H., ed. 1992. *Frauen und Bildung. Wege der Aneignung und Verwertung von Qualifikationen in weiblichen Erwerbsbiographien*. Bielefeld: KT-Verlag.

Krüger, H. 1991. "Doing Gender – Geschlecht als Statuszuweisung im Berufsbildungssystem." In D. Brock, B. Hantsche, G. Kühnlein, H., Meulemann and K. Schober, eds., *Übergänge in den Beruf*. München: DJI, 139-169.

Krüger, H. 1998. "Gendersensible Chancenforschung." WSI Mitteilungen 2:143-152.

Kuhlmann, M. and Schumann, M. 1997. "Patterns of Work Organization in the German Automobile Industry," In K. Shimokawa, U. Jürgens, and T. Fujimoto, eds., *Transforming Automobile Assembly*. Berlin: Springer-Verlag.

Kuwan, H., and Waschbüsch, E. 1996. "Zertifizierung und Qualitätssicherung in der beruflichen Weiterbildung." *Berichte zur beruflichen Bildung Heft 193*, Bielefeld: Bertelsmann.

Labour Market Trends 1995, November.

Landenberger, M. and Kuhlmey, A., eds., 1993. *Entwicklungsperspektiven der Kranken- und Altenpflege*. Tagungsband. Berlin/München.

Lauterbach, W. 1994. *Besufsverläufe von Frauen. Erwerbstätigkeit, Unterbrechung und Wiedereintritt*. Frankfurt: Campus.

Lawler, E. 1994. "Total Quality Management and Employee Involvement: Are They Compatible?" *Academy of Management Executive, 8 (1)*.

Lawler, E. 1996. *From the Ground Up: Six Principles for Building the New Logic Corporation*. San Francisco: Jossey-Bass Publishers.

Lawler, E., Ledford, G. and Mohrman, S. 1989. *Employee Involvement in America: A Study of Contemporary Practice*. Houston: American Productivity and Quality Center.

Lawler, E., Mohrman, S. and Ledford, G. 1995. *Creating High Performance Organizations*. San Francisco: Jossey-Bass Publishers.

Lehmann, U. 1996. "Dynamik und Beschäftigungsentwicklung der ostdeutschen Betriebe 1991-1995." *Mitteilungen aus der Arbeitsmarkt- und Berufsforschung*, No. 4.

Leigh, D. E. and A. M. Gill. 1997. "Labor Market Returns to Community Colleges: Evidence for Returning Adults." *Journal of Human Resources* 32(2):334-53.

Lemmermöhle-Thüsing, D. 1992. "Schulische Berufsorientierung (nicht nur) für Mädchen." *Ministerin für die Gleichstellung von Frau und Mann. Nordrhein-Westfalen, ed., 3 Bde.* Düsseldorf.

Lenske, W. 1997. *Die Berufsausbildung im Umbruch, Ergebnisse einer bundesweiten Unternehmensumfrage*, Cologne: Deutscher Instituts-Verlag.

Levine, D. 1995. *Reinventing the Workplace*. Washington, D.C.: The Brookings Institution.

Levy, J. 1999. *Tocqueville's Revenge: State, Society, and Economy in Contemporary France*. Cambridge, MA: Harvard University Press.

Lister, M. (TEC National Council Researcher) 1997. Data on Starts and Completions on Modern Apprenticeship, Youth Training and Training for Work schemes, 1993-7 (correspondence with author).

Local Authority Associations (LAA) 1996. *Memorandum submitted to the House of Commons Employment Committee on TECs.*

Local Government Management Board (LGMB) 1994. *Partnership in Action: Case Studies of Collaboration Between TECs and Local Authorities*, Luton: LGMB.

Luria, Daniel. 1996. "Why Markets Tolerate Mediocre Manufacturing." *Challenge* 39(4): 11-16.

Lüsebrink, K. 1993. *Büro via Fabrik. Entstehung und Allokationsbedingungen weiblicher Büroarbeit 1850 bis 1933.* Berlin: edition sigma.

Lynch, L. 1994a. "Payoffs to Alternative Training Strategies at Work." In R. Freeman, ed., *Working under Different Rules*, New York: Russell Sage Foundation.

Lynch, L., ed. 1994b. *Training and the Private Sector*. Chicago: University of Chicago Press.

Lynch, L. and Black, S. 1997. "Beyond the Incidence of Training: Evidence from a National Employers Survey." NBER Working Paper No. 5231. Cambridge, MA: National Bureau of Economic Research.

MacDuffie, J. P. and Krafcik, J. 1995. "Integrating Technology and Human Resources for High Performance Manufacturing: Evidence from the International Auto Industry." In T. Kochan and M. Useem, eds., *Transforming Organizations*. New York: Oxford University Press.

MacDuffie, J. P. and Pils, F. 1996. "From Fixed to Flexible: Automation and Work Organization Trends from the International Assembly Plant Survey." International Motor Vehicle Project Working Paper, 0109a.

Mahnkopf, B. 1989. "Betriebliche Weiterbildung – Zwischen Effizienzorientierung und Gleichheitspostulat." *Soziale Welt*, 40, pp. 70-96.

Mahnkopf, B., and Maier, F. 1991. "Flexibilisierung und Weiterbildung – Regulierungsdefizite und Regulierungsalternativen." In Semlinger, K. ed. *Flexibilisierung des Arbeitsmarktes*. Frankfurt, M.: Campus, pp. 225-248.

Mallok, J. 1996. *Engpaesse in ostdeutschen Fabriken*. Berlin.

Manske, F. 1995. "Arbeit, Umwelt und Gesellschaft: Zusammenhänge zwischen gesellschaftlicher Stabilität und 'ökologischer Modernisierung'." In W. Müller, ed., *Ökologischer Umbau der Industrie*. Münster/Hamburg,133-164.

March, J. G. 1994. *A Primer on Decision Making*. New-York: the Free Press.

Marcuse, H. 1964. *The one-dimensional man*. Boston, Mass.: Beacon Press.

Marsden, D. 1990. Institutions and Labour Mobility: Occupational and Internal Markets in Britain, France, Italy and West Germany. In Brunetta, R. and Dell'Aringa, C., eds., *Labour Relations and Economic Performance*. London: Macmillan. 414-438.

Marsden, D. and Ryan, P. 1991. "Initial training, labor market structure and public policy: Intermediate skills in British and German industry." In P. Ryan, ed., *International comparisons of vocational education and training for intermediate skills*. London: Falmer Press.

Marsden, D and P. Ryan 1995, "Work, Labor Markets and Vocational Preparation: Anglo-German Comparisons in Training and Intermediate Skills." In L. Bash and A. Green 1995.

Marx-Ferree, M. 1991. "Gender Conflict and Change: Family Roles in Biographical Perspectives." In W. R. Heinz, ed., *Theoretical Advances in Life Course Research (Status Passages and the Life Course. Vol. I)*. Weinheim: Deutscher Studien Verlag, 144-161.

Mason, G. 1996. "Graduate Utilisation in British Industry: The Initial Impact of Mass Higher Education." *National Institute Economic Review*, May.

Mason, G. 1997. "Back from the dead again? Production supervisors in the United States, Britain and Germany." National Institute of Economic and Social Research Discussion paper no. 120, London.

Mason, G. and Finegold, D. 1997. "Productivity, Machinery and Skills in the US and Western Europe." *National Institute Economic Review* 162, October 1997, 85-98.

Mason, J. 1987. "A Bed of Roses? Women, Marriage and Inequality in Later Life." In P. Allatt et al., eds., *Women and the life cycle. Transitions and turning points*. London: Macmillan Press, 90-105.

Maurice, M., F. Sellier, and J.-J. Silvestre. 1986. *The Social Foundations of Industrial Power*. Trans., A. Goldhammer. Cambridge, MA: Cambridge University Press.

Mayer, C. 1992. "… und daß die staatsbürgerliche Erziehung des Mädchens mit der Erziehung zum Weibe zusammenfällt." *Zeitschrift für Pädagogik*, 38. Jg., Nr. 5, 433-454.

Mayer, H. 1996. Die duale Berufsausbildung in der Zerreißprobe. Bildungswissenschaftliche Hochschule Flensburg (mimeo).

Mayer, K. U., ed. 1990. "Lebensverläufe und sozialer Wandel." *Kölner Zeitschrift für Soziologie und Sozialpsychologie, Sonderheft 31*. Opladen: Westdeutscher Verlag.

McKinsey Global Institute. 1997. *Removing Barriers to Growth and Employment in France and Germany*. Washington, DC.

Meifort, B. and Becker, W., ed. 1995. *Berufliche Bildung für Pflege- und Erziehungsberufe. Reform durch neue Bildungskonzepte*. Berichte zur beruflichen Bildung, Heft 178. Bundesinstitut für Berufsbildung, Berlin/Bonn, ed., Bielefeld: Bertelsmann.

Meyer, A., Tsui, A. and Hinings, C. 1993. "Configurational Approaches to Organizational Analysis." *Academy of Management Journal, 36* (6), December, 1175-1195.

Mincer, J. 1994. "Human Capital: A Review." In Kerr, C., and Staudohar, P. eds. *Labor Economics and Industrial Relations*. Cambridge: Harvard University Press, pp. 109-141.

Mishel, Lawrence and Ruy A. Teixeira. 1991. *The Myth of the Coming Labor Shortage: Jobs, Skills, and Incomes of America's Workforce 2000*. Washington, DC: Economic Policy Institute.

Mohrman, S., Cohen, S. and Mohrman, A. 1995. *Designing Team-Based Organizations: New Forms for Knowledge Work*. San Francisco: Jossey-Bass.

Mohrman, S.A. and Mohrman, A.M., Jr. 1997. *Designing and Leading Team-Based Organizations*. San Francisco: Jossey-Bass.

Möller, C. 1987. "Die haben wir dann sehr gerne, diese Damen …." *Beiträge zur feministischen Theorie und Praxis 19/1987, 37-54.*

Moy, Debbie. 1997. "San Francisco Hotels Partnership Project." San Francisco, CA: San Francisco Hotels Partnership Project.

Müller, W., Shavit, Y. and Ucen, P. 1996. "The Institutional Embeddedness of the Stratification Process: a Comparative Study of Qualifications and Occupations in 13 Countries." Paper presented at the 1996 Meeting of the American Sociological Association, New York City.

Müller, W., Willms, A. and Handl, J. 1983. *Strukturwandel der Frauen-arbeit 1880-1980*. Frankfurt/New York: Campus.

Münch, J. 1991. *Vocational Training in the Federal Republic of Germany*. 3rd edition. Berlin: CEDEFOP.

Naschold, F. et al.1994. "Germany: the concerted transition from work to welfare." In Naschold, F., and de Vroom, B. eds. *Regulating employment and welfare*, Berlin, New-York: de Gruyter, pp. 117-182.

National Association of Citizens Advice Bureaus (NACAB) 1994. *In Search of Work*, London: NACAB.

National Training Task Force (NTTF) 1992. *The Role of TECs in Local Economic Development and Enterprise*, London: Coopers and Lybrand.

Nave-Herz, R. 1997. *Die Geschichte der Frauenbewegung in Deutschland.* Hannover: Landeszentrale für politische Bildung.

Negt, O. 1997. "Gesellschaftliche Schlüsselqualifikationen. Sechs Kompetenzen zur Gesellschaftsveränderung." *Widerspruch. Beiträge zur sozialistischen Politik*, 17. Jg., Heft 33: 89-102.

Neubäumer, R. 1993. "Betriebliche Ausbildung 'über Bedarf' – empirische Ergebnisse und ein humankapitaltheoretischer Ansatz." *Jahrbuch für Sozialwissenschaft*, No.1, Mannheim.

Neuenfeldt, Phil and Eric Parker. 1996. *Wisconsin Regional Training Partnership: Building the Infrastructure for Workplace Change and Skill Development*. Washington, DC: AFL-CIO Human Resources Development Institute.

Nienhaus, U. 1982. *Berufsstand weiblich. Die ersten weiblichen Angestellten.* Berlin: Universitäts-Verlag.

Noll, I., U. Beicht, G. Böll, W. Malcher and S. Widerholz-Fritz. 1983. *Nettokosten der betrieblichen Berufsausbildung*. Eds. Bundesinstitut für Berufsbildung, (Schriftenreihe zur Berufsbildungsforschung, Vol. 63, Berlin.

North, D. 1990. *Institutions, institutional change and economic performance.* Cambridge: University Press.

North, D. 1993. "Institutions and Credible Commitment." *Journal of Institutional and Theoretical Economics (JITE)*, 149:1, pp. 11-23.

North, D. 1994a. "Economic Performance through Time." (Nobel Prize Lecture, delivered in Stockholm on December 9, 1993). *American Economic Review*, 84: 3, pp. 359-368.

North, D. 1994b. "Institutional Competition." In Siebert, H. ed. *Locational Competition in the World Economy (Symposium 1994).* Tübingen: Mohr, pp. 27-37.

Notz, G. 1989. *Frauen im sozialen Ehrenamt. Ausgewählte Handlungsfelder, Rahmenbedingungen und Optionen.* Freiburg: Lambertus.

O'Mahony, M. 1997. *Capital Accumulation and Manufacturing Productivity Performance: US-European Comparisons.* National Institute of Economic and Social Research Discussion Paper no. 124. London: NIESR.

OECD. 1994. *The OECD Jobs Study.* Paris: OECD.

OECD. 1995. *Income Distributions in OECD Countries. Evidence from the Luxembourg Income Study.* Social Policy Studies No.18. Paris: OECD.

OECD. 1997. *Employment Outlook.* Paris: OECD.

Offe, C. 1984. *Arbeitsgesellschaft. Strukturprobleme und Zukunftsperspektiven.* Frankfurt/New York: Campus.

Office for Standards in Education (OFSTED)/ Audit Commission 1993. *Unfinished Business: Full-time Educational Courses for 16-19 Year-Olds,* London: HMSO.

Office of Technology Assessment. *Worker Training: Competing in the New International Economy.* Report to the US Congress, Washington, D.C., 1990.

Oppenheimer, V. 1974. "The life-cycle squeezes: the interaction of men's occupational and family life cycles." *Demography Vol. 11,* No. 2, 227-245.

Osterman, P. 1988. *Employment Futures: Reorganization, Dislocation, and Public Policy.* New York, NY: Oxford University Press.

Osterman, P. 1994a. "How Common is Workplace Transformation and Who Adopts It?" *Industrial and Labor Relatons Review,* 47:2, 173-188.

Osterman, P. 1994b. "Internal Labor Markets: Theory and Change." In C. Kerr, and P. Staudohar, eds. *Labor Economics and Industrial Relations.* Cambridge: Harvard University Press, pp. 303-339.

Osterman, P. 1994c. "Strategies for Involving Employers in School to Work Programs." Paper prepared for presentation to a conference at the Brookings Institution, May 1994.

Ostner, I. 1989. "Zur Kategorie des "weiblichen Arbeitsvermögens." In P. Alheit, K. Körber and U. Rabe-Kleberg , eds., *Abschied von der Lohn-arbeit? Diskussionsbeiträge zu einem erweiterten Arbeitsbegriff.* Bd. 12. Forschungsschwerpunkt Arbeit und Bildung: Universität Bremen, 107-120.

Oswald, C. et al. 1996. "Die Teilrente: Zukunftsweisende sozialpolitische Innovation oder nur ein Alibi?" *Zeitschrift für Gerontologie,* 29: 5, pp. 343-347.

OTA (Office of Technology Assessment, Congress of the United States). 1990. *Worker Training: Competing in the New International Economy*. Washington, DC: U.S. Government Printing Office.

Parker, E. and Wever, K. 1997. "Projects and Institutions: Meso-Level Innovations in Germany and the United States." Manuscript. New Brunswick, NJ: Rutgers University.

Passmore, W. 1988. *Designing Effective Organizations: The Sociotechnical Systems Perspective*. New York: Wiley.

Pawlowsky, P., and Bäumer, J. 1993. "Funktionen und Wirkungen beruflicher Weiterbildung." In Strümpel, B., and Dierkes, M. eds. *Innovation und Beharrung in der Arbeitspolitik*, Stuttgart: Schäffer-Poeschl, pp. 69-120.

Pawlowsky, P., and Bäumer, J. 1995. "Konzepte betrieblicher Weiter-bildungsstrategien." In Heidack, C. ed. *Arbeitsstrukturen im Umbruch*. München und Mering: Rainer Hampp, pp. 145-161.

Pfau-Effinger, B. 1990. *Erwerbsverlauf und Risiko. Berufliche Stabilität und Instabilität im Generationenvergleich*. Weinheim: Deutscher Studien Verlag.

Pfau-Effinger, B. 1997. *Kulturelle und wohlfahrtsstaatliche Kontext-bedingungen der Erwerbsbeteiligung von Frauen in Westeuropa*. habil. forthcoming.

Pfeiffer, B. 1997. "Das Ausbildungsangebot der westdeutschen Betriebe 1995-Ergebnisse des IAB-Betribspanels." *BWP* 26:2.

Piechotta, G. Forthcoming. *Kompetenz und Sozialisation. Eine empirische Untersuchung zur beruflichen Situation von Pflegenden*. Bremen: Altera.

Pierson, P. 1993. "When Effect becomes Cause: Policy Feedback and Political Change." *World Politics* 45, pp. 595-628.

Pierson, P. 1994. *Dismantling the Welfare State?: Reagan, Thatcher, and the politics of retrenchment*. New York: Cambridge University Press.

Pierson, P. 1997. "Path Dependence, Increasing Returns, and the Study of Politics." Paper presented to the Seminar on the State and Capitalism since 1800, Center for European Studies, Harvard University, November.

Piore, M. and Sabel, C. 1984. *The Second Industrial Divide: Possibilities for Prosperity*. New York: Basic Books.

Porter, M. 1990. *The Competitive Advantage of Nations*. London: MacMillan.

Prais, S. 1995. *Productivity, Education and Training: An International Perspective*, New York: Cambridge University Press.

Prais, S. and E. Beadle 1991. *Pre-vocational Schooling in Europe Today*, London: NIESR.

Prais, S. and Wagner, K. 1988. "Productivity and Management: The Training of Foremen in Britain and Germany." *National Institute Economic Review*, 123: 34-47.

Prein, G., Kluge, S. and Kelle, U. 1993. *Strategien zur Sicherung von Repräsentativität und Stichprobenvalidität bei kleinen Samples*. Arbeits-papier Nr. 18 des Sfb 186. Universität Bremen.

Prognos AG. 1980. *Soziale Dienstleistungen als Träger potentiellen Wachstums und ihr Beitrag zum Abbau der längerfristigen Arbeitslosigkeit*. Basel.

Prognos AG and Dornier GmbH. 1989. *Angebot und Bedarf an Kranken-pflegepersonal bis zum Jahr 2010*. Vorstudie für den Bundesminister für Arbeit und Sozialordnung. Köln/Friedrichshafen.

Public Accounts Committee 1996. *Fifth Report to the House of Commons 1995-96*, London: HMSO.

Pyke, F., G. Becattini, and W. Sengenberger, eds. 1990. *Industrial Districts and Inter-Firm Cooperation in Italy*. Geneva: International Institute for Labour Studies.

Pyke, F. and Sengenberger, W., ed. 1991. *Industrial Districts and Local Economic Regeneration*. Geneva: International Institute for Labour Studies.

Rabe-Kleberg, U. 1993. *Verantwortlichkeit und Macht: Ein Beitrag zum Verhältnis von Geschlecht und Beruf angesichts der Krise traditioneller Frauenberufe*. Wissenschaftliche Reihe Materialien-Argumente Bd. 54. Bielefeld: KT-Verlag.

Rabe-Kleberg, U., Krüger, H., Karsten, M. E. and Bals, T., eds., 1991. *Dienstleistungsberufe in Krankenpflege, Altenpflege und Kindererziehung*: PRO PERSON. Bielefeld: KT-Verlag.

Rauschenbach, T. 1986. "Die verfehlte Wirklichkeit – Soziale Berufe im Zerrspiegel amtlicher Statistiken." *neue praxis 1, 57-75*.

Ravitch, D. 1995. *National Standards in American Education*. Washington DC: Brookings.

Regini, M. 1995. "Firms and Institutions: The Demand for Skills and their Social Production in Europe." *European Journal of Industrial Relations* 1: 2.

Regini, M. 1997. "Different Responses to Common Demands: Firms, Institutions, and Training in Europe." *European Sociological Review* 13: 3.

Reich, R. B. 1991. *The work of nations*. New York: Knopf.

Richardson, W. 1993. "Employers and an Instrument of School Reform? Education-Business 'Compacts' in Britain and America." In Finegold et al. 1993.

Richardson, W., and D. Finegold 1992. *TECs and Education: Report to the National Training Task Force* (mimeo, Sheffield University).

Richardson, W., J. Woolhouse, and D. Finegold 1993. *The Reform of Post-16 Education and Training in England and Wales*, London: Longman.

Richardson, W., K. Spours, J. Woolhouse and M. Young 1995. *Learning for the Future: Initial Report*, Warwick: Centre for Education and Industry, November.

Richter, R., and Furubotn, E. 1996. *Neue Institutionenökonomik.* Tübingen: Mohr.

Ritter, G. A. 1983. *Sozialversicherung in Deutschland und England.* München: Beck

Rogers, J. and Streeck, W. 1991. "Skill Needs and Training Strategies in the Wisconsin Metalworking Sector." Madison, WI: Center on Wisconsin Strategy.

Roloff, J. 1996. "Alternde Gesellschaft in Deutschland – Eine bevölkerungs-statistische Analyse." *Aus Politik und Zeitgeschichte B 35*, pp. 3-11.

Romer, P. 1986. "Increasing Returns and Long-Run GrowT." *Journal of Political Economy*, 94.

Romer, P. 1994. "The Origins of Endogenous GrowT." *Journal of Economic Perspectives* 8:1.

Rosenow, J., and Naschold, F. 1994. *Die Regulierung von Altersgrenzen.* Berlin: edition sigma.

Roullin-Lefebvre, V. 1997. "L'apprentissage en 1996-1997: La croissance se poursuit, ralentie." Article posted on internet server of the French Education Ministry: http://cri.ensmp.fr/dep.

RSFT (Report System on Further Training, by the BWBW). 1996. *Berichtssystem Weiterbildung VI.* Bonn.

Rüttgers, J. 1996. "Ist das System der dualen Berufsausbildung reform-bedürftig?" *Wirtschaftsdienst*, Zeitschrift für Wirtschaftspolitik, No. 8.

Sabel, C. 1993. "Learning by Monitoring." In *Handbook of Economic Sociology*, ed. Neil Smelser and Richard Swedberg. Princeton NJ: Russel Sage and Princeton University Press.

Sabel, C. 1994. "Turning the Page in the Industrial Districts: Some further thoughts on the reintegration of conception and execution and its implication for firms small and large." Paper presented at the Poitiers Conference, May 1994.

Sabel, C. 1995. "Bootstrapping Reform: Rebuilding Firms, the Welfare State, and Unions." *Politics and Society* 23:1.

Sabel, C., H. Kern, and G. Herrigel. 1991. "Kooperative Produktion. Neue Formen der Zusammenarbeit zwischen Endfertigern und Zulieferern in der Automobilindustrie und die Neuordnung der Firma." In H.G. Mendius and U. Wendling-Schroeder, eds., *Zulieferer im Netz – Zwischen Abhängigkeit und Partnerschaft*, Köln: Bund Verlag, pages 203-227.

Sächsisches Staatsministerium für Wirtschaft und Arbeit (SSWA). 1995. "Merkblatt" on the program for supporting training partnerships (*Ausbildungsverbünde*).

Sadowski, D. 1980. *Berufliche Bildung und betriebliches Bildungsbudget*, Stuttgart: Poeschel.

Sadowski, D., and Decker, S. 1993. *Vertragliche Regelungen zur Beruflichen Weiterbildung in Deutschland.* Berlin, Bonn: Bundesinstitut für Berufsbildung, ed..

Sattel, U. 1989. "Frauenerwerbstätigkeit und Arbeitsmarkt in der Bundesrepublik Deutschland." *Gegenwartskunde. Zeitschrift für Gesellschaft, Wirtschaft, Politik und Bildung,* H. 1.

Saunders, L., A. Lines, A. MacDonald and I. Schagen 1997. *Modern Apprenticeships: Survey of Young People – A Comparison of Modern Apprentices and Young People in Full-Time Education*, DfEE Research Brief.

Savage, S., R. Atkinson, and L. Robins, eds. 1994. *Public Policy in Britain*, Basingstoke: S. Martin's Press.

Saxenian, A. 1994. *Regional Advantage: Culture and Competition in Silicon Valley and Route 128.* Cambridge, MA: Harvard University Press.

Scharpf, F. 1997. "Employment and the Welfare State: A Continental Dilemma." Paper presented at the Center for European Studies, Harvard University, September.

Schettkat, R., ed. 1996. *The Flow Analysis of Labour Markets.* London: Routledge.

Schlüter, A. 1987. *Neue Hüte – alte Hüte? Gewerbliche Berufsbildung für Mädchen zu Beginn des 20. Jahrhunderts – zur Geschichte ihrer Institutionalisierung.* Düsseldorf.

Schmähl, W., and Gatter, J. 1994. "Options for extending the working period and flexibilising the transition to retirement in the German insurance industry – the current situation and assessment for the future." *The Geneva Papers on Risk and Insurance No. 73*, pp. 433-471.

Schmid, G. 1992: "Flexible Koordination: Die Zukunft des dualen Systems aus arbeitsmarkpolitischer Sicht." *Berufsbildung No 1,* pp. 55-59.

Schmidt, H. 1996. "Das duale System kann den Herausforderungen der Zukunft flexibel begegnen." *Wirtschaftsdienst,* 8, 397.

Schmidt, H. 1997. "Reformprojekt Berufliche Bildung, Kontinuität sichern – Kreativität entwickeln – Ausbildung für alle garantieren." *Berufsbildung in Wissenschaft und Praxis,* 26:4.

Schmitter, P. 1997. "The Emerging Europolity and Its Impact upon National Systems of Production. In Hollingsworth and Boyer 1997.

Schmitter, P. and Streeck, W. 1992. "From National Corporatism to Transnational Pluralism: Organized Interests in the Single European Market." In Streeck 1992.

Schober, K. and Chaberny, A. 1983. *'Bin tief enttäuscht. Werde mich aber weiter bewerben.' Untersuchung der bis zum 30. 9. 82 nicht vermittelten Bewerberinnen um eine Ausbildungsstelle.* MatAB 10, Nürnberg: Bundesanstalt für Arbeit.

Schömann, K., and Becker, R. 1993. "Participation in Further Education over the Life Course." Working Paper FS I 93-205, Berlin: Wissenschaftszentrum für Sozialforschung.

Schöngen, K. and Westhoff, G. 1992. "Berufswege der Ausbildung – die ersten drei Jahre." *Berichte zur beruflichen Bildung,* No. 156, Bielefeld.

Schumann, M., Baethge-Kinsky, V., Kuhlmann, M., Kurz, C. and Neumann, U. 1994. *Trendreport Rationalisierung.* Berlin: edition sigma.

Seidenspinner, G. and Burger, A. 1982. *Mädchen '82.* München.

Seigel, Beth and Peter Kwass. 1995. *Jobs and the Urban Poor: Publicly Initiated Sectoral Strategies.* Somerville, MA: Mt. Auburn Associates.

SESSI. 1996. "Décolletage." Publication of the French Ministry of Industry, December.

Seus, L. 1993. *Soziale Kontrolle von Arbeitertöchtern. Eine kriminologische Studie über junge Frauen im Berufsbildungssystem. Forschungen zur Kriminalpolitik.* Band 8. Pfaffenweiler: Centaurus Verlagsgesellschaft.

Shavit, Y. and Blossfeld, H., eds. 1993. *Persistent Inequality. Changing Educational Attainment in Thirteen Countries.* Boulder: Westview.

Sheldrake, J. and S. Vickerstaff 1987. *The History of Industrial Training in Britain,* Aldershot: Avebury.

Shimokawa, K., Jürgens, U., Fujimoto, T., eds. 1997. *Transforming Automobile Assembly.* Berlin: Springer-Verlag.

Skocpol, T. 1992. *Protecting Soldiers and Mothers: The Political Origins of Social Policy in the United States.* Cambridge: Belknap Press of Harvard University.

Sommer, B. 1994. "Entwicklung der Bevölkerung bis 2040 – Ergebnisse der achten koordinierten Bevölkerungsvorausberechnung." *Wirtschaft und Statistik No. 7*, pp. 497-503.

Sorge, A. 1990a. "A European Overview of work and vocational training." In M. Warner, W. Wobbe, and P. Broedner, eds, *New Technology and Manufacturing Management.* Chichester: Wiley.

Sorge, A. 1990b. "Unternehmensstrategien, Qualifikationsentwicklung und Erfolg von Wirtschaftszweigen." In D. Sadowski and U. Backes-Gellner, eds., *Unternehmerische Qualifikationsstrategien im internationalen Wettbewerb.* Berlin: Duncker and Humblot.

Sorge, A. and Streeck, W. 1988. "Industrial Relations and Industrial Change: The Case for an Extended Perspective." In Hyman and Streeck, eds., *New Technology and Industrial Relations,* Oxford: Basil Blackwell.

Soskice, D. 1990a. "Reinterpreting Corporatism and Explaining Unemployment: Co-ordinated and Non-coordinated Market Economies." In R. Brunetta and C. Dell'Aringa, eds., *Labour Relations and Economic Performance,* London: Macmillan,. 170-211.

Soskice, D. 1990b. "Wage Determination: The Changing Role of Institutions in Advanced Industrialized Countries." *Oxford Review of Economic Policy* 6:4.

Soskice, D. 1991. "The Institutional Infrastructure for International Competitiveness: A Comparative Analysis of the UK and Germany," In A. Atkinson and R. Brunetta, eds., *Economics for the New Europe,* New York: New York University Press, 45-66.

Soskice, D. 1994. Reconciling Markets and Institutions: The German Apprenticeship System. In L. Lynch, ed., *Training and the Private Sector.* Chicago: University of Chicago Press, 25-60.

Soskice, D. 1997. "German Technology Policy Innovation and National Institutional Frameworks." In Casper. and Vitols 1997.

Springer, R. 1997. "Rationalization Also Involves Workers – Teamwork in the Mercedes-Benz Lean Concept," In *Transforming Automobile Assembly.* Berlin: Springer-Verlag.

Statistisches Bundesamt, ed., 1994. *Statistisches Jahrbuch für die Bundesrepublik Deutschland.* Stuttgart, Bundesarbeitsblatt 1994, Heft 6. Metzler-Poeschel.

Statistisches Bundesamt, ed. 1996. *Statistisches Jahrbuch 1996 für das Ausland.* Stuttgart: Metzler-Poeschel.

Statistisches Bundesamt, ed. 1997. *Datenreport: Zahlen und Fakten über die Bundesrepublik Deutschland.* Schriftenreihe Band 340, Bonn: Bundeszentrale für Politische Bildung.

Steedman, H. 1990. "Improvements in Workforce Qualifications: Britain and France 1979-88." *National Institute Economic Review,* AuguS.

Steedman, H., G. Mason , and K. Wagner 1991. "Intermediate Skills in the Workplace: Deployment, Standards and Supply in Britain, France and Germany." *National Institute Economic Review*, May.

Steinmo, S., K. Thelen, and F. Longstreth, eds. 1992. *Structuring Politics: Historical Institutionalism in Comparative Analysis.* New York: Cambridge University Press.

Stern, D. et al. 1995. *School-to-Work: Research on Programs in the United States.* Washington, DC: Falmer Press, 1995.

Stevens, M. 1994. "A Theoretical Model of On-the-Job Training with Imperfect Competition." *Oxford Economic Papers* 46:537-62.

Stevens, M. 1996. "Transferable Training and Poaching Externalities." In A. Booth and D. Snower, eds., *Acquiring Skills: Market Failures, Their Symptoms and Policy Responses,* Cambridge: CUP, pp. 19-40.

Stooß, F. 1986. "Perspektiven der sozialen Berufe auf dem Arbeitsmarkt." In B. Schön, ed., *Die Zukunft der sozialen Berufe*, Frankfurt: Campus, 96-117.

Stooß, F. 1997. *Reformbedarf in der beruflichen Bildung.* Expertise im Auftrag des Ministeriums für Arbeit, Gesundheit und Soziales des Landes Nordrhein-Westfalen

Stratton, C. 1989, "The TECs and the PICs: The Key Issues which lie ahead." In R. Bennett et al. 1989.

Streeck, W. 1989. "Skills and the Limits of Neo-Liberalism: The Enterprise of the Future as a Place of Learning." *Work, Employment and Society* 3 (1): 89-104.

Streeck, W. 1991. "On the Institutional Conditions of Diversified Quality Production." In E. Matzner and W. Streeck, eds. *Beyond Keynesianism.* Aldershot: Edward Elgar.

Streeck, W. 1992. *Social Institutions and Economic Performance.* Newbury Park, CA: Sage.

Streeck, W. 1993. "Training and the New Industrial Relations: A Strategic Role for Unions." In *Economic Restructuring and Emerging*

Patterns of Industrial Relations, ed. S. Sleigh. Kalamazoo, MI: W.E. Upjohn Institute.

Streeck, W. 1996. "Lean Production in the German Automobile Industry: A Test Case for Convergence Theory." In S. Berger and R. Dore, eds., *National Diversity and Global Capitalism*, Ithaca: Cornell University Press.

Streeck, W. 1997. "The German Model: Does it Exist? Can it survive?" In C. Crouch and W. Streeck, eds., *The Political Economy of Modern Capitalism*, London: Sage.

Streeck, W., J. Hilbert, K-H. van Kevalaer, F. Maier, H. Weber. 1987. *The Role of the Social Partners in Vocational Training and Further Training in the Federal Republic of Germany*. Berlin: CEDEFOP.

Tan, H and C. Peterson 1993. "Postschool Training of British and American Youth." In D. Finegold et al. 1993.

TEC National Council 1995. *Submission to the Committee on Standards in Public Life.*

Tenkasi, R. and Mohrman, S. (1994). *Technology Transfer as a Collaborative Learning, G94-2 (245)*. Los Angeles, CA: Center for Effective Organizations.

Tessaring, M. 1994. "Langfristige Tendenzen des Arbeitskräftebedarfs nach Tätigkeiten und Qualifikationen in den alten Bundesländern bis zum Jahre 2010." *Mitteilungen aus der Arbeitsmarkt- und Berufsforschung*, pp. 5-19.

Teubner, U. 1989. *Neue Berufe für Frauen. Modelle zur Überwindung der Geschlechterhierarchie im Erwerbsbereich.* Frankfurt/New York: Campus.

The William T. Grant Foundation Commission on Work, Family and Citizenship 1988. *The Forgotten Half. Pathways to Success for America's Youth and Young Families.* Washington, DC.: Youth and Young Families. Final Report

Thelen, K. 1992. *Union of Parts. Labor Politics in Postwar West Germany.* Ithaca, NY: Cornell University Press.

Thelen, K. and Kume, I. 1997. Labor Politics and Skill Formation. Germany and Japan. *AICGS Policy Papers* No. 1. Washington DC.

Thon, M. 1995. "Demografische Aspekte der Arbeitsmarktentwicklung – die Alterung des Erwerbspersonenpotentials." *Mitteilungen aus der Arbeitsmarkt- und Berufsforschung*, pp. 290-299.

Thurow. L. C. 1996. *The Future of Capitalism: How today's Economic Forces shape tomorrow's World.* New York: Penguin.

Times Educational Supplement (TES) 1988. "Editorial." 16 December.

Timmermann, D. 1990. "Zukunftsprobleme des Dualen Systems unter Bedingungen verschärften Wettbewerbs." In Sadowski, D., and Backes-Gellner, U. eds. *Unternehmerische Qualifikationsstrategien im internationalen Wettbewerb.* Berlin: Duncker and Humblot, pp. 37-57.

Tirole, J. 1988. *The Theory of Industrial Organization.* Cambridge: MIT Press.

Training Agency 1989. *Training and Enterprise Councils: A Prospectus for the 1990s,* London Training Agency.

Tucker, M. 1995. "Skill Standards, Qualification Systems, and the American Workforce." In Resnick, L. and Wirt, J., eds., *Linking School and Work: Roles for Standards and Assessments,* San Francisco: Jossey-Bass.

Turner, L. 1991. *Democracy at Work. Changing World Markets and the Future of Labor Unions.* Ithaca, NY: Cornell University Press.

U.S. Bureau of Labor Statistics (BLS), (1992). *How Workers Get Their Training: A 1991 Update.* Bulletin 2407, Washington, D.C.: US Government Printing Office, AuguS.

United Nations. 1995. *International Trade Statistics Yearbook.* Department for Economic and Social Information and Policy Analysis Statistics Division, Vol. 1, New York.

Unwin, L. 1996. "Employer-Led Realities: Apprenticeship Past and Present." *Vocational Education and Training,* 48: 1.

van Lieshout, H. 1996. "Beroepsonderwijs in Duitsland. Een analyse van het Duits duale stelsel van beroepsonderwijs vanuit Nederlands perspectief." In Max Goote Kenniscentrum vor Beroepsonderwijs en Volwassenendeducatie, Report 96-13, Amsterdam.

Vaughan, P. 1993. *TECs and Employers: Developing Effective Links – Part 1, A Survey,* Sheffield: DfEE, Research Series No. 12, AuguS.

VDMA (Verband Deutscher Maschinen- und Anlagenbau). 1996. *Statistisches Handbuch für den Maschinenbau.* Ausgabe, Frankfurt: Maschinenbauverlag.

Visser, J. and Hemerijck, A. 1997. '*A Dutch Miracle*': *Job Growth, Welfare Reform and Corporatism in the Netherlands.* Amsterdam: Amsterdam University Press.

Vitols, S. 1997. "German Industrial Policy: An Overview." In Casper and Vitols 1997.

von Bardeleben, R. 1993. "Probleme der Berufsausbildung in der neuen Bundesländern aus der Sicht nichtausbildender Betriebe." In Degen 1993.

von Bardeleben, R. 1995. "Gründe für die Ausbildungsabstinenz." In Degen et al. 1995.

von Bardeleben, R., U. Beicht, and R. Stockmann. 1991. "Kosten und Nutzen der betrieblichen Berufsausbildung. Forschungsstand, Konzeption, Erhebungsinstrumentarium." *Berichte zur beruflichen Bildung,* No. 140, Bielefeld.

von Bardeleben, R., U. Beicht, and K. Fehér. 1995. "Betriebliche Kosten und Nutzen der Ausbildung." *Berichte zur beruflichen Bildung*, No. 187, Bielefeld.

von Bardeleben R., U. Beicht, and K. Fehér. 1997. "Was kostet die betriebliche Ausbildung? Fortschreibung der Ergebnisse 1991 auf den Stand 1995." *Berichte zur beruflichen Bildung*, No. 210, Bielefeld.

Wagner, K., D. Hitchens, E. Birnie. 1995. "Entwicklung der Produktivität und Investitionstätigkeit ostdeutscher Industriebetriebe." *Zeitschrift für Betriebswirtschaft*, 65.

Wagner, K., M. O'Mahony, M. Paulsson. 1997. "Standortfaktor Humankapital in Deutschland und die Aufholjagd der britischen Industrie." *Zeitschrift für Betriebswirtschaft*, 67.

Wagner,K. 1993. "Qualifikationsniveau in ostdeutschen Betrieben, Bestand – Bewertung –Anpassungsbedarf." *Zeitschrift für Betriebswirtschaft*, 63:2.

Weber, W. et al. 1994. *Betriebliche Bildungsentscheidungen – Entscheidungsverläufe und Entscheidungsergebnisse.* München und Mering: Rainer Hampp.

Weiß, R. 1994. *Betriebliche Weiterbildung – Ergebnisse der Weiterbildungserhebung der Wirtschaft.* Köln: Deutscher Instituts-Verlag.

West, C. and Zimmermann, D. H. 1987. "Doing Gender." *Gender and Society* 1/2, Beverly Hills/London/New Delhi, 125-151.

Wildemann, H. 1987. Strategische Investitionsplanung, Methoden zur Bewertung neuer Produktionstechnologien. Wiesbaden.

Wildemann, H. 1989. "Fabrik in der Fabrik durch Fertigungssegmentierung," In H. Wildemann, ed., *Fabrikplanung: neue Wege – aufgezeigt von Experten aus Wissenschaft und Praxis.* Frankfurt.

Williamson, O. 1985. *The Economic Institutions of Capitalism: Firms, Markets, Relational Contracting,* New York: Free Press.

Witte, J. C. and Kalleberg, A. L. 1995. Matching Training and Jobs: The Fit Between Vocational Education and Employment in the German Labour Market. *European Sociological Review* (11): 293-317.

Womack, J. and Jones, D. 1996. "Beyond Toyota: How to Root Out Waste and Pursue Perfection." *Harvard Business Review*, Sept-Oct, 140-158.

Womack, J., D. Jones, and D. Roos. 1990. *The Machine that Changed the World.* New York: Rawson Associates.

Wood, S. 1997. "Capitalist Constitutions: Supply-Side Reform in Britain and West Germany 1960-90." Ph.D. Dissertation, Department of Government, Harvard University.

Worcester, K. 1990. *From Tripartism to the Enterprise Culture: the Trade Unions, Training Policy and the Thatcher Government 1979-88*, Ph.D. Dissertation, Columbia University.

Working Partnerships USA. 1997. "Building Worker Representation in the New Economy: Brief Summary of Programs." San Jose, CA: Working Partnerships USA.

Yeandle, S. 1984. *Women's working lives: patterns and strategies.* London: Tavistock.

Yeandle, S. 1991. "Couples in the Labor Market: An Analysis of Work Histories Collected from Couples in South Wales." In W. R. Heinz, ed., *The Life Course and Social Change: Comparative Perspectives (Status Passages and the Life Course. Vol. II)*. Weinheim: Deutscher Studien Verlag, 169-184.

Zedler, R. and R. Koch. 1992. "Berufsschule – Partner der Ausbildungsbetriebe. Ergebnisse einer Unternehmensumfrage." *Beiträge zur Gesellschafts- und Bildungspolitik*, No. 178, Cologne: Institut der deutschen Wirtschaft.

Ziegler, J. N. 1990. "The State and Technological Advance: Political Efforts for Industrial Change in France and the Federal Republic of Germany, 1972-1986." Ph.D. dissertation, Department of Government, Harvard University.

INDEX